I0147974

Cradock

RECONSIDERATIONS IN SOUTHERN AFRICAN HISTORY

Richard Elphick, Editor

Cradock

How Segregation and Apartheid Came to a South African Town

JEFFREY BUTLER

Edited by Richard Elphick and Jeannette Hopkins

University of Virginia Press
Charlottesville and London

University of Virginia Press

Printed in the United States of America on acid-free paper

First published 2017

9 8 7 6 5 4 3 2 1

Library of Congress Cataloging-in-Publication Data
Names: Butler, Jeffrey, author. | Elphick, Richard, editor. | Hopkins, Jeannette, editor.
Title: Cradock : how segregation and apartheid came to a South African town / Jeffrey Butler ; edited by Richard Elphick and Jeannette Hopkins.
Other titles: Reconsiderations in southern African history.
Description: Charlottesville : University of Virginia Press, 2017. | Series: Reconsiderations in southern African history | Includes bibliographical references and index.
Identifiers: LCCN 2017024791| ISBN 9780813940588 (cloth : alk. paper) | ISBN 9780813940595 (ebook)
Subjects: LCSH: Segregation—South Africa—Cradock—History. | Cradock (South Africa)—Race relations—History. | Cradock (South Africa)—Social conditions—20th century.
Classification: LCC DT2060 .B88 2017 | DDC 305.8009687560904—dc23
LC record available at https://lccn.loc.gov/2017024791

Cover art: Detail of Cradock from the south, from Regent Street toward the town center, c. 1933. (Museum Africa, Johannesburg, South Africa)

CONTENTS

Editor's Preface *vii*
Author's Preface *ix*

Introduction 1
1 Landscape, People, and Politics: Cradock in the Age of Segregation 11
2 Lodgers, Layabouts, and Laborers: Access and Residence for Coloreds and Africans 28
3 Race and the Politics of Liquor and Beer 47
4 Water, Slops, and Night Soil: Sanitation for an Up-to-Date Town 64
5 Charity and Welfare in the Age of Segregation 87
6 "Is It Nothing to You?": Public Health in the Age of Segregation 105
7 Improvement or Removal? Segregated Public Housing 123
8 Apartheid Comes to Cradock 142
Conclusion: The Age of Segregation and the Age of Apartheid 185

Notes *195*
Index *225*

EDITOR'S PREFACE

This publication testifies to the high esteem that Jeffrey Butler and his scholarship enjoyed among his colleagues. He began his research in Cradock in 1977, and over the next two decades gave numerous presentations, most notably at the Yale-Wesleyan Southern African Research Program, that aroused intense anticipation among South Africanists for the promised book. Tragically, on 13 November 2001, he suffered a debilitating stroke that ended his involvement in the project. He died in April 2008.

By 2001, Butler had completed a manuscript that was heavily documented and publishable without additional research. But it required considerable cutting and editing. The renowned editor Jeannette Hopkins, then the director of the Wesleyan University Press, had worked closely with Butler in shaping the structure of his argument and was determined that the work should be published. She then produced meticulous line editing that became the basis for my own work on the manuscript. Sadly, she died in August 2011, long before her devoted efforts saw the light of day.

My principal goals were to streamline the manuscript while retaining Butler's distinctive voice as much as possible. At the final stage, Jeffrey Butler's daughter Katy, herself an eminent author, provided helpful suggestions on the entire manuscript. In light of the expert assistance I received from Jeannette Hopkins and Katy Butler, it is important to stress that I, as a historian of South Africa, made the final decisions on matters both major and minor. Thus, to the extent that errors remain that are not attributable to Butler, the blame is entirely mine.

It is not possible to know whom Butler would have thanked for helping him during his research, although it is certain that he would have effusively praised his wife, the late Valerie de la Harpe Butler, who had supported him heroically, both in good times and bad. And Fran Warren of the College of Social Studies at Wesleyan deserves thanks for expertly typing Butler's many drafts.

In part because Butler's memory is so widely revered at Wesleyan, I have been generously supported in this venture by a series of Wesleyan grants and by the moral support of numerous department chairs, deans, and provosts at Wesleyan University. I am particularly grateful to Judith Brown, Brian Fay, Joyce Jacobsen, Don Moon, and Gary Shaw.

The manuscript I inherited included numerous detailed endnotes. Admirably compact, they relied heavily on acronyms. Deciphering the acronyms was the first challenge faced by Susan Sturman, a retired librarian in Cape Town, who undertook the heroic task of identifying, first, the archives and, then, the relevant files where Butler had done his research, in order to fact-check both notes and text. It was a tiring, often dispiriting enterprise, which she undertook with determination, resourcefulness, and her characteristic good humor. She was assisted by the work of Adam Tinkle, an outstanding Wesleyan undergraduate, who checked several series that Butler had purchased on microfilm. Sadly, Sturman died in April 2016.

Butler left photocopies of many images he wished to accompany the book. Elizabeth de Wet, a retired archivist in Grahamstown, pursued clue after clue with relentless enterprise and managed to locate several of the originals. When, however, it became apparent that many of Butler's desired images had been lost, she worked with me to locate appropriate substitutes. The images we found are not as numerous or, in some cases, as germane as Butler had wanted, but we are pleased to present them nonetheless. She and I are both grateful to Brian Wilmot, curator of the Olive Schreiner House Museum, who helped immeasurably in searching for images in Cradock.

Mariah Reisner, under my direction, and with technical advice from Kevin Wiliarty, used the computer to produce the admirable maps that accompany this text. I am grateful for Reisner's ready grasp of the historical issues as well as for her technological competence.

I am greatly indebted to Katy Butler, who, as executor of her father's will, has provided not only cogent advice but also financial support from the estate to support publication. She also slightly amplified and amended the Author's Preface in light of her knowledge of Butler family history.

I received strong and unwavering support from Dick Holway, Mark Mones, and the staff of the University of Virginia Press. In particular, Bonnie Gill's understanding, good cheer, and efficiency helped me greatly in acquiring illustrations and permissions and in crafting acceptable copy for the maps. Jane Curran, my copy editor, was both meticulous and flexible in dealing wth the difficulties of editing a book by a deceased author. And Enid Zafran, quickly gaining a firm grasp of the intricacies of South African and Cradock governance, produced an admirably thorough and accurate index.

All translations are by Butler, unless otherwise indicated.

Richard Elphick

AUTHOR'S PREFACE

In mid-1977, after living and teaching for nearly four decades in England and America, I returned to South Africa on a U.S. National Endowment for the Humanities fellowship to collect material for a history of Cradock, the small town where I was born.

I reached the town from the south on a new national road along the wide, rocky, and nearly dry Great Fish River, which runs here on the edge of the Great Karoo semi-desert, a landscape of koppies (rocky outcroppings) and tafelberge (table mountains) rising from a thirstland of low gray bush. Here white settlers, from the Netherlands and the British Isles, established themselves from the 1780s on, marking out large sheep and goat farms on lands that had once been pasturage for the cattle of the Xhosa people, and building towns and garrisons fifty miles apart. To the left of the road, about six miles from Cradock and rising two thousand feet above the valley floor, was the familiar sight of Buffelskop (Buffalo's Head), where the South African novelist and feminist social reformer Olive Schreiner, author of *The Story of an African Farm,* was buried in 1923. When I was a child in the 1920s and 1930s, I sometimes accompanied my aunt Mary Butler, a Quaker nurse active in liberal causes in Cradock, on the expeditions she organized to Buffelskop for visitors and those of her nephews and nieces who had the interest and energy to make the climb. Often she would lecture us on the importance of Schreiner's ideals for the future of South Africa.

Schreiner's connection with Cradock—she had first arrived in the 1870s when her brother taught at our local school and returned later in life as well—was one of my birthplace's few claims to fame. Seeing Buffelskop again reminded me of her love of the Karoo and her prophetic and eloquent criticism of many South African policies and institutions—criticisms that lost none of their relevance during the era of informal segregation from 1910 to 1948, nor in the harsher, highly organized era of apartheid that dawned in 1948 and was still on full display upon my return in 1977.

Past the kop, I came upon two townships new to me, one on the left for Africans, another on the right for coloreds (mixed-race people), both with the dreary uniformity of most South African public housing: little boxes in straight lines, tightly packed in a dusty landscape, with no evidence of any attempt at a pleasing urban design. I could see no parks, no church steeples, and no main commercial street. Closer to the center of Cradock itself, I passed the old "location" that the townships had replaced, a neighborhood contiguous to the white town but dwelling worlds apart from it, where urban Africans and coloreds had been relegated (and regulated) since the 1840s.

All of my family's servants had lived in the location; like most white families, we knew the Africans who worked for us as gardeners, deliverymen, cooks, and house cleaners only by their first names. There was Jonas, September, Katrina, Susan, and Chrissie, a Sotho-speaker employed by my parents, first as a nursemaid to their two youngest children, and then as cook, becoming a counselor to us all. When Chrissie died suddenly in 1934, we went to her funeral in the wood-and-iron Basuto Methodist church, on the edge of town closest to the location. I was ten, and it was the nearest I had ever come to entering the location itself. There I learned for the first time, from a plate on the coffin, her family name: Marenge.

In those days, the old location was a dusty warren of small houses and huts, covered in early evening by a fog of smoke and emitting a genial hubbub we could hear from some distance in parts of the white town. On my return in 1977, the location was silent—an empty ruin of mud-plastered brick walls without doors or windows or roofs. It reminded me of the photographs of bombarded French and Belgian villages that I had seen as a boy in *The Times History of the Great War.* This devastating physical alteration in the town of my youth had taken place not as a result of a bombardment but by changes in South Africa's laws and dominant ideology: under the Natives (Urban Areas) Consolidation Act of 1945 and the Group Areas Act of 1950, Cradock's town government had relocated all the location's residents and allowed those wishing to build new houses to remove doors, windows, and timber from their old homes for reuse. My family's history was deeply entwined with this event: my great-uncle Charles was a mayor of Cradock in its age of segregation, and my liberal Quaker father, Ernest, long the publisher of Cradock's English-speaking daily newspaper, had served on the town council in the late 1940s when it presided over the destruction of the location and the removal of its residents.

The road then took me into the town's historic core, virtually unchanged from my youth in the 1930s. But the appearance of continuity was misleading. Although most of the buildings on the commercial strip of Church and Adderley streets survived, there were signs of decline and disturbing change. Empty shops and chain stores had replaced family firms, including Butler Brothers, where my great-uncle, grandfather, and father had once sold stationery, lamps, and sundries to Cradock's townspeople and to farmers from the surrounding countryside (or veld). Opposite what had once been my family's home, "The Poplars," lay a vacant lot marking the place where the Grand Hotel had burned down in 1966. Riot police in camouflage gear stood about town, and the Anglo-Boer War memorial in the Karoo Garden was marked by Xhosa graffiti attacking the government. It was 1977, after all, only one year after the Soweto revolt of 1976. Within eight years of my visit, Cradock would be known as an epicenter of resistance to apartheid in the Eastern Cape, and in 1985, four young African organizers, known as "The Cradock Four," would be kidnapped and murdered by government security forces.

The Cradock of my childhood in the 1920s was a sleepy town of some 6,800 souls, almost evenly divided numerically between whites on the one hand and Africans, colored people, and a sprinkling of Asians on the other. By 1977, Africans, once a minority in Cradock, now outnumbered all other groups combined: according to a local census conducted in 1969 there were 11,391 Africans; 5,666 whites (about 60 percent Afrikaans-speaking); 5,065 coloreds; and 64 Asians. In spite of the growing African majority living in the new township, Cradock proper was now politically and commercially an Afrikaner-dominated town. The British commercial and professional class into which I was born had lost its ascendancy, in tandem with English-speakers all over South Africa as they lost influence in national politics and with it their domination of jobs in local, regional, and national governments. Many of the English-speakers had left; so, too, had most of the Asians, Jews, Greeks, and Syrians I remembered from my youth, and many of the colored artisans and shopkeepers.

The decline of British presence and influence was intimately reflected in the history of my own family. My Quaker grandfather, James Butler, had come to South Africa in 1876, hoping that the dry climate would cure that Victorian affliction, a "weak chest" (most likely tuberculosis, but possibly asthma.) He married into a local farming family and with his younger brother, Charles, founded the *Midland News and Karoo Farmer* in 1891, an English-language daily newspaper that carried the Reuters wire service, often supported schemes for civic betterment and editorialized for better treatment of Africans and coloreds, and was read far beyond Cradock itself. My English mother, Alice Stringer, had come to Cradock to teach in 1909, and there she had met and married my father, Ernest, one of James's seven children. My father's sister Mary, my aforementioned unmarried aunt, had worked as a nurse in the old location in the 1920s and 1930s and had helped organize the town's "Joint Council," an unofficial reformist group whose membership, unusually, crossed racial lines. My great-uncle Charles, as mayor from 1937 to 1940, had played an active role in decisions that shaped both town and location just before the dawning of apartheid. My father, who ran the *Midland News* until his retirement in 1948, had sat on the town council during the imposition of the Group Areas Act, the apartheid law that rigorously allotted separate neighborhoods to four "races," defined by statute. By that time, I and my four siblings had left Cradock forever, pursuing careers and lives that would have been impossible had we stayed. With my father's death in 1965, and my aunt Mary's subsequent move from the family home to a home for the aged, the story of the Butler family in the town came to an end.

As a local boy returning after thirty years, the starkest visible change I noticed was the physical reconstruction of the town and its location. In the

1920s, when I was growing up, town and location had been a single contiguous settlement, legally bisected by Regent Street into a dominant town where whites and a sprinkling of coloreds, Asians, and Africans owned homes and land; and the "location," owned by the town, a place of unpaved streets, mud huts, and brick and tin shacks housing the bulk of the Africans and coloreds.

On my return in 1977, the location was no more, and three residential areas were now legally delineated by race. The town, much expanded, was now entirely white. Lingelilhe, a Xhosa word meaning "a place of worthy effort," was a new township housing all Africans; Michausdal, named after the sitting Afrikaner mayor of Cradock, Mrs. T. de la M. Michau, now housed all coloreds. The "mixed area" of the town of my childhood, a place where poorer whites and better-off colored, African, and Asian people had lived relatively harmoniously side by side, was now an entirely white neighborhood. There was no area for Asians in the new Cradock: they were regarded as too few to require a separate group area.

How had this remarkable destruction and reconstruction come about? How had town officials shaped life in the old location when our servants Jonas, September, Katrina, Susan, and Chrissie had lived there? How had my own liberal, civic-minded family helped shape, and failed to shape, what became the Cradock of the age of apartheid? And how had it come to seem normal to one small town, and by extension an entire society, to destroy the location and leave the remains standing so they looked bombed?

These are the questions that *Cradock: How Segregation and Apartheid Came to a South African Town* hopes to answer. It seeks to trace the town's path from the early 1920s to the 1960s to show how municipal and national authorities together shaped life in the location and ultimately implemented this drastic exercise in racially defined town planning. Like my brother Guy, who wrote *Karoo Morning: An Autobiography (1918–35)* (1977), I find stories of Cradock fascinating and eminently worth telling. Guy's work was largely the story of private lives; mine is a history of the politics and administration of the town and its location in which my friends and relations played intermittent but significant parts. The Butlers may have left Cradock, but they continue to write books about it.

Jeffrey Butler

Introduction

Race and Class in Small Towns: "Southerntown," USA, and Cradock, South Africa

In 1937, the American scholar John Dollard published *Caste and Class in a Southern Town,* a study of "Southerntown"—Indianola, Mississippi—in the 1920s and 1930s. The work has since become a classic.[1] For one who grew up in an equivalent South African small town in the same period, Southerntown is an achingly familiar world. Like Cradock, it had many of the traditional small-town virtues: simplicity, directness, decency, and order. And also, like Cradock, it was a place of poverty and structured racial discrimination and inequity. In both towns, people of color were poorer than whites, virtually disenfranchised, largely housed by race, receiving unequal education and municipal services, working in a discriminatory labor market, and subject to a racial hierarchy. People of color always approached white households by the back door, and whites, even children, addressed them by their first names.

On the surface, both towns seemed to be unambiguously structured by race. But in Southerntown, Dollard showed that further divisions arose from a complex interplay of "caste" (race) and class. Races were divided in ways that undermined group solidarity but also prevented alliances between white and black members of the same classes, especially workers. In Cradock, the divisions were even more complex: white people, Africans, coloreds (mixed-race people), and a handful of Indians and Chinese were implicitly sorted not only by race, ethnicity, and class, but also by language, regional and national origin, and political and civil status.

In Dollard's Southerntown, "nigger town" arose on one side of the railroad tracks; it survived without direct legal compulsion or a coherent plan to ensure that all people of color lived in the same place, or in a limited number of neighborhoods.[2] In Cradock, on the other hand, the very landscape was formally structured partially by race almost from the town's founding in 1814; Cradock's equivalent of "niggertown" was "the location," a far less spontaneous settlement. Legally established in 1840 on a piece of municipal land, it was a place where most people who were not "European" were to be "located" by the town government. Nobody could own land in the location: most of the plots were rented by the municipality to residents who could build mud huts, shacks, and small houses. That regime persisted into the age of apartheid.

The governance of the location had no equivalent in Dollard's Southerntown. The municipality exercised authoritarian control over location residents. They could not vote in local elections because they could not own land in the location and thus could not meet the property qualifications for the local franchise. The location was governed instead by a white superintendent—a landlord and police commandant rolled into one—who had no equivalent in town. After 1927, in compliance with the Natives (Urban Areas) Act of 1923, the Cradock town council established a Location Advisory Board made up of three Africans and three coloreds. This strictly advisory body had no control of taxation or expenditure and therefore could exert no pressure on town councilors to improve services or relax regulations. Its recommendations were often dealt with summarily by the town council, or simply ignored.[3] Only on occasion was it effective in influencing municipal officials.

Even though it had begun early in the town's history, Cradock's system of racial and territorial segregation was not rigorously planned or delineated until the mid-twentieth century. People of color were not required to live in the location: under the law of the Cape Province, of which Cradock was a part, they could buy or rent property in the predominantly white town if they could afford to. Town residents of color enjoyed a civil status denied to location residents: for example, they were not subject to the curfew enforced in locations. In the Cape, the national and provincial franchise were open to people of color if they could meet certain property or income qualifications; in 1925 men of color made up 15 percent of the town's electorate. By the 1920s, about 350 coloreds and half a dozen Africans lived in town, most of them concentrated in the area identified in this book as the "Mixed Area," located close to the location.

In the early twentieth century, in South Africa as in the United States, the racial or ethnic structure of an urban area had rarely been a subject of systematic national, regional, or local intervention. But in South Africa during the age of segregation, 1910 to 1948, and during the age of apartheid, 1948 to 1994, this slowly, and then dramatically, changed. This book is a study of that transition in Cradock, a small town in the Great Karoo, inhabited by an interracial population of whites and a few people of color, and a "mixed" location solely of Africans and coloreds. It is largely a book about how, in the 1920s, 1930s, and 1940s, South Africa's ad hoc system of segregation was shaped through the strengthening of municipal controls and the provision of municipal services in a complex interplay of local forces and intervention from the national government. And how, with the coming of apartheid in the late 1940s and 1950s, Cradock was physically transformed on a racial basis defined in national legislation. In the process, Cradock changed from a place that resembled Dollard's Southerntown to one that bore it little resemblance, particularly in terms of the housing and freedom of movement of people of color.

Until the early twentieth century, small towns in the United States and South Africa, including Southerntown and Cradock, had municipal governments independent in most respects from the central government and responsible to a local electorate, with real estate as the principal tax base. Local bodies—municipalities, school and hospital boards—engaged in limited building projects, funded mainly by local resources: a town hall, a public park with bandstand, and later schools and hospitals. Expressing what became known in Britain as "gas-and-water socialism," late nineteenth-century municipalities became providers of more services: improving water supply and later adding gas, electricity, and public transport. They also became town planners, subdividing municipal land into lots for sale and imposing standards for housing construction. Exercising extensive rule-making powers, they usually operated on their own, left alone by provincial and national governments, except for cursory audits of their accounts and legal vetting of their bylaws.

New Amenities and New Controls: "Normal" and "Abnormal" in Town Governance

In South Africa, this changed in the early twentieth century, with the emergence of an increasingly interventionist government. It began with the founding, in 1910, of the Union of South Africa, eight years after Britain's conquest of two Afrikaner republics in the South African (or Anglo-Boer) War of 1899–1902. The Union was to be governed by a new national parliament. It embraced the Cape Colony, which under the British had maintained a liberal tradition in racial matters, and three less liberal provinces to the north: the recently conquered Orange Free State and the Transvaal, and Natal, another former British colony.

With Union came the consolidation and reconciliation of conflicting laws and practices affecting everything from alcohol consumption to housing to patterns of residence.[4] Much of the legislative history of South Africa from 1910 to 1948 was dominated by national politicians' efforts to create a more consistently segregated political, economic, and social order.[5] Although Southerntown in the U.S. South remained segregated in the 1920s and 1930s while some other parts of the country slowly became more racially liberal, the reverse was true in Cradock. After union, throughout South Africa the civil rights and status of colored and African people were systematically eroded in different ways and at different times—their rights to vote in national elections, to work in certain occupations, to marry whom they chose, and to have equal access to places of residence.

Before unification, the parliamentary franchise in Cape Colony had granted the vote to males of any race if they were literate and had sufficient property or income. In the Union, this franchise was preserved only in Cape Province, where Cradock was located. The South African parliament eliminated the Cape franchise for Africans in 1936, for Asians in 1946, and for coloreds in 1956. African rights to own land in the countryside were limited in 1913 and further controlled in 1936; Africans continued to be denied the right to buy land in locations, and in 1937 they lost the right to buy land in towns or reside in them. From 1922 on, a color bar in employment and apprenticeship was further elaborated to secure jobs for the growing numbers of "poor whites," many of them displaced from rural areas. Formally designed to give whites preference over Africans, this color bar also became punitive to coloreds, who in the Cape Province were heavily represented in skilled trades. In 1927, an Immorality Act made sexual intercourse between whites and Africans illegal.

South Africa's age of segregation also involved systematic attempts to limit the settlement of Africans in towns. The Stallard doctrine was named after Colonel Charles Stallard, chairman of the 1922 Transvaal Local Government Commission, whose views on this subject became the national legislative standard. Stallard contended that Africans had no right to permanent town residence on the grounds that the "native," that is, African, urban population ought to be no larger than the local demand for labor required. In other words, unemployed African workers and their families had no right to stay in towns or their locations. The Stallard doctrine was enshrined in the Natives (Urban Areas) Act of 1923, but this was a permissive, not prescriptive act, and at first only fitfully applied. Its amendment in 1930 and tightening restriction on Africans in the 1937 Native Laws Amendment Act have together been characterized by Rodney Davenport as the "triumph of Colonel Stallard."[6] There is no American equivalent to South Africa's national policy of attempting by law to restrict movement and enforce settlement by race, a process later called "influx control." Municipalities like Cradock had their own reasons for welcoming the Stallard doctrine, particularly as a way of reducing the costs of housing Africans, of controlling a growing population, and of dampening the force of Africans' demands for political rights.

And from the 1920s on, national governments sought to restrict permanent African urban settlement, causing increasing interventions in local affairs.[7] But not all such interventions hurt the interests of location residents. The new South African state also began to press municipalities to provide better services to their racially delineated locations, such as improving water supply, providing electricity, drains, and sewers, and generally enforcing sanitary standards. Such involvement of the national government, a manifestation of international trends in nineteenth-century Europe and America, was largely provoked by public health crises in large cities. Industrializing states had become concerned about the political and social consequences of concentrated urban poverty and the related emergence of "dangerous classes": criminals, radicals, and untreated carriers of infection. Mid-nineteenth-century epidemics of cholera, then of smallpox, plague, and influenza, and a steady spread of tuberculosis led citizens around the world to demand that national governments finance improvements of public health that free enterprise and existing local authorities were manifestly failing to do.[8]

In South Africa, a public health movement, begun in the nineteenth century, received a powerful boost from the Tuberculosis Commission of 1914, which, responding to an alarming increase in tuberculosis among all ethnic groups, investigated conditions throughout South Africa in town and country, mine and farm.[9] This commission, consisting mostly of doctors, visited many towns, Cradock among them, and in public hearings harassed complacent town fathers and officials about the poor services and housing in their locations; they even charged that many towns (including Cradock) had actually made "a considerable profit" from their locations.[10] Partly as a result of the commission's report, a massive, consolidating Public Health Act of 1919 established the national Department of Public Health and the office of assistant medical officer of health (AMOH), a medically trained official who, among other duties, inspected towns and their locations. In the first such inspection in 1924, Cradock became the subject of a scathing and shaming report about deplorable conditions in its location.[11]

A related housing act in 1920 required, on paper, that local authorities provide housing for the poor, including people of color.[12] The Natives (Urban Areas) Act of 1923 provided loans to municipalities to build "dwellings" in locations and gave the Department of Native Affairs the authority to appoint inspectors of urban locations.[13] The department also drafted "Model Regulations" for locations, which it urged local authorities to promulgate.[14]

Medical officers and urban areas inspectors paid by the faraway Union government asked awkward questions and produced lengthy, informative reports far removed in spirit and substance from those of the Stallard Commission.[15] One goal of the current study is to trace the interplay of such "normal" interventions—common to many twentieth-century governments in the era of the founding of welfare states—with the "abnormal," racially discriminatory interventions peculiar to South Africa.

Some national policies, such as public health and influx control, had to be implemented locally by town governments, sometimes in collaboration with national authorities, such as the Department of Native Affairs and the South African Police. Cradock's administration, headed by a town clerk, was responsible to a nine-person council elected by owners and occupiers of local real estate. The council, white and all-male until 1934, annually elected Cradock's mayor from among its own members, all of whom served without pay. In some respects, the political order in Cradock was more liberal than that of the Union, especially in regard to the vote. In 1921, 40 percent of Cradock's voters in municipal elections were white women; 4 percent were women of color.[16] By contrast, the parliamentary franchise, which bestowed the right to vote in national and provincial elections, was granted to South African white women, but not to women of color, only in 1930.

Cradock town councilors had to tread a careful path, watched closely by a tax-averse electorate and dependent on revenue from "rates" (local property taxes) and from rents of municipally owned farms. They represented cautious small-town business people and the farmers they served; few costly projects were proposed, much less agreed to. Nevertheless, some local whites began, in the 1920s, to call for better municipal services to the location. In 1928, a small group of farmers, ministers, small businessmen, and other middle-class whites, some of them Quakers, joined with leading people of color to create a voluntary, multiracial Joint Council. The council, which had no legal authority, sought to inform whites frankly about conditions in the location and to influence the town council's decisions on specific welfare issues. This group, part of a national movement of voluntary Joint Councils, originated in Cradock through efforts by public-spirited white English-speaking women and a local philanthropist to persuade the town to provide better water supply, housing, and health services to the Cradock location.

Even though few people of color could vote, local Africans and coloreds attempted to influence town government through petitions, public meetings, new national organizations, a taxpayers group, and letters of protest to the local newspaper. Their protests invoked universal standards of humane treatment, as well as the historically more liberal Cape tradition. But there was division among Cradock's people of color. Even though most colored residents in the location shared the pervasive poverty and rightlessness of their African neighbors, leaders of the two groups, faced with issues that could have led to common political action, rarely allied. While the Joint Council and ad hoc location rights groups agitated for improved conditions for poorer people of color, a well-organized and effective group of white Afrikaner women focused elsewhere. With little cooperation from white English speakers, they organized relief work for a growing population of Afrikaner "poor whites" and began to object, privately and publicly, to the mixing of races in the Mixed Area close to the location.

Mounting Intervention: From Segregation to Apartheid

South African law had divided the population into "races," roughly by color. The four main categories were whites, Africans, Asian immigrants (both Chinese and Indian), and coloreds (mixed-race people). Unlike the United States, South Africa thus had a quadriracial, not a biracial, social order, which immensely complicated the devising of institutions. After the Union of 1910, "segregation" emerged as the theoretical model for this order; after the election of 1948, it was displaced by "apartheid." Both models embodied complex and not always consistent ways of adjusting, indeed enforcing, relations among the four races. Both affected almost all municipal regulations concerning people of color on matters of service—water supply, housing, liquor outlets, medical services—but also matters of control—over influx, access to liquor, and supervision of public health.

After the victory of the Afrikaner-dominated National Party in 1948, a central issue in local government was the imposition of "apartheid," a new term in local and national debate. This coherent and highly articulated theory was the product of enormous intellectual effort by Afrikaner intellectuals, ministers of religion, and politicians. It was not simply a continuation of what had come before. Although a powerful segregationist tradition had existed within the National Party since its founding in 1913, it was not embodied comprehensively in laws embracing all four races until the party's national victory in 1948. With the imposition of apartheid by the National Party, similarities between South Africa's Cradock and America's Southerntown lessened, and the differences between them dramatically increased.

Whether apartheid was merely a new term, or also a new policy, has engrossed politicians and scholars ever since 1948. Some scholars have argued that there was little material difference between the era of segregation and the era of apartheid. Deborah Posel in *The Making of Apartheid* (1991) argued that the apartheid regime did not start in 1948 with a new grand plan that it proceeded to enact. Rather, she writes, the plans existing in 1948 served to camouflage rather than resolve divisions within the National Party; policies that were essentially pragmatic later developed gradually, particularly in relation to African labor.[17] Similarly, Ivan Evans in *Bureaucracy and Race* (1997), in describing how "native policies" were elaborated and imposed, argued that little was done immediately after the 1948 election; it was not until 1953 that Dr. Hendrik Verwoerd, minister of Native Affairs from 1950 on, created a body of like-minded officials who could enforce a coherent set of policies.[18]

This book argues, to the contrary, that in Cradock the age of apartheid manifested important discontinuities from the age of segregation that preceded it. In some ways, it is true, apartheid continued and amplified the policies of the age of segregation: a racial hierarchy firmly under white control, with Africans' limited access to town, and much segregation and inequity in housing, employment, and municipal services. But, in other ways, apartheid was a signal departure, even a break from the past. A close look at Cradock shows that before 1948 the shaping of segregation proceeded without a plan and occupied no privileged place on the municipal agenda. In the post-1948 era, on the other hand, an interventionist national government—for whom rigorous segregation of the races in many areas of life, except in the economy, had become a high priority—imposed its racial blueprint on an initially reluctant Cradock town council.

The 1950 Group Areas Act imposed on Cradock was part of the National Party's utopian plan for complete residential and commercial segregation of all the races—whites, coloreds, Africans, and Asians. The act represented one of the strongest discontinuities between the ages of segregation and apartheid. Colored people had long lived in the racially Mixed Area of the town between Voortrekker Street and Regent Street, not far from the location border. Apartheid brought forced relocation of coloreds from their homes and shops in town and in the Mixed Area, with consequent loss of livelihood and neighborhood. Cradock town legally became entirely white. But these arrangements were not entirely new: throughout the age of segregation, colored artisans, grocers, and small shopkeepers had witnessed the steady erosion of their formal civil rights and an elaboration of a position as a separate and subordinate "race." From time to time officials had talked of segregated colored housing. But nothing had been done about it by 1948.

For Africans, apartheid brought another major change to the physical structure of the town and to the tone and intention of governmental actions and rhetoric. Cradock town in the 1920s had been predominantly segregated except for the Mixed Area, but it was also a part of a contiguous settlement. The "location" was separated from "town" only in name and by the width of Regent Street. The age of apartheid brought a much more drastic separation for Africans, a requirement by the national government that the municipality demarcate "buffer strips" around their African townships; the principal one was a no-man's-land five hundred yards wide to physically separate Africans from all other races.

In examining municipal life in Cradock this study endeavors to delineate, not only the continuities and discontinuities between the age of segregation and the age of apartheid, but also the complex processes by which policies in both eras were shaped and implemented. To what extent did policies originate in the municipality rather than nationally? Was the imposition of segregation and apartheid just another modern conflict in which a local authority resists the intervention of a wealthier national government bent on modifying old policies or applying new ones? And how were segregation and apartheid resisted, reshaped, or accepted by local politicians, local white liberals, and the Africans, coloreds, and Asians on whom they were imposed?

These processes were in fact messy, protracted, and surprisingly complex. This study provides little comfort to historians who yearn for a neat, linear narrative, who prefer to perceive a one-way causation from political ideology to practical implementation, or from the center of political power (the national government) to the periphery (local municipalities). Equally difficult is to discern how far municipal policy was a manifestation of South Africa's identity as a "very strange society," a label popularized by Allen Drury in his book of the same title in 1967. This study seeks to untangle the ways that the twentieth-century history of Cradock—its management of municipal services such as running water, electricity, sewage, public health, and public housing—represents a normal history of evolving town government that one could encounter in most parts of the developed world. It also shows where and how Cradock diverged from that history as it implemented South Africa's distinctive racial order—an order largely shared, at first, by U.S. Southerntowns, but less so as time went on—that for half a century attracted the interest and condemnation of the whole world.

1

Landscape, People, and Politics

Cradock in the Age of Segregation

The Founding of a Karoo Town

Cradock lies on the Great Fish River in a narrow flood plain next to a semi-desert, the Great Karoo. It is a region of high winds and capricious rainfall; the Second Escarpment parallel to the coast ensures that the moisture-laden south-easters drop much of their water before reaching the drier interior. In South Africa rainfall improves from west to east, and vegetation changes from the parched desert of the west coast to Karoo veld, with its cactus, tough grasses, and low gray bush. Sheep and goats can be pastured there, but raising cattle is difficult. It takes one morgen, or about two acres, to support a single sheep.

Water has long been a source of anxiety for both farmers and townspeople. Between 1881 and 1920, an average of only fourteen and a half inches of rain fell each year in the Cradock Basin, and droughts occurred every seven or eight years. When the droughts broke, heavy rains on parched countryside made the nearly dry Fish River "come down," as locals said, in a rich brown flow that carried large amounts of topsoil into dry river beds, coloring the sea for miles from the river's mouth.[1]

This climate, which scholars maintain has been in place since about 4000 BCE, has produced a landscape of large mountains, many of them grand mesas, remnants of a former plateau, with steep mountain slopes and flat lands of poor and shallow soils. Out of necessity, the Cape Dutch farmers who settled there from the 1770s created very large farms. That pattern has persisted: in 1929, the average size of the 502 farms in the Cradock district was 1184 morgen or 2,505 acres; today Karoo farms "are seldom below 1000 ha . . . [1167 morgen or 2471 acres] and usually much bigger in drier districts."[2] The Cradock Basin has never supported more than a small rural population, and Cradock, which developed as a market town and administrative center, has always been small as well.

The town itself was not a product of rapid economic growth, nor a magnet for eager immigrants. It was established, in 1811, by Sir John Cradock, the governor of Cape Colony, as a good place for a lockup and a garrison on an unstable frontier. British colonial authorities hoped that a string of forts along the Great Fish River would separate white settlers from Xhosa-speaking African farmers to their east. It did not work: the two groups would be in conflict over territory for much of the nineteenth century.[3] Soon after founding the town, the government built a weir and a furrow to irrigate small holdings along the river, but the settlement around the fort grew very slowly. When, in 1817, the colonial government conducted a public auction of thirty lots, the "most fertile arable land . . . forming the commencement of the new projected village," only eleven people, most of them Cape Dutch rather than British, bought nineteen lots among them.[4]

In 1824, Governor Cradock's successor, Lord Charles Somerset, labeled Cradock "a miserable place which could never advance."[5] Nevertheless, it did advance, if slowly, and from the start it was home to both whites and people of color. An 1825 tax roll of the "village" listed twenty-three white adult males, sixty-one "Hottentots" (the term, now derogatory, used to denote descendants of the Khoikhoi and San indigenes), and eleven slaves, the property of householders, presumably all of them whites.[6] In 1826, Cradock became the center of a new district, with a resident magistrate and civil commissioner, who presided over the court of first instance and represented the Cape Colony government administratively. The following year, Cradock became a municipality and hence responsible for a "location," a separate living place for Africans and other people of color who had come to Cradock in search of employment.[7] In 1844 the colonial government deeded to the municipality a commonage of 14,237 morgen (about 30,000 acres);[8] with these basic resources of land, water, colonial administration, and property-based local government, the settlement grew into a little town serving British and Cape Dutch farmers and townsmen, and their employees: Khoisan, freed slaves, and Africans. A "Plan of Cradock," from 1850, shows about a hundred buildings with a group of "Hottentot Huts" and a "Hottentot Burial Ground."

On the surrounding farms, Spanish merino sheep, first imported in 1789 by the enterprising Colonel R. J. Gordon, were replacing cattle and indigenous fat-tailed sheep. From the 1830s on, Cape exports of wool increased rapidly; by midcentury the Karoo had become "the major growth area" of Cape Colony and the Orange Free State. *The Cape of Good Hope Annual Register* in 1855 reflected a general sense of prosperity—Cradock, it wrote, had fifteen horse mills, forty-three water mills, two lime kilns, and four wool washeries.[9] By 1860, the magistrate called Cradock a "thriving bustling place." During the American Civil War, 1860 to 1865, which disrupted the export of cotton to Britain and increased the demand for wool, Cradock flourished.[10] The district's prosperous Dutch Reformed farmers built a substantial, austere, and classical church in 1868, modeled on St. Martin's-in-the-Fields in Trafalgar Square, London, acknowledging a pervasive British influence. The town soon followed

Fig. 1. Market Square and the Dutch Reformed church, Cradock, 2 April 1904. Photographer: W. W. Lidbetter. (Lidbetter Collection, © Rhodes University [Cory Library])

suit with grand buildings of its own: a public library, municipal offices, and a town hall (fig. 1).[11]

In 1881, the Cape Government Railway line came through the town, placing Cradock on the preferred route connecting Port Elizabeth to markets in the interior. But no important industrial development followed, much to the disappointment of local boosters. The town's fortunes continued to depend on the export of raw staples—wool, mohair, and ostrich feathers—which, until at least the mid-twentieth century, were processed outside the region and the country. Insofar as Cradock's fortunes depended on those of the region's "capital," Port Elizabeth, it may have shared in that port's decline. Designated the "Liverpool of Cape Colony" in midcentury, Port Elizabeth lost its leadership position from the 1880s on,[12] and Cradock was to remain a place on the way to somewhere more important.

There was, however, from the 1860s on, a remarkable growth of towns in the region.[13] In 1865, the Cape census listed only 9 towns with more than 2,000 inhabitants; but it listed 16 in 1875, 25 in 1891, and 48 in 1904. The proportion of the Cape's total population in such towns went from 15.5 percent in 1865 to 31.3 percent in 1904. As for Cradock, its population increased from 712 in 1875 to 8,381 in 1904, but fell to 6,453 in 1911. By the 1921 Union census, Cradock had grown into a multiracial urban settlement of 3,275 whites, 1,759 Africans, 1,659 coloreds, and 114 Asians.[14] Whites were divided (though not by the census) between Afrikaans speakers and English speakers; the Africans included Thembu and Mfengu, both Xhosa speakers, and Basuto, who spoke Sotho; the Asians included Indians and Chinese; the coloreds included indigenous Khoikhoi (then known as "Hottentots"), descendants of freed slaves, and people of mixed African and European descent. The four principal categories—white, African, colored, and Asian—would become the basis of segregation and its successor apartheid.

The Peopling of Cradock and the Making of Racial Categories

From Cradock's beginnings, its dominant whites had insisted on preserving their racial distinctiveness through marriage, though there had been frequent sexual contact between whites and people of color in the Cape since the beginning of white settlement in 1652, under the Dutch East India Company.[15] The racial attitudes of the Dutch, including a refusal to concede equality to Africans and mixed-race people, were largely shared by the five thousand British settlers who reached the Cape in 1820; their presence in the Eastern Cape, including Cradock, reinforced the already established structure of racial exclusiveness.[16] Such exclusiveness included the definition of the subdivisions of people of color, but it took some time to achieve consistency of terminology. For example, in 1855, "coloured people speaking the Dutch language" were included among those to be "located" in Cradock's location; this partially linguistic category was later dropped. The 1891 Cape census divided the population into "The Six Main Races: European or White; Malay; Hottentot; Fingo; Kafir and Bechuana; and Mixed and Other," categories that were repeated in the 1904 Cape census. The first all-Union census of 1911 reduced the "Main Races" to three—"European or White," "Native," and "All Other Coloured Races," which included Asians.[17] In the 1921 census, doubtless to accommodate demands by whites for the segregation of Indians, especially in Natal and the Transvaal, the number of races became four by a separation of "Asiatics" from the other "Coloured Races."[18]

By the 1920s, the term "coloreds" had come to include groups of differing appearance and historical origin: "free blacks" (that is, descendants of individuals who had gained their freedom before the emancipation of slaves under British rule in 1838); the "Cape Malays" (a Muslim community from various parts of Asia now largely concentrated in Cape Town), and the descendants of former slaves. Slaves had always provided the bulk of skilled labor at the Cape, and after emancipation in 1838 some of the former slaves probably became Cradock's colored artisans and skilled workers in the building trades. One large

Cradock family, for example, bore the name "Cupido"—a name that could indicate either slave or Khoikhoi origins.[19] The colored classification also included remnants of the indigenous Khoikhoi (earlier known as "Hottentots") and San (Bushmen), the first peoples in contact with Dutch settlers from 1652 on. These groups had lost their autonomous political and cultural life as a result of repeated military defeat at the hand of whites, in addition to a devastating smallpox epidemic in 1713 and loss of pasture and hunting and gathering lands. It took some time for governments to decide where to classify them. In Cradock's curfew regulations of 1902, "Hottentots" were included with "Natives," a rule that survived in the new location regulations for Cradock drafted under the Natives (Urban Areas) Act of 1923 and the Liquor Act of 1928. But the trend nationally, and in the Union census, was to include "Hottentots" with coloreds, whom the 1950 *Official Yearbook of the Union* would define as "mixed and other coloured . . . Cape Malays, Bushmen, Hottentots and all persons of mixed race."[20]

In the 1920s, Cradock's Africans were the town's second largest grouping after whites—primarily Xhosa-speakers who had been displaced by war and conquest from their farms and, for a century or more, had moved into Cradock seeking employment. They came in larger numbers after 1835 when the Cape government gave sanctuary to the Xhosa-speaking Mfengu ("Fingoes"), believed to be refugees from the military expansion of the Zulu kingdom. Cradock, like several other towns, established a "Fingo location"; other Africans probably came in on their own as laborers and domestic servants.[21] During "Mlanjeni's War" of 1850, named after a prophet who claimed that God would "help the black man against the white," part of the Cradock district was overrun by Thembu, also a Xhosa-speaking people. The war ended with a colonial victory, but the conflict between Africans and whites over land and cattle continued. In the mid-1850s, after a young Xhosa girl named Nongqawuse claimed that two men had told her in a vision that all living cattle should be slaughtered and all grain destroyed, the Xhosa slaughtered 400,000 cattle, and 40,000 people died in the resulting famine. By early 1858, 33,000 Xhosa men had moved into the Cape Colony as laborers on farms and in towns, accelerating the growing permanent involvement of Africans in the colonial economy and their residence in its towns. Some of their descendants live on farms in the Cradock district today, and in the 1970s Thembu constituted the largest African group in the town's African location.[22]

After 1900, Asians began to come to Cradock in small numbers, mostly to set up small shops. The 1921 census counted 114 Indians and Chinese, their household heads almost all shopkeepers. (That census noted that a "large influx of Asiatics" had led the Cape parliament to pass its first Immigration Restriction Act in 1903, certainly no expression of a liberal tradition.) The restrictions may have worked: in 1909 there were 16 Cradock Asians qualified to vote in parliamentary elections, and an identical number in 1925.[23] All Asians lived in town (not the location) but played no role in the town's political life. Their presence was a non-issue until the apartheid era, when, after 1950, the municipality and the government enforced the Group Areas Act.

There were also whites coming in from the countryside. When the railway came in 1881, Cradock's permanent skilled white working population grew. Its well-paid railway crews and artisans lived in the "Railway Camp"—more politely, the "Railway Reserve"—of fifty-four "cottages."[24] At the same time, with the advancing capitalization of agriculture, many white farmers and rural workers, English and Afrikaans speaking, were becoming impoverished in the Eastern Cape. In the 1890s an ideological shift occurred among policymakers: white poverty came to be seen as a problem to be remedied by state action, not by charity alone.[25] In time, these refugees from the countryside became predominantly Afrikaans speaking, and many settled in small towns. In Cradock some established themselves as transport riders with donkey wagons and lived in slums like "River Street." Local white poverty was already serious enough in 1893 for the Cradock Dutch Reformed church to establish a school for poor white children, formally the Wilson School but identified as the "Poor School" on Cradock's 1924 map.[26] In 1926, at a thirty-fifth anniversary celebration of the founding of the *Midland News,* managing director Ernest Butler, in a speech reflecting widespread anxiety among whites about white poverty, pointed with pride to the paper's employees—five apprentices, four printer's assistants, and six delivery boys, "all white."[27]

An "Up-to-Date" Town: Cradock in the 1920s

Cradock was two towns, not one—the town proper and the location. The town was predominantly white; in the 1920s the location was made up of nearly equal numbers of coloreds and Africans. Cradock had all the trappings of a modest modern market town. On market days in the nineteenth century, cart and wagon owners from outlying farms had unharnessed and fed their animals and slept overnight in the square. Afrikaner farmers had also camped there when they came to the Dutch Reformed quarterly *nachtmaal* (communion) service. In the 1920s, the town's square was still a genuine market square: open four days a week in the early morning to sell fruit, vegetables, flowers, and firewood by auction. With its market square, monuments, show ground, churches, and the Victoria Hotel with its wrought-iron verandah and balcony, Cradock looked much like many other little towns in the British Empire or in the United States at the time (fig. 2).

Whites were divided by language, religious denomination, and political loyalty. In Cradock, Afrikaners were always the majority among whites, as acknowledged in the central location of the Dutch Reformed church.[28] Still, signs of the political and cultural ascendancy of the English-speaking minority

Fig. 2. Market Square and Victoria Hotel in the early 1920s. Photographer: W. W. Lidbetter. (National English Literary Museum, Grahamstown, South Africa)

were everywhere: the Cradock park was planted in the shape of a Union Jack; the drinking fountain for horses in the market square was a memorial to King Edward VII's coronation in 1902. Nearby stood a cenotaph similar to the one in Whitehall in London that commemorates the dead of the First World War. The town's local government institutions were British. Its town council was elected by local owners and occupiers of property, its nine members recruited from among local merchants, professionals, and retired farmers. British-born mayors and town clerks were common: in the fifty-two years between 1869 and 1921, only three out of twelve mayors, and none of the town clerks, had been Afrikaners. Yet municipal politics were rarely conducted on the basis of white ethnic divisions, and there was no British "Quality Street," no separate area where wealthy white English speakers were grandly housed.

Cradock had two newspapers: the English daily the *Midland News and Karoo Farmer* (founded 1891), and the Dutch weekly *De Middlelandsche Afrikaander* (1903), which changed its name in 1933 to *Die Afrikaner,* a reflection of a shift from Dutch to Afrikaans in official use and in the Dutch Reformed Church. Both papers reflected the common interests of Afrikaans- and English-speaking farmers and townsmen in advertisements for land sales, fodder, and agricultural hardware; and both reflected national political conflicts. True to the Quaker principles of its founders, James and Charles Butler, the *Midland News* had endeared itself to many Afrikaners by opposing Britain's aggressive policy toward two Afrikaner republics before and during the Anglo-Boer War (1899–1902). But the *Midland News* was also a British settler paper, supporting the South African Party and its policies of Anglo-Afrikaner conciliation and often taking comparatively liberal stands on racial issues.

Die Afrikaner, on the other hand, founded immediately after the Anglo-Boer War, was strongly Afrikaner nationalist in sentiment, espousing such causes as a new flag for the Union without British symbols, a new national anthem, official bilingualism, and the welfare of poor whites, most of whom were Afrikaans speaking. *Die Afrikaner* expressed the racial and nationalist views of many of its readers: on 12 February 1926, it ran an advertisement from a vegetable dealer appealing to Afrikaners to support "jul eie nasie" (your own nation). On the same day, the paper reported the doings in Bloemfontein of the Industrial and Commercial Workers' Union of Africa, then a prominent African organization. At a time when "Kaffer," the South African equivalent of "nigger," was deeply resented by Africans, and South African officials were, by and large, avoiding it, the headline read, "Kaffers word al meer Parmantig" (Kaffirs are Becoming Even More Impertinent).

For most of the 1920s, Cradock's mayor was an energetic greengrocer, John Deary, the son of an Irishman who had settled in Grahamstown in 1864. Deary would successfully pilot important new water and electricity schemes through the town council, part of continuing efforts to draw new white residents to Cradock and to burnish its image as a thriving "up-to-date town."[29] Deary and his colleagues on the council were responsible to an almost wholly white electorate that expected them to attract new businesses and residents. At a turning-of-the-sod ceremony in 1926, the National Party chairman of the town council's Water Committee, an Afrikaner auctioneer named M. J. Hattingh, painted a rosy picture of Cradock's future. "The day would come," he said, "when they would be proud of their town, when factories would be established and an opportunity would be afforded to every citizen to earn a living." Similar hopes persisted throughout the decade, despite all evidence to the contrary: "No one could doubt that in the near future Cradock would be one of the greatest inland cities," said another Afrikaner councilor, H. P. du Plessis, in 1929.[30] Cradock never did become a hive of activity, but the promotion continued: in 1936, the town clerk sent a flyer to the Empire Exhibition in Johannesburg along with a display of local cactus, claiming that Cradock was "RECOGNIZED as the most-up-to-date town in the Midlands therefore the "*CAPITAL*." With its favorable site, "health-giving" climate, plentiful filtered water, cheap electricity, and dust-free "paved streets," the flyer continued, Cradock was "a delightful residential town."

Letter and Spirit in a Racially Mixed Town: The Cape Liberal Tradition

In the 1920s, as part of Cape Province, Cradock was heir to a long legal tradition of limited liberalism in matters of race. After the British occupation in 1806, the authorities in Cape Colony had given people of color better access to the courts, and Ordinance 50 of 1828 extended civil rights, including property rights, to free blacks, Khoikhoi, Africans, and freed slaves. The Cape Municipal Ordinance of 1836 extended self-government to towns by establishing councils elected on a franchise based on property, not on race.[31] And, in 1853, when the Cape Colony gained limited "representative" government, the parliamentary franchise was also defined, not by race, but by income (£50 a year) or occupation of property worth £25. While these reforms, the foundation of the "Cape liberal tradition," ensured that populations and their rights were not comprehensively defined by race, they fell far short of establishing a regime of equal rights for all.[32] Moved by the promises of Cape liberalism, coloreds in Cradock had vehemently taken the British side in the Anglo-Boer War (1899–1902), offering to serve in militias against the Boers. The liberal tradition began to erode during the making of the Union of South Africa in 1909–10—when, for example, the South Africa Act (the Union's constitution) decreed that members of the new parliament would have to be European, and limited the nonracial franchise to the Cape Province only. Much Union government action after 1910 was aimed at eliminating the liberal tradition altogether.

Two features of the Cape tradition were highly prized by white liberals and by the people of color who benefited from it—the right to buy land and developed property and the parliamentary and municipal nonracial franchise, for which one of the qualifications was possession of property. The Cape municipal franchise was available to all residents, male and female, who owned property valued at £100 or occupied property valued at £200; the lower Cape parliamentary franchise was granted to all *men* who were literate and who earned £50 per year or occupied property worth £75.[33] While most location residents were excluded from the parliamentary franchise by the property qualification, they could gain the vote if they acquired sufficient income. The 1925 parliamentary Voters' List of 1,013 Cradock voters included 132 colored, 56 African, and 16 Asian voters. Of these, 55 colored, 9 African, and all 16 Asian voters lived in town; 77 coloreds and 47 Africans lived in the location. The number of colored voters in Cradock had more than doubled from 1909 to 1925, from 51 to 132, but the number of these claiming the franchise on the basis of ownership or occupation of property (as opposed to income) had increased only from 28 to 31; thus 50 of the 81 new colored voters were qualified on the basis of income. The number of African voters had nearly quadrupled, from 15 in 1909 to 56 in 1925, but only 2 of the new African voters qualified by ownership of property, and 39 claimed the parliamentary vote on the basis of income. Asian voters had not increased in number between 1909 and 1925.[34] The increases in the number of people of color gaining the franchise alarmed those opposed to any coloreds, Africans, or Asians voting at all. The Cape franchise was to become a burning issue from the 1930s on.

In about 1924, to publicize Cradock as an eminently desirable place to settle, the town council prepared a blueprint, "The Township of Cradock." It showed the subdivision of the town into numbered building lots. A small rectangle at the southern edge was labeled "Location Lots," a misleading representation of what was in fact a large and contiguous African and colored settlement that housed almost as many people as the town itself, separated from the town proper by only the width of Regent Street. But Regent Street was not a strict racial boundary. According to a 1931 report by a health inspector, coloreds occupied about 57 houses in town, Asian and colored shopkeepers owned residential property and conducted businesses in the center of town, and the "tuck shop" of the Boys High School was owned by Piet Alexander, a member of a large and successful family of colored shopkeepers and artisans.[35]

As a matter of legal right, Cradock's building lots in town, but not in the location, were open to purchase by all races, and all properties there were listed and valued in periodic valuations.[36] On the municipality's 1929 valuation of land in town, £482,622, or 96.2 percent, was owned by whites, 1.9 percent by coloreds, 1.2 percent by Asians, and 1 percent by Africans. Residents could build houses based on freehold sites with approved plans. From time to time the municipality sold town lots at auction, and racial residential patterns tended to reflect economic inequalities between groups. In 1926, for example, when the municipality made available 31 large lots, (about two-thirds of an acre), in a new prestigious "New Township" on Victoria Drive, all were bought by whites.[37] A year later, the town auctioned 24 smaller, cheaper residential lots of about one-eighth of an acre each in the Mixed Area, close to the location end of the town; the purchasers were 18 whites, 4 coloreds, and 2 Chinese.

Mixed Living in Town and Location

Freedom to buy land, build houses, and occupy shops and houses led to the formation of the Mixed Area in the town: most colored and African town dwellers lived in a poor neighborhood between Carrington (later Voortrekker) and Regent Streets (map 1). This neighborhood, which had no official name, was precisely the kind of multiracial neighborhood that the Group Areas Act of 1950 would aim to eliminate. It was occupied, around 1924, by white (principally poor Afrikaner), colored, Asian, and African families. Quality houses occupied entirely by whites were on its upper slopes, while the houses of coloreds, and Asians especially, were concentrated downhill on three streets—Sprigg, Cawood, and Frere—that ran perpendicularly into Regent Street, the location border. In this downhill neighborhood of about 75 lots, 31 coloreds,

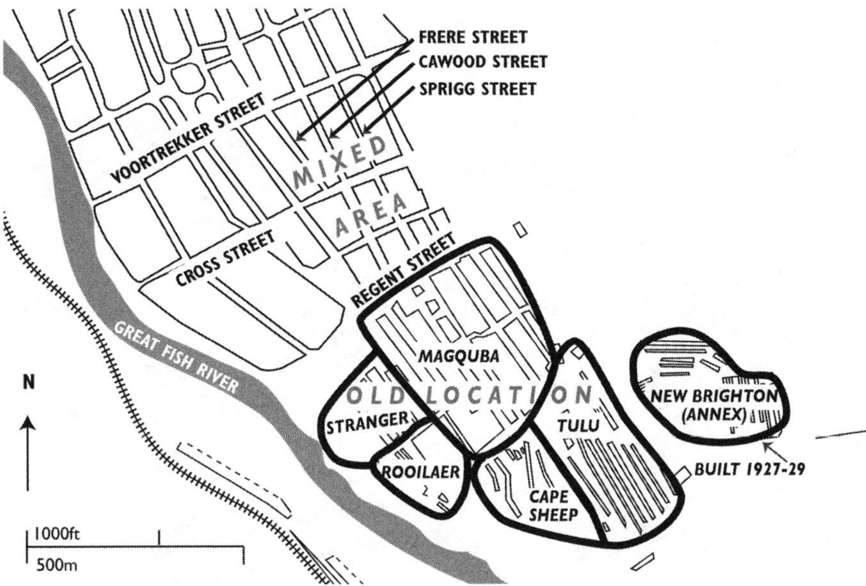

Map 1. Cradock Location and Mixed Area, 1926–29. (Map by Mariah Reisner, from reconstruction based in part on author's conversations with Patrick Mali and in part on "Cradock Location" enclosed in Annual Report 1946–47, Cradock Health Center, TBPA GES 1653 54/32, from which the author erased structures and roads built after 1926)

6 Asians, and 2 Africans owned houses; other people of color rented, making up the 57 houses officials believed to be occupied by people of color in town.

The Mixed Area was a place of modest one-story brick houses on unpaved streets. In the 1920s, it became the site of important institutions for location residents and people of color in town: the Immanuel Church, a Dutch Reformed Mission church for coloreds; the Holy Rosary Mission, a Roman Catholic church and its boarding school for colored boys and girls; the Coloured Methodist church; and the Basuto Methodist church, the only African church outside the location.[38] Closer to Regent Street were a handful of small shops serving location and town residents and run by a Syrian, two Chinese families, and three Indians.

There is no notable record of persistent racial conflict in the Mixed Area, although there were a few intermittent complaints by whites that coloreds were living in town at all.[39] Some colored residents, in the aftermath of the Group Areas Act of 1950, described the neighborhood in the age of segregation as a golden age, when interracial friendships abounded. In 1971, David Curry, the deputy leader of the colored national Labour party, who grew up in Cradock, recalled that coloreds "used to grow up amongst whites."[40] There was much

Fig. 3. "Fingo Location": wattle-and-daub beehive huts, probably in Rooilaer or Stranger, 1900. Photographer: W. W. Lidbetter. (Lidbetter Collection, © Rhodes University [Cory Library])

neighborliness—one colored woman informant told of a white neighbor, a police sergeant, who passed the time of day each morning with her husband and periodically put a glass of brandy on the wall separating their two properties.[41] Nevertheless, coloreds suffered discrimination: in 1924 they protested, to no avail, through their African People's Organisation (APO), against the marking of benches in the municipal park with signs for "Europeans only" and against the segregation of the taxi rank.[42]

On the southern side of Regent Street, the legal boundary of the town, lay the location—a crowded and meager living space for the nearly three thousand Africans and coloreds dependent on the town for work and subject to the municipality's control. It was a collection of small houses, shacks, and beehive huts built by its residents on land they could rent but could not own (fig. 3).

The 1920s location had none of the most modest features of planned town life; no paved roads, curbstones, drains, street signs, or lights; no street of shops or a market square (and no market); no memorials, public park, or playground; and few public buildings except a tiny one-room office of the location superintendent on rock-strewn Lwana Street. The only other public buildings were some almshouses, a few "isolation houses" for tuberculosis and venereal disease patients, and three African churches: St. Peter's Mission (Anglican), Lwana Memorial (Methodist), and African Methodist Episcopal, the first two of which doubled as schools.

Before the late 1930s, maps of the location appear rarely in official records. To reconstruct one in the 1920s, we must use a rough sketch map made by the municipality in 1946. The names of the quarters often referred to by officials and by location residents as individual "locations" have been superimposed on this map—Magq“uba, Stranger, Rooilaer, Cape Sheep, and Tulu (map 1). Even though the location was contiguous to the predominantly white town, no town street name continued on into the location. There were no numbered lots there—blocks of location sites were indicated simply by rectangles. In 1936, in an attempt initiated by the Location Advisory Board, the municipality strove to give the location more local character by naming a series of numbered streets outside the old core after six colored and twenty-one African local notables.[43] Though generally used by location residents to indicate where they lived, the quarters' names did not, apparently, become the basis of any organization's activity except that sports clubs were frequently identified by quarter.

In 1924, Dr. W. A. Murray of the Union government's new Department of Public Health, during his first "systematic sanitary inspection" of Cradock's urban area, described the location as "depressing and unsuitable."

> The Location is a straggling one composed of three different sections. . . . The uppermost section [that is, up the slope of the hill] is composed mainly of dwellings built of rough stone and mud with zinc [galvanized iron] roofs. . . . the houses in this section have no yards or gardens attached and are bleak and depressing to look at. . . . [From Ntimbela to Mona Street—the sections known as Tulu and Cape Sheep]
>
> The middle section of the location consists of rather better class houses inhabited by coloured people and having small yards and gardens attached which are very homelike. Many of these have their own sanitary conveniences. [From Taai Street to Taylor Street—Magqbuba]
>
> The third or last section contains about 150 round bee hive huts of wattle and daub often with petrol tin annexes. These huts while usually kept very clean are mostly dark and ill-ventilated. [From Minnaar Street to Sitela Street—Stranger and Rooilaer][44]

According to addresses on the 1925 parliamentary voters' list, the Magqbuba section, the closest to the town border, was, in spite of Murray's assertion to the contrary, inhabited by both African and colored people. This superior quarter, the town clerk said in 1923, had come into existence because certain coloreds and Africans wanted to separate themselves from the poor and had offered to pay higher rents for their fenced sites.[45]

In 1928, the location superintendent made a rough valuation of the buildings in the location. It shows 29 rooms in "buildings" (not described) valued at £34 per room, 308 houses valued at £20, 197 houses at £15, 13 at £10, and 38 at £3. Thus the location contained 585 "living units" for a population of about 3,068, an average of 5.24 persons per unit, most of them single-roomed huts. The total assessed value of buildings and improvements for the location was £11,869, which comprised 2 percent of the 1929 valuation of the town, the home of only a slightly larger population (3,275 whites and about 350 coloreds). The average value of a living unit in the location (£18) was under 3 percent of that of the average value of the 609 houses in town (£575).[46]

Although there was no enforced separation of coloreds and Africans within the location, coloreds tended to cluster in Magquba, the least poor neighborhood and the one closest to town. Neither law nor custom had ever required that all Africans and coloreds in Cradock live in the location, nor had the municipality ever separated the two groups residentially from one another. Despite this mixed character, local and national officials in the 1920s and later persisted in referring to it as Cradock's "Native location," at a time when "Native" was equivalent to "African" in official usage.

Location dwellers were subject to the authoritarian control of the town expressed in detailed location regulations that had evolved from the municipality's founding in 1837. Over time those regulations became steadily more precise and restrictive. After the office of superintendent was created in 1855, settlers in the location—Africans and coloreds only—had lots selected and pointed out to them by the superintendent. They had to show proof of employment, report all visitors, and mark their houses with numbered plates. Successively enacted regulations were cumulative, progressively tightening the letter of the law. Beginning in 1902, certain location residents were subject to a curfew, to be applied to members of named "native" ethnic groups—"Kafir, Fingo, Basuto, Hottentot, Bushmen, Koranna, Griqua, Bechuana, Zulu, and the like." Coloreds, notably, were omitted.[47]

In 1908, new regulations required adult males who were not already permit holders, along with their families living in location houses, to register with the superintendent and pay for a lodger's permit. These regulations neither excluded coloreds from the "native location" nor required that they live there, nor did it assign them to a separate section of the location. Under the regulations, an inspection by an official could ascertain whether "there are any natives living in or at the location who have no right or authority to be there," a provision that did not exempt coloreds from registering and paying the monthly fee.[48]

This regime of increasing regulation did not provoke African and colored leaders to create a single organization to represent their interests. Separate languages, cultures, and institutions sustained separate identities. Churches, the principal local nongovernmental institutions for Africans and coloreds, served one racial group or another. All the colored churches were located in the Mixed Area in town and owned in freehold the land on which they stood: the Holy Rosary Catholic Mission; a Congregational "Independent" church, the oldest church building in Cradock; the Sendingkerk (Dutch Reformed Mission); and the Coloured Wesleyan church. All their ministers lived in town and participated in the activities of the colored African Political Organisation, founded in 1902.[49] All African churches, on the other hand, were in the location, except the Basuto Wesleyan on its border. According to a list compiled by the location superintendent, G. P. Wilken, in 1935, 98 percent of African adults were Anglicans or Methodists: 400 attended St. James (Anglican), the largest church in the location, and 380 attended Lwana Memorial, the Methodist church.[50] Africans, whether church members or not, sent their young men and women away to the country for coming-of-age initiations.[51]

Unlike the colored ministers, African ministers lived in the location. In the early 1920s, the Rev. John Solilo of St. Peter's Mission (later named St. James), Cradock's African Anglican priest and a noted Xhosa poet, frequently appeared as a political leader, addressing the town council on behalf of a "Vigilance Association," which seems to have had an intermittent existence, usually called into life to protest particular actions by the municipality.[52] Solilo was succeeded in 1928 by the Rev. James A. Calata, who two years later established a branch of the African National Congress (ANC), the principal African political body in the Union, becoming a leader of national stature but living on in Cradock.[53] Throughout his forty active years in Cradock, Calata faced the difficult choices of a leader of a mixed, increasingly disenfranchised, community. Was he to be a location leader speaking for all residents, colored as well, or an African leader speaking for Africans only?

Divisions in education and sport paralleled those in religion. In no sport did whites and people of color compete against each other. The churches, not the municipality or the Union government, were the "managers" of African and colored schools; most churches served as schoolrooms during the week and became the principal organizers of sport for children. For most African men, rugby was the game of choice. The clubs seem to have been organized by location quarter: members of the "Blues" (1916) came from Tulu, the "Spring Rose" (1920) from Rooilaer. Coloreds were separately organized in the "Universals" and the "Chickens." African and colored rugby teams competed with each other and with their equivalents in other towns.[54]

In the late nineteenth century, Africans began to forge an African identity, rather than sustaining a number of the previous ethnic identities. The African National Congress was self-consciously African, resisting attempts by white authorities to emphasize ethnic differences among Africans.[55] But Africans and coloreds in Cradock did not develop joint organizations. Where English- and Afrikaans-speaking whites in town had little difficulty maintaining a common front on issues of segregation, the location's African and colored leaders frequently found themselves in substantial disagreement on questions of local governance.

By the 1920s, Cradock had established itself as a farmers' service center with a dominant white population looking vainly for investment and additional settlement of whites from outside. Municipal officials (all white) recognized the four categories—white, African, colored, and Asian—into which the town's population was now legally divided. The four groups were spatially distributed by race—all whites lived in town, virtually all Africans in the location, all Asians in town, and coloreds in town and location. Coloreds, alone of these groups, formed part of two racially "mixed" communities that straddled Regent Street—the Mixed Area in town and part of the location. Although the Mixed Area was accepted by whites as an aspect of the Cape tradition, that acceptance was reluctant. Mixed communities were accepted on sufferance; national and local policymakers in the age of segregation assumed that coloreds would one day be housed separately.

For a long time, local authorities were unsure whether, and how, to distinguish "natives" officially from "coloureds." Only in 1923 did the Natives (Urban Areas) Act try, hesitantly, to bring a semblance of consistency throughout South Africa. By its very name, the act defined urban Africans, and the locations they lived in, as special legal entities, but it did not specify or clarify the position of coloreds; indeed, the little it added to colored legislation was included almost as an afterthought to accommodate the Cape anomaly. In drafting the 1923 legislation, Union officials continued the practice of calling locations "native locations," although the wording was not correct for many Eastern Cape towns, and certainly not for Cradock. The act defined a location as "recognized by law as a place for the residence of natives," and by section 5 (i) gave the governor-general, that is, the Union government, the power, if it so chose, to require all "natives" in an urban area to reside there. The act also recognized that many locations were "mixed": section 4 (3) asserted a right for coloreds to live in locations "until [the local] authority has satisfied the Minister [of Native Affairs] that adequate and suitable accommodation is available for coloured persons elsewhere in the area." The act also, by section 28, exempted coloreds from the pass laws but made no mention of Asians, presumably because Asians had long been excluded from the locations anyway and were expected to live in town.[56]

The language of section 4 (3) implied clearly, however, that coloreds could some day lose their right to reside in a location. In the 1920s, terminology and practice were hardening in the direction of defining the colored "race" more rigorously: after 1921, "Coloured" was a specific racial census category, but a remainder category, a catchall for all who were not "European," not "Asian," and not "Bantu," the latter term increasingly used as synonymous with "Native." No longer was a location referred to as a "coloured village." Because the act made it possible for coloreds to stay in a location until provision was made for them elsewhere, a location was to remain “mixed” until the municipality, the provincial, or the national government or, more likely, all three together changed the law and found the resources to separate coloreds in towns from whites and coloreds in locations from Africans.

Devising a set of location regulations was an inherent aspect of controlling people of color. The overall spirit of regulation was consistently if not uniformly restrictive; policy aimed at keeping the African urban population small and its movements circumscribed. For coloreds in the location, the 1923 intrusion of the national government had somber implications: all residents of the location were now likely to be subject to the same confining rules as Africans, unless especially exempted. The act had barely been passed when an event in the Cradock location pointedly raised this central issue: would all location rules that applied to Africans apply to coloreds too?

2

Lodgers, Layabouts, and Laborers

Access and Residence for Coloreds and Africans

A Raid at Dawn

At 4:45 a.m. on 29 March 1925, before dawn on a rainy Sunday, the South African Police arrested about 80 men in Cradock's location and charged 76 of them with being in the "Municipal Nat.[ive] location without a Lodger's Permit." (A lodger's permit required a monthly fee of 1.5 shillings.) An unknown number of those arrested were the grown sons of location families living at home. The court record later identified 41 as "Kaffir" (African), 18 as "coloured," and 17 as "Hottentot" (Khoisan), representing the principal racial categories of the location's population.[1] After 74 of the 76 were convicted and fined 10 shillings each, a veritable storm ensued, with a sustained protest, led from the beginning by coloreds and some Africans and supported by a few sympathetic whites.

This police raid may have been the first in Cradock's history to reach such public notice. Later legislation and administration procedures would focus more narrowly on African male workers, seeking to limit their permanent settlement with dependents in towns, but in Cape province, with its "mixed" locations, a location raid directed at a nonracial category like "lodgers" necessarily drew in coloreds and "Hottentots" as well.

Five days later, "A Protest" appeared in the *Midland News,* signed by J. E. Manuel (painter), C. M. Sauls (messenger), D. van Jaarsveld (storeman), R. E. Butler (painter), and C. Antonie (laborer), all identified as coloreds in the town's 1925 Voters' List and all residents of the location.[2] They had been born in Cradock, they wrote, and "never in the history of this location has such a thing happened here. . . . The police went into the house and into every room, throwing their lights on the beds and getting all the occupants on their feet. . . . How dreadful to see your sons and visitors, no matter how respectable, marching four deep to the pound kraal [enclosure] on Sunday morning." Though they lived in a location, those arrested were law-abiding. Had they broken any law?

The "Protest" included a barely veiled attack on G. P. Wilken, an Afrikaner who was the acting location superintendent during the illness of A. J. Urie, the

English-speaking incumbent. "In Mr. Urie's time we had a gentleman superintendent and highly respected by all classes of residents in the location." The raid was "disgusting. . . . We can only term it most un-British." The lodger's fee, the protest concluded, was an unreasonable tax on adult children living at home.

Colored leaders from town held a "mass" meeting that same evening in the schoolroom of the Independent Church (the Congregational church for coloreds). In the chair was Thomas Rafferty, a tailor, owner of a shop in the town center and chairman of the local branch of the African People's Organisation (APO), the principal national colored organization. "He had been born and bred in Cradock," he said, "and he had never seen such a thing." A nurse named Plaatjes and "several women" complained at the way "the raiders walked in." P. C. Goodman, a colored teacher and town resident, an excellent speaker, and active member of the APO, questioned the authority of the police and of Wilken himself: "Who instructed the police to carry out this raid?. . . If Mr. Urie were well such a thing would not have happened (hear, hear)." Alfred Pokomela, the African court interpreter, took the assault on Wilken further; he was sure that neither the magistrate—"a man of understanding"—nor the district commandant was responsible. He drew some satisfaction from the whole affair: "He had always prayed," he said, "for something to happen to bring the location together." The meeting closed with a resolution to send a deputation of three coloreds and three Africans to approach the town council and the police commandant.[3]

The *Midland News* took up the cause of the protestors in an editorial on 8 April, "A Case for Inquiry," which commended the inhabitants for their "constitutional manner." The "Lodger's Law," the paper argued, had first been imposed "to keep undesirables from invading the precincts of the location," thus adding a new category of individuals—"undesirables"—that was heretofore unknown.[4] The editorial supported the protestors' objection to the taxing of sons living at home and their resentment of the "gross indignity" inflicted on "respectable" citizens early on a wet Sunday morning: "To put it very bluntly, would any local authority dare to treat a body of European people in the same manner?. . . It is a case of excessive zeal in which someone has blundered and blundered badly," a case for "the closest public inquiry."

In 1925, G. P. Wilken, at thirty-one years old, was at the beginning of a lifetime's work as a Cradock location official. He was clearly astonished, though unrepentant, that his raid should have occasioned such a fuss. He wrote to the town clerk on 14 April:

> On several occasions Mrs. A. Urie and Native Constable Edward complained to me, about the over crowding in the Location on Saturdays and Saturday nights, especially when it is the last Sunday in the month. Causing Rowdiness, Drunkenness and fights, and the adults residing in the Location not paying their Lodgers Permits & [Mrs. Urie and Edward] Asking me to try and arrange for a raid.

He had gained approval in advance for a raid, Wilken wrote, from "a number of Councillors." In the aftermath of the raid, permits "to the amount of £19 to £20 [253 to 267 permits] have been paid," sufficient proof that lodgers had been evading payment. An early morning raid had been essential because Wilken could not find evaders "at daytime on my rounds," nor in the early evening. On one such earlier round, a resident had "deliberately refused" to allow his son to pay; Wilken had "summonsed" him, but the magistrate had simply cautioned and discharged him. Another resident had said that "if he was not employed by the municipality . . . his Son would never pay." Denying that he had done anything "drastic," Wilken criticized the authors of the "Protest" for failing to report their visitors and lodgers, "as this is a well known fact to all Residents that no one is allowed to remain in the Location without the permission of the Officials." He took "more than ordinary exception" to the way "certain ratepayers interfere," and resented complaints that "the Official" was guilty of "allowing squatters and Vagrants about the Location."[5]

On the same day that Wilken presented his letter to the town clerk, the town council met a deputation from the APO, which, despite its name, represented colored interests at the council meetings—two coloreds from town, six from the location. The outcry in the "Protest"—"how dreadful to see your sons and visitors marching four deep to the pound kraal"—suggests that colored visitors to the location had been arrested, to the mortal embarrassment of their hosts. Wilken's raid had raised an issue, apparently for the first time: did children, male and female, African and colored, over the age of eighteen have the right to remain in the locations, or were they to be treated as "lodgers"? And were visitors, too, to be subject to arrest? The deputation objected strongly to the manner in which the law had been enforced, and asked for relief from the lodger's tax. The mayor, John Deary, replied that such relief was impossible "at present." He had decided, however, to bring Cradock under the Natives (Urban Areas) Act of 1923, and this required formation of a Location Advisory Board to give the colored and African populations a nominal voice in the running of the location. The regulations would then undoubtedly be relaxed.[6] Two weeks later, location residents, unmollified and vehement against the lodger's tax, held another mass meeting in the colored Independent church school room on the edge of town. "Excitement in the Location. Must Women also Pay?" read the *Midland News* headline. (If any women were arrested, they seem to have been immediately released, since none were charged on the following day.)

At the mass meeting, the hall was packed with five hundred residents. "At times there was restiveness," the paper reported, "because of the intense feeling." A committee had sent a telegram to the prime minister, General J. B. M. Hertzog, protesting application of the lodger's tax to location children over eighteen. Goodman, the colored teacher who had protested at the earlier "mass" meeting, now appealed for calm: if no reply came from General Hertzog by 1:00 p.m. the following day, he said, and if there had been further arrests, the committee should appeal to the magistrate as the government's representative. But such orderly and decorous process was unsatisfactory to a strong faction of those present, who advocated refusal to pay the tax. "In view of their previous experience in connection with the raid," said Joseph [Joel] Macombring, an African bank messenger, "there was [not] much use in going to the Magistrate." Another resident moved "amid applause that the tax be not paid."

This instance of colored and African militancy had emerged after a highly publicized breakdown of order in Bloemfontein in the Orange Free State, where Africans had destroyed the location police station, and white civilians had opened fire, killing five Africans. Goodman appealed again to the meeting: "I warn you of what has happened at Bloemfontein. . . . We do not want that sort of thing to occur in Cradock." The chairman of the APO, the colored tailor Thomas Rafferty, called on William Cursons, then editor of the *Midland News,* to address the meeting. An embarrassed Cursons replied that he could not "recommend" that they pass a resolution "pledging themselves willfully to break the law. . . . They must remember that the Premier was a busy man, and on the previous day when the wire was sent, he had been welcoming the Prince of Wales." They should accept Goodman's suggestion to go to the magistrate. The meeting closed with the singing of "God Save the King."[7]

The mayor and his councilors, probably just as astonished as Wilken at the location dwellers' vehemence, temporized; Mayor Deary announced, on 4 May, that the lodger's tax would be stayed until the next meeting of council; on the same day he wrote to the Department of Native Affairs asking for a ruling on the legality of the tax.[8] There was yet another public meeting on 15 May in the Independent schoolroom, again under colored auspices and leadership. C. Sauls, a colored painter, resident of the location, and member of the APO, was in the chair. The sponsors had invited the whole "establishment" of officials regularly concerned with the location. The mayor (J. Deary), the magistrate (W. J. Vlok), the district commandant (Captain Kuhn [Kunhardt]), the public prosecutor (Sergeant Jones), the white minister of the segregated Dutch Reformed Sendingkerk for coloreds (the Rev. J. A. van Niekerk), "and others" were on the platform. All deferred to the magistrate, who adopted the stance of a lofty and sympathetic neutral: he was not there, he said, to "stand between the Location residents and the Mayor and Councillors," but as a representative of the government to answer questions.

John Manuel, a colored builder, joint secretary of the APO, and a signatory of the original protest, complained of the burden of the tax. Deary replied at length, substantially agreeing with the protestors. "The idea in the minds of the Old Council [the council in 1908] in connection with this tax was to do away with lodgers living in the Location huts." Hardly a house had been built in the location in the last five years, he said, and with people "frequently" coming in, where were they to go? Wilken, he conceded, had been overzealous in applying the regulation "literally" to women, though "the Ordinance says

'Every adult.'" He had asked the Department of Native Affairs for a ruling on whether a charge for a lodger's permit was legal, and on whether the tax could be levied on "young men and women living with their parents."

The tenets of Stallardism held that Africans should dwell in towns only to the extent required by the local economy. But the mayor sounded a theme that would have great importance for Cradock's African location residents in years to come: location residents had security in Cradock, he said, because, unlike those in locations elsewhere, they had "fixity of tenure." "There were people in this Location who had owned houses for years and they had the right to sell and transfer them; the incoming tenants being recognized by the Council can take transfer of the house and the owner be paid for it." "Because Cradock's location was almost equal as regards Native and Coloured people," he thought that coloreds should have some say on the advisory board. Again he urged residents to wait for the advisory board to be formed: "he had no fear that when the board came into existence, the regulations in the location would be relaxed." Manuel, the colored builder, moved that the meeting accept the mayor's advice to wait for a reply from the Department of Native Affairs, "when no doubt the Mayor would address another meeting." The motion was carried "unanimously and with enthusiasm," and the meeting closed, as before, "with the singing of the National Anthem."[9]

The long-awaited ruling by the Department of Native Affairs arrived from Pretoria in mid-June. "No charge can be made for a lodger's permit since the issue of such a permit does not connote a service rendered," the secretary for native affairs wrote. Such permits, without fee, were, nonetheless, a legitimate means of "control . . . which the local authority would have the opportunity of refusing in the case of loafers or bad characters."[10] When it came to grown sons living at home, the magistrate, for his part, supported the claims of the protestors, because the lodger's permit "impairs parental supervision over children when parents are finding it very difficult to retain their hold." The permit would not, in the future, be required of "children of householders." Lodger's permits without a fee continued in new location regulations until 1940, when a fee for services was again required.[11]

"Reasonable and Suitable": Model Regulations for the Location

In 1925, while Cradock town officials had their hands full with protests over the lodger's tax, the national government was pressing them to resolve other location issues. First, to avoid past abuses, it required Cradock and other towns to pay all location revenues into a newly established Native Revenue Account, rather than into the municipality's general fund. Second, the municipality was to examine and possibly adopt location regulations using the Model Regulations proffered by the Union government. Third, the municipality was to establish a Location Advisory Board composed of location residents.

The Model Regulations had been drafted in 1914 by the Department of Public Health and sent to the Department of Native Affairs, which hoped to persuade municipalities to adopt them.[12] A 1924 circular from the Department of Native Affairs, enclosing a set of the Model Regulations, pointed out that, under section 27 of the 1923 Urban Areas Act, new regulations must be "framed and approved" by the end of 1924.[13] In mid-1925, before the protests over Cradock's lodgers' raid had been resolved, the secretary of native affairs noted that the deadline had passed; "the Cradock Municipality had no legally enforceable regulations for the control of its location."[14]

The national codification of location regulations—concerned with permits, curfews, passes, building codes, and access by medical officers to location houses—would force Cradock's council to face, once again, the uneasy position of coloreds living in a Cape location. Were they to be treated like Africans? And if not, would the codification of regulations erode coloreds' established rights to be treated differently?

The Cradock regulations were to define, at least on paper, a highly restrictive regime of permits for all location residents. All forms of residence were subject to permits—a site, a house, or the right to be a lodger. Permits were to be granted only to those persons the superintendent judged "fit and proper." Persons with no residential or site permits, if over eighteen, had to apply for lodger's permits. All "visitors or strangers" were to be reported within twelve hours, and all location residents were subject to curfew, opening the possibility that curfews and passes would be required of colored location residents, who had not been subjected to either before.

Though principally a set of rules and prohibitions, the regulations also set some standards and obligations for the municipality. Officials were to record births and deaths and submit a quarterly report on the "health and management" of the location and an annual report from the local medical officer of health (MOH) on health and sanitation. Some minimum housing standards were also set: sites had to be at least fifty by fifty feet, and houses had to provide at least three hundred cubic feet of "air space" for each resident over ten (half of that for those younger). Water and elementary sanitation, critically important services to the location, now became mandatory: "The Town Council shall provide a supply of pure water, and . . . sufficient . . . sanitary conveniences."[15] Yet the regulation provided no machinery or a regular budget to ensure that the municipality's responsibilities for services, or indeed its controls of movement and residence, would be enforced.

The Location Advisory Board was described in separate regulations. It was, indeed, to be an *advisory* board. Elected by registered occupiers of location houses who were up-to-date with their rent, the board was to be suitably deferential to the location superintendent. The superintendent would chair all meetings of the board, and "the speaker," the regulations stated, "shall address the chair standing." Mayor Deary, who was determined to give coloreds equal representation with Africans on the board, was granted his wish by the national government's Department of Native Affairs. Two coloreds and one African were to be appointed by the council, and two Africans and one colored were to be elected by "registered occupiers" of the location.[16] When P.C. Goodman, of the colored APO, with the support of the white Women's Civic Association, urged the council to appoint him as a colored representative, the council resolved that he could not serve because "he is not an inhabitant of the Location."[17]

Africans and coloreds seem to have been equally dubious about the benefits of the Location Advisory Board, on which Deary had set such store. Coloreds had objected to the notion that a mixed African-colored body could deal with the affairs of all location inhabitants. On 15 May 1925, at the public meeting on the lodger's tax, Walter Mentor—a teacher, member of the APO, resident of the location, and frequent writer of letters to the *Midland News*—addressed the mayor directly on the question. "The Bill [that is, the Urban Areas Act] was purely one for Natives," Mentor said, "and General Smuts [then prime minister] had stated that one for Coloured people would be brought forward. Why then did the Mayor desire to mix up the two?" He got no answer.[18] The council moved ahead. In September 1925, the Vigilance Association, the local African organization, nominated two Africans, and in November, the secretary of the Committee of the Location Coloured Residents nominated one colored to the board; the other three were to be nominated by the municipality.[19] The board did not, however, meet until 1927; it received no nominations for 1928, but was duly constituted for 1929 and 1930.[20]

In August 1925, when the municipality submitted the full draft of its location regulations to two representative location organizations, African and colored, the responses of each were hostile, though with different emphases. The Rev. John Solilo, an African spokesman for the Vigilance Association, raised a number of objections. Not every man over eighteen should be required to apply for a residence permit; rather, there should be a "civil legal age" of twenty-one. Moreover, "it would be better if [residence issues] were left to our usage and custom as natives." Medical officers should not have unlimited access to location homes, and residents should be given longer to report their visitors. The new curfew, Solilo asserted, "revives the pass laws to be extended to the voters and interferes with their privileges." The Vigilance Association was interested, too, in material welfare matters: a site of fifty feet by fifty feet for a house was too small; lots should be four times larger, and the municipality should make building materials available. "Rules and Regulations are not the means of oppression but modeling the character of people," Solilo concluded. "We now leave all to the prerogatives of mercy of our town fathers."

On the same day, three colored residents of the location wrote to "lodge objection," presumably on behalf of the APO, against lodger's permits, against the requirement that "all visitors or strangers" be reported within twelve hours, and against the curfew on location residents. The regulations "in as far as they apply to colored persons" were "inconsistent with Sections 28 and 29 of the said [Urban Areas] Act. We humbly pray that [these] Sections be made applicable . . . to Coloured residents of the Location." (Section 28 exempted coloreds from the pass laws, and section 29 defined coloreds as any person of "mixed European and native descent.")[21]

The 1902 curfew regulations for Cradock had provided that no "native such as a Kaffir, Fingo, Basuto, Hottentot, Bushman, Koranna, Griqua, Bechuana, Zulu and the like" could be "in the streets, public places or the thoroughfares" between 9 p.m. and 4 a.m. without a "pass or certificate." They had made no mention of coloreds.[22] Both coloreds and Africans regarded the curfew as equivalent to a pass law, but the coloreds, who had been explicitly exempted from passes under clause 28 of the Urban Areas Act, were particularly hostile to it.

The municipality, complaining that coloreds roamed the town during the night, desired "to confine them to a location the same way as natives." But the secretary of native affairs resisted such an expansion of the curfew. The intent of the Natives (Urban Areas) Act in exempting the coloreds from the pass laws was, he said, "one of liberation not restriction."[23] Still, having considered further evidence of colored drunkenness in the streets, his department agreed to a new regulation, number 38, that all location residents had to have written permission from the superintendent to be absent from the location between the hours of 9 p.m. and 4 a.m.[24] African *voters,* that is, owners of real property in town, and those with a "certificate of good character" from a magistrate were to be exempted from the curfew. This addressed one of the Rev. Solilo's objections, that the proposed curfew would encroach on the "privileges" of voters.[25] On paper at least, the curfew would, however, now apply to colored residents of the location.

Neither the department nor the municipality was prepared to offer concessions or even to discuss the issues with location residents. In November 1925, the secretary for native affairs wrote that "the Department regards the regulations submitted by the local authority as reasonable and suitable." In October 1926, curfew regulations and provision for the advisory board were adopted and promulgated.[26]

With the new regulations in force, the withdrawal of the lodger's fee, and the creation of an advisory board of equal numbers of coloreds and Africans, Cradock's coloreds had won a temporary and equivocal victory. Practically speaking, they had prevented the taxation of children living at home and had won an implied promise of no more lodger permit raids. They had yet to see the effects on them of the new location regulations and of the operation of the advisory board. If Goodman was typical, coloreds had been especially incensed at being treated by an Afrikaner in such an "un-British" way, and they had responded with sustained protests—two deputations and three mass meetings—between 29 March and 14 May. Wilken himself thought he was doing nothing new; he was simply using a customary raid to deal with recent disorder on paydays, disorder linked to the presence on weekends of numerous young African and colored visitors. Coloreds, it seems, both of town and location, were outraged to be treated as location residents on a par with Africans. They had assumed command of the protests throughout and dominated the proceedings in public meetings. Yet they formed no joint protest organizations with Africans and issued no joint manifestos. By securing equal representation on the location board, coloreds found themselves on a par with Africans, just as distant from the rights of whites as Africans were. And the new advisory board raised the possibility that town coloreds would be subject to a location body that Africans, through their growing numbers, would come to dominate if representation were to be based not on race—that is, with equal representation of Africans and coloreds—but on comparative numbers.

Searching for the Layabouts and the Unemployed

Both local and national governments were increasingly preoccupied with stemming the age-old townward "drift" of Africans who did not wish to work on the surrounding farms. Part of Cradock's attraction to others stemmed from its relatively high cash wages—higher, in particular, than wages on farms. In 1926, the thirty-one-year-old Rev. James Calata organized a "Natives and Coloured Peoples Conference" in nearby Somerset East, where he served as an Anglican priest. Delegates to the Peoples Conference compared farm wages in the nearby districts of Cradock, Graaff-Reinet, Adelaide, and Jansenville and agreed that workers were receiving only 8 to 10 shillings a month in cash.[27] In town, by contrast, male "gardeners and houseboys" were paid 20 to 60 shillings a month, "usually with some food." Even after paying a location site rent of at least 3s a month, they were considerably better off than farm workers.[28]

In 1937, the Department of Native Affairs set up a Native Farm Labour Committee to inquire comprehensively into the question of farm wages and conditions of work throughout South Africa. Two years later, the committee reported that, in the Eastern Cape, in-kind supplements to cash income had generally declined and labor tenancy had virtually disappeared, with many sheep farmers now objecting to their laborers grazing small stock on their farms. African and colored males in the countryside had become dependent on wages in cash and in kind (mostly rations); but cash wages on farms in the Eastern Cape, according to the historian Sheila van der Horst in 1942, had hardly changed over the previous fifty years.[29]

As South Africa industrialized, there were increased work opportunities even in a small town like Cradock. Builders, local authorities, commerce, and the railways all paid much higher cash wages than farmers did, even though they paid little, if anything, in kind. Africans were drawn to the Cradock location, too, by the lure of schools for their children. (There were few schools for colored or African children on the outlying farms.) In the fourth quarter of 1926, for example, 296 colored children were registered in public schools in town and 320 African children attended schools in the location. By contrast, only 44 African children were registered in schools in the surrounding district. One African child per 24 inhabitants in town went to school; in the district at large one child in 162 inhabitants did. Small though the town's African school population was, an African child had far greater opportunity for education in town than outside.[30] According to the Cradock Joint Council, "Children are sent into the towns to go to school and reside with relations and are ultimately followed by their parents."[31]

In 1931, the town clerk wrote to the Native Economic Commission that "there has been a fair influx of natives into our location . . . and this is mainly attributed to the farmers having fenced their farms." A reduction in their demand for labor, particularly for shepherds, had been the result.[32] Cradock's Joint Council, in its submission to the commission, stated that Africans in Cradock "nearly all belong to the Tembu Tribe." Newcomers came from Glen Grey, few of whom retained a home there, and from Cradock farms. "Natives sometimes leave Tembuland in parties to work at shearing on the farms and then drift into the towns."[33] Africans intended their migration from Tembuland, and from the farms, to be permanent—or so the Joint Council's submission implied.

After South Africa devalued its pound in 1933, the country experienced a boom generated by higher prices for gold and agricultural exports and by rapid secondary industrialization. With the improving economy, even more workers left the farms for towns, and Cradock's farmers began to complain once more that the location was a haven for "layabouts."

Many whites who considered themselves liberal, even before Union in 1910, regarded it as legitimate to control Africans' access to towns. James Butler, an idealistic Quaker who, with his brother Charles, had founded the *Midland News* in 1891, expressed in his editorials an ambivalence on the issue.[34] While generally sympathetic to Africans and coloreds on many straightforward welfare issues, Butler had long accepted the view that settlement by Africans in districts like Cradock ought to be limited.[35] In 1923, on James's death, his successor as editor, William Cursons, agreed that some kind of influx control was necessary, and in a 1926 editorial, he took the same line as his predecessor: Africans were "guests" of the town. They were there on sufferance, he implied, subject to the goodwill of their white hosts.[36]

At the beginning of the Depression in 1930, members of the newly organized Cradock Central Farmers' Association brought multiple pressures on the municipality to assure farmers of a labor supply by limiting the right of residence in the Cradock location. Constituent farmers' associations in the Cradock district complained about "leeglêers" (layabouts, loafers) in the location at a time when labor was "so scarce."[37] The council responded by setting up a special committee to investigate "all layabouts or unemployed" in the location. The town clerk, P. de K. van Heerden, tried to help by circulating a detailed questionnaire to eight farmers' associations to ascertain the number and gender of workers needed, with details on wages, accommodation, duties, and access to grazing. When eight farmers responded with particulars on their labor needs, Van Heerden tried but had limited success in helping them: "I have sent out families," he wrote, "but sometimes they are hired on the road by some other farmer and I am none the wiser."[38]

Although town officials continually denied that the location was a haven for the idle whose labor was in demand on farms, they and the local voters to whom they were responsible had their own reasons for not wanting the location to grow: they did not want to pay for more services without an expanding local economy. Hence, there was no real conflict of interest between the two contending white groups: the town fathers would have been happy to supply workers for the farmers if there were unemployed in town, and the municipality did try to exclude new African settlers from the urban area. But their task was made harder by the "fixity of tenure" that Deary had extolled in 1925, which provided security to those Africans who owned their houses and to those who bought them, and which also by implication included a right of those born in Cradock to stay there.[39]

During the Depression, the population of the location rose and fell. In 1933 Wilken's biennial location census reported a location population of 5,469 persons, 539 of them unemployed. By the next census in 1935, the population had fallen to 4,921, with only 119 unemployed, 100 of whom were "waiting on instructions to leave on Government Relief Works."[40] These were hardly the kind of figures farmers wanted to hear. In 1935, the government, responding to widespread anger among farmers, appointed the Young-Barrett Committee to inquire into the "Residence of Natives in Urban Areas" and to propose amendments to the Natives (Urban Areas) Act of 1923, which, so farmers and many municipalities had protested, was failing to enforce the essentials of the Stallard doctrine; that is, to limit the number of African males in a town to those needed for local labor.[41] While City Clerk Van Heerden was preparing his submission to the committee, a "very strong deputation" of farmers demanded strict control over Africans' access to the location. To this, Van Heerden responded that he had already instructed the location superintendent "not to allow strangers to reside or enter the location."[42] (Eight months later, he refused a lodger's permit to an Alfred Glovo because the council had decided to adopt a "definite policy not to permit strangers to enter the location.")[43]

Van Heerden's response to the Young-Barrett committee's questionnaire was based on Wilken's census of 1935, but though this census distinguished for the first time between coloreds and Africans in the location, Van Heerden concentrated on the latter. It was difficult, he wrote, "to obtain a true statement from the inhabitants of the location," to identify the "surplus" that many believed was responsible for a purported rise in stock theft. Thieves from the location apparently used bicycles "to carry away the carcass of the sheep," so the police could not "trace the 'spoor' [tracks]." Control of influx was a "practical impossibility unless we have a fair number of policemen." "The population of the location," Van Heerden wrote, "could be reasonably balanced with the requirements of the town . . . only . . . with the assistance of the government by taking . . . such surplus labour which will be available in the location from time to time."[44] Van Heerden had raised two central issues: how to find the alleged surplus and what to do with it if it existed. Though he denied the existence of a surplus, he put the burden of disposing of it on the central government.

"Closing" the Cradock Location

Completed in 1936, the Young-Barrett Report included a rigorous criticism of the entire Stallard approach.[45] It suggested amendments to relax the 1923 Native (Urban Areas) Act in several respects. This was not what farmer-dominated parties in parliament wanted to hear, and the report was not published. Nevertheless it did become the basis of important changes embodied in the Native Laws Amendment Act of 1937, a response from the Union government exasperated by the unwillingness or inability of small towns like Cradock to find and "do something" about their alleged labor surplus.[46] The 1937 act established a biennial census for all locations to identify native men "surplus to the labour requirements of the area" and empowered the minister of native affairs to remove them. Towns were urged to proclaim their locations "closed," using a rarely used power established under section 5 of the 1923 act. Municipalities could *require* all Africans in an area to live in designated townships. The act also eliminated the right of Africans to buy land in towns and empowered municipalities to fence their locations to control access and egress.[47]

Parts of the new act were enforced rapidly. By Proclamation 115 on 12 May 1938, Cradock, along with 106 other local authorities, was declared a "closed" area. "No native" could enter to seek work or live there unless going to a job, or "on a bona fide temporary visit," or seeking work with permission of the local authority "in view of the labour conditions then existing."[48] The "closed" nature of the location now gave the town clerk an all-purpose justification for refusing to allow Africans to move in.

Coloreds, too, became subject to exclusion from the location, even though the Natives (Urban Areas) Act of 1923 had provided that they had a right to stay in a "mixed" location until separate provision was made for them elsewhere in the urban area. In 1938 that right was eroded when the Appellate Division of the Supreme Court ruled that the 1923 clause had been intended to protect the rights only of those coloreds who lived in locations at the inception of the act, along with their descendants. The right was not "an absolute or unqualified right, but a right subject to the regulations applicable to the other residents of the location." The Department of Native Affairs sent a circular on the ruling to "all urban local authorities."[49] In fact, from the end of the 1930s, and even before the appellate court decision, the Cradock municipality had been prohibiting nonresident coloreds from moving into the location. For example, on 6 January 1938, Edward Hewett, writing from a town address, asked for "permission to reside in the location as a Coloured" and was turned down. In 1939, 1940, and 1943 there were further rejections, including a request by Elizabeth Rainers to stay only to the end of the war. Yet, in 1941, the town clerk advised the newly created Cradock Native Labour Advisory Board that "there is no fixed policy whereby coloureds can be forbidden to come into the location."[50] That is precisely what the municipality was, in fact, doing on an ad-hoc basis, even though no "fixed policy" had been adopted.

The 1937 act had signaled the central government's increased determination to limit the growth of the African population in towns and cities and to control those already there. A year later, P. G. Caudwell, one of the new urban areas inspectors appointed by the Department of Native Affairs, undertook the central government's first systematic inspection of the Cradock location and suggested that the municipality reinstitute a fee for the lodger's permit (at the time issued without charge) to augment "native" revenues, thereby limiting demands on general revenue.[51] At first, the municipality resisted, but then it agreed to a new regulation of June 1940, requiring an adult who had no residential or site permit to pay 1 shilling a month for "sanitary, water and other services." Such a permit removed the objection of the law officers in 1925, that a fee for a permit could be charged only if a service was rendered.[52] The lodger's tax now became a fixture, providing an average income of £311 per year from 1941 through 1947, a roughly 6 percent addition to native revenue. It derived from payment by about five hundred lodgers.[53] Besides new revenue, the new tax provided the municipality with more information on the location's population, including lodgers, who were now the only large category of adults other than holders of site and residential permits.

The enactment and initial enforcement of the 1937 Native Laws Amendment Act had taken place at a time when Cradock's farmers and the municipality were contending over Africans' access to the location and prevention of stock theft. In 1938, the location census required by the act found in the Cradock urban area 745 African males eighteen years and over; of these, 492 were employed there, 80 elsewhere; 36 were unemployed, 126 aged and unfit, and 11 were "bona fide" visitors. The town clerk set the "reasonable labour requirements of the urban area" at 500 workers, about the level of employment at the time, but he was "unable to state" how many "it is desired to be removed" because of the "extra-ordinary fluctuation of labour requirements."[54] Cradock's farmers continued their pressure on the municipality to enforce control of access to the location.

In 1939, the Native Farm Labour Committee recommended the creation of a

Native Labour Advisory Board in each district, made up of farmers chosen by their organizations and chaired by the magistrate. Cradock set up such a board in 1941.[55] It included J. H. Moolman, the local general of the Ossewabrandwag (OB), the militant quasi-fascist Afrikaner organization opposed to South Africa's participation in the Second World War; A. C. A. Lombard, a noted moderate; and Alex Bartman, a vehement member of the National Party. The mayor at the time, J. A. Cull—secretary of the Cradock United Party, pro-British and pro-war—complained to his party organizer that "not a single United Party member" had been appointed to the labor board.[56]

The board had before it two principal issues—wages for African farm workers and control of access to the Cradock location. The farmers recommended cash wages of 11 shillings a month "for a trusty native," plus rations, which they estimated at a value of 8.5 shillings. One Department of Native Affairs official wrote angrily that such wages were an "*aalmoes,*" a mere pittance.[57] The board had no executive powers, and we have no record of any increased wages provided by Cradock farmers. If the wages the farmers proposed were representative of current levels in the district, as is likely, workers were hardly attracted to the Cradock countryside by the generosity of their employers.

The question of access to the location raised the hackles of the farmers and the mayor at a special meeting of the council in March 1942. The council stuck to its established positions. According to Cull, the location could not be fenced because of wartime scarcities and the high cost of £500 a year for guards at the entrances. The council had tried "to introduce a system of Pass Laws" in 1940—the registration of service contracts—but the minister had refused to promulgate them because "we are going through very trying times."[58] After vigorous and public resistance by the municipality, the Labour Advisory Board seems to have stopped meeting, but the Central Farmers' Association itself kept up the pressure, prodding the council three years later to enforce the new consolidated Natives (Urban Areas) Act of 1945, especially section 29, directed at expulsion of the "idle" and "disorderly" from locations.[59]

One means to control the movement and settlement of African workers was the registration of service contracts provided for in Section 23 of the Natives (Urban Areas) Act. Such contracts were a form of pass, legitimizing a worker's residence in a location. A United Party councilor, G. L. E. Venter, obtained copies of regulations in force elsewhere, along with the recommendation that the municipality under Sec. 5 *bis* of the Urban Areas Act require that "all natives," except those exempted, "reside in a location."[60] When the council submitted draft regulations, including the registration of women, to the Cradock Location Advisory Board, the board of three Africans and three coloreds objected vehemently; the regulations would introduce a "bad system of passes" and burdensome fees, and, in addition, they smacked of "forced labour."[61] The Department of Native Affairs, which had called for tough enforcement, appealed to the council not to introduce "restrictive legislation applicable to natives which ought to give rise to a sense of grievance" during the "difficult time" of the war. (France had recently fallen to the Germans.) The council agreed.[62]

In 1945, as the war in Europe came to an end, the municipality revived the draft regulations for service contracts that the department had rejected in 1941, including a demand that registration be extended to women.[63] The department resisted the registration of women. Yet "no good purpose," the town clerk wrote "will be served in the Cradock area if male natives only are registered." The department stuck to its position but mollified the council with a promise that the matter would be dealt with in pending legislation.[64] When the Smuts government fell in May 1948, registration of service contracts had not yet begun in Cradock, even for men, but the question would be revived and acted on by the National Party government.

"Give Me the Village of My Father": Africans and the Right to Stay

Written applications by employers or residents for permission to live in the location are rare in municipal records before 1938, but the Second World War brought change: of fifty-six written applications from 1 January 1938 to May 31 1948 (all but seven made by whites on behalf of employees), forty-four were turned down.[65] The council also rejected the applications of four coloreds who applied to move from town to location.[66] Several employers applied on behalf of skilled long-term workers who could not be replaced locally.[67] Another eleven applications were from white women who were moving to Cradock to retire and wished to bring a trusted, often aged, servant with them; their pleading letters to the town clerk were nearly all to no avail.[68]

When discussing the lodger's fee twenty years earlier, the mayor, John Deary, had declared that Cradock's location residents had "fixity of tenure," meaning, presumably, that those who owned their *houses*—none were allowed to own the land—were entitled to buy, sell, stay, and bequeath indefinitely. But by 1941 some Africans were not so sure: they were afraid of losing residential rights if they left town for any considerable period—or so A. Akena, a Cradock school principal and member of the African National Congress, told the Native Labour Advisory Board.[69] In 1943, Cawood Hani, an African laborer, wrote to the location superintendent to claim his birthright after the death of his father, Moontlik, who, in 1940, had been living in "Hut number 345."[70] The junior Hani had left Cradock for a time but now cited his family's long connection with the area and with "Marthan Street 345," where his father's grandmother and mother had lived and where he himself had been born. "That's why I say this village is my place," he wrote, "Please sar give me the village of my father."[71] He succeeded in his appeal: in 1949 a house was allocated, and he was still in Cradock in 1958, when he applied to the Location Advisory Board to repair his house in Africa Street but was turned down.[72]

Hani's case raised the issue of the survival of a birthright, but it involved only himself and the municipality. Another case involving a local liberal lawyer and the Department of Native Affairs raised the question of the validity of location regulations—whether language imposing an obligation on the municipality could be enforced. In October 1946, Keith Cremer, a lawyer in Metcalf and Co., a firm that had long defended a liberal reading of Cape law, took up the case of Jan Tgintgi, a laborer born in the district. In 1939, when a Mrs. van Zyl, his employer, moved to town, Tgintgi had moved with her. She applied to the town clerk for a house for him, his wife, and three children, writing, "I know it's against the rules . . . to allow country servants to trek into town." The council turned her down.[73] Tgintgi first lived illegally in the yard of Van Zyl's town house and then, with the connivance of a location official, stayed in the location for three years. In 1946, Wilken ordered him to leave. "He had nowhere to go" wrote Cremer, "and when pointing this out he was told he could go to Kaffirland [Xhosa country]. . . . The suggestion is ridiculous. He has never been in Kaffirland, has no ties there and would starve to death if he went there." The council had refused to let him stay, Cremer continued, because the Cradock Location was now "closed."[74] The magistrate, G. Frank, clearly sympathetic to Tgintgi, forwarded Cremer's letter to the town clerk, but the council refused once more, whereupon Frank suggested that Cremer write to the secretary for native affairs "in view of the principle involved."[75] The department argued that the council, according to its own regulations in the case of someone employed, "shall grant" a site permit or a residential permit if a dwelling were available. Was there any reason to believe that Tgintgi was not a "fit and proper person"?[76]

The municipality, meanwhile, produced its own version of events. The town clerk wrote that, in 1939, the council had refused Tgintgi entry because of "numerous complaints that the Town Council of Cradock houses natives who could be employed as labourers on the farms." The municipality had prosecuted the location headman who had allowed Tgintgi to rent illegally; the court had sentenced the headman to six months' hard labor, and fined Tgintgi five shillings. "I trust," concluded the town clerk, "that this information is sufficient proof that the complainant is not entitled to be or to become a resident of the Cradock Location."[77] The secretary for native affairs refused to accept this contention; under the Natives (Urban Areas) Act local authorities had an obligation to house employed natives. Yet the council dug in its heels. The department apparently dropped the matter after the council voted, in September 1947, for the fifth time, to refuse entry to "strangers such as Tgintgi."[78]

This deadlock between the Department of Native Affairs and the municipality over the interpretation of the municipality's regulations reflected the growing sense of crisis among Cradock officials regarding the policy of influx control. With overall population, and especially that of Africans, continuing to grow, the municipality was in a panic. It learned that Wilken's count of the 1946 Location population, 6,391, was probably an undercount by 2,032;

the Union census figure that year was 8,423.[79] Cradock did not question the department's interpretation of the letter of its regulations; it simply insisted on excluding Tgintgi, no matter what its own regulations and Proclamation 115—which "closed" the location—said. The department itself, long divided over Stallardism and, if anything, opposed to it, saw Tgintgi's case as important from the beginning; it sent its first letter on the case, with the "relevant papers," to the secretary of the Native Laws [Fagan] Commission.[80] This commission, in its report just before the 1948 general election, would reject the Stallard doctrine, though without recommending entirely free labor and housing markets for Africans—thus enunciating what Rodney Davenport has called a "liberal aspiration rather than a policy." It was far from treating African workers as equal to white workers. The post-1948 apartheid regime would reject the Fagan Report outright, since it had explicitly accepted the permanence of African urbanization.[81]

In 1946, the Department of Native Affairs had to deal once more with lodgers' fees and with the rights of colored people to live in locations. The Department of Social Welfare, which had been given oversight of a new Coloured Advisory Council three years before, was raising such questions. "Coloured people as distinct from Natives are not compelled by law to reside in a Native location," the secretary of the Department of Native Affairs wrote. "So long as colored persons live in urban native locations, they must expect to be treated on the same footing as other location residents as to both control measures . . . and charges for rental and services." The department favored "the idea of complete separation of the natives and the coloured people. . . . Such separation presupposes that the urban local authority will make provision (e.g. in special townships) for the accommodation of coloured persons." Yet the department recognized that it had no power to "*compel* urban local authorities to embark upon housing schemes for coloured persons as distinct from Natives" (emphasis in the original).[82] So African rights to residence in town had disappeared, and coloreds who had settled in Cradock since 1923 had no *right* to live in a location. If decisions on access by coloreds during the recent war were anything to go on, and if coloreds were systematically excluded, the *town* was the only place for them to go to, an ironic outcome for those who favored rigorous segregation of whites from both coloreds and Africans. According to these officials at the end of the age of segregation, it was local authorities who controlled both access of coloreds to locations and the building of segregated housing for them. If there was no particular urgency for special housing for coloreds, the mixed location could stay mixed, and if the rights of those in the location in 1923 *and their descendants* were respected, that could be for a very long time.

From the 1850s, in most jurisdictions that would be part of the Union of South Africa, the law had allowed all citizens to buy and occupy land, both commercial property and housing in towns. Only in the Orange Free State was freehold denied to people of color.[83] In many small towns like Cradock, economic growth and a property law that was partly race-blind had led to some sorting by class between towns and locations: in Cradock a large number of coloreds and a few Africans lived in town, which was, however, still highly segregated. Neither law nor practice resolved the ambiguities of the 1923 legislation, which did not make a location a wholly "native" place, though it clearly envisaged such a future outcome. Whites, coloreds in town, and Asians after 1948, when the apartheid regime came into power, could still move about free of the curfew and could buy and rent property in town. Africans, however, by 1937, had come under increasing restrictive national legislation, and coloreds' access to locations had been limited by municipalities' rights to exclude them.

Wilken's raid in Cradock in 1925 seems to have had entirely local roots—the persistent disorder in the location on pay days. Yet it reminded coloreds living in the location that a territorially and racially defined regime in the location placed them under many of the same conditions as Africans. Coloreds living in town had not been caught up in the raid. The year after the raid, the Department of Native Affairs conceded to Cradock's demand that the curfew be applied to coloreds in the location but resisted applying it to town coloreds. Thus coloreds were divided into two territorial groups, with those in town having greater freedom of daily movement than those in the location. Although coloreds' immediate grievance about the raid was resolved when the lodger's fees were canceled, and although town and location coloreds later joined in a common political front on issues of access, Africans and coloreds did not do so, either at the time of the raid or later. If Wilken stopped raiding colored homes, as seems likely, a focal point for a colored-African front had disappeared.

For Africans themselves the definition of territory where they could reside became increasingly racial: only exempted Africans—a tiny group in Cradock, that is, those with the franchise, owners of property in town, or those with a certificate of good character—were to be free of the curfew, wherever they lived. The curfew made the location into a ghetto for virtually all Africans in the precise historical and legal sense used in parts of Europe—a place where they had to spend the night or explain their presence elsewhere. But whatever the municipality might try to do about "strange natives" who wished to settle in the location, it seems to have acknowledged, from the year of the raid on, the right of Africans born in Cradock to stay there. Even in 1941, the town clerk acknowledged to the Native Labour Advisory Board that some Africans had a right to stay: "when a strange native is found steps are taken to get them out . . . but the position in relation to natives born in this location and who have stayed here is different."[84] The right to stay could, by implication, be lost by absence, as Akena told the Labor Advisory Board, and as Cawood Hani feared in 1943. In 1952, national legislation recognized the right of those born in a town to stay.[85]

The Native Laws Amendment Act of 1937 denied Africans throughout South

Africa the right to buy land and property, or to reside, in towns. Cradock itself did not, apparently, seek power to deny these rights to coloreds. Cradock coloreds, at least until the late 1930s, could live in town or location and, indeed, according to the Natives (Urban Areas) Act, had a right to live in the location until the municipality made separate provision for them elsewhere. Few seem to have noticed that, for coloreds, the right to live in the location was a qualified right. But a year after the 1937 amendment, even before the appellate court had explicitly given town councils the power to do so, Cradock had begun to exclude coloreds from the location, though the main preoccupation of officials, local and national, was the growth of African population in urban areas.

In 1925, the Department of Native Affairs had brushed aside the objections of Africans and coloreds to the new location regulations. In the 1930s, it took a somewhat more liberal line, with some national officials attacking the Stallard doctrine root and branch. Yet they did not act as if they could enforce policies that local authorities or interests did not like. In 1946, the department and the magistrate took up the Jan Tgintgi matter, believing Tgintgi was entitled to stay in the location according to Cradock's own rules. Yet after the municipality dug in its heels, the department did not override local intransigence, perhaps because it had no sanctions to threaten and no bribes to offer.

An urban area's population could be legislatively divided into "races," counted accordingly, and treated differently; but to give each "race" its own territory and thus end residential and commercial "mixing" would take unambiguous intent, political will, and resources at local and national levels. Such a comprehensive enterprise would involve drawing and enforcing already sensitive boundaries, controlling access to residential areas and freedom of daily movement, and limiting access to liquor and other amenities. Neither the will nor the resources were available for such a project before the apartheid regime came to power in 1948.

3

Race and the Politics of Liquor and Beer

In September 1928, three years after the "lodgers' raid" in the location, the district commandant of the South African Police in Cradock, responding to unspecified "Complaints by the Public," ordered a white constable to report "on a Beer Raid duty." At 7 p.m. one evening, J. V. Kilian proceeded to the location, with one colored and two white South African Police constables and one African municipal constable in tow. In the first hut he entered, he found forty gallons of "Kaffir Beer," took a sample, found the alcohol content over 2 percent, dumped it all on the ground, and arrested the African owner. In the second hut he discovered a "large amount" of beer, poured it out, arrested the owner, and handed over his two prisoners, handcuffed together, to a "Special Native constable." The constable, Edward Quengwa, tried in vain to dissuade Kilian from raiding more homes, telling him that "the prisoners have escaped, Boss." Kilian continued on from hut to hut, finding "great quantities" of beer, but nobody at home to be arrested. Apparently, word had spread that he was on the hunt. By 9:30 p.m., Killian was back in the charge office with one lone prisoner. The next morning at 6 o'clock he returned to pursue those who had escaped the night before but "could not even ascertain their names." He did destroy "approximately 200 gallons of Beer which we found outside the huts in the veld." The "natives" had been "intoxicated, obstinate and threatening. Had it not been for the fact that I had them covered under a revolver at times, they would almost certainly have attacked us." For another raid, he recommended that "more men, Europeans, ought to be assigned."[1]

Kilian's 1928 raid, like Wilken's raid in search of unregistered lodgers in 1925, was part of increasing governmental intrusions into households, particularly African households, in the location. The lodgers' raid was directed at both Africans and coloreds, the beer raid at African beer brewers alone. From the 1920s on, such raids were often led by location superintendents, reinforced by municipal and national police. By 1942, Wilken regarded raids as routine: "I find the [street] lights inadequate," he wrote, "when I do my night raids."[2]

The Rise of Temperance and the 1928 Liquor Act

It had long been a rural African tradition to brew beer from sorghum, maize, or other grains and to drink at religious rituals and in celebration of the harvest cycle. Almost from the start, Europeans interfered with local custom. Under Cape law, since 1890 farmers in the Cradock district had the legal authority to forbid their laborers to brew.[3] In Cradock's location, brewing had been prohibited by municipal regulation from at least 1908.[4] Beer brewing was no longer an event controlled by the harvest cycle: sorghum and other grains could now be bought in any season from shopkeepers in town as well as in the countryside. Illegal brewing became a primary year-round occupation and the only source of income for some African women who had migrated to the location from farms and reserves, often after their husbands had deserted them.[5]

The Cradock beer raid fiasco took place in a changing political landscape where the drinking of alcohol—by any race—was under challenge. South Africa of the 1920s was experiencing a rapidly growing, church-based temperance movement, led by women and linked to similar movements active in Britain and the United States from the mid-nineteenth century. Their most spectacular victory was the 1920 enactment of prohibition in the United States. The strength of these temperance movements had inspired teetotaling South African whites, coloreds, and Africans, especially members of the "free" churches: Methodists, Baptists, Congregationalists, and Presbyterians. American speakers, among them the prominent William E. ("Pussyfoot") Johnson, toured South African towns, including Cradock, to bring news of the achievements of prohibition; they found eager listeners among members of the Women's Christian Temperance Union (WCTU), whose first South African branches had been founded in the 1890s. Like its counterparts overseas, the South African WCTU advocated both the prohibition of liquor and the enfranchisement of women.[6]

A successful temperance movement could be regarded as a mechanism of social control of new urban masses; members of the "dangerous classes" were likely, as Kilian had observed on his Cradock raid, to be "obstinate and threatening" when "intoxicated." In the United States, WCTU forays had singled out working men's saloons. In Cradock, the temperance movement was also a movement of social reform in which civic-minded citizens, particularly women, saw uninhibited drinking by male wage earners as a potent threat to family livelihood and stability and a source of domestic violence, misspent wages, and neglect of children. But in South Africa, those concerns were also viewed through the lens of race: national government policy permitted whites to consume liquor and beer, while controlling and prohibiting supply to an almost totally disenfranchised African majority. In urging the suppression of domestic brewing by black women, temperance advocates, wittingly or not, advanced the interests both of liquor producers, whose products could be consumed in lieu of African beer, and of the white farmers, who saw drinking as a threat to the efficiency of their labor. In Cradock, the temperance movement was supported by churches across the spectrum, from local white and colored members of the "free churches," including the Dutch Reformed church, to the town's small but influential band of socially liberal Quakers, including the publishers of the *Midland News,* which refused to accept any liquor advertising. The South African Temperance Alliance, a national umbrella body founded in Cradock in 1893, nearly persuaded parliament in 1924 to vote for "local option," which would have allowed towns to ban liquor sales to all races if a majority of local voters approved. The motion failed by only two votes—probably marking a high-water mark for the temperance movement in South Africa.[7]

In 1928, the South African parliament passed a consolidating Liquor Act to coordinate the varying liquor laws of the four provinces. Regional variations in regulating liquor supply to Asians and coloreds remained, but a Union-wide ban was placed on the sale of liquor to Africans; the old Cape liberal right of "exempted" Africans to buy liquor was abolished. The imposition of controls by race had been gradual. In 1908 the Durban municipality in Natal banned beer brewing by Africans, but a year later a Natal law permitted municipalities to exercise a monopoly of beer brewing for sale to Africans, the "Durban system." Under this system a local Native Affairs Committee used profits from running a beer hall to the cover costs of administration, housing, and welfare, while also increasing control of the African population.[8] The Natives (Urban Areas) Act of 1923 let municipalities choose among prohibition, domestic brewing, or a municipal monopoly beer hall whose profits would go to a new native revenue account. Cradock chose prohibition.[9]

Local licensing boards in the Cape, meeting annually, set hours of sale for everyone and designated how much a colored or Asian male could buy in a single outlet on any one day—one half bottle of spirits and one quart of any other liquor, wine, or fortified wine.[10] For whites the sole restriction on alcohol purchase, beyond controls on the alcohol content and purity of liquor and commercial beer, concerned time: typically liquor could be bought in hotels and bars from 10 a.m. to 10 p.m. and in "bottle stores" from 10 a.m. to 5 p.m., but never on Sundays except by those whites who were hotel guests. Farmers in the wine-growing regions of the Western Cape had had enough clout to preserve a legal exception for the so-called *tot* system, whereby they could give their colored workers a daily ration of wine to be consumed in their employers' presence. But that was a regional concession: Eastern Cape farmers would not consider it. "No person shall supply . . . any liquor to any native," the 1928 Liquor Act stated, "And no native shall obtain or be in possession of any liquor." It was illegal for anyone to take liquor into a location, a provision directed at whites, Asians, and coloreds, since it was illegal for an African to have liquor anyway. As it was illegal to supply liquor of any kind to Africans, anyone, of any race, who acted as a liquor courier was at risk, but especially colored residents of a location who legally moved in and out every working day.[11]

Only whites could hold liquor licenses under the 1928 act, and only for "bottle stores" or hotels more than half a mile from a location. White males could drink in "European" bars; white women had access to hotel "lounges." Colored and Asian males drank only in "Non-European" bars. A colored location resident who had drunk too much at, say, the Masonic Hotel, could walk past the Dutch Reformed church and across the market square to the Victoria Hotel, where he could drink some more, on his way home, as, of course, could any white. The law governing access and the geography of liquor outlets increased the probability of colored drunkenness in town. In 1926, the magistrate and the town clerk used colored drunkenness to support the extension of the curfew to all coloreds. Colored drunkenness became an issue throughout Cape Province and the subject of repeated commissions of inquiry, all of which, incidentally, recommended abolition of the *tot* system, but to no avail.[12]

Cradock's small police force could readily enforce the law that prohibited Africans from buying liquor in bars or bottle stores. But a colored man could buy the quota in each of six different stores (as of 1924) on the same day and cart the lot home to the location.[13] As a result, a number of coloreds became liquor couriers for location Africans, who often had no legal alternative. Coloreds were not required to carry racial identity cards or passes. The location was not fenced, and there were no defined points of entry. The new 1928 Liquor Act provided no effective means of coping with colored inebriation in public, reinforcing the widespread white stereotype of coloreds as feckless and degenerate drunkards.[14]

African women in the location brewed beer and "concoctions" far more potent than the 2 percent brew allowed by the 1928 act.[15] Earlier local and national officials had cracked down on drunks in the town streets, on colored couriers smuggling liquor into the location, and on the domestic production of sorghum beer and concoctions. From early 1924, the Cradock municipality sought a regulation to ban the sale and possession of sprouted grain, a brewing agent, in the urban area,[16] and in 1925, the government did ban outright the sale and possession of sprouted grain in Cradock, a ban extended to "fermenting agencies" like malted and liquid yeasts.[17] The police insisted, however, with the support of the Department of Native Affairs, that the Natives (Urban Areas) Act prohibited only the *sale,* not the possession, of sprouted grain.[18]

The Cradock Joint Council and the Case for Home Brewing

Several months before the raid, the Rev. James Calata arrived in Cradock to head the Anglican St. Peter's Mission in the location (fig. 4). He would prove to be a notable figure in Cradock and South African history. Calata considered brewing sorghum beer an African tradition that white authorities should leave alone. Born in 1895 near Kingwilliamstown in the Ciskei of Independent Presbyterian parents, Calata had become an Anglican and served as assis-

Fig. 4. The Rev. James Calata (1895–1983), priest at St. James Church, 1928–68. Portrait copied from picture in Calata House, Cradock. (Courtesy of Peggy Calata)

tant missionary at St. Stephen's in New Brighton, Port Elizabeth, clashing at times with his white superior who resented his independent style. In 1926 he had organized a conference on farm wages, the beginning of a long career of activism. As a liberal, he insisted that whites live up to their own principles and extend liberal institutions and policies to all of South Africa's people. As an Africanist, he composed hymns in Xhosa and acted as the chaplain of an order that celebrated the life of Ntsikana, the early nineteenth-century Xhosa Christian prophet.[19]

When Calata came to Cradock in mid-1928 seeking a dry climate for his "weak chest," he joined a small but unorganized group of liberals in establishing a Joint Council of about two dozen men and women concerned with improving the conditions of people of color in the location. The council met for the first time in early December 1928, with eight "European," six "Coloured," and nine "Native" members.[20] Mary Butler, a white nurse who ran the municipal dispensary in the location, became one of the most formidable members; she and Calata became joint secretaries of the council.[21] With some members teetotalers or simply loyal to the WCTU, the council was destined to divide over liquor issues.

In February 1929, the town council, under pressure from the national Department of Native Affairs, proposed a new location regulation: any superintendent, police officer, or constable who had "reason to suspect" that "Kafir-Beer" was "made, supplied or sold" could "enter [premises] and search without warrant . . . at any time of day or night. . . . The persons so searching" could seize any "Kafir beer found, and if the possessor was found guilty of infraction of the beer regulations, the beer could be destroyed." As required by the Natives (Urban Areas) Act, the council advertised its plan: objections were to be lodged at the town hall.[22]

Cradock's white WCTU branch, led by English-speaking women, promptly passed a resolution welcoming the effort to suppress the making and selling of "Kaffir" beer, but it had qualms. It shared location residents' resentment at the conduct of the police, who apparently had been conducting energetic raids even before the new regulation was passed. "The homes of innocent people," the WCTU said, should be protected by "the authority of the location Superintendent." The town council passed the regulation anyway, and the Department of Native Affairs approved it a year later. The mayor, M. J. Hattingh, announced that while prosecutions for beer brewing had quadrupled from 27 in 1927 to 106 in 1929, convicted offenders had not been deterred. Hattingh appealed to white social workers, ministers, the Location Advisory Board, and "the leading inhabitants of this location" to propose some new option. The Joint Council, he said, ought "not to look at the matter from the temperance point of view solely."[23]

Under Calata's leadership, the Vigilance Association, an African organization, had drafted two resolutions for the Joint Council's executive to consider in 1930. They were hardly temperance proposals. One proposed scrapping prohibition and introducing a permit system for home beer brewing, with African warders granted extensive powers to supervise the system. There would be no net cost to the municipality, since the council could "dispense with the services of a European assistant at the office." Three Africans could be hired for the price of one white clerk. The second resolution called on the Joint Council to sponsor a "Round Table" to discuss the permit proposal. The town council, the Women's Civic Association (WCA), "the Various Church Denominations," the WCTU, the "Non-European Vigilance Association," and the Location Advisory Board should be represented.[24]

At a public discussion that included the magistrate, the mayor, the commandant of police, and "a number of others," the Joint Council executive proposed domestic brewing by permit but did not mention dropping the "European assistant" or the appointment of the proposed African warders. The magistrate nonetheless opposed the idea, and the commandant of police took a clear prohibitionist and segregationist line: if brewing became legal, it would be impossible to keep the beer below the required percentage of alcohol. What was needed instead was "segregation of Native and Coloured, and . . . the license [to purchase and drink liquor] allowed the Coloured people [should] be seriously curtailed at once." The mayor was against both domestic brewing and municipal sales to Africans, but "if respectable Natives confined drinking to their homes they should not be arrested. . . . We have a right to raid, but not to raid respectable citizens."[25]

Joint Council members presented impressive written documents from the superintendents of Cape Town (Ndabeni), Port Elizabeth (New Brighton), and Bloemfontein locations, all of which permitted domestic brewing. When the Joint Council voted at the end of the meeting, the motion to allow home brewing passed by 12 votes to 2. But that vote concealed strong opposition. At another meeting, without public officials present, the issue was debated again. According to the *Midland News,* colored and African members had been afraid to talk freely with the mayor, police commandant, and magistrate in the room. This time vigorous opposition to brewing came from temperance-minded whites. The Africans, except for the Methodist minister, the Rev. J. Bam, were "solid" in favor of home brewing—"drinking of this beer was a national custom of the Bantu." The coloreds were almost all against it. The rest of the whites divided on sectarian lines—Methodists, the Baptist minister, and a member of the WCTU against brewing, the Anglicans and the Quaker Mary Butler, in spite of her vehement teetotalism, in favor. A motion to rescind the resolution in favor of brewing lost by a single vote.[26]

The three Africans and three coloreds on the Location Advisory Board refused to abandon support of "total prohibition," as did Mayor Hattingh. As a stock auctioneer and a leading Nationalist, Hattingh could not easily defy Cradock's organized farmers, who had loudly opposed relaxing beer sales in the location.[27] The town council itself would never agree to brewing, the town clerk told his contemporary in Queenstown, because brewing was "too dangerous."[28] So, despite the views of the Joint Council, prohibition remained the law in Cradock for the next five years.

The End of Prohibition: Cradock Gets a Municipal Beer Hall

In 1935, a Union government report recommended that municipalities like Cradock should no longer be allowed to prohibit beer brewing. Instead, they could set up a beer hall controlled by the municipality. Alternatively, they could "authorize any male Native of established good character to carry on business as a manufacturer and retailer of kaffir beer." The authority would rent "sites or buildings" to such entrepreneurs, a plan later known as the "hotel system." African entrepreneurs could sell only to "male natives over 18."[29] Further restrictions came under the 1937 Native Laws Amendment Act, which ended prohibition and provided for the sale of beer to all bona fide residents of locations, which in towns like Cradock included coloreds. Under this amendment, if no beer hall was opened and no Africans were licensed to manufacture and sell on their own, domestic brewing would automatically become lawful. It would also become lawful for African women "over the apparent age of twenty-one years," to buy beer from licensed Africans or beer halls.[30]

In Cradock, however, members of the Cape African Congress were unanimous in their disapproval of a beer hall. They were divided over legalized home brewing and the hotel system run by African entrepreneurs. Calata argued that home brewing encouraged the "illicit liquor traffic which was ruining Bantu *kwedinis* and *ntombis*" (uninitiated African boys and girls), and would require more police, while hotel keepers would have an interest in suppressing unlicensed brewers.[31]

But Cradock could not stand pat. General Smuts, then the acting minister of native affairs, had made it clear that prohibition was no longer an option for towns like Cradock; the choice was between a municipal beer hall, a hotel system, and legal domestic brewing. Cradock's town council voted unanimously "that licenses be granted to duly approved natives to control the beer halls."[32] The new mayor, Charles Butler, like his niece Mary, the location nurse, was a zealous teetotaler; he had forbidden the serving of alcohol at any mayoral function. Nevertheless, he did favor a municipal beer hall over the hotel system.[33] "It was his decided opinion," he said, "that the brewing of kaffir beer should be under the direct control of the municipality. . . . [It] would not be a wise policy for the Council to allow this profit to go into the pockets of private people." Such profit should go into the coffers of the municipality to supply services such as "streets, sanitation and housing" in the location.[34]

Wilken, the location superintendent, reported that Africans on advisory boards throughout South Africa were appalled at the failure of parliament to consult "native opinion" before passing the Native Laws Amendment Bill. They opposed beer halls as "alien to tribal law" and virtually unanimously demanded domestic brewing.[35] The African leaders in Cradock agreed, and Calata deplored the "ineffectiveness" of the Location Advisory Board in not resisting Butler's proposal. A. Akena, Calata's right-hand man, was shocked at the "council's somersault. . . . The Natives could not be blamed for their fears because they had been promised fine schools" and better salaries for teachers when the "poll tax was introduced [in 1925]," part of it to be spent on African education, but "not a single native school had been erected."

The president of the Joint Council, a liberal farmer named Owen Walters, convinced that "in the end the location would gain by Municipal brewing," suggested a management committee "elected by Natives," though not with "definite control." The other white members of the council joined in to support a beer hall, whereupon the town council voted, again unanimously, not to license Africans to produce and sell beer but instead to establish a beer hall it would manage itself.[36] A majority of the Location Advisory Board—three coloreds and one African—outvoted two Africans to support the town council. A public split between Africans and coloreds was the result.

With the hotel system a lost cause, the Cape African Congress shifted to demand legalization of home brewing. At a public meeting in the hall of Calata's church, a delegation of six, elected by "Native inhabitants of the Location all of whom adhere to membership of the Congress," signed a petition for "Home Brewing" and questioned the authority of the racially mixed "Native Advisory Board" (actually the Location Advisory Board) to decide on a purely African issue. (The board was half-elected, half-nominated; half-African, half-colored.) The three colored advisory board members who had voted for a municipal beer hall "do not come under the Act," the petition declared. The two "Native representatives elected by the inhabitants" were against the beer hall, and the only African who supported it was nominated by town officials. "We maintain that we have the right, as the section concerned, for whom the Amended Act was meant, to request the Council favourably to consider our humble petition."[37]

The next day, Calata acknowledged the risks of home brewing: it would certainly cause "dissatisfaction for the first year for when people obtain such privileges, such privileges will be abused to a large extent." The location committee of the town council considered a petition from fifty "Coloured Residents" requesting a "Municipal Beer Hall" that "will militate against the evils consequent on Home Brewing and will eventually produce more peace and order."[38] The committee quickly resolved to recommend a beer hall. It argued that domestic brewing would require additional policing that the native revenue account could not afford and might lead residents to "sell beer to inhabitants not residing in the location"; this was clearly a reference to farm laborers, and a gesture to farmers' fear that Africans who indulged in beer would be less reliable workers.[39]

Calata, who had risen in national politics to become secretary-general of the African National Congress, drew the municipality's attention to a resolution of the Native Representative Council, the new national "Native" body set up in 1936 to represent Africans. The council had asked the minister to ensure that "the municipal monopoly system [of beer halls] . . . not be forced upon urban natives until the other systems [hotel and domestic brewing] provided for in . . . the Act have been given a fair trial." Calata's protest seems to have elicited no response, and five years later, Cradock rejected a Cape African Congress proposal to permit Africans to brew a limited amount of beer (no more than four gallons at a time).[40]

There was a compelling local budgetary reason for ignoring the Africans' wishes. Cradock's town council, in 1937, was preoccupied with improving water supply, in particular with obtaining a loan for another reservoir, which required ratepayers' approval. The Union Departments of Health and Native Affairs were, at the same time, pressing the town to improve location housing, and local white groups were pushing for the construction of more public housing for poor whites. An exasperated town clerk had begun to search for ways to avoid asking for a modest loan to finance minor improvements in the location. It was, he said, difficult enough to persuade ratepayers to finance a water scheme largely benefiting whites: "ratepayers are opposed to pledge the assets of the Municipality for loans to be raised exclusively for the location." He was eventually allowed to build the beer hall by bank overdraft, that is, without ratepayer consent, certainly an illegal procedure.[41] Though the provincial administration insisted on a public meeting of ratepayers to approve any overdraft, the angry town clerk decided to put a stop to the now lengthy correspondence. He seems to have got his way.[42]

In 1939, the Cradock beer hall opened, right in the heart of the location, close to the Metcalf Health Clinic, and to the St. James and Lwana churches.[43] Beer halls were intended to be a source of revenue for municipalities, but between 1923 and 1937, according to a 1945 inquiry by the Department of Native Affairs, only forty-eight towns had built beer halls, only eight of them in the Cape.[44] Large cities like Bloemfontein, Port Elizabeth, and Cape Town had allowed domestic brewing; no towns or cities had adopted the hotel system. Councilors in some places, including Cradock, considered beer halls a source of revenue to improve the lot of location inhabitants; the law provided for "amenities" over and above services that regular expenditure did not cover. However, in justifying the beer hall, Charles Butler had spoken of spending on "streets, sanitation and housing," which were items of regular expenditure, and hardly the additional "amenities" the law specified. With the beer hall revenue to be deposited in the native revenue account, Cradock gained permission in 1941 to use the profits to reduce rents on new subsidized houses for whites. Despite provisions of the Native Laws Amendment Act of 1944—that "Kaffir Beer" accounts were to cover only costs of manufacture, plus new approved "social and recreation" amenities and interest on loans for "native welfare"[45]—by 1952, municipalities had won the right to use up to two-thirds of beer hall profits to balance their subsidized housing accounts.[46]

For all the talk of "Kaffir beer" as an African cultural tradition, a beer hall in a location like Cradock's was bound to serve all the location population, not "Natives" alone. In the case of Cradock's location in 1940, that meant serving about two thousand coloreds and four thousand Africans, and all of a designated age could drink and buy beer there. The municipality accepted department-drafted regulations to admit to beer halls only African males over eighteen, African females over twenty-one, and other bona fide residents of the location (that is, coloreds). In the hall, women were to be segregated from men.[47]

Deficits and Drunkenness in the Beer Hall Era

To prevent the beer hall monopoly from competing with illicit home-brewed concoctions, the town council proposed a new regulation in 1940, further restricting the sale of brewing agents, especially of sprouted grain.[48] D. L. Smit, the secretary of native affairs, instructed Cradock's magistrate to delay implementing such a regulation: "Natives throughout the Union are very much opposed to the imposition of regulations restricting the use of sprouted grain," and "the farming community who supply . . . this commodity have also made representations." It would be better to let things "stand over . . . until the international situation improves. . . . A good deal of enemy propaganda is being sown among our natives." The world, including the Union of South Africa, was at war. Smit's argument should have appealed to Charles Butler, an English speaker with close relatives in the armed forces and a supporter of South Africa's declaration of war against Nazi Germany, a matter of bitter dispute among whites. But the magistrate found the mayor "difficult to move. . . . He is seventy five years of age. . . . The beer hall is his particular baby." The mayor won out over the secretary of native affairs, and the new regulation went into effect on 14 November 1940.[49]

At first Africans boycotted the beer hall. Sales were sustained, for a time, by coloreds alone, but soon the manager complained that his "best" colored customers were leaving for military service. By spring of 1941, the boycott eased, and in 1940, its first full year, the beer hall grossed £830, with a profit of £429, a return of 107 percent on cost. (The next year, the profits went up, but so did costs, and net profit fell to £86.)[50] The following year, a Native Affairs Commission of inquiry proposed that coloreds should have access to beer halls but "only so long as they qualify for location occupation"; the commission assumed, it said, a "necessity for the gradual segregation of coloured urban communities."[51]

While colored Location Advisory Board members in Cradock had voted for the beer hall, several colored groups had opposed it at the time and continued to do so. The WCTU, with a number of committed colored members, had been against the beer hall from the beginning; in 1943 the Cape Coloured Defence Link Committee, an official body of coloreds that looked after the interests of colored servicemen and their families, asked for "Prohibition of the Coloured Dependents of Soldiers and all Coloured Attending the Beer hall." With colored drunkenness a constant topic of discussion by the Liquor Licensing Board, proposals to restrict sales were usually made by the white Anglican and Methodist ministers, often representing the WCTU. In 1945, the African Peoples Organization, representing the coloreds, appealed in vain to the council to ban all sales of beer to coloreds. Ten years before, it had asked Cradock's Liquor Licensing Board to ban sales of liquor to coloreds from 1 p.m. on Saturdays. Coloreds, of course, still had access—as Africans did not—to liquor in segregated bars in town where they could drink as much as they could pay for and had the right to purchase half a bottle of spirits and a bottle of other liquor at any bottle store.[52]

In allowing the beer hall, the Department of Native Affairs, despite its own preference for domestic brewing, had acceded to Cradock's wishes and overridden the wishes of the majority African population in the location. The tougher regulations on brewing agents made little dent in illegal brewing, however, and Cradock appointed three extra constables and divided the location into five wards for better policing. Quoting the conclusions of a 1937 commission of inquiry into riots at Vereeniging in the Transvaal, the department was now urging suppression of beer brewing as a municipal responsibility, with the location superintendent assigned to the leading role. In Cradock, the superintendent, Wilken (he of the 1925 lodgers' raid), with his constables and the South African Police, now took charge of raids of African homes looking for illegally brewed beer.[53]

At 4 p.m. on a March Sunday in 1941, a "skirmish" began between residents of the location neighborhoods of New Brighton and Tulu, with "throwing of stones and hitting with sticks." Location police stopped the fighting, but it resumed, and the South African Police had to step in. By Wednesday, "the children again came out . . . there was no parents present to try to stop [them]." The SAP arrested "a number." "There was a certain amount of Kaffir Beer about," Wilken concluded. "And when the children had a row, the older ones mixed in the melee. That is the only cause or reason of the disturbance."[54]

The opening of the beer hall may have created a new challenge to parental and church authority, perhaps even prompting young Africans to resist their parents' desire to boycott municipally produced beer. Although Cradock, unlike mining towns, did not have a large population of single African male migrant laborers, it did have many young people who were either lodgers, weekend visitors from nearby farms, or—a longstanding thorn to the town council—residents of railway "camps" across the Great Fish River that were not under municipal control.[55] Neighborhood loyalties in the location led to conflicts that white officials referred to as "faction fights."

The spring 1941 fracas had been entirely an affair of Africans in the location, with no spillover to town streets. As a result of the arrests and clampdown, Wilken believed that "peace and order are reigning as per usual."[56] When the council requested information on arrests and summonses, he reported that between 1 January and the end of May, 64 Africans had been arrested for being in the location without a permit, 68 for "riotous behavior," 76 for "Kaffir beer, querrie [a concoction forbidden under the 1928 liquor act] etc.," and 207 for default of rent.[57] This was probably "per usual" to Wilken.

But a deputation of white ministers was soon protesting to the council against drunkenness on the streets and, particularly, about "*dronk volk*" lolling at the entrance of the Dutch Reformed church in town.[58] These persons were almost certainly coloreds. In early 1943, Cradock appealed to the Union Department of Defence to station military police throughout the center of Cradock and in the location and annexes to deal with drunken colored soldiers on leave. The appeal was unsuccessful.[59]

Disorder in the location itself had became so regular that ministers of the town took up the issue. In 1944, the Rev. A. Karg, the white Methodist minister, invited about eighteen churches and organizations, most of them colored and African, and the location superintendent to a round table discussion in the colored Methodist church. He called on "members to state their complaints re the Lawlessness in the Location, people being frighten[ed] to go to church." A total collapse of "parental Control" was responsible, A. Akena responded. "Teacher Mvambo" offered a novel and plausible explanation: parents were frightened to interfere because "these children were supporting their parents." Other speakers, most of them colored, attributed the lawlessness to unruly *kwediens,* young Xhosa males, who were attacking coloreds. *Kwediens* had stoned a member of the Sendingkerk (the colored Dutch Reformed Mission Church) while he was driving his car; he had insisted that his assailants were "native children." Two members of the colored Sendingkerk told stories of other assaults by Africans—a Mr. Heffkie (colored) had been stabbed, but his assailant had been sentenced to "cuts only," that is, caning by the South African Police. Then an African church elder, Mr. Mango, shifted the debate: "the real Target" was the beer hall itself. "Anyone with 2d [2 pence] in his or her pocket can obtain beer." Calata returned to his original stand against the hall. "Drinking is to[o] excessive in the Location," he said, "especially among the boys. The residents . . . are used to have their own beer, they must and will have it whether allowed to or not. The Beer Hall is an additional place for drinking Beer. And it has not ceased or decreased the Beer and Concoction brewing, in fact it has increased [it]. . . . The women coming from the Beer Hall are disgraceful being drunk and half naked at times. I would suggest that the Beer Hall be done away with. The Council made an error in trying to teach the people how to drink beer." If the beer hall were closed, home concoctions, too, would diminish. Calata called on the council to close the beer hall "in order to combat the lawlessness of the children," and the Rev. A. B. Zambodla (Wesleyan) added an amendment "that Home brewing be allowed." The resolution passed. "I noticed," observed Wilken, that "only African people voted [for it]. One colored voted against."[60]

But the meeting had not been official, and no concessions came from the council. Raiding of location homes continued. In November 1944 Wilken and three of his staff arrested "a native spinster, domestic servant," Elizabeth Njawi, and transported her to the police station in town in a sanitary truck. She said later that a constable had struck her with a sanitary pail lid, forced her into a truck along with pails for the removal of "night soil," and had charged her with "wrongfully and unlawfully resisting arrest." The magistrate acquitted her, whereupon she sued Wilken and, in addition, Johannes Els ("lorry driver and special part-time 'Policeman'"), Eric Mdlimela ("Native Policeman or Headman"), Guqu Poni ("Ranger and Assistant Policeman"), and the municipality as the employer of them all. The case against the municipality was settled out of court, the municipality paying damages for injuries and insult, but Poni was found legally responsible.[61]

Njawi had sued with the energetic support of E. S. Mvambo, an active member of the Bantu Methodist church. Signing himself "Secretary of the Civic Association," Mvambo had urged D. B. Molteno, the representative for Western Cape Africans in the Union parliament, to intervene, but Molteno said he could do nothing until the civil case had been decided. After it was settled, Molteno asked for the council's assurance that it would not happen again. It had been "an isolated case," the town clerk assured him, and Wilken had been told to "stop this practice."[62]

Still the council stuck to its guns on the beer hall. To a Kaffir Beer Profits Inquiry in 1945, the town clerk insisted that home brewing could only be safely introduced in a "100% native location." Medicine Ngumbela, secretary of the Cradock Native Advisory Board, protested that beer was a "national drink and no one is qualified to brew it as [Africans] would do themselves."[63] The beer hall was seen as an institution imposed by whites, alien to African customs, and both provocative and corrupting in its effect.

By 1944, it was apparent that home brewing in Cradock's location had not diminished. As it had in 1940, the municipality persuaded the Department of Native Affairs to approve yet another regulation on sprouted grain, this time extending the ban on sale to "any native within five miles of the border of the urban area."[64] There was plenty of reason for the municipality to be concerned about the native revenue account's dependency on the profit from the beer hall. In six out of nine years from 1941 to 1948, it had run at a loss, with an accumulated deficit of £518.[65]

To move the native revenue account into the black once more, the council, in 1948, raised location rents from 4 to 5.5 shillings and lodgers' permits from 1 to 1.5 shillings. Through a program of cost cutting and more energetic rent collection, the £911 deficit of 1946 was transformed into a surplus. The beer hall itself also began to make a profit again. But still no promised "amenities" were provided as the law required. In this regard, O. H. Walters, a former president of the now defunct Joint Council now repudiated his old support for the location beer hall. In 1946, he became local chairman of the National War Memorial Health Foundation (NWMHF), founded in enthusiasm for "social medicine" with special emphasis on "peoples centres" for people of color. In a letter to member of parliament Donald Molteno, he said that, in 1938, Africans on the Joint Council "had been able to make no impression on the town council, the member of which principally concerned was old Charles Butler, a noted 'temperance' expert." Although the council had promised that "all the profits . . . would be spent on the location . . . what is now clear is that *the profits are being used at least in part to reduce the amount spent in the location by the Town Council* [that is, the regular services]. Actually . . . I see no particular increase in amenities other than an odd shower bath or two and . . . a few more water taps (making, I believe, 8 in all for nearly 8000 people)." "Saturday night sees an orgy there," Walters continued. "Coloured men get dop [spirits] in the town first and then go to the beer hall and scrap."[66]

Molteno replied that he had "never met a decent African who is in favor of a beer hall." He felt "sure that the minister would act on a resolution of council [to close the beer hall] addressed . . . to him." Home brewing had worked "perfectly satisfactorily in Port Elizabeth, Cape Town, Bloemfontein and countless small places. There is no reason why it should not work satisfactorily in Cradock." Walters remained stymied all the same. "I think the Mayor would be quite glad to see the B[eer]. H[all]. go, but his council has a very O.B. tinge now [Ossewabrandwag, a right-wing Afrikaner organization], and I am not very hopeful."[67]

By 1948, the South African government's attempt, through implementation of the 1928 Liquor Act, to control the production and distribution of liquor among coloreds had partially failed. While coloreds do not appear in the records as producers of liquor, they had participated in a considerable illegal trade in liquor with Africans. The attempt to prohibit the home brewing and sale of sorghum beer and concoctions was also a failure. It had long been clear, according to a 1942 Native Affairs Commission report, that beer halls had had no impact on the brewing of concoctions; the prohibition of sale to, and production by, Africans was, therefore, largely a dead letter. As the magistrate wrote in 1944, "any native who wants liquor can get it."[68] Africans protested, in 1945, that municipal beer was expensive—an average of 19 pence per gallon in the Cape Province, compared to a home brewing cost of 5 to 7 pence. That year, Cradock official beer cost 16 pence, a little less than the average but still much more than home brew.[69]

In 1944, Cradock's liberal magistrate, L. T. Philips, had urged D. L. Smit, the secretary for native affairs, to close the beer hall and permit domestic brewing under control of committees of Africans. His proposal, which was not accepted, was segregationist; he advocated separate housing, since Africans and coloreds, he said, ought not to drink together.[70] The council, on the other hand, was convinced that the beer hall helped to maintain order and to ease a shortage of municipal revenue at a time of rising costs. Besides, the electorate was resisting a boost in taxes (already at the statutory limit of 4 percent of municipal assets), and no one had explained how to replace the revenue that would be lost to domestic brewing. The town council and its successors therefore retained its monopoly on its beer hall until, in a time of rising African rebellion, Cradock's African schoolchildren burned it down in 1980.[71]

In the end the beer hall, which had opened in 1939, had solved nothing. The problem of colored *dronk volk* in the streets of the town persisted, but if anything, the beer hall had shifted some public drunkenness to the location. Whites' lives, in consequence, were little affected. But in the location, coloreds expressed resentment at being subjected to the same beer regime as Africans, as they had done in relation to the curfew and lodgers' fees in 1925. Location coloreds now had legal access to the Africans' sorghum beer, but they also had access to commercial "European" liquor, as Africans did not. Unlike their better-off colored contemporaries in town, they were soon in abrasive contact with Africans. The Cradock beer hall did not become a cozy pub; the Native Affairs Commission described "most beer halls" as "bleak and depressing places."[72] Cradock's location now became a site of random violence: the beer hall and the "scraps" in the location, the "faction fights" farther out in the district, and the regular weekend liquor raids. None of these had any equivalent in town.

No rift had emerged among Cradock's whites on the issue. White women in the WCTU, mostly English speaking, had supported the farmers, mostly Afrikaans speaking, in demanding both strict prohibition of Africans' access to liquor and a ban on domestic brewing. For local whites, the beer hall was a remote issue, except as a provider of about 14 percent of municipal "Native" revenue.

Coloreds, already privileged in their access to liquor, were in an ambiguous political position as to beer. Colored leaders in the location and on its Advisory Board invariably sided with the town council on the issue. In 1930 coloreds had supported the banning of Africans' domestic brewing. In 1939, the council, with colored support, had imposed the beer hall on the location African population. By the mid-1940s, location coloreds were no nearer an alliance with Africans on that issue, or any other, than they had been in the 1920s at the time of Wilken's raid.

The liquor issue intensified the belief of policymakers, and perhaps of local whites generally, that it was necessary to distinguish between Africans and coloreds, even to segregate them geographically. Most whites and officials probably considered it politically impracticable to prohibit colored access to liquor. But with the location and the beer hall providing opportunities for illegal liquor transactions and production of concoctions, the hostility of officials, local and national, to coloreds as purveyors of liquor to Africans had undoubtedly increased. Africans, many officials believed, ought to be protected from liquor and limited to their traditional beer.

The rising sentiment in Cradock for segregating coloreds from Africans occurred at the same time, from 1938 to 1948, as the National Party was intensifying its demand for segregation of coloreds from whites. Yet while public drunkenness by coloreds was a problem in town, reinforced by the required placement of all liquor outlets half a mile away from the location, the town's Mixed Area was apparently not a particularly disorderly place. Rather, it was in the "mixed" location, so local officials believed, that coloreds and Africans were corrupted by liquor brought in by colored couriers, and by concoctions made mostly by African brewers. But in Cradock's case, there was a further motive in the pressure from liberals, who, though themselves mostly teetotalers, wanted to open a beer hall for coloreds and women as well as for African men in the hope of gaining revenue for "amenities" in the location, as required by the 1937 act. But such a motive was not the principal reason why most whites reluctantly supported an end to prohibition for African brewing of sorghum beer. Whites wanted to maintain order, sustain an efficient African labor supply to Cradock's farmers, and increase municipal revenue by taxing the location's residents rather than Cradock's ratepayers for the meager services the location received.

4

Water, Slops, and Night Soil

Sanitation for an Up-to-Date Town

The "No-Stream" Policy: Water in the Location

W. W. Lidbetter, a businessman and Cradock's only photographer, often wrote to the *Midland News* to complain about the meager supply and the inequitable distribution of water in Cradock. At Christmas in 1915, Lidbetter used his photographer's skills and his ironic sense of humor to mail out a grim picture postcard, "The No-Stream Policy: Christmas Morning in the Cradock Location," showing Lwana Street, the bleak central road of the location.

In the photo on which the postcard was based (fig. 5), thirty or so residents had put down seventy or so buckets and four-gallon "paraffin tins," to reserve precious places in a queue reaching to a single water tap. The population of the location, Lidbetter wrote on the card, was "about 3000." The water supply consisted of "3 Taps running for less than 2 hours daily." Lidbetter had risen early Christmas morning to take his photograph—we can calculate from the longitude and latitude, and the ratio of shadow to object, that the picture was taken at 7.18 a.m. This Christmas morning was no leisurely "lie-in" for many location women and children but, as on every other morning, the occasion for a long wait for water. As the town itself woke to *its* Christmas morning, its demand for water would reduce the location flow perhaps to a trickle, even to zero. All houses in town had water "laid on" at least to a tap in the kitchen. Location dwellers, on the other hand, had to fetch their water either from the frequently contaminated furrow leading from a weir on the river, or from the three standpipes on the edge of the location nearest to town; those residents farthest out had to carry water about five hundred yards, almost a third of a mile. The location's pipes were at the far end of the mains leading from the reservoirs above the town; thus, the flow was reduced to a small stream at peak periods of town demand, even when plenty of water was in storage. Long queues, mostly of location women and girls, frequently formed throughout the entire day at all three taps. With washing of clothes in town supposed to be banned altogether by municipal regulation, many African and colored washerwomen carried the laundry of their town employers to the sulfur springs at Warm Baths three miles north of the town to wash the clothes in a large open

Fig. 5. The no-stream policy: Christmas Day, 1915. Photographer: W. W. Lidbetter. (Lidbetter Collection, © Rhodes University [Cory Library])

basin. In 1916 Lidbetter published another photo card, titled "Perseverantia Vincit (the Cradock Motto)," ironically dedicated to the "Long Suffering Ratepayers of Cradock." It was illustrated with his photographs of these "Cradock Washerwomen's Warmbaths Waterworks" (fig. 6).[1]

Lidbetter (fig. 7, p. 67) had left Britain at the end of the nineteenth century because, like many Victorians, he had a "weak chest," in his case, asthma. He went to South Africa in about 1903, set up shop in Cradock, and continued to work there as photographer until he retired in 1945. A soft-spoken, perceptive man, he had joined the small community of Quakers, previously limited to the four households of the Butler clan. He had an extremely limited command of Afrikaans but nonetheless assumed an active role in local politics, serving on the town council in the early 1920s and helping to found the unofficial interracial Joint Council in 1928. At his death in 1959, Lidbetter left an endowment for a meeting hall for location residents.[2]

In South Africa the supply of water and electricity in towns, following British practice, was almost universally a local government function—there were few private water and power companies, and none in small towns. In keeping with this pattern, the Cape colonial government had given Cradock its first water supply by building a weir on the Fish River in about 1814. In 1886, the municipality bought a farm, Holtzhuisbaaken, with a reliable artesian spring seven miles away, and installed Cradock's first mains there; these may have included the three location standpipes Lidbetter photographed that Christmas

Fig. 6. Washerwomen at the Warmbath, 1914. Photographer: W. W. Lidbetter. (Lidbetter Collection, © Rhodes University [Cory Library])

morning in 1915.[3] But this scheme gave only a brief respite to a growing town located in the middle of a semi-desert, and by 1900, the search was on for more water. For decades, the town was divided between those who wanted a dam and those who hoped for a cheaper solution—to find another spring. By 1913, Lidbetter was arguing that the only solution was not to search for new springs or pump more from the existing springs at the Warm Baths, but to dam a river. A proposal to build a dam was agreed to in 1914, but construction was postponed "because of the present crisis"—the First World War had just begun.[4]

"Nothing Short of a Scandal": Cradock's Urgent Need for Water

From the founding of the town, Cradock's inhabitants of all colors had searched constantly for reliable sources of water, but supply depended on geographical conditions over which they had little control. Cradock is situated in a region of low, capricious, and sudden rainfall, high temperature, and sustained winds. This is not a climate to produce a countryside of close settlement like the cozy villages and market towns of Europe or the clusters of African houses in the better-watered eastern coast of South Africa. In the Karoo, water courses can be traced more by dark lines of bush than by the glint of the sun on regularly flowing streams: babbling brooks are unknown, features of a green European world that South Africans read about in books.

Fig. 7. W. W. Lidbetter (1874–1959) self-portrait, 27 October 1937. Photographer: W. W. Lidbetter. (Lidbetter Collection, © Rhodes University [Cory Library])

Failing such water supply, most Karoo farmers were doomed to pastoralism. Shortage of water limited them to staples like wool and mohair, placing inescapable limits on rural income and hence on human populations, which, in turn, limited the growth of towns and cities. Some of Cradock's white farmers, however, refused to concede that their district's economy must, of necessity, be based on stock farming. In the second half of the nineteenth century, they set up small irrigation systems on the Fish River and its tributaries—weirs and canals to entrap and distribute intermittent flood waters—that enabled them to grow lucerne (alfalfa), which in turn made profitable ostrich farming possible. In 1912, eager to attract white settlers, the parliament of the new Union passed the Irrigation Act to encourage and provide loans for the building of conservation dams. In the 1920s, thanks to the efforts of an engineer turned farmer, C. E. Lawford, farmers near Cradock set up the Great Fish River Irrigation Board; the board raised loans from the Union government to build two dams (Grassridge and Lake Arthur) in the Cradock district. Officials in London used Lawford's optimistic 1922 pamphlet, "Facts about the Valley of the Great Fish

River," to attract immigrants to Cradock.[5] In 1924, the *Midland News* issued an equally optimistic special illustrated supplement, "Cradock—The Lake District of the Midlands. Irrigation Development in the Fish River Valley."[6] And the next year, the region's leading daily paper, the *Eastern Province Herald* of Port Elizabeth, published a series of articles on "The Miracle of the Great Karoo: Whole Future of the Great Fish River Valley Changes."[7] But even as the large dams were completed, the municipality was still wrestling with the problem of adequate water supply for town and location.

When it came to expensive water schemes, many farmers were in direct conflict with townspeople. For townspeople, especially Cradock's boosters, a better water supply was paramount. An "up-to-date" town in the 1920s had to have potable and safe water piped to individual houses if it were to attract and hold a white middle-class population that demanded "civilized standards."[8] Such a town also had to provide electricity, increasingly regarded as a necessity for cooking, space and water heating, lighting, and power. But safe water was more crucial to survival and health. In the nineteenth century, water had been identified as a frequent bearer of lethal infections to urban populations: cholera, typhus, diphtheria, and typhoid fever.

Cradock also depended heavily on a regular safe water supply for its public services. The town had built the Queen's Central Hospital in 1897, in hopes of serving a region beyond its own district, and, by 1924, it had installed X-ray equipment, adding electricity to its needs along with water.[9] The town could legitimately claim to be an "education center" for whites with the founding of a teachers' training college, boarding dormitories at the boys' and girls' high schools, and hostels for poor white children. In 1926, 1,539 pupils studied in segregated town and location schools; 793 of them were white, 225 at schools for poor whites.[10] Such a medical and educational center could hardly function, let alone compete successfully with other towns, without proper water and electricity supply. In many nineteenth-century cities and towns the installation of water-borne sewerage had further enhanced the importance of adequate water; by the mid-1930s, Cradock politicians had begun seriously to discuss a sewerage scheme of their own.[11]

Since the turn of the century, the spring on the Holtzhuisbaaken farm had, at its maximum flow, been barely sufficient for the growing town; in times of drought, the town's water mains were often opened for as few as four hours a day. The spring project had been financed by a loan funded by an annual "water rate" on real property in town rather than on metered consumption of water; by 1926, this rate accounted for £2876, or 14 percent of the municipal revenue.[12] Many ratepayers paid the water rate reluctantly and resisted any attempt to increase it, especially farmers—most of them Afrikaners—who owned a town house as a pied-à-terre for shopping expeditions and for their quarterly visits for *nachtmaal* (the Dutch Reformed church communion). Accustomed to regular water shortages in the country, they had little interest in expanding the water supply of the town itself if expansion would raise rates on the urban homes they used only intermittently. In the 1920s, town councilors and officials often blamed the "nachtmaal vote" for their difficulty in raising money for any water scheme.[13] In 1925 a provincial engineer, J. Kirby, persuaded the town council that the new dam at Grassridge would provide the necessary increased supply.[14]

Debates over increasing the town's water supply, largely technical discussions about the practicality of various engineers' proposals, paid no attention to the uneven distribution of water between the location and the town. The location regulations of 1908 had clearly specified that "The Council shall provide a sufficient and available supply of pure water" to the location, but when the regulations were rewritten in 1926, "sufficient and available" was omitted.[15] The very nature of municipal services provided multiple opportunities for territorial discrimination by race: clean streets, safe and plentiful water, adequate street lights, and cheap electricity could exist only when whites arranged for them. These could easily stop at Regent Street, on the edge of town.

Achieving equality of any service throughout a municipality has always been a matter of politics even in racially homogeneous societies, with inequity often a matter of class. In Cradock, race was more contributing and controlling than class; voters, 90 percent of them white, were preoccupied with the level of services to the town where they themselves lived, not with service to the adjoining location. Before the Location Advisory Board was set up in 1926, location residents had no link to municipal government, and no channel for petitioning the town council for better service. In 1924, the African People's Organisation (APO) did protest, on behalf of resentful colored ratepayers in town, against the racial segregation of taxis and benches in the town park, itself a municipal service. But coloreds do not seem to have taken up such issues in an organized and persistent way.[16]

From the beginning, location residents had to fetch water by pail from the standpipes, the river, or the town furrow dug in 1814. The river was closer than a tap for many, but it was muddy during flood season, often brackish, and invariably contaminated (fig. 8).

A nearer and better water supply must have been one of the principal advantages for people of color who managed to live in town rather than in the location. While we have no record of a colored or African family's making a move to town because of the water supply, in 1944 eight colored residents who applied for houses in a proposed colored housing scheme did list "tap in yard" as desirable.

Because of the shortage of water, vegetables could be grown in the location only on a few small holdings irrigated from the furrow; the commonage—public land outside the town—provided only limited grazing. Without water, residents had to buy any food they ate to supplement the rations supplied by their employers. For heat and light, location residents bought coal, kerosene,

Fig. 8. Standpipe near the river, 28 September 1904. Photographer: W. W. Lidbetter. (Lidbetter Collection, © Rhodes University [Cory Library])

or wood if they could afford it. Otherwise, the women and girls collected cattle and horse manure (used as fuel as well as flooring) and firewood (under permit from the municipality) from the commonage; in the early evenings, they ran home through town with long bundles of wood on their heads. Throughout the long public debate in the 1920s and 1930s over increasing the town's water supply, distribution to the location itself was only occasionally addressed, and then perfunctorily.

In the early 1920s, municipal politics was apparently deadlocked over the water issue, with various factions pressing for the virtues of a particular dam site. After the devastating worldwide flu epidemic of 1918, Lidbetter seems to have persuaded James Butler, editor of the *Midland News,* to take up the issue of water supply in the context of newly awakened interest in public health. In 1919, the South African parliament passed the Public Health Act making the municipality subject to the attention of a new inspectorate of health and sanitation.[17]

Lidbetter soon gained another Cradock ally in Mary Butler, James's earnest and dedicated eldest child. She had left Cradock to study at Sidcot, a Quaker school in England, returning in 1899 just as the Anglo-Boer War began. Mary Butler then took up nursing and returned to Cradock around 1913 to practice as a private nurse and midwife in town. She was widely known in Cradock for her interest in "native" affairs, and contributed to the "Sister Marion" column in the *Midland News,* a weekly discussion of health and family issues. In a characteristic "Sister Marion" piece in 1923 she explained to her readers that servants were often late because they had to queue at standpipes to obtain a day's supply of water before leaving for work.[18]

The new editor of the *Midland News,* William Cursons, made an issue of the location's shocking water supply, writing an editorial on 17 October 1923: "It was nothing short of a scandal . . . that children were in the school there [i.e., in the location] apparently hard put to it to obtain a drink of water. Anyone who cares to take a walk into the location and see the long line of buckets . . . knowing that in all probability the last in the queue after waiting for hours may not be able to obtain a supply. . . . Many coloured [he meant all people of color] have to beg from the white people in the town," he continued. There was a "menace to health, not alone in the location but to the whole community"; it was encouraging that the council and ratepayers were showing some determination to put Cradock among "other up-to-date towns." The location issue brooked no delay: "Would it be possible to give another [connection to the town main] from, say, Hospital Street?"

The magistrate W. J. Vlok, forwarded the editorial to the Department of Native Affairs in Pretoria, asking it to "assist in improving a somewhat disgraceful state of affairs." Thereupon the acting secretary for native affairs, J. S. Allison, wrote to the administrator of the Cape and to the secretary for public health urging intervention; the secretary for health did as he was asked and wrote back to the town clerk.[19] Unaccustomed to being hectored by government departments and the provincial administration, the town clerk, G. B. Paterson, replied with a scarcely credible statement, which read in part: "The supply to the location is fair and reasonable and . . . town and location are supplied with the same quantity." The department, clearly skeptical, inquired almost by return mail about "details of the scheme proposed and the amount per head per day of water supplied to the native population of the location." But Paterson did not have such "details." Replying to the provincial secretary, he acknowledged that the location suffered from a shortage of water "to a certain extent" but defended the town council and blamed ratepayers for turning several water schemes down.[20] There, for the moment, the Department of Public Health was prepared to let the matter rest, though one official wrote, "I suggest we bring up the matter again in six months' time."[21]

"A Systematic Sanitary Inspection" and Defeat of the Nachtmaal Vote

The official was as good as his word: in July 1924, Dr. William A. Murray, an assistant medical officer of health (AMOH), a position created by the Public Health Act, arrived to conduct a "Systematic Inspection" of Cradock—town,

Fig. 9. Dr. W. A. Murray, assistant medical officer of health (1922–34). (Graaff-Reinet Museum Archival repository/Photographic Collection/Murray)

location, and hospital. Murray (fig. 9), born in 1874 and raised in Graaff-Reinet, ninety-five miles west of Cradock, was the grandson of the Rev. Andrew Murray the elder, and son of the Rev. Charles Murray, both members of a powerful line of Dutch Reformed Church ministers. After graduation from the University of Edinburgh, William Murray worked at a Dutch Reformed Church Mission hospital until 1912.[22] He returned to South Africa after brief military service and joined the Department of Public Health soon after its founding in 1919. After gaining a diploma in public health at the University of Cape Town, he rose rapidly in the new department. He was to have a distinguished career, writing an important health report for the Carnegie Commission in 1932 that denied that climate played a large role in the "degeneration" of South African poor whites. In 1924 he vehemently castigated the Cradock municipality for the state of its location and the location's meager water supply.[23]

Despite his background and experience, Murray seems to have had little knowledge of the Africans in towns; he spoke to Cradock town councilors as if Africans were an entirely migrant population.[24] In his "Report on Systematic Sanitary Inspection of Cradock Municipal Area," an eleven-page single-spaced foolscap typescript of numbered paragraphs, Murray showed how rudimentary Cradock's sanitary inspection staff was and how limited sanitary control had been. Sharing with most white South Africans the unexamined view that the Africans and coloreds in the location were a health threat to whites, he recommended the "entire removal" of the Cradock location "further away from town." But the principal emphasis of his report was on water and the implications for health of poor supply *and* distribution for town and location. Supply was "utterly inadequate," he wrote, with even the "upper part" of the town—the houses up the hill below the water works—receiving only a three-to-four-hour supply daily in the summer months.

Lidbetter's graphic portrayal of location residents queuing for water would have been a useful enhancement to Murray's presentation: "Four standpipes are erected on the town side of the location . . . but the water merely dribbles. . . . Poor water supply invariably increased personal uncleanliness and disease." The Cradock medical officer had given Murray no figures on infantile diarrhea but had acknowledged a high infant mortality rate: a reported mortality of 229 African and colored children under five in 1923. "This points strongly to the prevalence of bowel diseases which is always an indication of defective sanitation and water supply." And the existing system of washing clothes in a large open pool at the Warm Baths "increased the danger of the conveyance of infection to Europeans."

Murray's recommendations were urgent and specific: "The most serious defect in Cradock is the want of an adequate supply of pure water, and this *must* be remedied without delay." For twenty years the council had been trying to augment the supply, "and almost every engineer of note in South Africa has advised them." "About a dozen" schemes had been decided on, but the ratepayers had thrown them all out: "It is said that the deciding factor . . . has been the so-called 'Nachtmaal' vote." Councilors were considering "two or more schemes" but "seemed to be hopeless as to the possibility of getting the ratepayers' sanction to any scheme." Murray called for immediate action to improve water supply to the location either by means of additional taps or a borehole "in or near the location." Somewhat optimistically, considering his discouraging description of local politics, he concluded: "When the new water supply has been obtained it is presumed that the water supply of the location will be entirely adequate."

On washing and laundering, Murray would have eliminated the three-mile walk of washerwomen to the Warm Baths; he advocated a "wash house near the municipal power house to which water from Warmbaths could be laid on" with a separate room for "laundering" (by which he meant ironing). Women servants would then have hot water, presumably in separate basins; such a laundry, he hoped, would keep the washed clothes of European employers out of the location.[25]

Murray's report, which arrived in Cradock in mid-September 1924, outraged the councilors. Their feathers had already been ruffled the previous July when Murray had publicly rebuked the mayor, John Deary, at the end of the two-day inspection: "The opinion was expressed by the Mayor," said Murray, "that Cradock was equal to any town in South Africa as regards cleanliness and health generally. I regretted I was not able to agree with him."[26] Cradock's medical officer of health, Dr. P. de Wet, a part-time official, reacted heatedly to the remarks of that "hypercritical AMOH." "The high death rate in Coloured infants is not due to bad water or poor environment . . . but chiefly to lack of knowledge and unsuitable diet." "It was hardly necessary," De Wet continued, to tell "us that . . . we . . . need . . . additional water any more than we are urgently in need of rain." He brushed aside the proposed wash house and laundering room: the wash house would not improve conditions, and "the laundering room would not be used by the washerwomen."[27] The Sanitary Committee, too, sharply disagreed with Murray on water supply and the washing of clothes: "The location shares [water] equally with the town. . . . We have our washdams which have been in use for the last 50 years or more." If all Murray's recommendations were carried out, it concluded, "the cost of the town would run into four figures."[28]

Cradock's inadequate water supply had become something of a cause célèbre—even the *Cape Times* in Cape Town carried an article on it.[29] In 1924, on the eve of a local election, the editor of the *Midland News* urged Cradock's ratepayers to make their wishes clear: "It [is] the bounden duty of every ratepayer to support only those candidates who are . . . pledged . . . to secure an adequate water supply."[30] In an editorial headed "Water!," the paper quoted Dr. Viljoen of the Cape Education Department. No new schools, Viljoen had said, had been allowed to open in Cradock during the past two years. "We have been stagnating. . . . I appeal to you: is this a suitable centre for education when you cannot even get a bath?"[31]

In April 1923, M. J. Hattingh, later to be mayor, was elected to the council; by the beginning of 1924, after consulting an expert of his own, he had reached the conclusion that attempts to improve water supply solely from springs must be abandoned.[32] An Afrikaner Nationalist lawyer, Hattingh was the secretary of the Cradock Board of Executors, an Afrikaner organization based in many towns that sought to break British dominance of the management of real estate and livestock sales by conducting stock and property auctions. In 1925 he proposed to build a new dam to impound Fish River water, pumping the water above the town and filtering and chlorinating it before distribution. An allocation of water from the river would be required: according to the 1912 Irrigation Act, the council had to apply to have 200 morgen (423 acres or 171 hectares) of town land scheduled for irrigation under the new Grassridge dam to entitle it to a regular allocation of water. The land was duly scheduled and approved by the council; Hattingh's scheme was to be paid for by a loan of £37,000.[33]

Ratepayers had to approve the loan and several times earlier had rejected

Fig. 10. Opening of the first reservoir, Cradock, 16 May 1928. Photographer: W. W. Lidbetter. (Lidbetter Collection, © Rhodes University [Cory Library])

similar measures. This time the Cradock ratepayers, weary of a debate that had continued for at least twenty-five years, were finally won over. At the public meeting of ratepayers, which was required by the Cape provincial ordinance for approval of such a loan, Hattingh explained his scheme in detail and was rewarded with a unanimous vote.[34] The dreaded "nachtmaal vote" of Afrikaner farmers had at last been overridden. Cradock would now have a water supply based on two sources, not one, though its problems were not over. Though it had added facilities to convert river water for home use, that use would depend on the reliability of supply from the Grassridge dam and floodwater from the Great Fish River.

The new water plan required considerable electric power to pump the water from the riverbed to the works above town. In 1914, the municipality had opened an oil-driven direct-current power station, not financed by rates (that is, by a tax on property); instead, it functioned as a municipally owned business, raising its own loans, setting its own tariffs, and intending to show a profit.[35] Facing a long-term steady growth in demand, the Electricity Department, unlike the Water Department, was not subjected to the opposition of "nachtmaal" voters. In the early 1920s, it was planning a new alternating current station to replace its out-of-date facility. In 1926, the contractor, who was to supply the electric pumps to raise the water 131 feet (40 meters) from the settling dam on the river to the filtration plant at the top of the hill, advised the council to scrap its oil-driven electric plant. The council arranged to build a new steam generator adequate to meet all the town's power needs, with the municipality continuing in its role as a supplier of water and electricity to the railways. By the beginning of 1928 the new water and power operations were functioning (fig. 10), and, thereafter all visitors arriving in Cradock by rail could see the bold legend on the roof of the power station: "Cheap electricity for domestic and commercial purposes at 1d [one penny] a unit."[36] In 1929, Hattingh, by then mayor, celebrated success: the water supply was "practically unlimited. . . . I trust that the growth of population will soon warrant the construction of another reservoir."[37] The supply might have been "practically unlimited" for town dwellers. It was still wholly inadequate for coloreds and Africans in the location.

Standpipes and Taps: Water Supply in an Expanding Location

The voters of Cradock had addressed the problem of overall water supply, but not the equity of distribution between town and location. Murray had been over-optimistic when he predicted that the new scheme would give the location "adequate" water; in 1930, the municipality added four standpipes to the existing three in the location, but these were hardly enough. In 1931, the national government's Department of Public Health again took up the specific issue of the distribution of water in the location: Murray, irritated by the Cradock medical officer of health's cursory annual report for 1930, placed Cradock on his department's "Reinspection List,"[38] and in late 1931, yet another health department medical officer, Dr. F. W. P. Cluver, visited Cradock on Cradock's invitation. He complimented the town on its new water scheme and on the location's four new standpipes, but he noted that water supply was adequate for the town only: the location's seven standpipes were "quite inadequate for a population about 5000." Location householders in New Brighton, a block of 145 new single-roomed houses built in 1929, still had to walk a full six hundred yards, more than a third of a mile, to fetch water. Cluver suggested that the council "take immediate steps" to provide an additional main to New Brighton, three tanks, each with four taps, and a borehole.[39] Cluver's report was published in the *Midland News,* but the council did not respond; almost a year later, in a rare show of exasperation, a Health Department official suggested that "we threaten to stop payment of refund contributions [presumably a subsidy for the salary of the location's nurse] until a reply is received."[40]

The municipality had not, however, been sitting on its hands: it built two tanks, each with eight taps, in the location. By the end of 1932 the tanks were supplying twenty-four outlets. "Great relief has been given to the native population," wrote the town engineer in support of an application to charge the £55 cost to the native revenue account, duly approved by the Department of Native Affairs in December (fig. 11).[41]

Fig. 11. Washerwomen with new wash troughs, 27 July 1931. Photographer: W. W. Lidbetter. (Lidbetter Collection, © Rhodes University [Cory Library])

Cluver had noted that the planners of New Brighton, built in 1929, had made no provision at all for water. These new houses were farther away from standpipes than were the homes in the rest of the location. In 1930, the council had raised rents to pay for better water supply, but no better supply had been forthcoming, provoking a heated discussion in the Joint Council in 1932. The Rev. James Calata noted that frequent violent incidents were occurring around the taps. The grievance persisted: in 1935, sixteen residents of New Brighton petitioned the council for more access to water. When they went to fetch water, they wrote, they often encountered hostile residents from other districts in the location, and "we or our children are even assaulted." Their rents, they protested once more, had by now been raised from 5 shillings (for a one-room house) and 10 shillings (for a two-room one) to 5.5 and 11 shillings, respectively, "on the understanding that water was going to be laid to New Brighton."[42]

This time the municipality responded, but only after Alfred Metcalf, Cradock's leading lawyer and patron of a wide variety of causes, came forward with a charitable grant. Taking up the old suggestion of William Cursons, editor of the *Midland News* in 1923, the municipality, in 1937, extended the main from Hospital Street to New Brighton.[43] But the following year one of the new inspectors of urban locations, P. G. Caudwell, in the first intensive examination of Cradock's location by the Department of Native Affairs, discovered that water was available at only six points in the location, five separate standpipes, and one tank (five thousand gallons) with four taps. A second tank built in 1930 was not functioning at all, "apparently because the water supply is not sufficient to supply the two tanks," hardly surprising because the town's water supply at the time was available only from 7:00 a.m. to 12:00 noon and from 4:00 to 7:00 p.m. (The tanks were supposed to fill overnight.)[44]

In 1942, the consulting engineer on a proposed sewerage scheme, J. Clinton, claimed that a twenty-four-hour supply *could* be achieved. Assuming thirty-seven and a half gallons per day per head for four thousand Europeans and ten gallons per day per head for six thousand "non-Europeans," Clinton argued, a sewerage scheme was possible if overall water consumption were reduced through metering existing supply.[45] The council did install meters in town, and by 1950–1951 consumption was down from 1947 by 32 percent.[46] But Clinton did not address the problem of inadequate distribution to the location itself beyond proposing enlarged mains in town, to increase supply to the location.[47]

Some real improvement for the location was, nevertheless, achieved. After a two-day inspection of the location in 1946, G. I. Nel of the Department of Native Affairs reported there were now ten standpipes and four tanks each with six taps, thirty-four taps in all, though none yet in individual houses. Nel applauded the promised quadrupling of standpipes and urged supplying water to each location house in the future, an ambitious proposal at this time. "The supply was said to be adequate" he wrote, "and the Native Advisory Board voiced no complaint about it."[48] It is difficult to assess what Nel's opinion was worth, and more important, how many of the reported outlets were functioning at any one time—no visiting official had checked on all of them. Consequently, the number of taps visiting officials reported was often twenty-two, a figure taken, it seems, from earlier reports.

By 1948, the gap in water supply between town and location had been only slightly narrowed, and no location house at all had running water while each house in town had had running water since the early 1920s. We have no figures for bathrooms, but we know that the municipality had been subsidizing the sale of bathroom water heaters in town through a local retailer since at least 1929.[49] The basic inequality between town and location remained—there were now more taps than before in the location, but the women still had to wait in a queue each day and then carry water from a distance.

It is probable that there had been real improvement in terms of higher water pressure and a shorter average distance from house to standpipe. If Nel's 1946 report of thirty-four taps was accurate, that was progress from the three taps Lidbetter found there in 1915. But piped water to each location house did not come until long after 1948, and washerwomen continued to lug laundry three miles to the Warm Baths and back. Water was preeminently an issue for the location's women, and the all-male advisory board members failed to raise the issue with Nel at all.

Slops, Night Soil, River, and Veld

Urban populations have always created formidable quantities of wastes—urine and feces, waste water ("slops"), and garbage (animal, vegetable, and mineral)—that threaten human health if not appropriately disposed of. Ordure and urine—human, bovine, and equine—are the most threatening to human health because they provide breeding grounds for carriers of intestinal and respiratory diseases. In the interests of the health of the community as a whole, the municipality was responsible for removal of such wastes, for the provision of adequate public and private lavatories for town and location, and for ensuring sanitation of dairies, bakeries, stables, and garbage dumps.

In 1924, Cradock had no sewer system at all. One night a week, in town, the municipal health department removed a twenty-gallon pail from each house—the "night soil"—and replaced the soiled pail with a clean one, the so-called double-pail system. Houses in town had a hinged wall flap from which the worker removed the pails and replaced them. Weekly removals from houses in town were required by municipal regulations, as were more frequent removals from hotels and schools, paid for by an annual sanitary fee. Each day, municipal mule-drawn tank carts also collected "slops"—waste water and urine—from individual premises in town—private, public, and commercial. Both forms of collected waste—night soil and the slops—were dumped by the municipal workers across the Great Fish River about a mile south of the town. The night soil went into large trenches in Sondagshoek (later a proposed site for first a colored and then an African township), which was covered over about once a week. The slops were poured out on open sandy soil near the municipal abattoir, a practice the national health official Murray criticized as dangerous to health.[50] These dumping sites were out of sight or smell from the town and hence largely out of mind; waste removal from town was not a persistent public issue among Cradock's property-owning ratepayers, whose fundamental needs were met. Each house in town was required to have at least one lavatory, but the municipality later encouraged town householders to provide a second lavatory for their servants by offering households an extra weekly removal at a reduced rate.[51] In 1910, a local pharmacist, Charles Tapp, later a member of the Joint Council, had complained to health authorities in Cape Town that many employers in Cradock made no provision for their white female shop assistants and clerks. After some badgering of the municipality, the problem had been solved, though for white women only, with businesses that had facilities sharing with those that had none.[52]

According to Dr. Murray in 1924, "a few" households did provide separate lavatories for their servants. Others allowed their black female staff to use the household's lavatory but required their garden or house "boys" to use the veld, or the river half a mile away.[53] Cradock was necessarily a "walking town"—

there was no public transportation—for all people, black and white, going to and from work. Thus, many of those who needed a lavatory during the day had extra miles to walk. There were only two public lavatories, both in the market square, one labeled for "Europeans" and one for "natives"—actually for all people of color.[54] By 1931, according to Cluver, the health department AMOH, Cradock had built "a number of sanitary conveniences on the outskirts of town for the use of coloureds and natives," primarily those domestic and commercial employees whose employers provided none of their own.[55]

In the location in the late 1920s and early 1930s, all households had to use water sparingly, and with no slop barrels for waste water, dirty water was simply poured out on the ground. As to lavatories, the 1926 regulations for locations stated that the municipality "shall assign and provide sufficient and suitable sanitary conveniences" for males and females. Site holders could put up a pail closet behind their hut with a weekly fee of sixpence (half a shilling) for "the weekly removal of the night soil," a charge that would have raised the average site rent of 3.5 shillings in 1927 by 60 percent.[56] Unlike in town, where a lavatory was required for each dwelling, in the location there was no such requirement, no doubt since few location dwellers could afford to build their own lavatories or meet the weekly removal fee. Because most of them, whether at home or at work in town, had to use the ground outside their shacks, or walk out to the veld or river, there were many stinking areas where one had to walk with care. "Several spots in and around the location," Cluver noted, "were being used by the inhabitants as places of defecation." He had calculated in 1931 that the municipality had provided "91 pails and 3 pit closets . . . totally inadequate for the present population," thus about 1,533 persons per closet, or 49 persons per pail. The pit closets, he argued, should be closed down altogether.[57] (A pit closet is a hole, eight or ten feet or so deep, with wooden planks across it. Persons using it had to squat on the planks over the hole.) In contrast, by the mid-1920s, those in town had at least modest modern sanitary services and could perform their bodily functions in private and in conditions whose cleanliness they controlled.

A New Sanitary System for the "Up-to-Date" Town

Apart from boosters' interest in projecting an up-to-date image for Cradock, the demand for a modern sewerage system was initially triggered by the inadequacy of the system of slop removal in which water barrels were emptied daily into mule-drawn municipal tank carts. The slops themselves were not the problem: rather, it was waste water from washing, bathing, and cooking that was allowed to run directly into street storm-water gutters or into gardens. Soapy water left an offensive smell. It seems that the waste water in street gutters grew in volume as town residents washed more, many using the electric water heaters energetically promoted by the municipality's electricity department since 1929.[58]

In November 1935, Cradock's town clerk wrote to the chief health officer at the Department of Public Health to complain of the "severe smell nuisance . . . [from] bathroom water . . . in drains . . . constructed at some remote date," and the department dispatched an assistant medical officer of health to undertake another systematic inspection. The drains, the officer reported, were "causing loss to business in certain areas"; he regarded the problem as essentially one of engineering, to be solved by a "rational waterborne scheme."[59] An engineer from the national Public Works Department told him there was "no cure, short of reconstructing the drainage system with salt-glazed pipes, laid to a self-cleansing velocity."[60]

As mayor of Cradock, Max de Kock, an enterprising Afrikaner Nationalist businessman, attended an annual Municipal Congress in 1936 and was impressed by the new local sewerage system in Worcester, the site of the congress; he invited its town engineer to visit Cradock.[61] Worcester, with a population of 8,641 as of 1931, was a near analogue for Cradock, with its population of 6,807. The engineer reported that Cradock was "ideally suited for a water borne sewerage scheme." "Since labor, material and money is as cheap as it will probably ever be this is a most opportune time to undertake the scheme . . . an absolute essential in a progressive town."[62] Thereupon the town council contracted with Stewart, Shand and Oliver, a Johannesburg engineering firm, to study the feasibility of water-borne sewerage and were advised that such a scheme could be undertaken with meters to reduce water consumption, most of it in the town. "The sewering of locations is always difficult," the engineer wrote, presumably because many municipalities would be unwilling to pay for service to a location. He urged Cradock to limit the nonwhite population to 150 percent of the white population: "otherwise the town's progress will be seriously hampered." The growth rate of the nonwhite population was a variable that he believed Europeans could and should control. For the short run, he proposed keeping the old location on the double-pail system, but dumping the contents in a trench at a new site "below [i.e., south of] the location" to prevent "the present night traffic through the town." The old location's housing was due to be demolished in several years, he said, and so suggested sewering only the new Wilken Township of 288 houses for coloreds and Africans, which was farther away from town.[63] Under his proposal, every house in the new location would have water. Yet, when the town sewerage plan was actually completed in 1946, houses in the Wilken Township got only a pail closet in an outhouse.[64]

Murray had noted in 1924 that some location residents "of the better class" had already provided themselves with pail closets. In 1928, the town clerk wrote that a weekly removal of a pail cost a resident £3.5 a year (more than the average location rent of £2.1), and that only 23 removals were being made from the location each week.[65] (Even that figure may be an exaggeration: from 1934 to 1939, when a lower removal fee of sixpence, or half a shilling a week was in effect, total fees averaged £15.5 per annum, and there were about 14 removals per week.)[66] When a Native Affairs Department urban areas inspector suggested, in 1938, lowering the "comparatively heavy charge of sixpence per removal," the municipality resisted, offering instead to build twenty more *public* pail closets and twenty more public urinals. The option of pit lavatories for individual houses was said to be unrealistic also, because the lots in the old location were too small to house them.[67] Yet the number of private lavatories rose abruptly during the war; in 1949 Cradock's health inspector marked 70 public lavatories on a map of the location, and listed 175 private lavatories on individual streets, a total of 245.[68] With the lavatories in the new township of Wilken, that added up to 533 lavatories for a location population of about 6,391.[69]

A sewer main to the new location in Wilken was not built after all; the pail system continued for location public lavatories, for the 288 new houses in Wilken Township, and for the 175 private lavatories in the old location.[70] By 1946, the municipality's housing program for people of color had stalled altogether, primarily because of the difficulties of building housing location residents themselves could afford to rent or to buy.

Water-borne sewerage had brought the issues of waste removal and water supply together and had created an opportunity to narrow the racially discriminatory gap in quality of service between town and location. Its arrival in Cradock, however, demonstrated once more the ease with which a new service could stop at the town's edge, increasing, not diminishing, inequality between town and location. The installation of individual lavatories for each house in Wilken Township was a considerable achievement, even though they were using pails not flushing water; future housing might be expected at least to meet the "Wilken Township minimum." Although the town council wanted to imitate other "up-to-date" towns, it resisted pressure toward that end from national government departments and apparently did not believe that poor services in the location were inimical to the interests of Cradock as a whole.

Public Health and Infant Mortality

Medical officers of health were required to report annually to the national Department of Health on sanitation and housing; their reports reflect the discrepancy between the relative physical well-being of the town, on the one hand, and the location, on the other. A. H. Budler, eager to give Cradock literally a clean bill of health, submitted casual and inaccurate reports between 1927 and 1939. In 1927, for example, he reported that overcrowding had been "dealt with," housing was being "improved," and most of the typhus (lice-borne), typhoid (water-borne), and tuberculosis cases reported had been "imported" from outside.[71] His mortality figures and population totals are almost certainly underestimates. Yet they are revealing, especially for the death rates of children of color compared to those for whites (table 1).

Beginning in 1931 with Cluver's report, the statistics became more reliable

Table 1. Death rates among whites, coloreds, and Africans in Cradock, 1931 and 1946

	Whites		*Coloreds*		*Africans*	
	1931	*1946*	*1931**	*1946*	*1931**	*1946*
Overall mortality: per 1,000 living	13.35	9.28	81.46	18.67	81.46	56.81
Infant mortality: 0–1 year per 1,000 live births	80.35	30.00	737.59	105.77	737.59	186.38
Infant mortality: 0–1 year as % of all deaths in race group	18.75	9.38	32.82	20.00	32.82	20.97
Child mortality: 1–5 years as % of all deaths in race group	12.5	3.12	35.58	21.81	35.58	38.71
Child mortality: 0–5 years as % of all deaths in race group	31.25	12.50	68.40	41.81	68.40	59.68

Source: "Report on Systematic Inspection of the Health and Sanitary Conditions in the Municipal Area of Cradock conducted by Dr. F. W. P. Cluver on the 27th of November, 1931," 30 Dec. 1931, NAR, GES 627, 123/13; "Report on Re-Inspection of the Municipal Location Cradock and Matters connected therewith, on 7th and 9th September, 1946," by G. I. Nel, NAR, NTS 4266, 114/313 Main File, vol. 3.

*In 1931 the MOH did not distinguish between coloreds and Africans in infant and child mortality rates, so the two groups are treated equally for that year in this table.

and more alarming. Among whites all mortality rates declined from 1931 to 1946, but among coloreds and Africans the overall death rate remained at least double that of whites. The most shocking figure is the 1931 mortality rate of 737.59 per 1,000 African and colored live births combined—three-quarters of African and colored babies died before the age of one. Cluver noted: "Of the total of 114 deaths of infants under one year [in 1931], 100 occurred in the location."[72] The child mortality figure (one to five years) for coloreds and Africans combined accounted for more than 20 percent of all deaths in 1931. In 1940, G. O. Thornton, Cradock's first full-time MOH, noted that deaths of children five or under among "Non-Europeans . . . were still more than fifty percent of all deaths." He noted a small improvement—while in 1938 and 1939 there had been no natural net increase in population among Africans, there was a small increase in 1940, due, he believed, to the services at the prenatal clinic in the location, which opened in 1937.[73]

Table 2. Principal causes of death by racial group, Cradock, 1944

	White	*Colored*	*Asian*	*African*	*All races*
Enteritis and diarrhea	6	38	—	82	126
Pneumonia and bronchitis	5	37	—	47	89
Diseases of the heart and circulation	35	10	—	10	55
Tuberculosis (all forms)	2	16	—	26	44
Whooping cough	0	4	—	9	13
Malnutrition	1	1	—	6	8
Rheumatic fever	—	2	—	5	7
Prematurity	—	2	—	4	6
Diphtheria	—	—	—	3	4
Enteric (fever)	—	—	—	3	3
Typhus fever	—	—	—	2	2

Source: Medical Officer of Health (Cradock) Annual Report, 1944, NAR TBPA GES 565 123/13/B.

In 1941, 1942, and 1943, "Native deaths" again exceeded live births: "The native in this area is dying out," Dr. B. J. van Rensburg, the new MOH, wrote in 1943. "When a native baby is weaned it has very little chance of survival."[74] After 1943, live births among Africans barely exceeded deaths. The colored infant mortality and child mortality rates in 1946 (105.77 and 21.81), though much lower than the African (186.38 and 38.71), were dramatically higher than the rates for whites (30.0 and 3.12). In explaining these great differences in mortality between whites and people of color, all the annual reports emphasized malnutrition, sanitation, and housing and shied away from attributing high infant mortality to the ignorance of blacks, as an angry Dr. de Wet, the MOH, had done in 1924.

In 1944 Van Rensburg ranked diseases in descending numerical order of deaths among all groups, using the medical terminology of the time (table 2). Van Rensburg noted that of a total of 364 non-European deaths, 239 occurred in children under five. Fifty-six percent of all deaths among people of color were caused by two categories of disease: enteritis and diarrhea, or pneumonia and bronchitis. Enteritis, diarrhea, diphtheria, and typhoid fever, diseases most closely linked to poor water supply and sanitation, accounted for 135 deaths, 35 percent of all deaths of people of color (no deaths of whites). In 1945, the figures were almost identical.[75]

Van Rensburg's reports invariably linked high infant mortality to sanitation and water supply. Reacting to an outbreak of typhoid fever in 1943 north of the town, Van Rensburg wrote: "There is no sanitary accommodation on farms for Non-Europeans and insufficient [sanitary] accommodation for domestic servants employed in Cradock. The result is that the veld is fouled and the furrow and river water grossly contaminated."[76] In 1945, he complained, "The incidence of typhoid fever is a good index of the sanitary state of the community." Lavatory facilities for people of color had to be improved, he said, urging "the early incorporation" of the new "Non-European" housing plan into the municipal sewerage system. "The tragedy of these childhood deaths," he wrote, "is increased by the fact that they are largely preventable."[77]

In the twentieth century, Cradock was no longer an isolated village writ large as it had earlier been. It was no longer simply a market town providing limited services to a surrounding agricultural population. It had become a provider of utilities, an eliminator of wastes, and an inspector and enforcer of sanitary standards. Residents demanded that these services be safe and reasonably cheap, but providing them required engineering and investment—which were not cheap—and the maintenance of technical standards imposed by remote regional and national governments. Local politicians, competing with other towns for industry, commerce, and, consequently, white population, publicized the services and amenities of an "up-to-date" town.

But Cradock's boosters were discriminating in whom they tried to attract. At no point in the debates over water supply and sanitation did anyone argue that a well-housed, well-watered, and well-sewered *location* population of coloreds and Africans, and consequently a stable, healthy, and contented body of employees, could enhance Cradock's attraction to business. The "up-to-date" town fathers tried to attract white-owned businesses and residents by stressing the *town's* amenities, which were unavailable to most coloreds and Africans. Indeed, the consulting engineer on the sewerage scheme in 1942 had urged Cradock to limit the "Non-European" population of the town to 150 percent of its white population, an extended Stallardism that regarded all persons of color, not Africans only, as having limited claims to live permanently in an urban area.

No one in town was directly affected by the location's abysmally poor water supply or sanitation regime. The thirty-eight "Non-European" municipal voters of 1921 (all coloreds who owned premises of £100 or more or occupied premises of £200 or more) did not take part in any ratepayers' groups or participate in ratepayers' meetings, which were required by law to ratify municipal borrowing on the security of the town property. Although the multiracial Cradock Joint Council, a nongovernmental group, advocated improving water and sanitation from 1929 on, its only tools were moral suasion and publicity in the *Midland News*. It was unable to forge a business-political alliance strong enough to move a town council beholden mostly to white municipal ratepayers. The agitation for a more reliable water supply succeeded after 1924 only because the dominant white electorate, weary of frequent shortages and seemingly interminable debate on the matter, saw that the general water shortage affected their own interests. Despite his interest in fostering bilingualism—a deeply divisive issue among whites—Mayor Hattingh, as an Afrikaner Nationalist businessman, had no desire to preserve Cradock as a somnolent *dorp* (rural town). He made common cause with his English and Jewish counterparts, and the "nachtmaal vote" of Afrikaner farmers was finally overridden. The white population had now finally given priority to its own broader common interests. The pattern was repeated in 1936, when Max de Kock, another Nationalist modernizer, took up the cause of water-borne sewerage, once more without improving distribution in the location.

The most telling inequality between town and location remained the absence in the location of clean piped water. Open standpipes no longer existed in the town in the 1920s, and we can assume that all town houses, by then, had at least one inside faucet. In the location, the town had used river water from the polluted furrow built in 1814 to irrigate the first lots along the river; by now it was used by whites strictly for their gardens but by location inhabitants for other purposes. Water was a bearer of diseases, which became endemic among Africans and coloreds, contributing to their appalling and persistently high infant and child mortality rates. Sanitation, too, was unequal. Every white house in town was required by law to have at least one lavatory. No such requirement was in effect in the location, though the four location lavatories in 1924 grew to more than five hundred in 1948—an important change. For many—coloreds and Africans—the choice remained between public lavatories, frequently fouled, and the open *veld,* itself fouled, on the borders of the location.

Between 1926 and 1948, improvement in supply and distribution of water to the location was frustratingly slow, mitigating but not removing the burden. Location women, many of them full-time housewives and/or brewers of beer, still had to engage in a daily search for water and fuel. To have to carry water only fifty yards after the building of the new location in 1944, rather than the six hundred yards for many in the 1930s, was a welcome improvement; but there was still a queue, the water still had to be carried a distance, and it still had to be used sparingly. For a woman from the location to gain access to piped water would have been to escape an important burden of her race.

The growing national concern for public health could well have been an equalizing force, at least in the sense of enforcing equal sanitary standards even between racial groups segregated by residence. But though they put pressure on the municipality, national officials had only limited success in persuading local officials that there were common interests between the mostly white town and the African and colored location. They repeatedly made improvements in water supply and distribution and in sanitation, but with limited success. Two settlements lived side by side, with a wide inequality of services and sanitary standards that the dominant whites, both English and Afrikaans speaking, were happy to ignore.

5

Charity and Welfare in the Age of Segregation

While local and national governments provided water and waste disposal, many social services to people of color were, until the 1920s, provided only by voluntary organizations. Initiatives by nongovernmental institutions—religious bodies, private charities, and temperance organizations—were often led by white women. This was an expansion of women's traditional role long before they gained the vote in 1930. The dominant white community generally agreed on the necessity for social welfare policies, but also on the necessity for white supremacy. Such services were provided on a segregated basis. The whites responsible for them were themselves divided between two ethnicities based on historical memory, language, and religious denomination: roughly the Afrikaans speakers on the one hand, and the English speakers on the other. Health and welfare programs, thus, were shaped not only by racial segregation but also by ethnic suspicions among whites.

In the new South African state founded in 1910, less than a decade after Afrikaners' defeat in the Anglo-Boer War, deep divisions persisted among whites. Among contentious issues that continued into the 1920s were membership in the British Commonwealth, competing national symbols—the flag and the anthem—and bilingualism and mother tongue instruction in primary schools. Yet English and Afrikaans speakers collaborated cordially in a large number of nongovernmental activities: Cradock's white bourgeoisie often united to sponsor "cultural" events. Sport was rigidly segregated by race; but within the white community, golf, bowls, and tennis attracted both Afrikaans- and English-speaking middle-class men and women; rugby, a national obsession among white men, was genuinely cross-class and multiethnic, though not multiracial. Much philanthropic effort, too, involved white inter-ethnic collaboration. Voluntary organizations such as the Women's Christian Temperance Union (WCTU), the Red Cross, and the St. John's Ambulance Brigade had both English- and Afrikaans-speaking members and joined with churches and the ACVV (Afrikaanse Christelike Vroue Vereeniging, or Afrikaans Christian Women's Association) in public activities. The annual agricultural show and the hospital ball, open only to whites, were joint Anglo-Afrikaner enterprises that remained politically neutral.

In the 1920s, churches were the most important nongovernmental organizations for all the races, but they were segregated by race and by language. In 1926, as the owner of 64 percent of all church property in Cradock and the spiritual home of 4,419 adherents (70 percent of Cradock's white population), the Dutch Reformed church was larger than all the English-speaking churches combined. After the Dutch Reformed church, the largest denominations were the Anglican (around 800 members) and the Methodist (450). Protestants of all sorts constituted 90 percent of the white population.[1] None of the denominations actively competed with the others for members, nor did they compete for government subsidies for ethnic or denominational schools. (The only denominational school in Cradock was the Roman Catholic Convent of the Sacred Heart; some of its teaching was subsidized by the Cape Provincial Administration, but that was not a local issue.) The Dutch Reformed church had virtually no English-speaking members; the Methodist, Anglican, and Baptist churches each had only a few Afrikaans-speaking members, and many of these were anglicized, speaking English at home. Though the basis of cooperation in the WCTU was a common Protestant Christianity, religion did not otherwise mitigate ethnic conflict, nor did it produce a united movement to respond to the welfare of the poor, however "poor" was defined. Joint religious activities across the language divide were rare, limited largely to occasional joint services in the Dutch Reformed church to pray for rain. From time to time, evangelical preachers from overseas preached in English at public services in the Dutch Reformed church, which had the largest available auditorium.[2] All the white churches and their related organizations were geographically remote from their separate affiliated churches for coloreds (in town) or for Africans (in the location).

Uplifting the Poor White: Afrikaner Women Mobilized

Afrikaans- and English-speaking women defined "the poor" differently in the 1920s. Those in Dutch Reformed churches were part of a cultural nationalist movement that sought to gain "real" independence from Britain, to preserve the Afrikaans language, and to provide welfare to Afrikaners, many of whom lived in sordid poverty in the countryside or drifted to towns where they were ill-fitted by education and training to earn adequate incomes. These "poor whites" became the object of vigorous organizations, among them the ACVV, a formally Christian organization dedicated to supporting the Dutch Reformed church (fig. 12).[3]

English-speaking women took on a broader mandate, with fewer ethnic limitations. They were active in organizations with national and international connections promoting temperance (the WCTU), child welfare (the National Council of Child Welfare, NCCW), and health. Given that there was no glaring poverty in the English-speaking population like that among Afrikaans speakers, they turned to the location. Shocked by the data on infant and child

Fig. 12. Second Congress of the ACVV, held in Cradock in 1906. (H. C. Hopkins, *Die Nederduitse Gereformeerde Kerk, Cradock, 1818–1968*; Courtesy of the Dutch Reformed Church Archive, Stellenbosch, South Africa)

mortality in Cradock's location in 1924, English-speaking women created a modest secular humanitarian movement, a public health organization directed specifically at serving the location. They had no great resources at their command, nor were they formally connected to a single church like the ACVV. Before they gained the vote in 1930, English-speaking women had little claim on the South African Party for which their husbands voted; as the party of Anglo-Afrikaner conciliation, it was not concerned with the welfare for the poor of any color. These women founded the Lady Volunteers for the Location Movement, which, as the Women's Civic Association (WCA), and with the help of a single local philanthropist, established the first dispensary (clinic) for the African and colored residents of the location.

Both groups of charitably minded white women tacitly agreed on the necessity of separating whites from people of color. How they thought this should be arranged affected each group's provision in welfare and in health services for the poor. From the middle of the nineteenth century, the Dutch Reformed Church included a "mission" church serving segregated colored Dutch Reformed congregations and later a church for African congregations as well.[4] In 1925, a missionary, the Rev. J. A. van Niekerk, established the Immanuel Church for coloreds in Cradock; he raised his own funds, obtained land from the municipality, and built a church in town close to the location edge (figs. 13, 14).[5]

Ten years later, in 1935, Van Niekerk opened an orphanage for colored girls, the Immanuel Te-Huis, (Immanuel Home), but he died suddenly a few weeks

Fig. 13. The Rev. J. A. van Niekerk and the Church Council of the Immanuel Church for Coloreds. (H. C. Hopkins, *Die Nederduitse Gereformeerde Kerk, Cradock, 1818–1968*; Courtesy of the Dutch Reformed Church Archive, Stellenbosch, South Africa)

later on a fund-raising foray in the Transvaal.[6] Until this point, the *moederkerk,* the mother Dutch Reformed church for whites in Cradock, had provided no resources for his activities. Now faced with a leaderless mission church, school, and orphanage, the *kerkraad* (church council) intervened, committing itself to support Van Niekerk's projects, and appointed the Rev. J. P. Jacobs, a white missionary.[7] Jacobs's mission began at a time of rising Afrikaner nationalist consciousness, and ministers like him were placed in a difficult position: they had to reconcile the demands of a racially exclusive Afrikaner nationalism with the welfare and religious needs of their colored congregations. Jacobs was an ardent participant in Afrikaner nationalist activities and supported the National Party in Union politics. In 1937 he refused to pay the municipal bill of his church because the town clerk had rendered it in English. He became a prominent participant in the Voortrekker centennial celebrations held from 1936 to 1938 in honor of the Great Trek, the epic withdrawal of about fifteen thousand Cape Dutch from the British Cape Colony a hundred years previously (fig. 15). Under his ministry, Van Niekerk's orphanage and school for colored girls closed down.[8]

The ACVV had its roots in the three-year South African War that ended in Afrikaner defeat in 1902. Supported by "pro-Boer" English-speaking notables such as Olive Schreiner, the novelist and prominent feminist; Emily Hobhouse,

Fig. 14. Immanuel Church in 1930, presumably with the Rev. van Niekerk in the Cape cart. (H. C. Hopkins, *Die Nederduitse Gereformeerde Kerk, Cradock, 1818–1968*; Courtesy of the Dutch Reformed Church Archive, Stellenbosch, South Africa)

Fig. 15. Great Trek reenactment in Cradock, March 1938. Photographer: W. W. Lidbetter. (Jeffrey Butler Papers)

the daughter of a noted British liberal, Lord Hobhouse; and J. A. Hobson, author of *Imperialism: A Study,* Afrikaner women and men throughout the Cape Colony (the predecessor of the Cape Province) condemned British policy and mobilized to help the victims of the war. A group of women whom the military had banished from Cradock during the war became the leaders of this new Afrikaner women's organization; it was to outlive the political situation that gave it birth.

The Dutch Reformed Church and public-spirited Afrikaner laymen had long been aware of chronic rural poverty among their own people, but Afrikaner politicians and churchmen only took up the issue in a determined and systematic way after the South African War.[9] There were class divisions among Afrikaners, ranging from wealthy sheep farmers to dispossessed "poor whites." As John Dollard wrote of the American South in 1932, there were classes within the castes of whites and people of color.[10] But class divisions among Afrikaners were not very sharp. Only rarely did the Afrikaner middle class express concern that poor whites might threaten their own positions. The Dutch Reformed church had taken some responsibility for poor whites since the 1880s—the Cradock church had founded a "poor school" (the Wilson school) in 1893—and each congregation had its *armesorg* (poverty relief) commission. With the founding of the ACVV in 1904, middle-class Afrikaans-speaking women made the welfare of poor whites their special responsibility.[11]

Some of the founders of the ACVV tried to create a liberal and feminist movement that would unite English speakers and Afrikaners, but it soon became a specifically Afrikaner ethnic, unilingual organization. By 1907 it was insisting on the use of Dutch at meetings; it opposed the admission of English speakers to membership and, in 1910, took a vehement stand against the enfranchisement of white women, a stance that divided its members from their English-speaking equivalents.[12] Believing the survival of the Afrikaner people (*volk*) to be endangered by pervasive poverty, the ACVV worked intensively for the *opheffing* (uplift) of poor whites, and the progress of the Afrikaans language, under threat from the spread of English. To keep alive the memories of Afrikaners' struggle with imperial Britain, they engaged in symbolic acts such as tending graves of anti-British rebels in Cradock's white cemetery. *Opheffing* became even more necessary in the 1920s. In 1926, the Cradock ACVV faced the reality that poor whites were begging for food; in 1933, four years after the onset of the Great Depression, white beggars still appeared at farmers' houses in the Cradock district.[13]

Elizabeth Jordaan, wife of a retired farmer, made the ACVV her life's work (fig. 16). Under her firm and focused leadership over forty years—she was ACVV president from 1904 to 1906, and from 1911 to 1944—the ACVV in Cradock achieved formidable continuity and concentration. Concerned with the dismal prospects of young Afrikaner women in the countryside, the ACVV made the education of girls one of its special obligations. It established Cypressenhof (Cypress Court) in Cradock in 1917, a "hostel" for indigent girls,

Fig. 16. Elizabeth Jordaan (1859–1950), president of the ACVV, Cradock. Portrait copied from picture in the Elizabeth Jordaan Tehuis, Cradock. (Elizabeth Jordaan Tehuis, Cradock, South Africa)

most of them from the countryside. In 1922 the *kerkraad* founded a similar hostel for boys, Toekoms (Future), but it did not prosper under its male control; four years later, in 1926, after a critical report by a provincial inspector, the ACVV took it over. The *kerkraad* tried, the next year, to persuade the ACVV to close the boys' hostel in town lest it take boys away from a rural hostel of its own at Elandsdrift in the Cradock district. The ACVV executive brusquely refused, implying that there were more than enough poor whites to go around.[14]

At the ACVV annual provincial congress in Cradock held in 1926, Jordaan tried to solve the problem by urging wealthy whites to hire young Afrikaner women as domestic servants. But most young Afrikaner women from poor homes were ill-equipped to play the authoritative role of an English nanny or governess, and in any case, both professions were in decline. And even though many employers separated the semi-privileged (white) servants from those they regarded as the true subordinates (Africans or coloreds), whites could lose status by taking servants' posts. At the same ACVV congress, a speaker protested that white domestic servants "are treated on the same footing of equality [with servants of color] and during the lunch hour are forced to have their lunch in the same room or go into the street."[15]

Jordaan, no doubt influenced by such concerns, soon shifted her focus from domestic service for Afrikaner women to vocational education for both women and men. Unlike many Afrikaner men, she seems to have concluded that policies such as "back to the land" for white men and domestic service for white women were unrealistic in urbanizing South Africa, and that the state, not a private welfare body, should provide the appropriate training for the future. In 1929, as president of the Cradock ACVV, and with the help of her son-in-law, Dr. S. F. N. Gie, who was secretary of the Union Department of Education, Jordaan founded the Cradock Handelskool (Commercial School) to train young whites, especially women, for urban occupations, with instruction in typing, shorthand, and commercial arithmetic. The ACVV was also combating, quite self-consciously, the *Roomse Gevaar* (the Roman Peril). As early as 1912, the *kerkraad* had deplored the fact that Afrikaans Dutch Reformed children were going to the Roman Catholic Convent for music, art, and commercial instruction. In the 1920s, commercial education was still available only at the Convent of the Sacred Heart, but Marijke du Toit argues that this "peril" was largely a "figment of platteland imaginations": Afrikaner students did not frequently convert to Catholicism at the Cradock convent.[16]

In the 1920s, the ACVV took up welfare issues such as children's health, a campaign against alcoholism, and school feeding—helping with the midmorning distribution of subsidized cheese and milk at white primary schools. The minutes of the ACVV's executive show an organization run with an iron hand—presumably Elizabeth Jordaan's—and with an extremely effective committee network. If information on a problem was lacking, an ad hoc committee was appointed at once and charged to report back by the next meeting. Some sense of the flavor and content of proceedings, and the level of distress the ACVV was trying to address, can be gained from these two abbreviated entries:

> 10 July 1926. Saturday. Gewone Bestuur (Regular Executive). Ten blankets for boys' hostel. A few members said Mrs. Barnard was sending her children out to beg. Mrs. Hattingh and Miss Haarhoff to go and see her. Some think the Fourie family does not need so much help. . . . Resolved: to ask the Kerkraad to give £30 out of the Susan Schoeman Fund to Wilson School feeding.
>
> 31 July 1926, Saturday. Gewone Bestuur. Fourie family need food. Husband denies he has TB and is careful about the risk of spreading it. Mrs. Barnard denies begging. Says she's in a tiny room in backyard of Mrs. van Heerden who promises to see Mr. O'Connor [the building inspector].[17]

Much of the ACVV's activity—an old people's home, hostels for indigent children, and the commercial school—was subsidized by the government. Its executive had an exemplary knowledge of those it was helping, an important resource when dealing with Union and provincial officials with skinflint ideas of economy. It was efficient in raising money privately for its own activities and for the church generally; it made itself responsible for the annual *dankfees* (thanksgiving) bazaar, a device for fund-raising employed by all white churches in Cradock. It also became an unofficial public caterer, arranging luncheons, teas, and dinners for the municipality, the divisional council, or congresses, at times driving a hard bargain for fees with the mayor, and usually realizing a considerable profit.[18] In doing such work for a fee, the ACVV women seem to have had little competition from their English-speaking Methodist and Anglican counterparts, who lacked the numbers and resources, and perhaps the zeal, to do much more than run their own annual bazaars and picnics for their Sunday schools.

Devoting its principal efforts to the future of poor Afrikaner youth, the ACVV took advantage of the annual health inspections undertaken by the Cape provincial administration of all white children in school, which identified infections and alerted parents to the need for treatment. English-speaking doctors contributed their services. In one case, the *bestuur* (executive) sent a child to a noted specialist in Port Elizabeth for free eye testing; Gert Jordaan provided transport, and the ACVV paid for the spectacles prescribed. It helped twenty-five children with treatment of eyes, tonsils, and teeth in 1935.[19] Its work on behalf of poor white children was not in principle ethnically exclusive—the fact that schools and school feeding were subsidized precluded that—yet, because of the structure of white poverty in Cradock and its district, the beneficiaries of the ACVV were, in fact, almost entirely Afrikaans speaking. Its welfare initiatives were cross-class within a racially defined ethnic fold, and decidedly not cross-race. As for the Cradock location, the ACVV's interest in public health seems to have been limited to demanding segregated facilities for colored and African TB and venereal disease sufferers there, a response to a widespread fear in the 1920s that domestic servants might spread such diseases to whites.

Both English-speaking and Afrikaans-speaking middle- and upper-class people were more shocked by white poverty than by poverty among coloreds and Africans. The English-speaking churches in town had only slightly closer ties with their branches in the location than the Dutch Reformed church had with the Immanuel Church for coloreds. White, colored, and African Anglicans and Methodists were members of the same denominations and attended annual synods together, but, in the 1920s, white Methodists and white Anglicans in Cradock and elsewhere frequently held separate meetings for their "Native" clergy.[20] The white English-speaking ministers of town churches, most of them from Britain, were far ahead of their laity in willingness to acknowledge the poverty of the location population and its general lack of municipal services. In 1931, an Anglican layman, Alfred Metcalf, of Cradock's principal legal firm,

Fig. 17. St James church, Anglican, with the Rev. James Calata. (Historical Papers Research Archive, University of the Witwatersrand, Johannesburg, South Africa; Courtesy of Peggy Calata)

gave £350 to the new St. James church in the location, a sum he had originally set aside for a new nave for St. Peter's, his church in town, to commemorate his son, killed in Flanders in 1916. Such individual generosity to the location was rare, however, and did not signal the beginning of closer ties between white and African Anglicans (figs. 17, 18).

The Afrikaner community was in a stronger position to provide organized services to the poor. The two principal English churches—Methodist and Anglican—together had only 1,250 nominal adherents compared to 4,419 for the Dutch Reformed church, in town and district, and much less money. The ratable value of their urban property gives a rough indication of the relative poverty of the English-speaking churches—£7,115 for the Methodist and Anglican churches combined, compared to £34,945 for the Dutch Reformed church. Throughout the 1920s and 1930s the Anglican church struggled to meet the stipend of the rector; it was unable to buy him a car before 1948, thereby limiting his contacts with his country parishioners.[21] Although there appear to have been no religious disputes between Methodists and Anglicans, there was no intensive institutional cooperation either: no equivalent "Association of British Christian Women"; no organized preoccupation with the English language and cultural survival; no shared concern for the welfare of the English-speaking poor. Perhaps, above all, there was no English-speaking equivalent of Elizabeth Jordaan.

Fig. 18. St. Peter's, a white Anglican church. Photographer: W. W. Lidbetter. (Lidbitter Collection, © Rhodes University [Cory Library])

"Your Location Makes Me Weep": "Lady Volunteers" and Reform in the Location

There were, however, a number of women in the British community who played crucial roles in promoting the welfare and health of the poor. In Cradock's English-speaking community, social welfare initiatives were spearheaded by women involved in the international temperance movement; the Women's Christian Temperance Union, with headquarters in Evanston, Illinois, had founded its South African branch in 1893. As explicitly Christian as the ACVV, the WCTU was informally linked to what were called the Nonconformist churches in England—Methodist, Baptist, Presbyterian, Congregationalist, and the Salvation Army—all of which insisted on teetotalism, or total abstinence from alcohol. The WCTU was strongly represented in Cradock, with white, African, and colored branches. Some WCTU members, such as the Cradock branch's president, Mrs. L. Brown, were early advocates of founding a location dispensary; in 1927, the newly appointed dispensary nurse, Mary Butler, gave a paper in honor of Frances Willard, the WCTU's American "organizing genius."[22] Temperance was a serious issue in town and in the location as well, but it was public health that brought women advocates of temperance and health together.

The worldwide Spanish influenza epidemic of 1918 had hit South Africa hard. One historian has described the influenza epidemic as South Africa's worst demographic disaster. In its aftermath the *Midland News* carried endless reports of new outbreaks of "flu" and of other threatened epidemics of whooping cough, typhoid, enteric illness, smallpox, and plague. In 1922, the flu returned, this time in a less fatal Asian variety. (Such reports of threatened epidemics frequently concerned De Aar, a railway junction 190 miles northwest of Cradock, where on one occasion an outbreak of spinal meningitis was noted, later attributed to "natives from the Rand.")[23] A constant sense of alarm was sustained by traveling officers of the nation's new Department of Public Health, who contributed to a weekly public health bulletin that the *Midland News* regularly quoted. For months, Cradock was cited as a place where cases of typhus had occurred, and later, of both typhus and smallpox. In 1924, after plague was reported in several places, and nine months later, when an African victim of the plague was identified only ten miles outside Cradock, the municipality banned nonresident Africans from entering the location, posted guards, and distributed materials for fumigating houses and destroying vermin. A similar sequence occurred two years later, after another African died of the plague, again only ten miles outside town.[24]

To many Cradock whites, the location, with its African and colored population, seemed a standing threat to the health both of the town and the location, which were separated only by the width of Regent Street. Each day, cooks, cleaning women, nursemaids, and garden "boys" were in close contact with members of white households they served, particularly with the women and children. Since most white households had their main meal at midday, their domestic workers who lived in the location walked to work in town early every day and returned home in mid-afternoon. (Few servants lived in their employer's home in Cradock.) The daily ambulation increased fears that whites would be infected. Nevertheless, these fears did not prevent whites from employing people of color as domestic servants, and especially as nursemaids for their children.

Just before the publication of Dr. W. A. Murray's alarming 1924 report on health and sanitation in Cradock, Mary Waters, a daughter of Anglican missionaries in the Transkei and an instructor at the Cradock training college for teachers, issued a call to action. The WCTU had asked her to address its annual meeting on the subject of (sexual) "purity." Temperance advocates saw prohibition of liquor, quality of housing, health, and "purity" as closely related;

they perceived a breakdown of moral sanctions among the African women who came to town, illegally brewed beer and "concoctions," or became prostitutes. Waters, however, apparently surprised her hosts by delivering not a temperance address but a vigorous call for "Social Reform in the Location." Sketching Durban's efforts to build hostels and "eating houses" for migrant laborers, she stated that the first problem in Cradock was housing in town and location. Servants, she said, were women's special responsibility: she intended to address other local bodies to call for women "volunteers," to "investigate and to outline policy." Several women in the audience promptly volunteered. To show its support, the *Midland News* ran this headline: "New Local Movement: Women Volunteers Wanted."[25] Waters had widened the discussion of location issues to include improving housing, water, and the welfare of women, but she had scarcely touched on subjects of moral uplift, such as temperance or "purity."

The response from Cradock's council was hardly friendly. The mayor, John Deary, promptly criticized Waters for citing Durban as an example of "what a location should be," since Durban had financed its hostels on "Kafir beer" sales. Embroiled at the time in discussions with national authorities over improving Cradock's water supply, Deary argued that nothing could be done about housing until this problem was solved. Waters responded that a moral issue was at stake: the degradation of women servants was a direct consequence, or so the location inhabitants themselves believed, of crowded and filthy housing. She quoted Dr. Charles Loram, a prominent educator and a member of the Native Affairs Commission, as saying at a meeting in Cradock that "Your location makes me weep." Europeans, Waters charged, had deprived urban Africans of their own "native code of tribal morality," and they, therefore, had a duty to replace it. The mayor then criticized Waters's emphasis on housing, which was insufficient by itself, he said, to solve the moral issue. Moreover, housing would require funds beyond the loans available under the Natives (Urban Areas) Act. Cradock's ratepayers would have to be persuaded of its necessity. And, supposing new dwellings were built, would location householders be able to afford higher rents?[26]

Deary's cold bath of economic realism forced the newly organized "Lady Volunteers" to some rethinking. They focused first on the water issue the mayor had raised. But then, across white ethnic lines, a committee of six women, among them Martjie van Rensburg, Mary Waters, and Hester de Kock (wife of Max de Kock, a National Party leader) forwarded a petition to the mayor and councilors to "take steps for the improvement of the conditions in the local Native Location." In the previous twelve months, 174 "Native [that is, colored and African] infants" had died: "for this enormous death rate the European population is indirectly responsible as no effort is made to assist them [that is, Africans] in their fight for existence." The committee urged hiring a "trained European Nurse" to work in a "free dispensary in the Location for the benefit of the children only." An excellent "local lady," approved of by the "local Natives," was available.[27] The Volunteers' committee attended the next council meeting, but they failed to move the council. "We must say," the town clerk wrote a week later, "that we are not in anyway impressed by the Petition signed by certain ladies. . . . We require no outside support . . . save monetary. . . . This petition is only meant to convey that we are grossly neglecting our duties."[28]

"Staggered" by the council's insensitivity, the Lady Volunteers acknowledged the "good work" of the council in the location but said that since Cradock's medical officer of health had attributed the high infant mortality to ignorance and malnutrition, the "obvious remedy" in the Volunteers' opinion, was to hire a nurse.[29] The Volunteers then enlarged the scope of their proposal. Agreeing that the council could not afford a nurse for the location alone, they noted that "the Poor Whites are in as great a need for a nurse as the Location and we wish to suggest that you appoint a nurse for both sections. . . . In view of the outbreak of plague at De Aar . . . we feel the great need of a nurse to report suspects," and not only of plague. "We view with alarm the increase of venereal disease in the Location and the consequent increasing danger to which we are exposed." Yet, at a special meeting, the council concluded brusquely that there was no need for a nurse.[30]

The Lady Volunteers now gave themselves a wider mandate. A Miss Dorman, vice president of the Union-wide Women's Enfranchisement Association of the Union, suggested to a meeting in Cradock (as Clara Abrahamson, a farmer's wife, had done earlier) that wives should refuse to help their husbands at election time unless they supported the vote for women. The meeting then took a detour: Abrahamson had proposed that women should get out of the home into public life, take part in "the work of the town," and "help" the town council. She now suggested setting up a Women's Civic Association (WCA). The meeting did so, electing Hester de Kock as acting honorary secretary, but they apparently dropped the enfranchisement issue altogether.[31] Abrahamson had inadvertently launched an association more interested in local welfare issues than in the franchise.

The decision to concentrate on local welfare issues came at the same time as a change in the ethnic and political character of the WCA. The first Lady Volunteers committee had been bi-ethnic, with three Afrikaans-speaking and three English-speaking members, but only Mrs. de Kock was from a National Party household, and her family was politically divided; she was not an active Nationalist like Elizabeth Jordaan. None of the prominent National Party women were members. The WCA now became a civic association with a few non–National Party Afrikaans-speaking members but overwhelmingly English speaking in membership—Mrs. de Kock's name disappeared. It conducted its proceedings and correspondence in English. Later, however, it occasionally recruited prominent National Party women, like Mrs. Hattingh, wife of the mayor from 1928, as members of deputations to the town council.[32] The Lady Volunteers, never more than an ad hoc body, went out of existence.

Mrs. L. Brown, wife of a commercial traveler and an eager member of the WCTU, and Mrs. Nicolina Best, a nurse and practicing midwife, became the first leaders of the WCA. They soon discovered that Cradock whites would not readily join a vigorous initiative to help the "sick and poor," particularly if the "poor" were people of color. The *Midland News,* on 16 January 1925, reported a petition to the council protesting that poor whites needed help just as much as poor people of color. That did not dissuade the WCA. The building of a location dispensary and the appointment of a nurse became a multiracial and cross-gender enterprise.

It was not clear, at the beginning, whether the poor inside and outside the location were to be treated by the same nurse. Wrangling around this issue proved to be a critical stumbling block. Two African ministers in the location (the Rev. John Solilo, Anglican, and the Rev. Charles Msikinya, Methodist), and two coloreds (P.C. Goodman, a teacher, and the Rev. Adrian Hendrickse, the Congregational minister) wrote to the council that poor location housing was a cause of the high death rate, and they also requested a municipally funded nurse and dispensary. A healthier location "would mean greater health security to . . . employers."[33] There followed a period of energetic organization by coloreds and the WCA. Goodman took up the cause, but he had the specific interests of coloreds, not African location residents, in mind. He organized and chaired a meeting of seventy coloreds that passed a resolution in favor of "the Coloured nurse and a dispensary." At this same meeting, Nicolina Best lectured her audience on "the need for the location sections [that is coloreds and Africans] to cooperate . . . and on the advantages of beginning the movement by self-help instead of waiting to have all done for them." The colored women had responded, Best reported, by organizing a bazaar, from which £15/3/3½ (that is, £15.26) had been banked. But Africans were far behind the coloreds, Best said.[34]

The touchy town council now received an offer it found impossible to refuse. After the WCA persuaded the council to more than match any funds they raised, the WCA received, in 1926, an "anonymous" gift of about £75 from Alfred Metcalf, the Anglican layman.[35] The town engineer then drafted a plan for a single-room dispensary to cost a maximum of £75; the council accepted a bid for £90, and a small building, fourteen by twelve feet, was ready for occupancy by the end of the year. It stood in the center of the old location in Lwana Street, close to the spot from which Lidbetter had taken his photograph, "Christmas Morning in the Location," in 1915.[36]

Since the days of the Volunteers in 1924, these English-speaking women had wanted Mary Butler to be the nurse (fig. 19). She had agreed to come at £13 a month, but since £13 was more than the municipality was prepared to spend, it advertised for a "Coloured" at £7 and appointed R. M. Benjamin, who, however, turned them down four days later.[37] The WCA countered with a suggestion of £14 a month: "as [the nurse] will attend to white patients as well

Fig. 19. Mary Butler in nurse's uniform. Photographer: W. W. Lidbetter. (National English Literary Museum, Grahamstown, South Africa)

as coloured and native, is it not possible to draw on other funds beside location funds to make up the deficiency?"[38] The council balked again, agreeing to try for a part-time (three hours per day) "European" at £10, but no one applied.[39] It had meanwhile become clear to the WCA that the proposal of a single nurse to serve white and black poor would have to be abandoned because, as Mrs. Brown of the WCTU wrote, "no white person would like to employ a nurse who was spending the morning attending to native and coloured people."[40] With no other practical option, the council then appointed Butler at £14 a month full-time, £1 above her original offer, but to work in the location only.[41]

The dispensary opened on 1 January 1927. Immediately the WCA began to agitate for an increase in the municipality's financial contribution. But the council stuck to its commitment to contribute, over three years, £1 10s (1½ pounds) for every £1 raised by the WCA, with a maximum of £100 in any one

Fig. 20. Enlarged dispensary. From photograph album compiled by Mary Butler. (Guy Butler Collection, © Rhodes University [Cory Library])

year and a total of £166.[42] The WCA pressed for an extension to the dispensary and for a telephone; once more, the philanthropist Metcalf put up money, this time for an additional room, twenty-two by twelve feet, that would nearly treble the dispensary's size and equip it with a sink, hand basin, hot plate, and five-hundred-gallon water tank. The enlarged dispensary was formally opened by the mayor's wife, Mrs. Hattingh, in March 1930 (fig. 20).[43] But the telephone was not installed, an omission that that would become a poignant issue later on.

The Depression of 1929 and subsequent years dramatically increased the numbers of Afrikaans-speaking poor in Cradock. For them, there was already a functioning if incomplete private welfare system for whites, run by bodies like the ACVV, the Dutch Reformed Church's all-male Armesorg Kommissie (Poverty Relief Commission), and Helpmekaar (Help One Another). Those bodies raised funds locally, exploited and helped expand government subsidies to white public schools and hostels, organized the follow-up of the regular medical examination of all white children at school, and provided clothing and even food for needy cases. It was not a comprehensive "safety net" in the modern sense, and it was limited entirely to whites, whose male members were likely to vote for the National Party, itself informally linked to the ACVV.

The ACVV had an overwhelming advantage in raising resources for the welfare of its uncared-for "own." Active in Cradock's welfare problems from about 1904, the ACVV, by 1929, owned hostels and an old people's home in Cradock valued at £5235. It was effective in raising money and in gaining provincial and national subsidies.[44] The English-speaking groups, in the absence of a poor white English population, were concentrating on coloreds and Africans, almost none of whom could vote or stimulate public expenditure on their own behalf.

The WCA was only two years old when it opened the dispensary in January 1927 and was eager to gain subsidies for its work. But without a self-conscious ethnic base, an affiliation with a major political party, a language to be defended, a church to be cherished, or a racially and ethnically defined poor needing help, it lacked the assets of the ACVV. In consequence, the WCA's demand for a nurse and a dispensary, though encouraged by an "enlightened" national Department of Health, was a modest proposal. The WCA had no resources to give regular supplements to the income of individuals and families, and no clinical facilities. In 1927, the municipality did open a soup kitchen in the location, with £30 a year allocated to the three main English-speaking churches with approximately eight hundred children in schools for which they were responsible—Anglican (African), Methodist (African), and Congregational (colored).[45] But that was not the beginning of a sustained program.

It was the coloreds who first asserted a public role for location residents, promoting the dispensary in 1925 and then in raising money for it. In 1924 P. C. Goodman had made the dispensary his cause. But now in 1930, with the opening of the enlarged dispensary, residents of town, both white and colored, had embarked on an enterprise to improve health facilities in the location, and Africans and coloreds in the location were organizing to support it. The location up to 1927 had been a racially defined, neglected, urban settlement with no governmental institutions beyond a superintendent with a tiny office and a house, concerned almost totally with control, not with providing normal municipal services. Now for the first time, a position had been created for a professionally trained official with a tiny dispensary, concerned entirely with the health of location inhabitants and with bringing to bear some of the resources of modern medicine, on however limited a scale.

Although the WCA had no connection with a church, it depended on the loyalty of members of Cradock's Protestant churches, standard-bearers of a humanitarianism that led them to go beyond the needs of their "own," to seek an expansion of vital municipal services rather than merely an imposition of more controls. While the ACVV had simply to carry on with resources already mobilized to nurture Afrikaner nationalism and look after the Afrikaner poor, the dispensary, meagerly financed from the start, faced an uncertain future, particularly since enthusiasm among whites for the welfare of the location people, generous in the first days of the Lady Volunteers, had largely evaporated by 1930. Yet the enlargement of the dispensary would turn out to be a beginning, not an end of a road, as the national government's interest in public health expanded from the 1930s on.

6

"Is It Nothing to You?"

Public Health in the Age of Segregation

Cradock's First Location Nurse and First Interracial Council

On 14 February 1931, the *Midland News* published a harrowing piece by nurse Mary Butler on the devastating infant mortality rates of the Cradock location: "Is It Nothing to You? A Day in the Location Dispensary" listed nine children who had died in one day, 5 February 1931. During December, twenty-four "Non-European" babies of one year and under had died; during January, twenty-three. "There has been an epidemic of measles in town too but not one death of a European baby was recorded in December or January."

It was one thing to portray misery in the location, another to make invidious comparisons between whites and people of color. Mary Butler's eloquent article was already in proof when Ernest Butler, the publisher and her brother, worried about local white reaction. In light of the shaky financial foundation of the paper, he consulted the town magistrate A. G. Oakes, a liberal like himself. Oakes objected to the article on prudential grounds. The offending paragraph was amended and the column published in censored form. Mary Butler, frustrated by this timidity, gained some grim satisfaction from the fact that the paper included another short article on white poverty. The fact that Mary Butler was in Cradock's location as a municipal nurse at all was something of a miracle, but that miracle could not be sustained. Six years after her reproach to Cradock's white majority almost appeared in her brother's paper, she would resign her post.[1]

Since qualifying at the Somerset Hospital in Cape Town in about 1914, Mary Butler had worked as a private nurse in Cradock and had no experience of running a clinic. A woman of tenacity, she had a sustained sense of the injustices suffered by South Africa's people of color and the burdens imposed on location women by poor water supply, poor waste disposal, and the distant facilities for washing clothes. She worked as location nurse in the location from 1927 to 1937 without much help from doctors, administrators, or nursing colleagues. But when Cradock appointed a trained African nurse as her colleague, the two women were soon at odds. The reverberations drew in the Rev. James Calata,

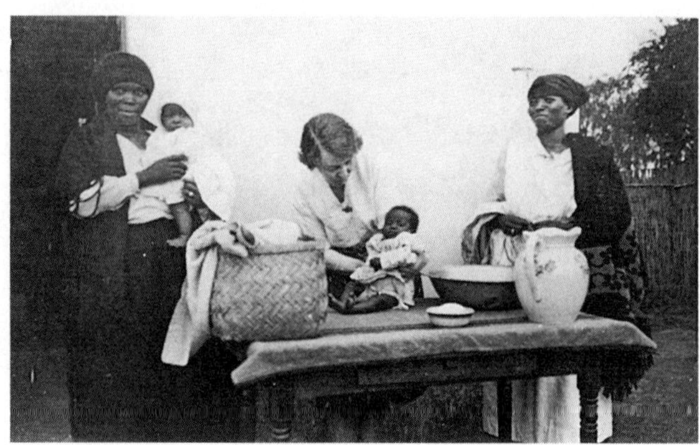

Fig. 21. Instruction in washing a baby at the dispensary. From photograph album compiled by Mary Butler. (Guy Butler Collection, © Rhodes University [Cory Library])

leader of the Cape African Congress in Cradock, and brought about the collapse of the Joint Council, Cradock's first and only venture in multiracial politics.

When the location dispensary opened in 1927, it had extremely limited resources: one small room and a modest budget to purchase medical supplies and pay the trained nurse in charge (Butler) and a "native assistant" with no training. Its hours were modest—Cradock's regular business hours—9:00 a.m. to 5:30 p.m., five days a week with a half-day on Wednesday (fig. 21). Its work was to be supervised by the town's part-time medical officer of health (MOH), who was in attendance once a week. Costs were charged to the native revenue account, established under the Natives (Urban Areas) Act (1923). Though a municipal enterprise, the health clinic was not to burden the municipality's own general revenue. The parsimonious electorate of ratepayers, 90 percent of them white, had little to fear. The clinic cost them nothing.

The Union Department of Public Health was largely a supervising and inspecting body; its assistant medical officers of health, such as Dr. W. A. Murray, brought the prestige of science to their "systematic" inspections of local public health regimes. In 1927, the department had only just begun to enforce higher standards of health and hygiene in South African towns, and Murray's highly accusatory inspection of Cradock in July 1924 was still fresh in public memory. Cradock's Queen's Central Hospital had been founded in 1897, the year of Queen Victoria's Diamond Jubilee (fig. 22), but by 1923 it had only twenty-eight beds for whites and twenty-two for "Natives"; by 1946 it had virtually no more, though the population had grown rapidly. The hospital was always in financial difficulty—at the end of 1923 it had an overdraft of £1,891, almost half its budget, when demand for services was increasing every year. Its grant

Fig. 22. Opening of the Queen's Central Hospital, 1899. Photographer: W. W. Lidbetter. (National English Literary Museum, Grahamstown, South Africa)

from the Cape provincial government of £1,750, which had been set in 1921, was far from adequate.[2]

The town clerk set out Mary Butler's duties: she was to work in close cooperation with the location superintendent, "guiding him in hygiene, prevention of overcrowding etc."; to "employ her knowledge as a Nurse to raise the domestic life of Natives where such is necessary"; to "assist in the reduction of the infant mortality rate by supplying correct feeding and advice where necessary, in deserving cases only"; and, with the "Native Clergy," to hold "lecture evenings to inculcate knowledge re prevention of disease," to "stock drugs in bulk for the common diseases," and to encourage the use of the "outpatient medical supervision at the hospital."[3]

This program recognized political realities. As the embattled Cradock MOH had maintained in 1924, the town clerk, and presumably many councilors, blamed location dwellers' poor health and that of their children on their own ignorance and immorality, not on low income, inadequate nutrition, tainted water supply, and crowded and poor housing. Cradock's approach was moral, judgmental, and palliative rather than generous, material, and fundamental. It avoided the central question of poor housing, a decent sewer system, and adequate water and food. Its reference to "correct" feeding of children made no suggestions of sources for such feeding. Nor did it indicate a source for the "drugs in bulk."

From the beginning, Butler was critically short of funds. She appealed to location residents for "their voluntary financial support again this year [1927]."[4] The Women's Civic Association, hard put to meet its own annual obligation of £68 for Butler's salary, (Metcalf's roughly £75 had been a one-time gift toward the capital cost of the building), did set up a Medicine and Nourishment Fund and in 1927 asked the town council if it could hold an annual street collection. Since many of Butler's patients were dependents of itinerant workers such as shearers and fencers, she also approached farmer-employers for contributions.[5]

Butler made the dispensary committee multiracial and established a quarterly meeting that was "to consider the work that is being done, any suggestions from location residents, and finance."[6] In creating this Combined Location Committee, Butler had established Cradock's first multiracial body of Africans, whites, and coloreds to discuss matters of public policy. Mrs. L. F. Brown, WCA president and chair of the committee's quarterly meetings, proposed a commitment of £15 from each of the colored and African communities. It was a commitment the poorer Africans found far more difficult to meet than coloreds did. An energetic school teacher and colored leader, P. C. Goodman, raised 106 shillings in a month, the Africans only 5 shillings.[7]

At the second meeting of the Combined Location Committee, Goodman asked whether a "child welfare branch" could be set up "under the auspices of the WCA," but Butler thought this would require a separate body.[8] Goodman persisted, raising issues of public health and high mortality from TB, poor housing, and the need for "a Coloured nurse" as a "helper" for Butler. Mrs. P. J. J. Coetzee, wife of Cradock's South African Party provincial councilor, made a forceful plea for a child welfare society to deal with infant mortality and child care. She had been involved in the Child Welfare Society (CWS) for twelve years and suggested a branch in Cradock to help "rich" and "poor" children resist especially the ravages of "pulmonary T.B." She repeated Goodman's plea for an assistant colored nurse to help Butler.

The campaign for a child welfare society was now heightened by intervention of an African leader: Florence Makiwane Jabavu, wife of the distinguished African scholar D. D. T. Jabavu, at the South African Native College, Fort Hare. Jabavu proposed to the Combined Committee that a child welfare society for coloreds and Africans be set up; it was part of her campaign "round the country," she said, to establish "Non-European Child Welfare societies" to instruct young mothers so as to prevent the "death of numberless children . . . by sheer ignorance." Again, the emphasis was on the victims' ignorance, not on society's inequities. They would have to choose, Jabavu continued, between "one European [committee], and one non-European, or one combined. But the natives are very suspicious regarding what the white people do for them and they prefer committees of their own." Others, Butler among them, resisted this proposal. She maintained that Cradock was not ready for a Child Welfare Society, but perhaps for a "Health Society—Location Health Society." The meeting, taking her advice, decided on a "Health Society . . . to have native and colored helpers under the guidance of Europeans."[9] The Health Society flourished. By May 1928 it had divided the location into "districts" and set up a "Visiting Committee" of location residents. The white Methodist minister from town served as its president. The society had sufficient sense of its importance to produce a banner and to have itself photographed.[10]

Why did Butler argue that Cradock was not "ready" for a Child Welfare Society? Perhaps she feared the consequences of having a competing organization dealing with the health of location children; perhaps she was reflecting her own increasing interest and that of others in a Joint Council, which would have a much wider mandate than the Child Welfare Society. Miss L. M. Mackenzie, organizing secretary to the National Council of Child Welfare, visiting the clinic, saw no conflict of interest between a Joint Council and other bodies and urged the health society to contact Joint Councils outside of Cradock.[11] At the end of November 1928, the dispensary quarterly meeting ceased to function and a Joint Council was established "forthwith."[12]

Goodman had inquired what the position of coloreds would be on a Joint Council. Butler, also concerned about the position of coloreds, wrote to J. D. Rheinallt Jones of the Institute of Race Relations, the organization that fostered the founding of Joint Councils, about the delicate question of a name. To affiliate with the Joint Council movement was it necessary to be called a Joint Council? "Would it meet the case if we called ourselves a 'Non-European Health and Welfare Society'?"

Butler's desire to avoid the term "Joint Council" in favor of "Non-European Health and Welfare Society" undoubtedly reflected her awareness of coloreds' dread of being linked in institutions with Africans, just as they had been in 1925 in the case of the Location Advisory Board. Rheinallt Jones's reply suggests that Joint Councils had taken little interest in coloreds and Indians and were, in fact, usually preoccupied with the problems of Africans. Nonetheless, any federation of Joint Councils, Rheinallt Jones wrote, should include bodies "working both amongst Indians and Coloured as well as among Natives."[13] But as Richard Haines has pointed out, such bodies were rare in South Africa; it can be added that councils, like Cradock's, involving whites, Africans, and coloreds were rarer still. In any event, Butler's anxieties and those of Cradock's coloreds were alleviated. The Combined Location Committee formally dissolved itself and was replaced by a Joint Council of eight "European," six "Coloured," and nine "Native" Members.[14] An attempt to include Afrikaners on the committee appears to have been abandoned.

A Nurses' War and the Intervention of the Cape African Congress

In the first years of the dispensary, Butler appealed to the public to save medicine bottles for reuse at the clinic. Her duties had included an injunction to "stock drugs in bulk for the common diseases" and after the extension of the dispensary in 1930, the municipality persuaded the Department of Native Affairs to spend £100 a year out of Cradock's native revenue on "stock medicines." The dispensary was to supply these to residents "free of charge to those unable to pay, and to make a nominal charge for those who are in a better position, and the better class still would, of course, purchase their medicines from the chemist shops."[15] The policy involved some risks for Butler, putting her in the position of deciding who would pay and how much, and in particular, it put her in possible, even probable, collision with members of the "better class," who were expected to pay for their own medicines.

The Rev. James Calata, then not yet a resident of Cradock, had attended the combined Location Committee as a visitor and had admired, he said, Cradock's "multiracial meeting." He became a close friend and ally of Butler's; the two shared a number of liberal attitudes, and Calata depended on her for medical help for his own tuberculosis from time to time. Alone among liberals in Cradock, he had had some prior experience with a multiracial body—the Native Welfare Society in New Brighton in Port Elizabeth—so his move to Cradock at the end of 1928, just as the Combined Committee was pondering a Joint Council, was a coincidence that gave him some standing in Cradock.[16] The minutes of Cradock's Joint Council to 1934 show a cordial cooperation between Butler and Calata—they were joint secretaries for a time. But they were about to face an issue in which their interests were so divided that it would destroy the council and end their relationship.

In July 1933, without warning, a bomb fell. Two colored members of the Location Advisory Board, noting the depletion of the native revenue account, proposed helping the superintendent collect outstanding rents. This was a politically astounding proposal, one likely to be resented by Africans as affecting them more seriously than coloreds. One of the two proposers, C. Sauls, suggested that Mary Butler serve "the Europeans in the town" while the location's needs would be better served by "a native and [a] coloured nurse," living in the location and paid "a joint salary of about £11 [£5 10s, or £5.5 each] against the £17 paid [Butler] at the present moment."[17] An African and a colored nurse could assess the "needs and wants" of "their own people . . . more accurately." The dispensary should also be open longer hours, 6 a.m. to 6 p.m. daily, instead of 9 a.m. to 5:30 p.m., and one nurse would be available all night.[18] In the meanwhile, "pending the appointment of the coloured and native nurses," the council should instruct nurse Butler to be on hand on Wednesday afternoons, a day when shops and offices closed early in Cradock, and also on Sunday afternoons.[19]

Early in 1934, the district surgeon, Dr. W. Scholtz, and the MOH, Dr. A. H. Budler, entered the ring against Mary Butler as well. The council had earlier resolved that "written application" had to be made to the council before she could deliver indigents' babies at government expense. Scholtz exploded: "If you could . . . arrange for a confinement [childbirth] to come off till after the approval of the Council has been obtained, I could see some sense in such a resolution." He proposed closing the dispensary and appointing two "district nurses." For his part, Dr. Budler suggested "two or three fully qualified native nurses . . . in place of the present European Nurse"; the next year he declared that "the present clinic serves no good purpose whatsoever" and would "continue to be a failure until accommodation can be provided for infectious diseases patients."[20] For reasons unclear, the council did not respond to the two doctors' rigorous criticism of Butler and the dispensary. Residents of the location were not taking the same side as the doctors—they were not asking for abolition of the clinic but only for a change in personnel—removal of Butler from the location and her replacement by a colored and an African nurse—and an extension of dispensary hours. The coloreds' preferred their own nurse; a deputation from the APO, including Sauls, one of the originators of the colored protest, appeared before the council to request "coloured nurses for the coloured people in the location." But the council announced that it could not appoint a colored nurse "at this stage."[21]

Then Africans, too, began to raise grievances. In two difficult deliveries in African households, they said, Butler had delayed too long in calling for assistance, and both babies had been born dead. The municipality's stingy refusal in 1928 to place a telephone in the dispensary had now borne bitter fruit. Butler had to obtain the town clerk's permission to summon the MOH, but without a dispensary telephone, she had to go the location office. In one case, she phoned, but the town clerk was in a meeting and could not be disturbed. In the second, the location office was locked after hours, and Butler could not use the phone. As a result, medical help came too late.[22] To make matters worse, the Rev. N. Mhlomi had complained to the location superintendent, apparently questioning Butler's authority to impose a fee of 10s. on better-off location residents for her nursing assistance at childbirths. Africans also claimed that Butler had refused treatment to residents who owed money to the dispensary.[23] She was under siege.

In August 1935, Metcalf, the generous Cradock philanthropist, broke the stalemate by, again "anonymously," donating funds to build a larger clinic and to pay the first year's salary of a full-time "Native" nurse (at £9 a month).[24] Butler drafted a plan for Metcalf's donation to enable the municipality to take over the location superintendent's house in the location and renovate it as a clinic to be staffed by a white nurse, an African nurse, and an African assistant—the Africans to be supervised by the "European nurse" and by the council, with professional oversight from the MOH. A reluctant town clerk, fearful of political consequences, pointed out that this project would cost the council £355 a year, instead of the current £150, and suggested raising location rents by threepence (a quarter of a shilling) per month, about 10 percent, to meet the increase. "Last year," the council had resolved "to grant relief to the poorer section of the European community. . . . Nothing has been done and it would be just as well to consider the matter when this report comes up for discussion."[25] Location rents were a touchy issue, just as the lodgers' fee had been in 1925, and the Location Advisory Board reacted vehemently. The location superintendent, Wilken, who chaired the board, offered to leave the room so that the discussion could proceed more freely. The board refused, and with the colored members taking the lead, rejected the plan as too costly: the proposed "native" assistant at £15 a year was not necessary; "a native and a coloured nurse" could "be given preference to work among their own people"; and such nurses "would be on the premises at all times." Without the white nurse, the location would save "approximately £100 in salaries per year."[26]

Metcalf and Butler were still prepared to move ahead on their proposal to hire a single African nurse. Helen Mtombeni was appointed, but she soon resigned, without saying why. Next, a white committee, including Butler and Metcalf, hired an experienced African replacement who had worked in the Langa location in Cape Town.[27] Nurse Osary Hokwana and Butler were soon arguing; Hokwana also complained to the town clerk about her living and working conditions. Nor would Butler agree to a subdivision of the location to give each nurse clearly defined, separate responsibilities. Soon, the two nurses were, apparently, barely speaking: "Latterly she has refused to tell me where she was going," Butler wrote, "or to report on what she had done."[28]

The Cape African Congress (CAC), the Cape branch of the African National Congress, was already exercised over the issue of the "Native Nurse." John Sitela, CAC secretary, raised several issues: "whether [the Native Nurse] should charge for confinement cases or not," particularly in view of "the large amount of births of illegitimate children and the uncontrollable state of some of our young men and women." Also, "who is the controlling authority to whom complaints about nurses should be made?" And lastly, could individuals who owed money to the dispensary be refused treatment? Who had control of the money? The "Advisory Board . . . or some other board" should account for all moneys including those from sale of medicines, donations, and "Location Revenue."[29] The Congress was hardly modest in its demands for a redistribution of power over money, including location rents. Nor was it conciliatory in implying that Butler might be making illegitimate use of funds. The town council, in turn, was hardly willing to compromise; its Location Committee responded curtly that all complaints were to go directly "to Council." Disposition of medicines was "left to the discretion of Nurse Butler and . . . all monies are accounted for to the municipal office." Moreover, the council was "unable to assist Congress in regard to illegitimate children born in the Cradock location." The committee instructed Hokwana explicitly to "take her instructions from Nurse Butler."[30] Hokwana then resigned. When Butler saw the full statement of the CAC's grievances, she too resigned, citing "personal reasons" and her opinion that "it is a legitimate ambition on the part of native and coloured people to have their own nurses."[31]

The council's attempts to sustain Butler's authority had backfired. Sitela wrote again to the council on 8 May "taking exception . . . for the manner in which the dispute between the nurses was heard and protesting that the council had allowed the uncle of one of the nurses [Charles Butler], to be the chief spokesman on behalf of the council." Sitela called on the council "to close the Location dispensary if the Native nurse leaves Cradock."[32] The African members of the Location Advisory Board then resigned, citing the council's "ignoring of the board. . . . [It] seems the more strange in view of the fact that the present Government, under the new Native Representation Act [1936] has conferred on all Adv. Boards a definite political status . . . and we had hoped . . . for . . . greater official recognition from our Council."[33] The council then appointed a special committee of councilors, with Mayor Max de Kock as chairman, which in turn called a plenary meeting of councilors and residents in the location. At a "very lengthy debate," the "inhabitants" submitted a list of "requests": that at least two "Non-European" nurses should be hired, one "Native" and one "Coloured," that both should be required to live in the location in accommodation provided by the council, and that the nurses were not to "discriminate [among?] the inhabitants of the location."[34]

By the time the special committee met again, the Africans had won *all* their points: the council was already writing to the Department of Native Affairs about subsidies for the salaries of *two* "Non-European" nurses. The council accepted Butler's departure with "extreme regret" and reappointed Hokwana to take "full charge" of the dispensary "until such time as final arrangements have been made." She became an official location nurse, and the council advertised for a colored nurse.[35] Africans had dominated that stage of the debate—no colored leaders had had anything to say even though it was the colored members of the Advisory Board who had made the original motion two years before to hire two "Non-European" nurses. The colored members had not resigned in sympathy with their African colleagues, and the CAC had referred only to "grievances of the Bantu Location Inhabitants." The African members, returning to the Advisory Board, passed an eloquent motion, thanking the outgoing National Party leader, De Kock, for his work as mayor.[36]

Butler's resignation had a profound impact on the Joint Council and on Calata's relations with liberal whites in Cradock. Butler left Cradock to work in a mission hospital in the Transvaal and did not return to public life in Cradock for a decade, at the end of the Second World War. The dispute had shown how helpless the Joint Council was; it had played no part at all in the nurses' dispute, because Calata had chosen not to involve it. Its president in

1937, Owen Walters, a British-born farmer, was outraged at Calata's behavior but concluded that the Joint Council had little real role to play.[37] Yet Walters hosted a meeting including Calata on his farm in 1938, just at the time that he and other white members were supporting the municipality on the opening of a beer hall, against the determined opposition of Cradock's Africans. As Walters feared, without Mary Butler's involvement, the Joint Council had little chance of survival. Dorothy Butler, Mary Butler's niece, became joint secretary but resigned when she married a year later. In 1940 Rheinallt Jones of the Institute of Race Relations wrote to Charles Butler, now mayor, to ask whether "the Joint Council . . . is really dead."[38] It was indeed, and the effort to maintain a multiracial institution to inform Cradock whites about location affairs and to discuss wider issues of policy died with it.

The Coming of "Social Medicine" to Cradock

Mary Butler may have been deeply hurt by her extrusion from the location clinic, but she had nevertheless set something of value in motion. The conversion of the location superintendent's house into the Metcalf Clinic, which Butler had proposed, was already far advanced, and the new premises were opened in September 1937. With Butler's hiring a decade before, Cradock had established municipal clinical services for the location before it had done so for the town. (In a longstanding pet project of the ACVV, a social worker/nurse was appointed in 1939 for indigent whites, to work out of a clinic in the town hall.)[39] The possibility of subsidy for a full-time combined medical officer of health (MOH) and district surgeon (DS), provided for by the Public Health (Amendment) Act of 1935 was being considered; this official would oversee the public health needs of the municipality as a whole, in both town and location, replacing a full-time MOH, but would also attend to the needs of the rural area under the divisional council, as well as the needs of Union government officials (the South African Police, prison staff, and civil servants), previously the responsibility of the part-time district surgeon.[40] Thus the Cradock location had the Metcalf clinic (named for its first philanthropist), staffed by two nurses, one an African in charge, the other a colored, both to be employed by the hospital, their salary subsidized by the Union government, and supervised by the new full-time MOH/DS.

The new appointment of a MOH/DS produced important benefits. Dr. G. O. Thornton wrote far more informative and hard-hitting annual reports than those of his predecessors. He complained about the "gross contamination" of the irrigation furrow running through the town and pointed out that infant mortality rates for "Asiatics," "Eurafricans" and "Natives" were ten times those for "Europeans."[41] At Thornton's death in 1943, Dr. B. J. van Rensburg of Cradock, a member of a prominent United Party family, succeeded him, bringing even greater energy and enthusiasm to the post. Van Rensburg faced considerable obstacles to improving clinical services: the number of doctors in Cradock had declined, and the demands for medical services from the government increased, especially for military personnel, Italian prisoners of war working on farms, and the police. The population of the town was growing rapidly: between the censuses of 1936 and 1946 the number of whites increased by 21 percent, from 3,690 to 4,477; of Africans, 57 percent from 3,569 to 5,606, despite the harrowing loss of infant and child deaths; of coloreds, 53 percent from 1,951 to 2,084; of Asians, 4 percent from 50 to 52. Whites had declined as a proportion of overall population from 40 to 27 percent, and Africans had risen from 39 to 46 percent.[42] Farmers, complaining that rates of tuberculosis and venereal disease were rising among their workers, demanded visits by doctors to the rural areas and access to the location clinic for their workers of color.

In November 1944, the government published the report of the National Health Services Commission, named after its chairman Dr. Henry Gluckman MP, a document remarkable in its framing of South African health problems as those of a single people rather than an assemblage of races. It was also something of a pioneer in the modern intellectual movement for "social medicine," reflecting in some respects Britain's Beveridge Report of 1942. "Health services in the Union," the report stated, "are not organized on a national basis, are not in conformity with the modern conception of health and are not available to all sections of the people." To the familiar categories of curative and preventive medicine it added "promotive" services including adequate wages, nutrition, and industrial hygiene; and "rehabilitative" services, both medical and educational. The preventive services, crucial for municipalities, were subdivided into nonpersonal services concerning sanitation and the environment (housing, water, removal of wastes, and food handling) and personal services (periodic examinations and immunizations, in a system of clinics with trained personnel). Combined, these services would constitute an institutional reconstruction of a town. The great innovation proposed was a community-based "health center": the commission proposed that four hundred of these be established in the Union as the foundation of a national health service, with each center to serve 25,000 people. With Cradock's town and district population at 26,733 in 1946, a Cradock center and rural subcenters would need a staff of six to eight doctors. The whole ambitious enterprise was to be financed by a new national health tax.[43]

The publication of the report was the beginning of an attempt by a Union department to intervene in local jurisdictions in the interests of new reformist policies. Social medicine had been promoted from the late 1930s by a remarkable group of senior health department officials, among them Dr. George Gale, who was to become secretary for health in 1946 and to play an especially significant role in opening Cradock's new health center.[44] Their proposals were attractive to many in Cradock's government who hoped to see a new institution that might make of Cradock something of a health "Capital of the Midlands." At the fourth annual meeting of the Cape Midlands Development Association, in 1944, Cradock's mayor, J. A. Cull, urged establishment of a center "at Cradock more fully as stated in the Gluckman Health Commission's report." The town clerk supported the mayor with a boosterish letter: Cradock was "ideally situated," had "perfect climate . . . and controls no less than eight towns within a radius of 90 miles and is also the capital of the Midlands . . . [with] regular train services from north and south." It would soon "boast a modern sewerage system," he continued, and had plenty of pure chlorinated water and cheap electricity. The municipality would make land available free of charge for an isolation hospital and provide services there at very reasonable rates.[45] Cradock boosters' ambition for the town to become a vigorous regional center had long been expressed in such labels as "Capital of the Midlands" and in the title "Queen's Central Hospital" (1897).

Public bodies were also now aware of a serious deficiency in clinical services, especially to the location. Since 1937, when Mary Butler left, the Metcalf Clinic, like the former dispensary, had served only coloreds and Africans and was staffed by two African nurses and the full-time MOH/DS. Many location residents bypassed the clinic and went directly to local physicians in town who were willing to treat them on a cash basis. As population grew and the number of doctors declined from five to four, and sometimes only three, the remaining doctors increasingly limited themselves to white patients, urban and rural. Africans complained at a 1944 meeting of the Cape African Congress that people of color could not get medical attention even though willing and able to pay. When Donald Molteno MP, the "Native Representative" in parliament for the Cradock area, addressed a meeting in the Cradock location, residents made their resentments clear: "When location residents seek attention from local doctors the latter refer them to the [Metcalf] clinic . . . ; when they go to the clinic they are told by the District Surgeon that he can only attend to them if they are paupers." Molteno therefore urged the minister of health to open a health center. The minister (H. G. Lawrence) replied that he had set up a committee to consider such a health center; he also deplored the physicians' refusal of medical services to paying coloreds and Africans.[46]

The town clerk supported the proposal that "the Government" establish a health center. Previous efforts, he said, had failed to get help from the Department of Native Affairs. "A non-European child of about 12 years of age actually bled to death in the streets . . . [because] the parents were unable to obtain medical attention."[47] Van Rensburg, the new MOH/DS, pointed out that a town and district population of 22,300 was served by "a fifty-bedded hospital" and two clinics—one for whites with one nurse, one for people of color with two nurses, and only four doctors for 6,600 "Europeans," 6,500 "non-Europeans" in the location, and 9,200 in the district. The combination of MOH/DS was not working, and therefore he now suggested "two completely separate appointments."[48] But "our financial position cannot stand it," the town clerk wrote. "The position is getting out of hand, more especially tuberculosis and unless some form of relief is granted by the Central Government . . . it might also become beyond the control of the government."[49]

Gale, the secretary of public health, came to Cradock and expressed support for "either a full-time Assistant DS . . . or a Health Centre"; but taking "local opinion" into consideration, he recommended a health center as the more ambitious course.[50] Representatives of the Queen's Central Hospital Board, the municipality, the divisional council, and the two rural nursing societies—Mortimer and Baroda—sent a petition for a health center.[51] At the end of March 1946, Dr. Van Rensburg resigned as MOH/DS to accept an appointment as head of the Cradock center.[52]

"The Tuberculosis Menace in Cradock"

Van Rensburg promoted social medicine with enthusiasm. A Cradock farmer, Mrs. Margery Cooper, had made a now-familiar complaint: the divisional council, the Metcalf Clinic, and the hospital all refused to pay to treat an African woman on her farm who was suffering from TB.[53] Anxiety over tuberculosis had a long history in Cradock, whose dry climate enhanced its reputation as a suitable refuge for persons, especially from England, suffering from the disease. Nineteenth-century discussions portrayed TB as a menace to whites rather than to people of color.[54] However, some witnesses to the National Tuberculosis Commission of 1914 saw whites as bearers of the disease to Africans and to coloreds. James Butler, who had "come out [from England] on account of chest trouble" in 1877, said TB had long been "rife" in Cradock among "Natives," and "three or four of the coloured nurse girls employed in his own family had died of consumption."[55] TB, along with venereal disease, became the focus of repeated demands for an isolation hospital, but several such efforts, by the Women's Civic Association in 1930 and by the Joint Council in 1930 and 1934, had failed to secure such a hospital.[56]

In the 1940s, public officials were becoming increasingly restive about the spread of TB among coloreds and Africans. In 1944, when urging the opening of a health center in Cradock, local officials emphasized the TB problem. In 1946, the municipality resumed the practice of hiring only a part-time MOH, Dr. L. V. Oosthuizen, who produced, clearly at the request of the municipality, a memorandum that included a table on "The Tuberculosis Menace in Cradock" (table 3). The death rate from tuberculosis was 4.5 per thousand in 1946. Oosthuizen's figures were part of a public relations statement detailing Cradock's inadequate TB facilities for "isolation," "diagnosis," and "after care" that was intended "to persuade the Health authorities to build a Sanitarium or a Regional Hospital." His letter included a statement of Cradock's excellent

Table 3. Tubercular cases in Cradock

	White	*Colored*	*Asian*	*African*	*Total*
1940	5	14	1	16	36
1941	5	16	–	28	49
1942	3	11	–	20	34
1943	2	13	–	26	44
1944	2	16	–	26	44
1945	–	12	–	37	49
1946	–	13	–	37	50
TOTAL	17	95	1	186	299
MEAN	2.4	13.5	0.1	26.5	
MEAN Non-European					40.2
MEAN European					2.4

Source: L. Oosthuizen, "The Tuberculous Menace in Cradock," 30 Apr. 1947, NAR GES 1035, 43/17. [Date may be incorrect.–Ed.]

"facilities"—adequate water supply, cheap power, a "delightful residential area," a pending water-borne sewerage system, and an offer of twenty morgen of land for a "Regional Tuberculosis Hospital" to be built in seven years.[57]

Responding to this plea, B. A. Dormer, the Department of Health's chief tuberculosis officer, visited Cradock and drafted an ambitious plan in the best spirit of social medicine: Van Rensburg should be given equipment "so that he can apply standard technique to his whole population and find out the degree of tuberculosis infection in it." There should be a "Mass Radiographic X-ray Survey" of the *entire* Cradock population, "European" and "Non-European," with provision for "isolation houses," care of children, provision for sheltered employment after treatment, and transfer of treatable cases to the King George V Hospital in Durban, a noted tuberculosis treatment center. There should be future mass surveys, at first "not less than yearly." Cradock, Dormer wrote, had agreed to build isolation houses and to provide twenty morgen of land for a regional hospital. "We can demonstrate how simple it is for a small community with a Health Center and with the help of the Tuberculosis Division [to] ascertain exactly its Tuberculosis Problem and control the disease cheaply and efficiently without great cost to itself or the state." He set up a team, including himself, for the mass radiographic survey.[58]

Van Rensburg moved energetically to collect demographic and epidemiological data. He defined an "Intensive Area" in the new Wilken Township as a pilot project, with three newly appointed native health assistants, each assigned forty houses for regular visits and collection of information on population, pregnancy, natality, mortality, and morbidity.[59] The Mass Radiographic Survey was conducted by canvassers, including ministers and teachers, who moved systematically street by street. To Van Rensburg's delight, his staff examined 8,300 persons, a figure "in excess of the figures obtained in [the] 1946 [census] for the urban Non-European population!"[60]

The first report of the health center, for the first six months of 1947, gave statistics on deaths from tuberculosis, venereal disease, and whooping cough. It pointed out that in Wilken Township's Intensive Area there was no gardening because of poor soil and no water, and that only two taps served the 120 houses; thus drinking water "is collected and stored in open buckets and paraffin [kerosene] tins," increasing the risk of infection. There were no washing facilities, and lavatories were "inadequate." Out of 372 residents in 79 two-room houses, 249 lived in households of five or more individuals, so no separation of sexes was possible. Van Rensburg found it "anomalous" that even in the "recently constructed housing scheme for Africans—Wilken Township"—a majority of dwellings would be "condemned if the second schedule of the Slums Act could be applied." (The Slums Act of 1934 had deliberately excluded African housing from its remedial provisions.) The report had sections on location schools and the need to test *all* children.[61] Finally, there was a section on the need for cooperation with other agencies—with the Department of Social Welfare and the schools on school-feeding schemes; with the municipality on the sale of cheap vegetables from municipal gardens, and the provision of land for gardening; and with charitable organizations—the Red Cross, and the National War Memorial Health Foundation, which was hoping to open a "Peoples Centre" next to the health center to take over "promotive" health services; and with a recently formed Adult Education Movement.[62]

A Health Center Rises in Cradock

Van Rensburg had started with a staff of nine, including one doctor (himself), two "Native Sisters," and two "Native Health Assistants." Soon this number expanded to thirteen, including another doctor, another "Native Staff-Nurse," and another "Native Health Assistant"; to nineteen by 1947–48; to twenty-one by 1950–51. From the beginning Van Rensburg acknowledged that the Cradock health center was serving an African and a colored population, and he complained of the lack of colored staff until the two staff nurses were added in 1950–51. Van Rensburg and his successor, Dr. Ethel Froom, complained of a persistent shortage of midwives, made worse when the Hospital Board withdrew its three nurse/midwives at the center's opening at the end of 1946. Yet, by 1951, there was progress in staffing nursing services and with publicity of the opening of the center and the Mass Radiographic Survey, an "avalanche of Out-patients" appeared at the "curative clinic."[63]

Table 4. Attendances at Cradock health center, 1947, 1947–48, and 1950–51

	*Cases**	*Prenatal*	*Mother and baby*	*Syphilis*	*Total*
1947 (first 6 months)	4,975	739	310	1,859	7,883
1947–48	18,379	1,971	2,972	3,012	26,334
1950–51	19,271	2,633	1,671	4,571	28,146
Change 1947–1950	+892	+662	-1,301	+1,559	+1,812
Percent Change 1947–1950	4.8	33.58	-43.77	51.75	6.8

Source: Cradock Health Center Annual Reports, NAR, GES 1918 5/54/32.2.
*Cases of disease, excluding venereal diseases.

Each year, the health center had to submit a massive report on disease, prenatal care, mother and child care, and syphilis treatment (table 4). The table shows a rapid increase in attendances immediately following the center's opening and a sustained increase (34 percent) in prenatal visits. However, there was a large drop (44 percent) in prenatal attendances at the mother and baby clinic, almost certainly due to shortages of staff. In 1947 Van Rensburg complained about the too-frequent use of "gamps," unqualified and unregistered midwives. Assuming that a midwife could handle an absolute maximum of 120 cases a year, he claimed that about three additional well-trained African and two colored midwives were required.[64] A native staff nurse and two colored staff nurses had been added by 1950; in 1950, Froom could report that 327 births (of a total of 410) had been handled by center midwives, a jump from only 164 the year before, and a reduction in the activity of "gamps."[65]

Between 1947 and 1950 the number of visits of syphilis patients had risen by 52 percent. Women made up 76 percent of such visits in both years; new female cases virtually doubled in two years. Froom's report for 1950–51 showed that 63 percent of all cases had been sixteen years of age or less. The treatment of syphilis depended crucially on sufficient numbers of doctors to provide regular treatment at the two rural nursing society clinics. With the increased demands on the center itself, the needs of the countryside simply could not be met, and in 1954 the secretary of the Mortimer Rural Society complained that doctors from Cradock had come for scheduled visits in 1953 far less frequently than needed.[66]

Dormer's ambitious intervention, of which the Mass Radiographic Survey of 1947 was part, had at long last produced a concrete result when the municipality built an isolation hospital in the location. The MOH, once again a

Table 5. Infant mortality and general death rates, Cradock, 1946 and 1953

	Infant mortality rates per thousand births					*General death rate per thousand people*
	White	*Colored*	*Asian*	*African*	*All*	
1946	30	105.77	00	180.38	136.36	26.19
1953	28.04	114.29	00	283.78	183.08	20.13

Sources: Medical Officer of Health (Cradock), Annual Reports 1946, 1951, 1953 NAR TBPA GES 565/123/13C.

part-time municipal official, had high expectations of reducing TB infections by effective isolation, but the 1953 figures gave officials little to cheer about. Comparing the means for 1950 to 1953 with those of 1940 to 1946, one finds increases in deaths per thousand across the board from 43 to 53; increases in "Non-Europeans" from 40.2 to 50.3 and in "Europeans" from 2.4 to 2.8. The death rate from TB went from 3.89 deaths per thousand in 1946 to 5.09 in 1953; the rate for Africans in 1953 was 6.37, for coloreds 12.23, for whites .021. The position, wrote the MOH, Dr. G. de V. Morisson "is unchanged and unfavorable."[67]

The health center idea had been developed by a small group of officials, and by individuals like Emily and Sidney Kark, who had achieved remarkable results at Polela in Natal from the early 1940s, even before the Gluckman report was published. When Dormer came to Cradock in 1947, he wrote, "We should use this town [Polela] based on the Health Centre as a demonstration that tuberculosis can be controlled in small Local Authority areas, simply, efficiently and economically."[68] Gale, secretary for health at the time, wrote later that at Polela "the general death rate was reduced by a half, and infant mortality by two-thirds in 5 years."[69] As for Cradock, by using the figures on mortality from the annual reports of the Cradock MOH, we can construct table 5 covering the first years of the center's operation, 1946 to 1953. This mixed report—a decline in the general death rate and an increase in infant mortality—is hardly a fair test of the Cradock center's first seven years: Polela was staffed by the Karks, exceptional people with no equivalents in Cradock, and it was a rural, almost entirely African, area. Yet the comparison may suggest that because crucial policies affecting women and children in particular had not been maintained in Cradock, social medicine was unlikely to produce quick results.

In his report of the first systematic inspection of Cradock in 1924, Dr. Murray had proposed a better water supply and segregated housing for Africans, but he had made no proposals for clinical facilities in the location. Yet soon thereafter, in 1927, the government, municipality, and members of the public played an increasing role in local affairs, and a dispensary was founded. Cradock's town fathers saw in Gluckman's proposals of 1944 yet another opportunity to persuade national authorities to support a new, nationally financed, regional medical facility in their small town. But local support of Gluckman was not based on a well-mobilized electorate aware of the pioneering character of the proposals. The United Party government did not make social medicine part of its program. Health centers were poorly financed and few in number by 1948.[70]

The new apartheid government did not promote the health centers after 1948. Many National Party members were hostile to such centers, and by 1960 most had been closed or downgraded.[71] Although in Cradock there was a rapid and sustained increase in staff and attendances from 1948 to 1950, by 1951 there was a change in the tone and content of the reports, from Van Rensburg's enthusiasm of 1947 to Froom's brusque and cursory communication of data. The useful data on Africans collected in the Intensive Area of Wilken Township seem to have gone into storage: "Owing to pressure of work at the Centre, the Health Assistants were unable to carry out accurate statistics in their field work." Hopes for adult education, vegetable growing, and collaboration with other bodies had disappeared or were not regarded as important enough to comment on. The densely packed 1947 report of ten pages had been reduced to three in 1951, leaving the reader with little idea of what had actually happened.[72]

In its first years, the center had brought location residents into touch with town residents who were organized in public voluntary bodies like the Red Cross. We have no evidence of the impact of such activity, nor of attempts to organize support for increasing social contacts between people of different races. Still, even though National Party members were opposed to many aspects of social medicine, the centers did survive and conducted clinical operations on a scale previously unheard of—nine workers in 1946, twenty-one in 1950. The health center took over the Metcalf clinic, leaving the municipality to continue the limited clinical functions defined by statute—primarily recording vital statistics, reporting disease statistics, and sanitation conditions. The social medicine movement had hoped to create a single national, adequately funded, health service. This was not achieved for Cradock.

7

Improvement or Removal?

Segregated Public Housing

"The Native and Coloured People Should be Separated"

In 1926 Cradock ventured warily into building its first public housing since 1903. For the first time it confronted the question that would not be resolved until the age of apartheid: should Africans and colored be separated residentially? In October 1926, John Deary, then mayor of Cradock, called a special meeting of the town council to propose building separate new locations for Africans and for coloreds. "The idea of this Council, and it has always been my own idea, is . . . that the Native and Coloured people should be separated. If we are going to build houses let us build a Native location and a Coloured location. . . . Both the past and the present [Union] government advocated a policy of segregation so if the Council was going to spend money let it rather follow the policy of the government and separate the two peoples." That was Deary's preference, but the council had another choice to make: "whether they should move the location or build new houses on the present site." The *Midland News* headline, "Future of Cradock's Location: Improvement or Removal?" identified the crux of the issue.[1]

"Improvement," the more modest option in the age of segregation, could be undertaken by adding new homes or refurbishing old houses on a piecemeal basis, leaving the location racially "mixed," but with Africans and coloreds in separate neighborhoods within it. "Removal," a more ambitious and comprehensive plan favored by Deary, would enforce the official national distinction between Africans and coloreds—not based on skin color precisely since a number of coloreds were black. It would require investing in planning and drainage, building about six hundred new houses, perhaps some distance away. The drastic and ambitious plan was not to come to pass before 1948, when the age of apartheid began.

The Cradock municipality had built a block of twenty-nine single rooms in the location back in 1903. It was now about to build the first post-1903 public housing, first for Africans in the location and then for poor whites, many of them elderly, in town. The housing it built up between 1927 and 1948, financed by loans from a mildly interventionist national government, did a little to increase the residential separation of coloreds and Africans in the location, but not much. Even less did it further the segregation of whites from coloreds in the Mixed Area of town, which was adjacent to Regent Street, the boundary between town and location.

After the First World War, as South African towns and cities confronted a persistent influx of African and colored people, many towns faced the question of improving or removing racially designated locations. For many local governments, the in-migration of Africans was especially alarming. A shortage of housing for whites, anxiety over the spread of "contagion" after the 1918 influenza epidemic, and a new awareness among local and national officials of the grave state of housing in crowded locations and city slums provoked both national intervention and local demands for action.[2] The state of locations became a heated moral issue for the Women's Christian Temperance Union: at the WCTU national convention in 1922, Mrs. Julia Solly, a recent immigrant from England, proposed a program of housing and child welfare. Drink, she said, was not responsible for slums; slums were responsible for drink.[3] Africans, especially women, were at risk, temperance advocates believed: their wretched living conditions in segregated locations had driven many into illegal beer brewing and prostitution.

In response to such mounting concerns, the Public Health Act of 1920 and the Housing Act of 1921 established the machinery of health and sanitary inspection and offered government loans to enable local authorities to encourage private construction or to directly build housing for all racial groups. The Natives (Urban Areas) Act of 1923—which by its very name acknowledged the existence of a new "problem" social category, the urban African—provided money for housing loans specifically in locations. But it also declared that Africans could not own houses there in freehold, and thus, in the Cape, it limited Africans' access to the franchise in local and national elections. The act indirectly influenced the housing policies municipalities would later adopt.[4] Municipalities became the local agents for implementing a national housing policy with segregationist as well as ameliorative intentions. The local medical officer of health was now required to submit to the Department of Public Health an annual report on housing, as well as on health and sanitation.[5]

Authorized grants of housing loans always came with racial qualifiers—"Native," "European," and "Coloured." The last of these terms could create confusion in Cape Province, with its racially "mixed" towns and locations like Cradock's. At first, loans were often clustered in only two categories, "European" and "Natives and Coloured." Only later would "Native" (African) and "Coloured" be effectively separated from each other.[6] South Africa's rulers did not contemplate using housing to erase the racial divisions of South African society. There were to be no intentionally multiracial housing schemes—quite the contrary. Housing plans sustained two principal racial divisions—between whites and all people of color and, to a growing extent, a subdivision between Africans and coloreds. When Cradock embarked on its own housing schemes in the 1920s, the fine division between whites and all the rest was strictly observed, but before the 1940s, Cradock's officials would, despite Mayor Deary's views in 1926, show much less interest in creating or enforcing a subsidiary boundary between Africans and coloreds.

National intervention in Cradock's housing question began with the scathing 1924 report by Dr. William A. Murray of the Department of Health. In the several years before Murray's inspection, there had been much discussion in South Africa about water supply and housing, with frequent references to "overcrowding," a core subject of Murray's report. Murray said flatly that nothing short of the location's "entire removal to a more suitable site . . . and the erection by the council . . . of suitable separate dwellings for native and coloured families" would suffice. A "native village" with "properly laid out . . . streets and blocks and a minimum standard type of dwelling should be insisted on."

Although Murray called the location a "native village," he did not press for immediate separation between Africans and coloreds; the Natives (Urban Areas) Act acknowledged the right of coloreds to stay in locations until the local authority provided them with separate areas. Nor did Murray propose any plan for separating the 350 or so coloreds in town from Cradock's whites, implying, correctly, that the ruling whites had given tacit, if perhaps reluctant, consent for some coloreds to stay in town.

Murray did, however, propose some elementary concepts of broad town planning. His "properly laid out village," with "decent homes and surroundings" and with houses of a "minimum standard," was prophetic of the thousands of "little boxes" to be erected in South Africa (and elsewhere) before and after the Second World War. His proposals were intended solely to provide minimally adequate housing to replace the existing location dwellings with ones that would "ensure some measure of privacy." Each new house was to have its own latrine and a fenced lot. Moreover, enforcement of the "Model Regulations" dispatched to municipalities under the Urban Areas Act would achieve minimum standards in construction, especially in space requirements per person. But Murray suggested no provision for people to build their own houses in what would later be known later as "site-and-service" schemes. African housing, unlike colored housing, was to provide for a largely transient male labor force, and Murray therefore suggested that the town apply to the Department of Native Affairs for a housing loan.[7]

As the new era of government intervention began in 1926, Cradock's first Afrikaans-speaking town clerk, P. de K. van Heerden, was in a strategic position. He was born and raised in Cradock, and his only training had been thirteen years in a local law office, beginning as a clerk. A humane and efficient official, and an active member of the Dutch Reformed church, he had a shrewd sense of what could be done fiscally. Van Heerden energetically explored the possibilities of government loans. Loans for native housing were then administered by the Department of Native Affairs; loans for all other houses—for whites, coloreds, and Asians—by the Department of Public Health. No doubt influenced by Murray's stern report, Van Heerden wrote to the Department of Native Affairs to pose a crucial financial and political question: if Cradock undertook to build public housing under the Urban Areas Act, would the loan be "a liability of this Council's Rates and Assets?" If the housing loan were to be considered a "private liability of the Location," he wrote, "there would be very little difficulty." The secretary replied that "provided the Native Revenue Account is in a position to bear these charges, there would be no objection. . . . But this is a matter that will be determined in relation to the rents to be charged."[8] Thus the national departmental secretary was allowing the municipality to separate the financing of location capital expenditure from that of the town, a step toward limiting the town's responsibility and financial liability for its location. When Van Heerden reported to Cradock's council that £10,000 would be available from the government, councilors agreed to look for a site, complimented him on his energy, and raised his annual salary by £100.[9]

It was not easy to design a building whose rent location residents could afford. The town engineer, S. J. Kelly, proposed building 30 houses of two rooms, each 10 by 10 feet, with a *dagga* (mud) floor, which was strongly preferred by Africans because cement floors were cold. These houses were to rent at 12.5 shillings a month, but Van Heerden pointed out that this was well beyond what location residents were then paying: "Cradock location is looked upon as one of the cheapest . . . in the Cape Province, the rents ranging from 2½s to 5½s."[10] Kelly negotiated further reductions with the Central Housing Board and produced two plans: for a two-room dwelling renting at 11 shillings, and a one-room at 5.5 shillings.[11]

The council's appointed Location Committee chose a rocky site just southeast of the old location for an "annex" to be called New Brighton. Kelly planned 52 (later 56) new houses in rows on unfenced lots, with little semblance of Murray's "properly laid out village." There were no planned open spaces, except for a small playground of about 150 by 50 yards, and no sites reserved for public buildings, shops, or churches. Kelly's layout plan (unfortunately now missing) baffled the secretary of the Central Housing Board: "the peculiar lines of the roads . . . [appear to have] no particular reason . . . such as the nature of the ground." In response, the town clerk simply noted that "only a small portion" of the roads would be built "at present." The board approved the plan "subject to a window in each room being placed in the wall opposite the door so as to secure proper through-ventilation."[12] In what became an issue later, no standpipes for water were proposed or added. The new houses did not approach even a minimum standard of privacy. They were merely rectangular huts made of modern materials. Kelly's plan for rooms 10 by 10 by 8 feet provided 800 cubic feet of air space, much less than the 1,200 cubic feet required under the recently adopted Cradock location regulations for a family of five.[13] Yet there was to be one notable advance: each house was to have its own outdoor pail closet, as Murray had urged. Yet when it came to actual building, the closets were eliminated and replaced by separate public lavatories for men and for women.

The average location rent in 1927 had been 3.35 shillings; 84 percent of all rent payers were paying between 2.5 and 3.5 shillings; only 14 percent paid 5.5 shillings, the highest rent. Yet Cradock's council went ahead with the engineer's design and, by early 1929, had completed a plan for 132 houses, 22 of two rooms to rent at 11 shillings, and 110 of a single room to rent at 5.5 shillings. The cheapest was still 64 percent above the average rent previously paid in the location. The addition of these 132 houses at the top of the rental distribution, and a simultaneous 0.5 shillings (15 percent) boost of rents of the old location in 1927 to balance the native revenue account, increased the average location rent to 4.5 shillings in 1930, a 28 percent increase above 1927. New Brighton houses therefore remained expensive, and in 1935, during the Depression, the council found itself unable to rent many of its 22 two-roomed houses and converted 13 of them into single-roomed ones.[14]

After Cradock built the first 56 houses, the town clerk sought a second loan, writing that "the housing question of the location is still appalling."[15] The Department of Native Affairs, when it provided loans for "native" housing, had been concerned not only to improve location housing but also to support the principle of Stallardism, which sought to limit urban Africans to the number needed for labor locally. In considering the second loan in 1928, the secretary for native affairs required Cradock district's magistrate to certify that the new houses were "necessarily required for natives actually employed and permanently resident in the Urban Area." The magistrate did so certify, and all the new houses were let.[16] Knowing that it could borrow £5,000 more to build, and with the job of rebuilding the location only about one-fifth done—132 houses added to the 570 permits issued by 1927—the council went no further.

It is not clear how the first tenants of New Brighton were selected, and especially how strictly the colored/Native distinction was enforced. The new township was formally a "Native" one—the magistrate had certified that the first tenants were employed Africans—but Cradock apparently did not always take that certification seriously. By 1935 New Brighton had some colored tenants; in 1944 several New Brighton residents would apply for inclusion in a proposed colored housing program.[17] These small dwellings were not part of the radical plan for separate locations for coloreds and Africans that Mayor Deary had envisaged in 1926. They were in his words, simply "new houses on the present site," a modest ad hoc "improvement," with no space set aside for a proper location.

Housing Europeans of the "Poorer Class"

If large numbers of whites in Cradock in the 1920s wanted a more systematically segregated municipality, as Mayor Deary, Dr. Murray, and the *Midland News* had assumed, they gave no public expression to their wishes, either by pressing for an all-white town or for separate locations for Africans and for coloreds. At the time of the founding of New Brighton, the town clerk, Van Heerden, and the council seem to have been almost unaware that the Pact government of 1924, a Nationalist and Labour coalition, was making the welfare of the white, primarily Afrikaner, poor its special concern. Cradock seems to have accepted at face value Dr. Murray's statement that the town itself had no slums, although he did report some "overcrowding" in back yards. Murray had not pointed to the white poor in Cradock, only to coloreds and Africans as a threat to health.[18]

In July 1929, after being rebuffed in an application to build middle-class housing for whites, the town clerk submitted a new application for £5,000 for housing for "poorer class Europeans." This time approval came quickly. As it had done in the location, the municipality lowered its sights: a penciled note in the town clerk's hand read: "10 cottages for £2000. Option by Council build addition [*sic*] ten cottages." Kelly, the town planner, designed a three-bedroom cottage as a model, and the council awarded the contract to P. L. van Heerden, the same contractor as for the location, and again the lowest bidder.[19] The new project, like its immediate African housing predecessor, New Brighton, was not part of an overall planning blueprint, but a modest plan to add ten houses at a building cost of £245 each for whites somewhere in the town or on its edge, houses that achieved minimal standards of privacy. It is instructive to compare the more generous new housing provided for poor whites with that built for location residents: The average size of the ten lots for whites was 3,150 square feet; in the location, 2,500 square feet.[20] The houses for whites enclosed 6,183 cubic feet in five rooms (three bedrooms, kitchen, and living room); in the location, most of the new houses had only 1,152 cubic feet in their single room. The houses for whites had electricity, bathrooms with a tub with piped-in water, a pail closet in the yard, and water in the kitchen. Location houses had none of these, and water had to be carried about a third of a mile.

Choosing a site for the new buildings proved to be more difficult than the council anticipated, provoking expressions of class animus among many of Cradock's better-off white homeowners. In the late 1920s and early 1930s, Cradock could be divided into eight zones (map 2).

> 1 and 2. The oldest parts of the town, including shops, some grand old houses, the market square, the town jail, and the Dutch Reformed church were almost entirely white in population and separated from the old location by Regent Street.

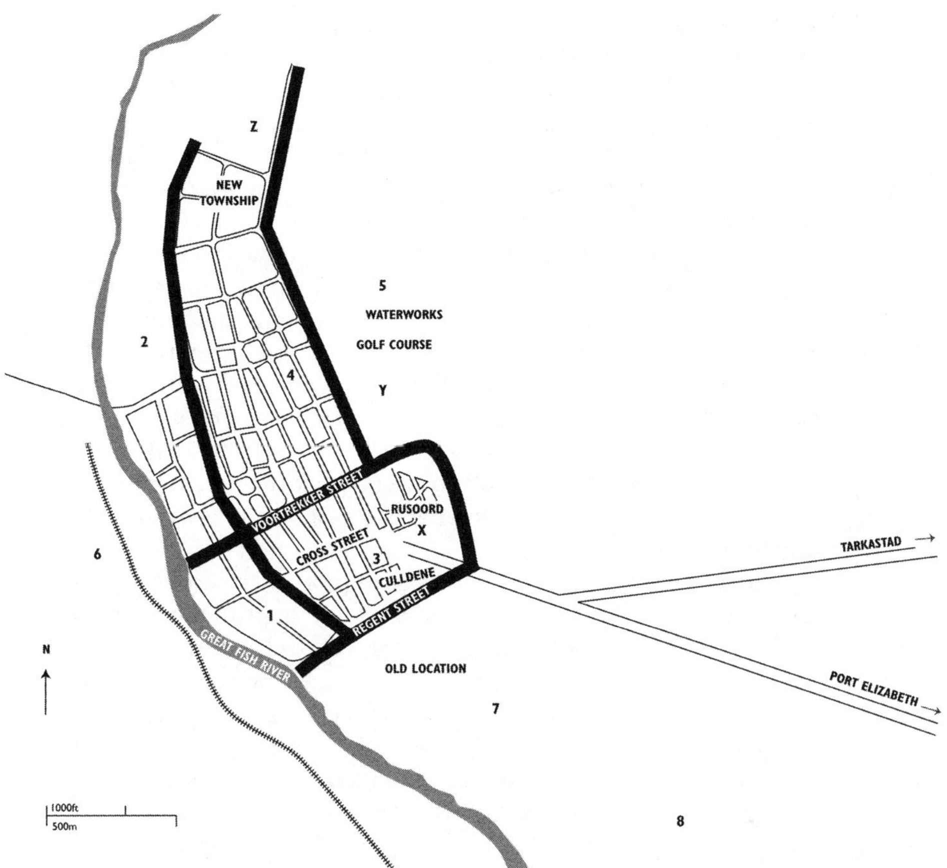

Map. 2. Cradock Residential Zones, 1929. (Map by Mariah Reisner, based in part on a map showing sites for proposed sub-economic housing, c. 1945, CAR 3/CDK 4/1/31, European Housing, 1945–1949)

3. The Mixed Area, was racially mixed in population and directly abutted the northern edge of the location.

4. An almost entirely white zone, including the prized "New Township" of large lots for private housing of the most affluent whites, on the northwest edge of town.

5. A prime white residential area, much of it undeveloped, close to the golf course and the waterworks.

6. The "Railway Reserve," often sneeringly called the "Railway Camp," on the west bank of the Fish River, including mainly houses for white railway staff and artisans as well as the railway station itself, the freight or goods yard, the new municipal steam power station, and the agricultural show grounds.

7. The old location and New Brighton, its annex.
8. A municipal commonage, available for future town expansion.

In 1929 there were two feasible options for placing the ten new houses for the white poor: lay out a compact housing estate on the edge of Cradock, with space to build a further ten later; or purchase already available vacant lots within the town itself, of which there were about thirty in 1929, most in the Mixed Area. The ACVV, the influential Afrikaner women's organization, appealed to the predominantly English-speaking Women's Civic Association (WCA) to help it prevent the building of the houses for white poor close to the location.[21] The town council acknowledged the difficulty and, with the ACVV's approval, considered building instead on the edge of town at one of three possible sites: a piece of land (X) at the top of Carrington (later Voortrekker) Street in the Mixed Area; on the top of the hill (Y) near the waterworks in the prized new white residential area near the golf course: and at the northern edge of town (Z) beyond the New Township where lots for the white well-to-do had only recently been sold.

Various persons petitioned against each of these proposals; petitioners were predominantly middle class and professional, thirty English speakers and fourteen Afrikaners. The first petition, against the Voortrekker Street site, was signed by nineteen residents who sought to protect their own area, "the best and most select residential part of the town." The second petition opposed the site above the waterworks, saying it would block Cradock's eastward expansion. Furthermore, "it is undesirable to confine tenants of this type [that is, poor whites] to a colony. They will feel they are isolated as undesirables and this will tend to lower their self-respect. . . . Such a colony being away from any restricting or refining influence, may easily develop into a nuisance or even a danger." A third protest, against the site in New Township, came from twelve owners of vacant lots there; it was forwarded to the council by a building contractor who had speculated by buying several lots offered by the municipality in 1926: "Small houses . . . are to be erected at a cost of £200 each [actually £245]; it will seriously affect the value of our properties. . . . The fact that these proposed cottages will be screened off with trees will make very little difference."[22]

This class-based dispute continued through the Christmas season with no resolution. In early February 1930, a committee of council called in the prominent Cradock attorney Alfred Metcalf (the philanthropist who helped the health clinic) to mediate. Like a benevolent squire anxious to camouflage but respect an awkward social reality, he suggested several sites but in the end recommended the land at the top of Voortrekker Street: "When the belts of trees (towards the cost of which there is already a movement to collect funds) skirt those grounds the site will be practically hidden from view. The situation is a healthy one, with a cheerful outlook for the cottagers."[23] Thereupon a deputation from the golf course and waterworks district repeated its opposition;

Fig. 23. Cradock from the south, from Regent Street toward the town center, c. 1933. (Museum Africa, Johannesburg, South Africa)

the neighborhood would suffer the traffic of "wagons, donkeys etc."; to build all the houses in one place would make it look "more or less like a compound." Residents would be ashamed to live there, just as they "are ashamed to say that they live in River [Canterbury] Street." Max de Kock, a member of council and supporter of the proposal, took the petitioners to task. Talk of pollution and the damage done by poor people walking past respectable houses, he said, was "*alles kaf*" (all rubbish)—he lost nothing, he said, by having "poor children walk past his house to school." The National Party mayor, M. J. Hattingh, also supported the proposal; it was, he said, the product of a joint meeting with the ACVV and WCTU. There would be no pollution or donkeys, he said, and as Metcalf had indicated, the houses would not be "visible."

The council finally accepted none of these proposals and opted for use of vacant lots in the Mixed Area, the site the ACVV had opposed, but it bought four lots from private individuals, a perfectly safe course that avoided mixing the white poor with the white well-to-do. The ten houses were to be placed in two groups on Parade Street in the Mixed Area, one street north of the Regent Street border of the location (fig. 23).[24] While the debate continued, the municipality had circulated a questionnaire calling for applicants for the new municipal houses (whose number, cost, location, and nature, whether for sale or for rent, were still unclear). Of the thirty-six residents who applied for the ten houses, thirty-two had Afrikaans names. It is obvious that the project was not intended for the very poor, since the questionnaire included an option to buy rather than to rent, with a down payment of £49 (20 percent) on a £245 house. The applicants were already paying, on average, a rent of 52 shillings, or almost a third of an average income of 166 shillings a month, and formed a relatively prosperous group: only six of them earned the lowest wages paid to white laborers on the railways (about 91 shillings a month).[25] Even that was above the income of most colored and African laborers, many of whom earned less than 78 shillings a month.

The rents of the new houses were set at 48s a month, more than half of the wages of a white railway laborer. The successful ten applicants chosen were not among the poorest: their average income was 155s a month. The town clerk seems to have picked them on his own criteria of character and on estimates of the degree of overcrowding they were suffering; three were widows with children.

Having successfully completed ten houses, the council now decided, as they had done for the location, to build no more houses, even though they had been given loans to do so. They would wait until "the financial condition of the country improves." In that case, the secretary of the housing board told the town clerk, the funds would be "reallotted" to another town "in urgent need of funds." Cradock's town clerk was not swayed by the threat, and the available loans were rescinded.

Local authorities would have been reluctant in any circumstances to take on ambitious housing projects in 1930, the early days of the Depression. But after South Africa left the gold standard in 1933 and economic recovery began, the new United Party government, formed by a 1934 "fusion" of the National Party and the South African Party, began again to encourage municipalities like Cradock to borrow for housing. In 1936, it announced subsidized loans to house the poor (both people of color and whites) and an additional program for housing the aged white poor; but the health committee of Cradock's council decided that the ACVV's old people's home was sufficient.[26] It seems that the town clerk and the council were also operating on a fallacy that because few applied for subsidized loans there was no genuine housing shortage. But in 1938, the council received a petition from 125 whites interested in new housing; more than half applied, and most were picked as deserving tenants of a Special Economic Housing Scheme. All but one had Afrikaner names; only one submitted his application in English.[27]

The condition of Cradock's housing for whites and people of color became a prominent issue when the Cradock medical officer of health filed his report for the year ending in mid-1938. He labeled six "dwellings" in town and 145 "huts" in the location "unfit for human occupation" and said they did not "conform to the requirements of the [Slums] Act 53 of 1934." A shocked council resolved to apply to the Union Health Department to add Cradock to the first schedule of the Slums Act. This would have given Cradock officials more authority to inspect houses and require owners of bad housing to repair or demolish it.

But the Slums Act did not apply to the location, so it was the town's white housing that became the object of determined national government intervention.[28] It took three years for the Cradock council to negotiate housing plans for both town and location that satisfied both the Central Housing Board and the Department of Native Affairs. The council applied for a subsidized loan, (a "sub-economic" loan) for the fifty-two white applicants who could not afford unsubsidized rents.[29] At last, the council seems to have devised a scheme that *did* reach the very poor, that is, the aged white poor, many of whom had probably been left behind by younger Afrikaner family members who had gone to the port cities of Port Elizabeth and East London in search of better jobs.[30]

In siting the new "European" houses, the council continued its 1929 policy of taking parcels of land in the old town, all in low-status areas, that is, in the Mixed Area, close to the location.[31] One such site of twenty new houses, named Culldene after J. A. Cull, the mayor from 1940 to 1949, shows that the council was more interested in providing housing for poor whites at the lowest possible cost than in advancing any thought-through policies to advance segregation; yet the program, in the end, did enhance racial concentration. Culldene was on the site of a former "Coloured Sports Ground," a piece of land recently legally incorporated into the location and reincorporated into the town in 1940 to accommodate this new housing for whites.[32] The town clerk told a skeptical provincial secretary that the site was eminently well suited: a large number of Europeans lived in the area, and no other suitable site existed.[33]

Impressed with its highly efficient housing department, the council now moved to rehouse even more of the white poor and built another group of thirty-six detached houses for aged whites in a valley close to Culldene and invisible from town, a site earlier suggested by Metcalf. The choice provoked some of the same residents who had protested in 1929, once again to no effect. By August 1945, Rusoord (literally "resting place") had been completed, its name acknowledging its role as a village for old people.[34] The municipality had behaved like other local authorities whose revenue base was real estate, following its electorate's assessment of the value and desirability of property and resisting the complaints of nearby residents.

By 1948, the council had built 108 houses for rental to whites whose poverty had been confirmed by a means test. Of these houses, 102 were in the Mixed Area of town, much to the continuing disapproval of the Afrikaner women's organization, the ACVV. In 1937, complaining that the town clerk had not put up a promised name plate calling the first 10 cottages "Uitkoms" (Deliverance), Elizabeth Jordaan, president of the Cradock ACVV, noted that the housing project was frequently referred to as a "wit lokasie," a white location.[35] Her complaints did not deter the council; in the 1920s, it had intensified the multiracial character of the Mixed Area by permitting the opening and expansion of the colored Convent of the Holy Rosary and the building of the colored Immanuel Church and its orphanage. In planning for the future Rusoord in 1943, it did include a row of trees to screen Culldene (and the Convent) from the location to the south. That was the extent of its deference to ACVV anxieties about housing whites near the location. Since only whites were eligible to rent in the new housing cluster, and since many of the whites moved to Culldene and Rusoord from elsewhere in the Mixed Area, the schemes did achieve segregationist objectives; whites were consolidated by moving from mixed areas to all white ones. These were programs of voluntary "removal," as manifested in the houses' widespread popularity with their new tenants.[36]

The Increasing Differentiation of Colored People

The ACVV's concerns about racial residential mixing were expressed in a national political climate that was becoming more explicitly hostile to the rights of people of color. This hostility had surfaced particularly harshly in the so-called Swart Gevaar (Black Peril) election of 1929, when the Afrikaner-dominated National Party accused its South African Party opponents of working to hand over power to Africans. During the election, an attempt by Nationalists to court colored voters in the Cape Province failed, and the National Party turned increasingly to developing segregationist statutes that its successor, the Purified National Party, consisting of former members of the National Party who opposed fusion with the South African Party, was able to enforce more strictly when it came to power in 1948.[37]

After the 1934 "fusion" of the South African Party and the National Party into the United Party, the national government began to restrict further the voting and residential property rights of Africans and to differentiate colored people from them. In 1937, by the Native Laws Amendment Act, Africans lost the right to own land outright in urban areas. Colored children lost the right to go to mixed schools in Cape Province, and coloreds were barred from apprenticeships in building and other trades, where they had been competing with Afrikaner poor whites who had recently left the countryside.[38] A 1938 letter from Cradock's ACVV to the organization's provincial office reported with disapproval that Cradock's Mixed Area was occupied by forty-three whites, fifty-nine coloreds, two Asians, and two "Grieke" (Greeks); as well that two colored schools and two colored churches were located there. (Twelve coloreds lived elsewhere in town.) The next year, the Cradock ACVV repeated the complaint: on five streets "the living together is very undesirable," and it demanded, "in the strongest terms," an "improvement."[39] Also in 1939, the Cradock African Political Organization (a colored body) sent a deputation to the town council to protest a provincial draft ordinance empowering local authorities "to enforce compulsory Residential Segregation based on colour." The council said that the draft proposal had been dropped, but it was a significant straw in the wind nonetheless.[40] The issue of enforced residential segregation was being considered in both the ruling United Party and the opposition Purified National

Party. The door to the "removal" rather than the "improvement" of nonwhite neighborhoods had been opened.[41]

In 1937, the Cradock council instructed the location superintendent to estimate the value of all location buildings for a discussion of "proposed removal." At the next meeting of the location committee, "removal" was postponed without explanation.[42] Later in 1938, P. G. Caudwell, a government inspector of urban locations, completed the first comprehensive inspection of the Cradock location by the Department of Native Affairs, one analogous to Dr. Murray's first health inspection of 1924. Caudwell criticized the location's layout, its limited sanitary facilities, and particularly its housing—260 houses there had been condemned by the council itself. A plan should be instituted at once, he wrote, to replace the condemned houses.[43] The council consulted the Location Advisory Board and urged the Native Affairs Department to approve a £5,000 loan to help location householders improve existing housing.[44] The department insisted on a much larger scheme, a loan of £15,000 for 144 new houses with space for future expansion. It agreed to lower rents on the new location houses by using revenue from Cradock's new beer hall. Incidentally, to reduce costs, the Central Housing Board insisted that the work be done departmentally, rather than put out to contract—an attempt, it seems, to evade white trade union intervention on wages.[45] There was no mention at all of making a distinction between Africans and coloreds.

The removal of the location and the separation of coloreds from Africans were long-term objectives of the town council, seldom spelled out in local policy discussions, but referred to repeatedly in reports by Union government officials. In 1940, F. W. Jameson of the Central Housing Board, on a visit to Cradock, noted disapprovingly that coloreds and Africans had lived together "in the same location" for a long time. He remarked that "better paid Coloured persons" required "different handling," and that "the council are alive to the need of assisting those persons to own their own houses on a suitable site," but "that time [is] not yet." For the time being, the council should confine its attention to providing homes for the "most needy and poorer section of Coloured and Native people."[46] The council, with Jameson's clear approval, was now regarding the colored population of Cradock as a "race" distinct from Africans and whites, and also distinguishing among coloreds between the "better paid" and the "needy and poor."

In 1941, the Rev. James Calata and Alfred Pokomela, in a specifically African request, asked Jameson that some of the new houses have warmer floors of brick rather than concrete, because African location inhabitants were so poor they could not afford furniture and had to sleep on the floor. Jameson conceded unwillingly, and thus a minor distinction in building was to become the basis of a future allocation of houses by race. By mid-1943, a clear distinction between colored and African housing appeared in an application for another set of subsidized loans—£15,000 for "European" housing, £5,000 for "coloured" housing, £10,000 for "African" housing; and from a fund for the aged poor, £2,000 for Europeans, £1,000 for coloreds, and £2,000 for "aged poor natives."[47] The building from 1941 on of what became Wilken township—a location annex of 288 houses near New Brighton—made explicit once more that the location was to continue to house both coloreds and Africans. Even though the town clerk insisted that he was administering a single township, the Wilken annex became racially subdivided.

Colored Demands for a Separate Township

In the 1920s, there was little public involvement in housing plans by Cradock residents—African, white, or colored—with the exception of the ACVV's appeals and other white protests over the siting of housing for the white poor, and African requests for warmer brick floors in new houses in the location. Racial sorting had been low on the list of priorities expressed by the municipality and most Cradock residents: in its new housing, the council had sited poor whites close to coloreds in the Mixed Area of town and had only begun to sort colored from African housing within the location on a piecemeal basis. But in the 1940s, housing policy became a major bone of contention in national white politics as demands for further segregation arose—and especially for separating coloreds from whites. In the increasingly harsh racial atmosphere, governmental pressure to separate colored and African housing schemes increased, but so did demands from Cradock coloreds for a separate colored township. Since at least the 1920s, coloreds living in the location had sporadically protested, with little effect, against being lumped together with Africans there, where they were subjected to curfews, lodgers' raids, and other controls of private life. Not until the 1940s did their protests coalesce into an organized movement for a separate township, a movement that can be traced partly to the municipality's refusal to allow new colored residents to settle in the location since 1938. In 1943, the national government created a Coloured Advisory Council (CAdC), a first step toward separate political and administrative institutions for colored people. In localities like Cradock, the CAdC, operating under the umbrella of the Department of Social Welfare, began to push for greater funding for housing and welfare and to protest against lumping coloreds together with Africans in the location.[48]

In 1944, a group of colored town residents, led by W. E. Lawn, a tailor, with the support of the CAdC, asked the council for separate colored housing. The town clerk then circulated a form, "Sub-Economic Houses—Application Form (Coloured)." Of forty-five applications he received, he put thirty-four on a consolidated list, presumably relying on his own judgment of character and capacity to pay. On the invitation of the town clerk, another deputation of five colored men met the housing committee; all were town residents—Lawn; M. W. Curry, the principal of the colored Independent school; E. C. Carolus, a teacher; A. K. Sauls, a bank messenger; and J. Lottering, a contractor. The housing committee chairman and mayor, J. A. Cull, told the deputations that the rents the applicants had offered to pay were much too low: about half had specified 15s or less a month, while 50s was the rent paid for poor whites' new houses. Curry again requested, in addition to rental housing for poor coloreds, a "an area to be occupied exclusively by the coloured community . . . where they could purchase their own ground," that is, where they could possess land and houses in freehold.

In February 1945 the council examined sites and committed itself to a colored township on the left of the Tarkastad road, which, if it had been built, would have for the first time placed a main road between African housing and colored housing.[49] The colored deputation now reoriented its cause from housing for relatively well-off coloreds to housing for the poor, and with an explicit segregationist objective. It produced a petition of 213 names, apparently all from coloreds, collected in the location, giving "hearty thanks . . . for all that the Council has done for us as a community" and making "a friendly and civil request" that the council turn over part of the old location (from Taai Street to the river) to the colored community.[50] The petitioners were laying claim to the entire historic core of the old location. Nothing further was heard of such a possibility until it was revived more than a decade later, at the beginning of the age of apartheid, when the Group Areas Act of 1950 was about to be implemented in Cradock.

Demands from coloreds for a separate colored township reflected shifts in national colored politics. Ever since publication of the Cape Coloured Commission report in 1937 and the United Party's establishment of the Coloured Advisory Council in 1943, the colored community throughout Cape Province had become more deeply divided. New organizations appeared, some to support, some to oppose the CAdC. In 1945, dissident colored members of the long-established African People's Organisation (APO) had founded the Coloured Peoples National Union (CPNU), which, while committed to equality with whites, took a strong stand for a racial identity separate from Africans. In general, it supported the CAdC, its constitution setting out its aims to promote "social, economic, civic and educational needs . . . ; to combat compulsory segregation; [and promote] closer relationships between European and coloured persons . . . in order to enlighten European public opinion." It did accept separate housing schemes for coloreds because of urgent need.[51] In March 1946, Lawn and others who had first asked for a separate colored township in 1944 established a branch of the CPNU in Cradock. A. Sauls, the secretary, wrote to the town clerk that it represented "the interests of the whole Coloured population of the town of Cradock inclusive of the location."[52]

The new CPNU persevered with its policy of conciliation with whites and actively sought the help of the CAdC, which, in turn, used the Department of Social Welfare as its official intermediary with the Cradock municipality. In

1946, H. A. C. Cloete, a teacher and member of the CAdC for the Cape Midlands, came to Cradock to lead a deputation of local citizens to press "the case for the Coloured people of Cradock, on the question of separate Housing in a coloured Township." Colored people in Cradock, the deputation said, "have no desire to reside in Native locations where they are subjected to serious restrictions that do not normally apply to them as a coloured race." Citing the support of the Department of Native Affairs for a separate colored township, it urged "more attention to their [that is, colored] social requirements and upliftment." Colored residents of the location, Cloete's petition said, suffered from numerous "social handicaps," among them that "the Beer Hall . . . is more frequented by coloured women resident in the location than the natives"; also, that when "respectable Coloured people come from church . . . they are compelled . . . to keep their heads covered, for fear of being stoned in the dark by unruly natives. Natives according to their custom have services and parade through the location singing at any hour, the most popular days being Saturday and Sunday." Further, "the location Police just enjoy coming into the homes occupied by coloured people . . . a coloured girl was roughly handled, stripped naked by the police and taken in one of the sanitary lorries." Sanitary buckets were removed during the day in the location (not at night, as in town) causing an "unpleasant smell." At "communal water taps . . . coloured people . . . [are] pushed away by Natives who make them understand quite clearly that it is a Native Location."[53]

The mayor, J. A. Cull, and other officials met Cloete and his deputation, which now offered to pay rents of 30s a month, an advance on their previous offer.[54] But rents were not the only sticking point. The apparent, and surprising, lack of any serious conflict within the Cradock colored community now came to an abrupt end. W. A. J. van Heerden, a teacher, town resident, and secretary of the "newly established" Non-European Ratepayers Association (NERA), wrote to the town clerk requesting "closer consultation" on the "interest of Non-European Property Owners and Ratepayers." The NERA, Van Heerden wrote, had unanimously decided "to inform your Council that we view the proposed Coloured Township with the gravest misgivings. . . . We dissociate ourselves entirely from the few Coloured men who made representations in support of the said scheme." The letter persuaded the council. "We cannot . . . proceed with this scheme," the town clerk wrote to Cloete, "in view of the fact that we have received a letter from the local Coloured Ratepayers Association strongly opposing the layout."[55]

Cloete vigorously denounced the Non-European Ratepayers Association, whose members, he charged, had never shown any interest in the location's colored residents.[56] The criticism appears to have some foundation. NERA members by definition did not live in the location, and none had put their names on lists for the new township; in 1951 they would, however, press the council to provide better roads, drains, and stop signs near the colored schools in the Mixed Area in town.[57] In the NERA's view, a better strategy for town coloreds would be to lobby the council for more housing, facilities, and services in the Mixed Area while asserting their economic and political interests as property owners and ratepayers entitled to the municipal franchise. Cloete's group seems to have made a different political calculation: that a separate colored freehold township might hold off the day of the dreaded "compulsory Residential Segregation based on colour," whose possibility the APO in Cradock had first protested against to the council in 1939.

In March 1950, with the new National Party government in power, the council applied for a £70,000 loan for subsidized houses for coloreds: "Natives and Coloureds live deurmekaar [mixed up] in the Native location," the new town clerk, G. W. van Rooyen wrote. "Instead of building extra houses in the location, the council intends to set up a separate neighbourhood for coloureds."[58] Improvement of the location was rejected, and some kind of removal was envisaged. The earlier position of Cloete and the CAdC had won out.

But national events would soon outstrip the council. In 1950, the National Party in parliament passed the Group Areas Act, directly aimed at towns like Cradock that had racially mixed locations and mixed areas in town. In 1951, Cradock's town clerk applied to the Department of the Interior to begin the process of applying the new act to Cradock, noting that the town had a "well-off class of coloureds in a part of the white residential living area."[59] In referring to the mixed town as being in a "white" area, the town clerk was raising a central objective of apartheid: the legal definition of ownership and occupation of property by race, not by class.

Cradock's public housing schemes had begun in the 1920s when the national government began both to encourage and to bribe local authorities to build housing for those too poor to build on their own. From the beginning, however, government financing of public housing drew, and reinforced, a distinction between whites, on the one hand, and all people of color, on the other. Loans for municipal housing were administered by the Central Housing Board, under the government's Department of Public Health. In Cradock, those loans were directed entirely toward housing of poor whites. Significantly more money was spent on this housing than on housing for people of color, and higher rents were charged. There was, in theory, no reason why a municipality could not have built houses for coloreds inside the town proper, but such a project, though legally possible, was politically and economically unfeasible. Loans for housing in locations, including those for "mixed" locations like Cradock's, on the other hand, were made through the Department of Native Affairs even though technically the department had no responsibility for colored people.

The Natives (Urban Areas) Act of 1923 had contemplated a day when locations would be homogeneously African and distant from town, and coloreds would be housed separately in their own townships. But in practice, in the 1920s and 1930s, the Cradock town council did little to sort Africans from coloreds in its location. Housing in the first new location township, New Brighton, came to be occupied by both colored and African families; from 1943 on, as an afterthought, separate areas of the new Wilken township were earmarked for coloreds and for Africans. The "mixed" location remained mixed, and Cradock's officials, while they might complain of the corrupting effect of coloreds supplying liquor to Africans, showed no alarm at such mixing and took no actions to end it. The municipality took few actively segregationist steps of its own, but rather accommodated, and certainly did not resist, segregationist initiatives from the national government and from others. In 1944, when a group of coloreds made an attempt to define coloreds as a race and to stop their assimilation with Africans, the municipality readily accepted the proposed colored township as a legitimate notion and was prepared to make land available for freehold lots for coloreds. In seeking, from 1944 on, to create an exclusive colored township, the colored leaders had stepped onto a hazardous path, and the municipality did not resist them. Their proposal was one step away from a compulsory regime that would soon require all coloreds in any urban area to live in a designated place or places.

What is remarkable about the history of the issue in Cradock is the almost total absence of public debate among whites on the very existence of the Mixed Area, the multiracial neighborhood on the location edge of town. Apart from a few complaints by individuals, and by the Afrikaner women's group, the ACVV, the record shows no organized white group ever pressing the municipality to remove coloreds from the area. And Cradock's own colored leaders, nearly all of them town residents, never seem to have sought reassurances from the town fathers that their position as owners and ratepayers was secure. They had seen Africans lose ownership and occupation rights in town in 1937, but many seemed to believe that they could prevent such a process in their own case. In hindsight we can see the futility of their hopes; but we should not ignore the fact that they were trying to do something radical: they wanted to end their ambiguous status as part of the subordinate population of Africans and coloreds by getting coloreds out of a "native location" overseen by the Department of Native Affairs and into the town, acquiring full municipal rights. Some colored leaders seem to have confused two processes: a separated colored township might well have limited their assimilation with Africans but would not have contributed (and whites did not want it to contribute) to their assimilation, or equal civil status, with whites.

Much of the status of coloreds was as yet undefined when the age of apartheid arrived. No coherent published master plan, no conception of the ideal town, had emerged in the age of segregation. In the 1940s, the governing United Party had not committed itself to colored townships in every town or to the compulsory segregation of existing mixed areas within towns. The national government accepted the four statutory racial divisions into which South Africa's population was divided, but it did not rigorously define or enforce membership of each racial group. Throughout South Africa, housing projects had been built on an ad hoc basis, with municipalities making proposals for siting on municipal land and for local financing before clearing the proposals with government departments and the housing board. If Cradock's record is typical, there was little determination on the part of municipalities to make full systematic use of national resources offered. Invariably, Cradock resisted making use of all the loan funds it could have had for whites, aged and poor, and for people of color. Since the towns were the established agents, the Union government could cajole and promise but lacked a coherent urban vision and a political constituency that could have mobilized the resources to develop a neat, well-housed, and clearly segregated town.

The United Party government of the 1940s, was deeply divided on policy, aware that it was losing the Afrikaner vote and fearful of losing crucial Cape seats if there were insufficient loyal colored voters. Throughout this period, the party never played a vigorous local role in Cradock. Its members of parliament did not take up the cause of loyal African and colored ratepayers and parliamentary voters or attempt to increase the number of Africans and coloreds on local and parliamentary voters' lists. Nor, in the 1948 election, did the party exploit, in Cradock, the superb record of J. A. Cull, the English-speaking United Party mayor, who cared about housing for everyone. On the contrary, it passed legislation that had the effect of restricting the number of colored voters, which fell from an all-time high of 54,134 in 1945 to 47,804 in 1949.[60] The United Party never seemed to regard qualified colored and African voters as a political resource worth cultivating; it took their loyalty for granted and was more concerned with retaining Afrikaner supporters and with subsidizing the immigration of whites, particularly Britons, who could be relied on to vote against the anti-British Purified (later Re-United) National Party.

A radical racial restructuring of towns like Cradock would have to wait for the development of a coherent ideology by the National Party that would also accommodate the demands of more conservative English speakers in Natal and the Transvaal and those of others who had long mobilized to demand statutory urban segregation. Up until that point, housing programs for the poor of particular racial groups had incrementally extended and deepened segregation, but such developments were not part of a broad and comprehensive plan based in ambitions to segregate. They were, rather, fragmentary expressions of most whites' desire to live lives separate from nonwhites according to the principles of J. S. Furnivall's "plural society": a society where racial groups meet intimately in the market place, but nowhere else.[61] In Cradock, the "improvement" of housing for the white poor and aged, with no disruption of the town's racial and class pattern, had been piecemeal; so, too, the "improvement" of the location for Africans and for coloreds. Mayor Deary's 1926 vision of "a Native location and a Coloured location," involving drastic "removal" and an end to "mixing," was an idea, in 1948, whose time had come.

8

Apartheid Comes to Cradock

APARTHEID: A BLUEPRINT FOR FRICTIONLESS LIVING

The United Party and the Waning of Stallardism

On 17 February 1947, HMS *Vanguard,* the last big-gun battleship to be added to the Royal Navy, docked in Cape Town carrying the British royal family—King George VI, Queen Elizabeth, and their two young daughters, Elizabeth and Margaret. It was the beginning of a grueling tour to all parts of the country and an attempt by the prime minister, Jan Smuts, to arouse enthusiasm for South Africa's role as a Commonwealth country and thereby to counter National Party propaganda for a South African republic. The tour did not include Cradock, but that did not stop many of Cradock's white residents from participating: the *Midland News* offered prizes for essays on the occasion, and a Cradock farmer sent three horses to Port Elizabeth so that the princesses could ride if they chose. "Yesterday morning Cradock was a deserted town," wrote the editor of the *Midland News* on the day of the royal visit to Grahamstown, a hundred miles away. "The Royal Family . . . in but a few days have endeared themselves to all."[1]

The royals may well have "endeared" themselves to many blacks and whites, but the impact on voters, especially Afrikaner voters, was still to be seen. There had to be a general election by May 1948, and the royal visit was part of the government's preparation for it. Smuts, an Afrikaner born in Cape Colony in 1870, had fought in the South African War (1899–1902) as a general on the Boer side, later becoming, in 1910, one of the founding fathers of the Union of South Africa. When General Louis Botha, South Africa's first prime minister and Smuts's mentor, died in 1919, Smuts became prime minister and leader of the South African Party, dedicated to preserving white supremacy, to advancing the "conciliation" of Afrikaans- and English-speaking whites, and to retaining South Africa's membership in the British Commonwealth.[2] In 1948, relationships with the Commonwealth remained an issue, but domestic issues, and general questions of race, would determine the outcome of the election.[3]

The major parties shared a commitment to white supremacy; the urban policies of all national governments from 1910 to 1948 had been segregationist.

The Stallard doctrine, adopted by both the National and the United Parties, maintained that Africans should leave a town when their labor was no longer needed.[4] Yet, by the end of the age of segregation, sections of the United Party and its government rejected the Stallard approach and were brimming with social-democratic ideas.[5] Henry Gluckman's pioneering report on public health and an interdepartmental committee of 1942, chaired by D. L. Smit, the secretary for native affairs, proposed a restructuring of the local government of Africans, more generous financing of new housing, and employment of African contractors and workers on location housing schemes.[6] And the Fagan Commission, appointed to inquire into laws affecting urban Africans, proposed, just before the election of 1948, that the Stallard doctrine be abandoned and urban housing be provided for African workers and their families. The commission recognized the impossibility of limiting urban African populations by administrative fiat, a view already expressed publicly by the prime minister in a much-quoted speech to the Institute of Race Relations in 1942: "Segregation has fallen on evil days."[7] But the government did not make Smuts's speech the basis of a new urban policy. According to Rodney Davenport, it "preferred to allow the segregation policy to run down."[8]

Stallardism concerned Africans, not coloreds. A 1937 Commission of Inquiry Regarding the Cape Coloured Population of the Union had recommended better houses and education for coloreds, but any such public housing would have been segregated since all government housing loans were racially allocated. But in 1938 the United Party government, responding to the pressure from many Cape municipalities, drafted a bill—never enacted—that would have enforced segregation of coloreds at the behest of local whites; if 75 percent of owners in an area wanted it, the area could be declared entirely white, and municipalities could enforce it.[9] In 1946, G. I. Nel, a Department of Native Affairs urban areas inspector, recommended separating coloreds and Africans in Cradock—an aspect, he wrote, of a longstanding department policy.[10]

United Party members frequently declared that separation of coloreds and whites should be "voluntary," yet the party was in fact moving in the direction of enforced segregation of coloreds—the 1938 proposal would have involved compulsory movement. The Coloured Advisory Council, established in 1943 under the Department of Social Welfare, was a step in the direction of a separate Coloured Affairs Department. To many politically active coloreds, this meant treating them like Africans, who, from 1910, had been under the jurisdiction of a separate Department of Native Affairs. Even though the United Party hoped to retain Western Cape seats in which the colored vote was crucial, it supported legislation urged by its conservative members and also by the National Party, that would make it more difficult for colored men to register as voters.[11]

The United Party's 1948 election manifesto declared its commitment to the "maintenance of white civilization," that is, to white supremacy.[12] It attempted to counter the National Party's central charge that it could not be trusted to preserve white power against the African majority. The manifesto suggested an undefined enlargement of the "rights and functions" of the Native Representative Council, a body created in 1936 in hesitant recognition that Africans needed some representative institutions at the national level. But the most important change in "native policy" envisioned in the United Party manifesto was a general, undefined commitment to implement the Fagan Commission's finding that permanent African urbanization was inevitable and Stallardism impracticable. This would have important implications for local government, since there would be "separate Native townships for permanent residence . . . progressively administered by the Natives themselves." As for the coloreds, the United Party repeated its long-standing but evasive recognition of them as an "appendage" of the "European community," an acknowledgment that coloreds were not African in culture but European, and a judgment that they ought to be attached to whites in some way, but without full equality. The manifesto also affirmed the 1946 Asiatic Land Tenure and Representation Act, a controversial measure that limited Asians' urban property rights, while providing them limited political rights; it made no proposals about Asians in the future.

The United Party fought the 1948 election without a mobilizing slogan or central issue. At most, it promised, as Newell Stultz put it, "adjustments in the pattern of South African race relations."[13] Crucially, for local governments, it advocated no racial "mixing" and "a policy of social and residential separation." In a cautious reference to "regulated native industrial organization," its manifesto envisioned the recognition of African trade unions. Though tantalizing, these hinted possibilities were far from meeting the demands of Africans, coloreds, Indians, and white liberals; they amounted to no coherent program of social reform.[14]

The Foundations of Apartheid

Some scholars have asserted that the National Party came to power in 1948 with only general ideas, not a master plan, as many scholars had long assumed. Deborah Posel's 1991 book, *The Making of Apartheid, 1948–1961,* while investigating labor policies and "influx control" as "a central pillar of the Apartheid system," directly challenged the claim that a master plan existed. Posel argued that "the nationalist government was thrust to power with some of the fundamentals of Apartheid still a source of controversy and uncertainty."[15]

Yet the outlines of the apartheid policy had already been approved a number of years before the 1948 election. In May 1944, Dr. D. F. Malan, the party's national leader, appointed a commission, chaired by a member of parliament, P. O. Sauer, to examine the "policy of the National Party towards the coloureds" in the Cape. The report of this, the first Sauer Commission, was issued in 1945;

it pointed to two principal issues in the Cape: a rapid increase in the number of colored voters, which was alarming to whites, and a breakdown of relations between whites and coloreds. Grasping a legal nettle that National Party politicians had avoided in the 1920s, the report urged a practical, legal definition of "coloured" that would enforce racial identities and prevent coloreds from "passing" as whites. The privileged position of coloreds compared to Africans would be preserved, a national colored consciousness would be developed, and coloreds would be separated from Africans as well as from whites.[16] Included in the 1945 Sauer report were principles of racial identity, separation, and "own state," all central to the doctrine of apartheid.

The Union-wide National Party then appointed Sauer to head a "Kleurvraagstuk Kommissie" to deal with the "colour question" of the country as a whole. What became known as the Sauer Report (actually the second Sauer report) proposed goals that formed the basis of the "Race Relations Policy of the National Party" in its 1948 election manifesto.[17] The party's policy entailed "preserving and safeguarding" the racial identity of the "White population" and of the "indigenous peoples" as "separate racial groups." Intermarriage between whites and all people of color—colored and Indian as well as African—was to be prohibited. For coloreds, the manifesto proposed "total apartheid—that is social, residential, industrial and political—between [the coloreds] and both the Bantu [African] and the non-white [presumably Malay and Asian] communities." No longer would coloreds who met property qualifications be able to vote on the common roll in the Cape; instead, three elected white members of parliament—one senator and an elected Coloured Representative Council—would represent them. Coloreds would be given "their own boards" to manage in their own areas.

The National Party's "Bantu policy" would similarly focus on "segregating the most important ethnic groups . . . in their own areas," so that each could "develop into a self-sufficient unit." A system of councils in all the reserves would "uphold the authority of the tribal chiefs and enlist the services of educated Bantu." The existing representation of Africans in the Native Representative Council, and of Cape Africans by three elected white members of parliament, would both be abolished; African "boards . . . in urban locations . . . shall have no prospect of developing into self-governing bodies. "Bantu" in towns would be recognized only as "migratory citizens not entitled to political or social rights equal to those of Whites." The state, with the help of municipal bodies, would control "the entire migration of Bantu," who would dwell in "separate residential areas." When Africans became "redundant" in town, they "should be returned to the original habitat in the country areas or the reserves." The party's electoral manifesto also reiterated the Sauer report's hostility toward those missionaries responsible for African education, who had, purportedly, indoctrinated their students with ideals of racial equality. Under a Nationalist government, education would become state controlled; it would "have moral purpose" and "inculcate national consciousness." Africans would "progressively . . . assume responsibility for financing and controlling their own education under White supervision."

As for Indians in South Africa, the manifesto said they could never make South Africa their own; they were a "strange" and "foreign" element that could not be assimilated into the "South African set-up." No further immigration from India would be allowed, and Indians already in South Africa would, if possible, be sent back to India. Separate residential areas would be "allotted" to Asians, while "trading facilities . . . outside their own areas will be drastically curtailed." The limited franchise granted to Indians in 1946 would be abolished.[18]

For Cradock, as for any Cape town, the National Party's program was to involve abolishing those rights for coloreds that had survived from the Cape liberal tradition. Cradock's colored male residents had had the same right as whites to vote in national and provincial elections.[19] They could also buy and occupy land anywhere in town or countryside on the same freehold tenure as whites; those who owned and occupied sufficient property in town could vote in local elections. Most leisure and religious activities had been segregated in Cradock by custom, but not by law. Embracing both a "mixed" town, with colored and white property owners and occupiers, and a "mixed" location set aside for Africans and coloreds, Cradock would become a prime target of the comprehensive scheme the National Party now advanced.

The *Midland News,* no longer a vigorous daily but now a weekly with limited coverage, saw the impending election in traditional United Party terms; it urged conciliation between the white groups (Afrikaans and English speakers) and extolled the indispensability of Smuts's leadership in a hostile world. It advocated "cooperation of all races in South Africa,"[20] though "there will be no mixing of blood lines, no social intermingling."[21]

The campaign in Cradock was extraordinarily low-key, a reflection of limited conflict among local whites, as well as the town's "honourable tradition of orderly meetings." There were no polemics from either side, and the candidates hardly mentioned each other by name. Both James Cull, the English-speaking candidate for the United Party, and Gerard Bekker, the National Party candidate and sitting M.P., campaigned on an ambitious scheme to divert water from the Orange to the Fish River. But Bekker, who persistently attacked Britain in the House of Assembly ("Britain had been swallowed up by a lot of Bolsheviks"), said it was his duty to "preserve South Africa as a white man's land." Campaigning on Bekker's behalf, N. Malan, a National Party member of the Cape Provincial Council, defined the principal issues of the upcoming elections as the "coloured problem [he meant the problem of color generally], communism, and internal administration." Apartheid was a system, Malan continued, in which "Natives would be removed to land given to them and would have their own police, civil servants, schools and so on."[22] But he did not spell out the meaning of apartheid at length, or with precision.

On questions of race, United Party speakers in Cradock repeatedly offered themselves as effective guardians of white supremacy: "Europeans must continue to be the leaders in South Africa," said one. They thus implied that apartheid was nothing new, that white supremacy and social segregation had long been agreed to by South African white voters. Still, the National Party seems to have convinced many voters that apartheid *was* new and better, and Cull lost badly, by 5,038 to 3,560 votes. Yet, he was reelected as mayor four months later, along with the same town council.[23] Despite the National Party's victory in Cradock and in the country at large, five councilors out of the nine selected were United Party members, four of them English speaking. Among municipal staff the long transition from English to Afrikaans speakers continued. At the beginning of the National Party regime, in 1948, Cradock had a new, energetic, and able administrator, G. W. van Rooyen, who was in sympathy with the new urban policies about to emanate from Pretoria and Cape Town. Van Rooyen soon changed most of the working language of Cradock's local government to Afrikaans, a rapid shift reflected also in correspondence with government departments. In 1951, the council, by now with a National Party majority, moved the municipal bank account from Barclays Bank to Volkskas, the first and most important Afrikaner national bank.[24]

The Nationalist victory of 1948 caught virtually everyone by surprise: the United Party had conducted a campaign characterized by the serene self-confidence of its leader, Smuts; even the Nationalists themselves anticipated merely reducing Smuts's majority. An editorial in Cradock's *Midland News,* underestimating the energy and discipline of South Africa's new rulers, declared that their small majority would compel them to schedule another general election soon.[25] The Nationalists' five-seat margin of victory was indeed small, but this did not stop the new regime from vigorously pursuing its goals. The new government identified two principal adversaries: the politically organized English-speaking whites and the 20 or so percent of Afrikaners who voted for the United Party; and the people of color, especially Africans, whose strength in numbers alarmed the dominant white minority, English and Afrikaans speaking alike. John Lazar has pointed out that much of the National Party's actions in its first few years in office were concerned with the consolidation of power, not with implementation of the grand apartheid design.[26] Yet consolidating power and enacting the design were not mutually exclusive. The government used its slim majority to do both. It turned at once to changing the constitution in ways that favored the National Party: in 1949, it established six seats in the House of Assembly for South West Africa (later Namibia), requiring, for each new seat, less than half the number of voters required for ordinary Assembly seats. The party not surprisingly won all six of these new seats at the next election, in 1953.[27] A new Citizenship Act, also in 1949, lengthened the waiting period for enfranchisement for British immigrants from eighteen months to five years, effectively disenfranchising recent immigrants in the next election.

The Separate Representation of Voters Act (1951) took the Cape franchise away from colored men (colored women had never had the vote), and provided, instead, that they could vote on a separate roll for four white representatives in the Assembly, one in the Senate. While this act implemented a National Party policy adopted as early as 1936, it also aimed to improve the party's electoral prospects in about twelve Cape constituencies where colored voters, likely supporters of the United Party, could determine the outcome. The Appeal Court declared this measure unconstitutional. The resulting crisis was not resolved until 1956, when the government packed the Senate, giving itself the two-thirds majority of both houses it needed to amend the law to limit colored voting rights.[28]

The apartheid project was neither amorphous nor vague, and it had not, in fact, been placed on the back burner. From its inception, the new government released a continuing torrent of racial legislation. The Asiatic Laws Amendment Act, passed just four months after the 1948 election, abolished the limited franchise only recently bestowed on Asians, while retaining the restrictions on Indian ownership and occupation of real estate enacted by the United Party in 1946. The Population Registration Act of 1949 established a national register listing each person's racial identity; later the regime required the carrying of an identity card that specified the holder's "race." The Prohibition of Mixed Marriages Act, also in 1949, made it illegal for whites to marry members of other racial groups. And, in 1950, parliament passed the Group Areas Act, which aimed, according to Davenport, at "nothing less than a complete unscrambling of the residential pattern in South African towns."[29]

Much of the new legislation was intended to define more clearly the position of Indians and coloreds, who were inserted in the South African order uneasily between whites and Africans. But it was in African affairs that the new government was to have its greatest impact. In 1950, the able and energetic Dr. Hendrik Verwoerd became minister of Native Affairs and radically reorganized the department's operations in both the urban areas and the reserves.[30] The Bantu Authorities Act of 1951 set out to transform the political institutions of African societies in the reserves, later called "homelands," by bolstering the powers of chiefs. Two years later, the Bantu Education Act enabled the state to take over existing African schools run by missionaries and establish other schools that would deliberately promote a narrower ethnic pride—for example, a Xhosa rather than an African nationalism—partly through mother-tongue instruction. It was a deliberate attempt to persuade Africans that their political institutions were to be separate from the existing national governing bodies. The ineffectual Native Representative Council, set up in 1936 and refusing to deal with the government for some time, was abolished and replaced by a "pyramid of Bantu Authorities."[31]

The Group Areas Act: "By Compulsion If Necessary"

To create the new institutions, ethnically homogeneous "own areas" had to be identified and legally defined, and in some cases created; this was relatively easy for the African ethnic communities still resident in the "reserves," but more difficult for the coloreds and Asians, who had never been assigned reserves. In cities and small towns, Africans from many ethnic groups had long lived in *racially* segregated townships ("locations") and compounds, but few of those townships were ethnically sorted, either spontaneously or by authority. It was in some of the larger towns of the Cape, Transvaal, and Natal that the most intense *wrywing* (friction), had occurred between whites and Asians or coloreds. Immediately after the 1948 election, the South African Railways had segregated its suburban lines in Cape Town, an action planned before the election to meet the vehement demands of whites. Preventing such friction was the public rationale for the Group Areas Act of 1950.[32]

Cradock was still, as it had been in 1926, a "mixed" town—whites and coloreds owned and occupied real estate in town—with a "mixed" location of Africans and coloreds cheek by jowl across Regent Street, the town's southern edge. Cradock had not been wracked by the *wrywing* of Cape Town or Port Elizabeth. Cradock's town clerk said, in early 1955, that he assumed the required separation of all racial groups could easily be accomplished because virtually all town coloreds, except for one family in a house owned by an African, lived in the Mixed Area between Cross and Regent Streets.[33] The logical choices for any apartheid planner, assigned to rid Cradock of "mixing," were to subdivide the town itself into white and colored "group" areas; or to declare the town set aside for one racial group, with all others moved to a fresh site outside of town—a policy of "removal." If removal was to be the policy, the power of whites, and their overwhelming ownership of real estate in town, ensured that it was colored owners and occupiers who would most likely be displaced, either to a new "colored area" within the town, which could also involve forcing some whites to move, or to an entirely new site outside the town. Cradock was to toy with each of these alternatives.

In 1946, a total of 4,557 Africans and 3,191 coloreds lived in Cradock's location, so the problem of defining separate areas for each group posed different dilemmas from those in town.[34] Cradock could create an area for coloreds outside the location that included freehold in land, but not such an area for Africans, because, under the Natives (Urban Areas) Consolidation Act of 1945, they were barred from purchasing land in town and could now be *required* to live in a racially restricted location. Cradock officials could move location coloreds out to a new colored area, perhaps to join coloreds evicted from the town itself, thus leaving the location homogeneously African; or they could move all Africans to a new site and give all or part of the old location to coloreds. In Cradock the problem was complicated by an additional 994 Africans who were not in the location and hence not under municipal control; most of them were wives and children of employees of the South African Railways, living poorly housed with minimal sanitation facilities on railway land, known among Africans as "Loco," across the river from town and location.[35] Thus, any site for a new African location would need to provide for a population larger than that already housed in the old location and its annex in the Wilken Township built during the war.

Separating "mixed" populations was a central part of the National Party manifesto, to be applied everywhere and to all races whether in a state of *wrywing* or not. Under the former United Party regime, ad hoc separation of location and town populations had frequently been realized by housing some residents in racially homogeneous neighborhoods, but no systematic policy of segregation had been enforced. Now racial sorting was the ideology of a victorious party with the political will to ensure its systematic enforcement throughout the Union.

The Group Areas Act of 1950, a highly technical piece of legislation, provided "for the establishment of group areas, for the control and acquisition of the immovable property, the occupation of lands and premises and for matters incidental thereto."[36] The minister of the interior, Dr. T. E. Dönges, emphasized that the act's central goal was to establish "separate areas for the different racial groups by compulsion if necessary." The demarcation of group areas would not be immediate, Dönges said soothingly, because of the economic disruption it would cause. The new law "merely creates the necessary machinery for doing so over a period of years and in a fair, equitable and judicial manner."[37] To justify such national legal intrusion into ownership and occupation, and, therefore, into local municipal affairs, Dönges recounted the experience of Natal and the Transvaal since the 1880s in controlling and restricting Indians' acquisition of property. In inquiry after inquiry, he said, almost all witnesses had argued for compulsory segregation as the second-best alternative to the wholesale repatriation of Indians. Just before the 1948 election, even the Cape Municipal Executive had begun to demand compulsion when it sought legislation "empowering local authorities to declare areas predominantly occupied by Europeans as European areas, within which no Coloured person or company may acquire fixed property or reside." Dönges maintained that the Cape should, therefore, "fall into line with Natal, the Transvaal, and the [Orange] Free State."[38] This was a sweeping attack on a remnant of the Cape liberal tradition, which, since 1828, had preserved the right (in theory) of anyone to acquire property regardless of race.

In the parliamentary debate on the Group Areas Bill, a divided opposition was unable to adopt a clear stand on compulsion. J. G. N. Strauss, having succeeded Smuts as the leader of the United Party, asserted his party's belief in the "principle of social and residential separation" and the avoidance of "race intermixture" but argued that the Cape Municipal Executive had been asking for a kind of local option. Problems of segregation should, he said, be handled by local authorities in concert with the provincial councils, not by an interventionist national government. Dönges interjected: "When are you going to deal with the question of voluntary or compulsory application?" Strauss would not commit his party to a voluntary policy, perhaps because many, perhaps most, of the United Party's white supporters favored residential segregation and hence could easily be wooed to support the National Party.[39]

The Group Areas Bill was introduced as a short-term stratagem for a by-election, but it was also part of a comprehensive national long-term apartheid plan. "This Bill," said Dönges, "is a major measure towards the realization of one of the main objects of the policy of apartheid, namely the elimination of friction between the different races of the Union, by providing separate areas for the different races." It divided South Africa's peoples into three groups—white, "native," and colored. In "controlled areas," home ownership and residence would be regulated by a system of state-issued permits; no property could be sold to a member of another racial group unless sanctioned by permit. A similar rule applied to occupation; each "group area" would be owned and occupied by a single racial group. Since enforcing control of both ownership and occupation at once would have caused enormous dislocation in mixed areas like those in many Cape towns, provision was made for delay—those who owned or occupied property in an area assigned to another group were now to be labeled "disqualified persons" and allowed a number of years to move, the length of time to be decided by officials. Eventually, the plan envisaged that all South Africans would live in an area entirely occupied, and, in some cases owned, by members of a single group.[40]

The machinery devised to enforce the act reveals profound continuities between the age of segregation and the age of apartheid. The three northern provinces had long tried to restrict Indian ownership and occupation: in the Transvaal starting in 1885; in Natal, in the form of sustained agitation for "class areas" legislation in the 1920s and of the passing of a "Pegging Act" in 1943; and in the Orange Free State, which had excluded Indians altogether from 1891 on.[41] In 1946, the United Party had further restricted Indian property rights in Natal and the Transvaal. The Group Areas Act made these sorts of restrictive laws national in scope and applied the same logic to coloreds. A Land Tenure Advisory Board, later to become the Group Areas Board (GAB) or Groeps Gebiede Raad (GGR), was to enforce the act. The board was subdivided into regional committees, with Cradock under the jurisdiction of the Eastern Cape Committee.[42] Each regional committee, after receiving locally made proposals and holding public hearings, was to forward its own proposals for group areas to the national board in Pretoria. In 1951, in the Cape, Transvaal, and Natal, the Chinese (originally defined as coloreds) and Indians were declared to be separate groups.[43] From then on, the whole of the Cape Province was a "controlled" area, with all property transactions between members of different races, and much leisure activity as well, under official control—attendance at a theater could be defined as an act of "occupation."[44] The days were over when the national government was reluctant to intervene in municipal affairs or to press local authorities into compliance.

The national government was soon to learn, however, that pressure had its limits even when local authorities were controlled by members of the National Party. The definition of "group areas" in Cradock would be a protracted battle, not to be resolved until 1971. Numerous schemes would be proposed, altered, and abandoned, as officials struggled with the realities of topography and local politics to advance two intertwined goals of the new national government: to replace Cradock's mixed location with a purely African "location" distant from the neighborhoods of other racial groups and to unscramble the areas of town where whites and coloreds had long lived close to one another.

A NEW "NATIVE VILLAGE": UNSCRAMBLING THE MIXED LOCATION

Boundary Lines and Buffer Strips: Cradock's First Group Areas Proposal

In Cradock, apartheid required new racially defined boundaries. Africans and coloreds shared the location; whites, coloreds, and Asians, the "mixed" town. Regent Street had historically marked the boundary between town and location, but it had never demarcated racial living areas precisely. In 1947, Cradock hired a town planner, J. H. C. Hofmeyr, to help locate Cradock's first industrial areas and a distinct colored township as well. The town clerk had sent the Department of Native Affairs a rough map of an expanded location, whose new boundaries were approved and proclaimed in December 1948.[45] Apartheid planners, however, were determined to separate *all* "Non-Europeans" into separate "areas" for ownership and occupation of property, for the conduct of business, and as the locus of schools and churches. Thus, a year after the change of government, Hofmeyr was writing in general segregationist terms: "Every effort," he wrote, "should be made to make Regent Street the defining line between Europeans and Non-Europeans."[46]

After Dr. Hendrik Verwoerd was appointed as minister of native affairs in 1950, the national government intervened energetically in large and small towns, Cradock among them.[47] J. van Heerden, the Cape's chief native commissioner and a fervent supporter of apartheid, frequently sent his officials to nudge reluctant local authorities into action. In May 1952, the urban areas commissioner, G. A. Brand, visited Cradock to discuss demarcation of its location and its enlargement to house all Cradock's Africans—including those

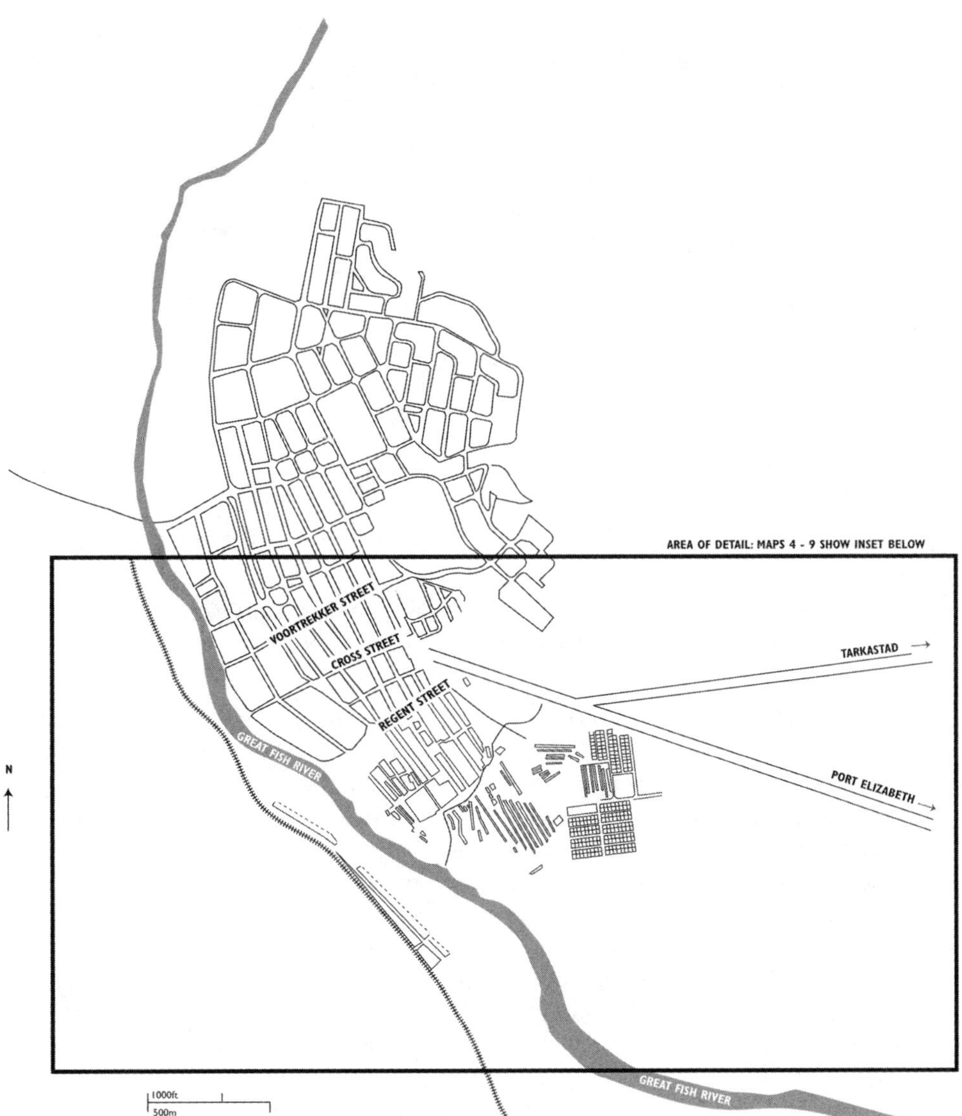

Map 3. Cradock. (Map by Mariah Reisner, based on an undated aerial photograph in the author's possession)

then living at "Loco," the South African Railways land outside the location. As a result of Brand's report, Van Heerden declared that a location solely for Africans could be established only after the coloreds had been removed. A separate colored area was, therefore, a top priority. First, the new commissioner for Coloured Affairs had to be consulted on colored housing, and then

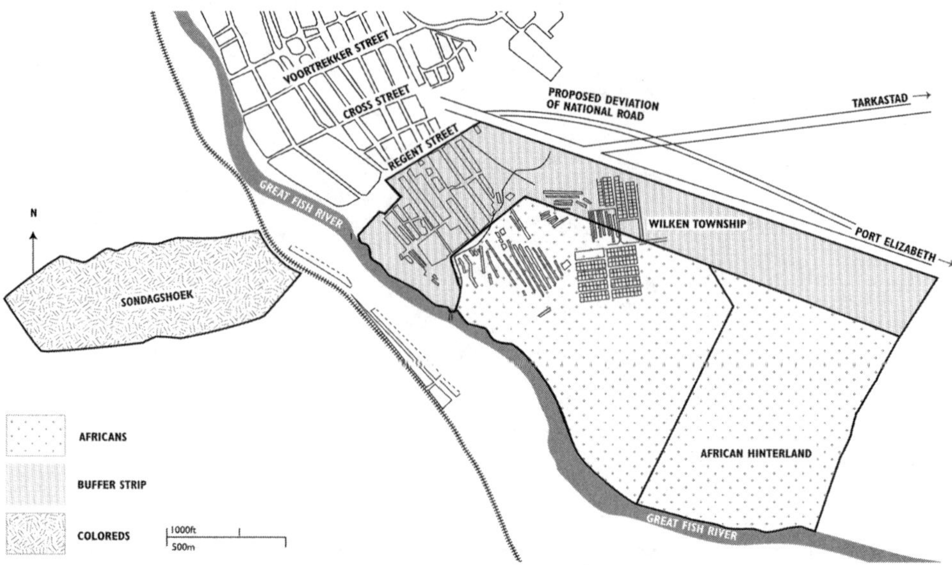

Map 4. The Chief Commissioner's Plan, 1953. (Map by Mariah Reisner, from Chief Native Commissioner to Town Clerk, 26 Mar. 1953, NAR, DNA 114/113 N, vol. 1, 185)

a representative of the Central Housing Board would arrange financing. Four months later, officials agreed to expand the "native location" and build a new "coloured township" across the Great Fish River in Sondagshoek, as proposed by Cradock's new town planner.[48] Three months later the town clerk dispatched a map delineating the proposed new location's boundary.[49] Under the plan, Regent Street would continue to separate the "Existing Native Location" from the town; and beyond the location would lie the required "Hinterland" for future expansion of the African population (map 4).

Van Heerden, the chief native commissioner, now peremptorily instructed the municipality to "extend" and "circumscribe" the African location to meet "the following requirements of the [Native Affairs] department": "a 500-yard buffer strip between the white area and the built-up part of the location, [and] a similar strip along the national road; both strips ultimately to be clear of all obstructions and to be included within the location's boundaries; and a hinterland sufficient for another fifty years' growth." A 500-yard strip ultimately would have to be cleared south of Regent Street. No more building would be permitted in the strip. Furthermore, a buffer strip along the "provincial road" meant that the National Road Board would have to move its road "as far as geographical factors would allow." Van Heerden reported that the minister, Dr. Verwoerd, would agree to re-proclaiming the location's boundaries only if these requirements were met as closely as possible.[50] Regent Street would now be the boundary between town and buffer strip, not between town and location.

By demanding "buffer strips," the Department of Native Affairs was enormously complicating the issues in order to produce more systematic distance between whites and Africans. Virtually all of Wilken Township, the 288-house township built between 1941 and 1948, was in one of the proposed strips. The provision for housing for coloreds now also stood in the way; the secretary for native affairs wrote impatiently to find out if any progress had been made with "the establishment of a coloured housing area and the removal of coloureds from out of the native location." The Cradock council, still struggling to find a site for colored housing, and not to be hurried, delayed a decision, opting for a multistep procedure provided for by the Group Areas Act. Thereupon an exasperated chief native commissioner appealed to the town clerk: why was the drawing of the location boundaries held up?[51] The council refused to budge: "the laying out of a coloured housing area, and the elimination of the coloureds from the location is a necessary preliminary to finding out the size of the future native location."[52] "Council has for years been talking of the elimination of the coloureds from the location," the chief native commissioner wrote to his superior, "and has done nothing about it. . . . Is there anything further I can do to compel the Town Council?"[53]

Meanwhile Cradock had been negotiating with the South African Railways to buy back the "Loco" land for the proposed colored township in Sondagshoek; it would then move the Africans now on railroad property into the new location. In an extended interview in March 1954, the town clerk, Van Rooyen, put the project in the context of apartheid policy regarding Africans. The Department of Native Affairs, he said, wanted to abolish all privately owned locations, including sites owned by the railways, and house all "non-whites" in an area controlled by local authorities. Separate colored housing would stop coloreds from smuggling liquor to Africans, and new African housing would replace slums in the location. Moreover, coloreds and Africans themselves preferred segregation, or so Van Rooyen asserted.[54]

In July 1954, a circular letter from the Department of Native Affairs instructed all local authorities, magistrates, and other officials to monitor the building of roads near old and new African locations, and stated that, in addition to buffer strips, a "separate access road from the location to the town should be constructed for the exclusive use of location inhabitants."[55] By such a scheme, Africans would not encounter whites as they walked to work in towns. In Cradock, a 500-yard buffer strip along Regent Street and a colored township across the river would have separated Africans, whites, and coloreds from each other; but to leave the bulk of the African location on its old site, as Cradock preferred to do, would not only make the "old location" part of a buffer strip that must be cleared, but it would also leave the national road a mere 100 yards from the edge of the recently built Wilken Township. The council could preserve Wilken Township or insert the buffer strip, but not both. Hence, it sought to persuade the Department of Transport to move its road so that it was 500, not

100, yards from the edge. Transport officials refused; the road had been built in 1940, and funds were available only to tar it. A National Party councilor, J. J. Gerber, protested, but in vain.[56] To the fury of a Native Affairs official and the Cradock council, the Transport Department proceeded to tar the road in place.[57]

Pressed by the Land Tenure Advisory Board to announce its group areas proposals, Cradock's council decided, in March 1955, that Africans, not coloreds, would be moved to Sondagshoek, and that the present location would be assigned to coloreds instead.[58] Since "no buffer strip is required round an area occupied by Coloured persons," the chief native commissioner wrote, the need to divert the national road "would fall away."[59] Cradock's first proposal for the required group areas was now, at last, submitted.[60]

Who Will Move? The Battle over Sondagshoek

Africans were far better organized than coloreds in responding to the imposition of group areas. Immediately after the 1948 election, the Rev. J. A. Calata, secretary-general of the Union-wide African National Congress (ANC) and a Cradock resident, advised his followers not to take the change of government too seriously; he implied that both major parties were supporters of white supremacy and hence Africans could expect little from either—"nobody cares for our support." Yet Calata deplored crude anti-Afrikaner attitudes. He called Cradock's National Party MP, Gerard Bekker, a "real gentleman farmer," and at the death of the town clerk, P. de K. van Heerden, he led his esteemed ANC choir at the graveside service in the Dutch Reformed cemetery.[61] In 1948 Calata resigned as secretary-general; the ANC, he said, was moving in a radical direction he did not like.[62] Two years later, with the approval of the ANC leadership, he kept Cradock's Africans out of a National Day of Protest.[63] His moderation earned him little credit in government circles; in 1952, national officials banned Calata from teaching and, in early 1956, indicted him among 156 leaders of all races for "high treason"—though, on his arrest, he was granted bail and released early in the trial.[64] Two years later, he was to play a public role in opposing the move of Africans to Sondagshoek.

Location Africans had been especially exercised by rent increases in 1947, 1948, and 1953. With the native revenue account in persistent deficit, most location rents had gone up by about 30 percent since 1946. Beer hall revenue had risen, and the meager £1,000 annual subsidy from general municipal revenue, much resented by white ratepayers, continued; in 1953 the location again ran a deficit.[65] Ernest Butler, now a councilor and chairman of the Location Committee, argued for a location community hall to be financed by a loan and by beer hall funds; he reminded ratepayers that his brother Charles Butler, as mayor in 1940, had promised African residents new "amenities" to override ANC objections to the opening of the beer hall. Thereupon the council raised location rents again.[66] The proposed loan for a community hall, which required ratepayer approval, was debated in the midst of a national "Defiance Campaign" by the ANC and the South African Indian Congress against "unjust laws."[67] Cradock's ratepayers rejected the proposal, because, some said, riot insurance on a public building would be unobtainable.[68]

In 1954, the town clerk raised the issue of compensation, explaining that "several native inhabitants" wanted to improve their houses, even if, because they were located on buffer strips, these houses might be demolished later; the inhabitants were prepared to forego compensation. The Native Affairs Department was "totally opposed" to any such improvements.[69] At a special council meeting the following year, F. H. Brownlee, the urban areas commissioner, announced that in view of the planned new African location in Sondagshoek, no "improvements or additions" would be allowed to houses in the old location. Some councilors, including Ernest Butler as chair of the Location Committee, persisted nonetheless in arguing for allowing improvements if applicants indemnified the council against compensation. Van Heerden, the chief native commissioner, reminded the town clerk that the cost of such improvements would be borne, not by the Union government nor by the municipality's native revenue account, but by the town's general revenue; that is, by the town's ratepayers, who were, of course, overwhelmingly white.[70]

By 1956, the Cradock council had learned that a new location would have to house 6,930 Africans—not, as originally planned, 3,326 coloreds. Moreover, the town clerk reported "the hostile attitude of the natives—especially in some circles."[71] Three bodies represented the Africans in Cradock: the ANC, the ANC Youth League, and the Location Vigilance Committee (or Association). (There was some bad blood between the ANC and the Vigilance Association; many in the Youth League regarded the Vigilance Committee as incorrigibly conservative—on its nine-member committee were three traders, a health worker, and a teacher, all upper class in location terms.) The Vigilance Committee requested street lights, taps, and lavatories, whereupon the council proposed yet another increase in rents, which Youth League members termed an "outrageous" and "sinister" attack on Africans: "South Africa owed its prosperity to the sweat and blood of the African people."[72] Soon after, the location office burned down, and the town council, blaming the ANC, banned all ANC public meetings except for certain religious occasions.[73]

An embattled town council announced that F. H. Brownlee, the urban areas commissioner for the Eastern Cape, would come to Cradock to explain government housing policy to Africans. At a "continuous" public meeting in the hall of the St. James church (Calata's church), the mayor, Charles Osche, announced that the council had decided to improve conditions in the location "by transferring the African inhabitants to a new site where a new Township would be laid out on modern lines." Brownlee added that the cost of improved housing would be borne "mainly by the employers through the Service Levy" under the terms of the Native Services Levy Act of 1952, to "provide the funds required for services such as water, lights and sanitation and roads etc." Under a "site and service" scheme, the council would build the first room of each house in the new township; "additional rooms would have to be built by the occupant."

"Why must the African inhabitants be the ones to move?" asked a memorandum that Calata presented to the council meeting. If more land were required for Africans, "why not extend the present Location EASTWARD beyond Wilken Township?" Sondagshoek was "quite unsuitable. . . . We . . . understand that it had previously been offered to the Coloured people. We do not want it too. . . . We . . . understand that the chief reason for applying the Group Areas Act in the way suggested, is that the 41 Coloured families, who live among the Europeans, must be sent out of town. . . . Why not send them to a new place? Why move 1200 families to make room for 41?" If local authorities "are compelled by Law to implement the 'Apartheid' in this way . . . we . . . submit that "THE LAW IS MADE FOR 'MAN' AND NOT 'MAN' FOR THE 'LAW.'" "The removal of the Mission Churches and Halls . . . will create an adverse sociological effect on the Christian inhabitants of this town. These institutions are rallying places for the congregations of the town and districts, and it would require, at least, some £40,000 to £50,000 to rebuild them. . . . A good portion of the land on which they stand is FREEHOLD. There is NO guarantee of Freehold Tenure elsewhere."[74]

The mayor pledged that the council would "give careful consideration of the places dear to the Africans such as their churches etc." Brownlee said that the law required that more land be made available to Africans than to coloreds—presumably a reference to the required buffer strips—and "this makes it necessary to move the Africans." The law did not "provide for compensation for churches but the Mayor had promised the Council's careful consideration of this matter." Local authorities were not "compelled to promote apartheid," Brownlee said. Toward the end of the meeting an African speaker walked to a vacant space in the middle of the hall. "We are not interested in the Council's proposal, nor are we in favor of being removed from here, we want to stay here." The mayor thanked Calata for his assistance in securing a reasonably civil hearing for Brownlee and suggested that the meeting close "with the singing of the African National anthem."[75]

Letters of protest from both Africans and whites soon appeared in the *Midland News.* Ernest Butler resigned as chair of the Location Committee: "He would never have proposed the building of the new location," he wrote in the *Midland News,* "if he had known there would be no compensation for Native Churches." Furthermore, Brownlee's statement that "local authorities are not compelled to promote Apartheid came as a complete surprise to me." If this was correct, there was "no necessity for immediate action."

Local pressures to abandon the buffer strip policy increased. Buffer strips were forcing the council to go for the most expensive solution—a new African location over the river. A letter from Butler in the *Midland News* proposed that if buffer strips were abandoned, "a start could be made in improving the worst parts of the existing location."[76] Better to delay, the town clerk wrote to the secretary of native affairs: "My Council feels that if it is not absolutely necessary now . . . they would rather postpone this matter as long as possible." Hostile "propaganda" by blacks and whites in the local paper made things "very difficult."[77] Besides, added J. J. Gerber, the Nationalist deputy mayor, the buffer strip was "policy" but not "law." L. L. Scheepers, also a National Party member, agreed: no other town was being compelled to impose a buffer strip; at one township in Johannesburg "the buffer strip consists only of a barbed wire fence next to the road. The distance is only 10 feet." In Cradock, "the Coloureds and Africans have been living side by side for years. They are used to one another. So, leave them alone." The mayor reported that the council was unanimous in wanting to allow "Non-Europeans to live where they are now." Still, practicalities must be faced: "We must have governmental help and unless we play in with them we won't have their help." The town clerk agreed: "unless we can get the Department to relax their policy slightly, and obtain their support at the same time, we are lost."[78]

Passions were escalating among Africans throughout the country. African women campaigned against the government's extension of passes to women under the Natives Abolition of Passes and Coordination of Documents Act. African ministers, Calata among them, opposed the Bantu Education Act of 1953, a bitterly resented intervention of the Union government's Department of Native Affairs in African schools, which were virtually all managed by missions and churches. The ANC Youth League held "concerts" as a means of avoiding a ban on meetings. W. Lombard, the Cradock location superintendent, went to such a "concert," in St. James's Hall and reported a display of posters proclaiming "*A suja e Sondagshoek*" (roughly, "Sondagshoek get out of here") and "We want houses, we do not want money."[79] The council, reacting to a letter from the Youth League, defended its recent raises of rents and denied that it had planned to build houses in the new location in Sondagshoek on top of old "stercus pits"—trenches for burying sewage.[80] Citing "insulting behavior" and "threatening language" by Youth League members, the council handed the Youth League letter to the police, who, over one weekend in mid-1957, brought in one hundred police reinforcements from surrounding towns.[81] Not to be intimidated, the Youth League began an effective boycott of the municipal beer hall in February 1957, causing its surplus to turn into a deficit.[82] Yet the government did not lose control of the Cradock location; the extra police were sent home promptly. The beer hall boycott ended within a year.[83]

At a special council meeting in April 1957, the mayor, five councilors, and three municipal officials met Van Heerden, the chief native commissioner, and Brownlee, the urban areas commissioner, hoping to soften the Africans' hostility to the moving of the location. The verbatim record, eleven foolscap single-spaced pages, appeared in the *Midland News*. The proposed move of the location, deputy mayor Gerber told the meeting, was a consequence of the Group Areas Act and the demand for buffer strips. If only the buffer strip provision could be eased, a start could be made to improve houses in the existing location. Still, improvements raised a further problem: if they were allowed now and the location were later moved, residents would feel inadequately compensated for the cost of improvements, and Cradock's ratepayers would have to foot the bill. Van Heerden was intransigent: the buffer strips were "applicable to the whole of the Union of South Africa." "I have not known the Minister [Verwoerd] to deviate one inch from the policy and I make bold to say that he will not deviate from that policy." Van Heerden refused to explain why no buffer strips were required between "other non-Europeans and Europeans," noting that his department had nothing to do with coloreds. Buffer strips *were* required between Africans and coloreds, and there was no room in the existing location for properly separated African and colored areas.

At that council meeting, Butler asked if it was "compulsory for local authorities to carry out the 'Apartheid' laws." Yes, said Van Heerden, the government itself had the power to build townships, as it had done in Johannesburg—"we had to clear Sophiatown of the natives"—but it preferred municipalities to do the job. The government could refuse loans if a council built "a location where the Department does not want it," and ratepayers would have to pay the compensation for expropriated location houses out of general revenue, not out of the native revenue account. Nor did the law provide for compensation to churches. Indeed, under the Group Areas Act, coloreds could no longer use their present churches in town or even churches in the location they had been using jointly with Africans.

Van Heerden had little sympathy for appeals for delay. He threatened "to be at the Council all the time until something is done"; it was "absolutely against the Law and against the Native [*sic*] Urban Areas Act to have natives and coloureds residing in the same location." "Under no circumstances" would the department sanction a loan to implement "something . . . in conflict with the set policy." Brownlee added: "if the Department of Public Health 'condemned' the location, I will have to ask that all further loans to Cradock for any purpose whatsoever be withheld."[84] In the view of the *Midland News,* such threats by Native Affairs officials were a new feature of apartheid, "unknown in the segregation era."[85]

Van Heerden's blunt speech stepped up the pressure for a Sondagshoek location. At a council meeting, the mayor laid on the table a detailed report by Cradock's chief health inspector, P. S. Coetzee, which calculated that, assuming an average of five persons per house, Cradock needed 1,100 houses for 5,500 Africans already in the location.[86] The council voted to accept, "in principle," the Sondagshoek proposal. It authorized drawing up plans and estimates and approved negotiations with the railway administration to erect houses for "all their native labourers."[87]

Group Areas Proclaimed: Cradock and the Union Government in Agreement

The town engineer, T. Kleefstra, apparently began at once to draw up the "plans and estimates." His report, coming two months later, on 1 July 1957, was a bombshell. The Sondagshoek area was unsuitable—in the opinion of "most" councilors, the location superintendent, and himself. The cost of services would be "tremendous": water would have to be piped two miles, a costly "overhead bridge" would have to be built, and there would be "heavy traffic and pedestrian congestion." Kleefstra expressed "much pleasure in submitting a revised plan" (map 5). Part of the old location, site of the proposed first buffer strip, next to the town along Regent Street, could be set aside for coloreds. A new buffer strip of five hundred yards could be laid out in "the *worst* portion in the present location . . . [which] should as a fact never have been built on at all." A new location for Africans could be built on 174 morgen of land beyond the buffer strip, with "215 morgen for hinterland." The location, he noted, had been "gradually extending in this direction" anyway. As for the buffer strip along the national road, the houses in Wilken Township were "all only approximately 15 years old and in very good condition. I suggest therefore that the Council approaches the Government with the request to keep those homes

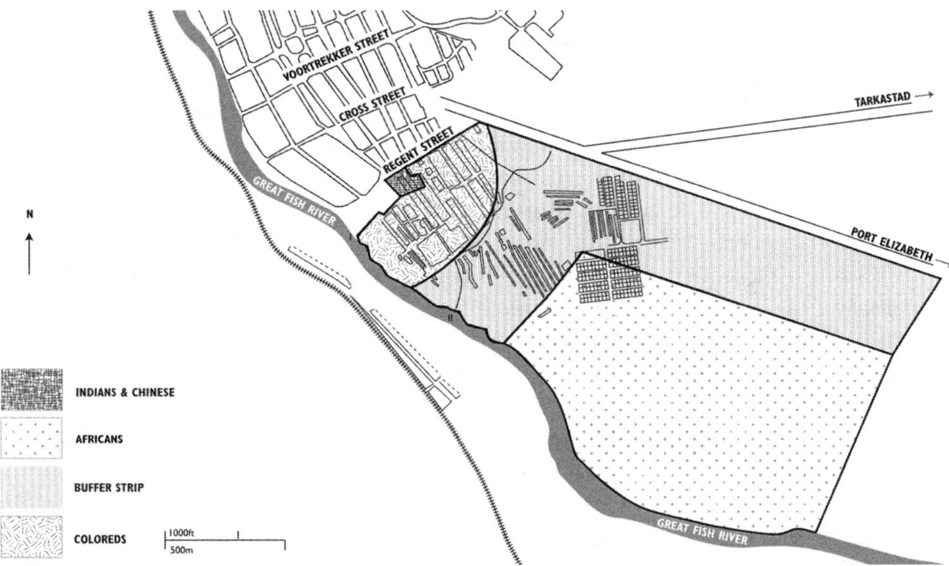

Map 5. The Town Engineer's Plan, 1957. (Map by Mariah Reisner, from Provincial Secretary [Cape] to Secretary of Native Affairs, 14 Aug. 1957, NAR NAD 114/113 U, Medical and Clinical Services, 40, with additions by the author)

occupied until in years to come they also come into such a state that they are unfit for human habitation."[88]

The council moved rapidly to accept Kleefstra's proposal: the Location Committee voted to abandon Sondagshoek and to ask the department for a three-hundred-yard buffer strip, rather than the five-hundred-yard strip, along the national road and for compensation for churches and halls.[89] The town clerk appealed to the chief native commissioner once more for a relaxation of buffer strip requirements: because Wilken Township had been built before the national road, Cradock hoped the houses there could remain. To prevent traffic between the colored and African areas, as was required by law, a service road would be provided to the east of the proposed colored area and the buffer strip marked off with "an appropriate fence" to avoid "necessity of intercommunication" between the two races.[90]

For Africans, the town's abandonment of Sondagshoek was a crucial victory, even though they were to lose land south of Regent Street to a colored area and the new buffer strip. They had helped shape the decision, not least by frightening officials and councilors, who frequently alluded to their hostility. Though municipal policies toward Africans were not formally negotiated, the council had at least been prepared to have a public discussion of the Sondagshoek scheme. The abandonment of the scheme was a victory for those who wanted to preserve the best houses in the location—Wilken Township—and for those in the location who wanted to improve their houses. Many Africans probably regarded the decision to scrap Sondagshoek as a triumph, even a major one.[91]

To the Cradock council's annoyance, however, an official in the office of the chief native commissioner now insisted that the area allocated to coloreds would be sufficient only for the 2,757 coloreds from the existing location. Where would the coloreds go? Commissioner Brownlee was prepared to recommend the council's plan, but the area planned for coloreds in the old location was insufficient.[92] The council responded by allocating another 64 morgen for coloreds between the Tarkastad and national roads.

In July 1958, Van Rooyen formally applied to the Department of Native Affairs for approval "in principle" of the proposal to proclaim a new location and the two group areas for coloreds. Two maps were delivered to the chief native commissioner's office in Kingwilliamstown, one of them the basis of map 6.

Demarcated were the following:

1. *Boundaries.* The future white group area north of Regent Street; two colored group areas (one of 35 morgen, the other of 64 morgen); and one "New Location" (157 morgen). Sondagshoek was abandoned as a location site. No Asian area was defined.
2. *Buffer strips.* The new location was enclosed by the strips, separating the colored area of 35 morgen from the new African location. Most of

Wilken Township was included in the strip. (Note that the new colored area of 64 morgen did not need a buffer strip between it and the national road.)

3. *Hinterlands.* The future expansion of each separate group area was indicated: (a) Europeans to the north; (b) coloreds to the southeast into the hinterland beyond the 64 morgen; (c) the "Native location" to the southeast into a hinterland of 215 morgen.

Concessions from the government were needed because the 35-morgen colored area had no contiguous hinterland. The proposed 64 morgen along the Tarkastad Road for coloreds in the future was separated from the 35-morgen area by a road and a buffer strip, an obstacle for apartheid planners eager to demarcate *aaneenlopende* (unfragmented) racial areas. For the time being, Cradock would have two separated colored group areas, only one with a hinterland for expansion. The Cradock municipality wanted another concession to preserve the 209 houses of Wilken Township, now in the buffer strip, and doomed, sooner or later, to demolition. "It was sincerely hoped that this request would be met because the Council in fact cannot see their way open to demolish these houses at this time."[93]

Brownlee acknowledged to his chief that the abandonment of Sondagshoek meant jettisoning a piece of apartheid theory: that Africans be "near the in-

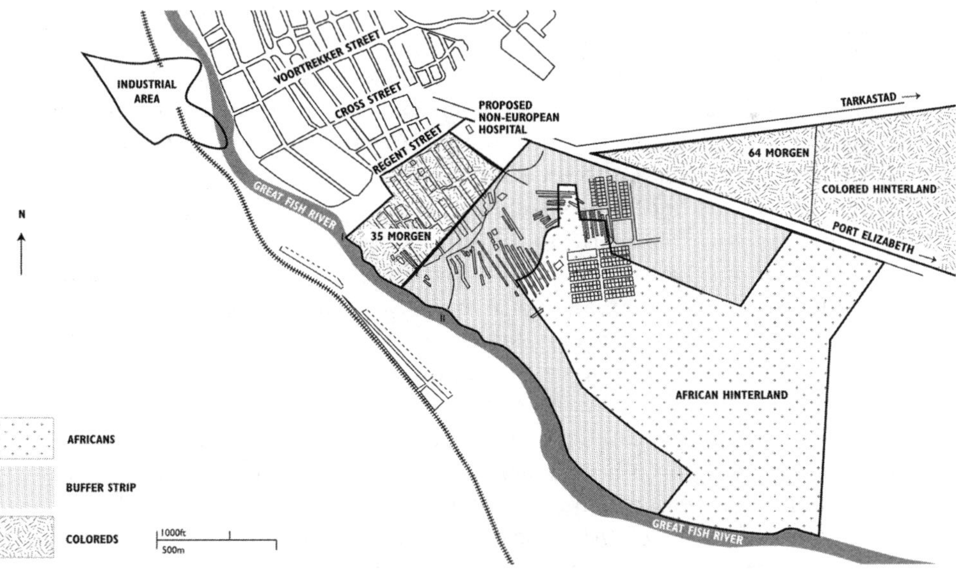

Map 6. Cradock's Final Proposals: Group Areas Proclaimed, 1960. (Map by Mariah Reisner, from sketch by Valerie Butler from maps T82 and T83 enclosed in Town Clerk to Chief Native Commissioner, 29 July 1958, Port Elizabeth Repository, CNC N 9/15/3/23)

dustrial area and completely segregated from the town." But, he noted, no repairs would be allowed to the well-built houses in Wilken Township in the buffer strip; and as soon as the council began to build new houses for Africans, African occupiers of inappropriate areas would be moved and their present houses demolished. The "zoning of the town into racial group areas" would "gradually cause native house owners in the proposed coloured area to move to the new location"; and the provisions of the Natives (Urban Areas) Act (1945) would secure the removal of twenty-two colored owners in the "proposed boundary belt" of the new location (that is, the buffer strip). The new location, Brownlee recommended, should therefore be approved "in principle."[94]

A few months later, the Group Areas Board in Pretoria gave final approval and so did the minister of Bantu Administration.[95] A proclamation was issued in May 1961, "defining, setting apart and laying out by the municipality of Cradock . . . a location and Native Village." Unlike some other territorial demarcations in Cradock, much of this would survive.[96] It had taken thirteen years, since 1948, against broad resistance from African activists and white sympathizers, to determine location boundaries acceptable to both local and national policy makers. Every racial group would be separated from every other, as the apartheid system required.

Industry, Churches, a Hospital, and "Sauntering through Town": Group Areas in Action

It was one thing for the government to define territorial boundaries, another to ensure that the boundaries were respected and achieved their purposes. Group areas were intended, not only as segregated places of residence, but also as segregated places of business. Hence, in 1952, the Cradock council and Union officials had hoped to establish industrial areas on the west bank, with a new colored township nearby so that colored workers would not have to walk through town on their way to work.[97] By 1960, the council had established a plan for an industrial area (map 6), but now it had no colored (or African) township on the west bank. Van Heerden had written, "if it is at all possible, the industrial area should be on the same side of the town as the location to prevent natives going to work sauntering through the town."[98] As of 1958, no such industries had appeared on the west bank; Cradock's African and colored workers were employed in commerce, local government, the railways, and domestic service, all of which required access to town.

Long before 1948, only Africans could conduct businesses inside the established locations. Under apartheid, the policy continued: in 1953 the secretary for native affairs had refused to allow a quarry in the location area "unless the ground is to be hired to a native, or the business is run by the local authority and . . . the income therefore be put in the Native Revenue Account."[99] Brickmaking, on the other hand, had long been undertaken in Cradock by Africans, coloreds, and whites, using clay on the east bank of the Great Fish River, which was now declared a buffer strip. In 1959, the secretary for Bantu Administration wrote to Cradock's town clerk: "though Bantu . . . are given more or less a monopoly to trade in such areas they are not allowed to establish industries there. They are allowed to do certain limited necessary services like shoemaking, washing, etc. in the Bantu township for the location inhabitants. . . . Except for his own use, a location Bantu is not allowed to make bricks in a Bantu township and not on the plot that has been given him."[100] When Sam Thallie, an African who had made bricks in Cradock for thirty years, wished to renew his lease, the town clerk wrote: "My Council feels it would be unjust to cancel the leases." The Department of Bantu Administration (the newly named Department of Native Affairs) was not moved: "There can be no concession in relation to the two old Bantu brickmakers because it would be against policy and against the provisions of Article 6 of Act 25 of 1945 [the Natives (Urban Areas) Consolidation Act]. It is suggested that the two Bantu brickmakers be taken into the employ of one or two of the white brickmakers or the coloured brickmaker on brickfields outside the new Bantu townships, (unoccupied buffer strips included)."[101]

The siting of a new hospital for Cradock exposed yet another quandary for apartheid planners: hospitals, even more than businesses, created problems because they mixed people of different races. According to a Cape hospital official in 1957, a population of about 25,000 was required to sustain a hospital, about the same as the total population of Cradock's town and district.[102] The Cradock Hospital Board had sought to build a regional hospital ever since the founding of the Queen's Central Hospital in 1897. After Charles Osche, an energetic Afrikaner nationalist, was elected mayor in 1950, he made a new hospital his own particular cause. The project was far advanced in 1957 when the Cape Provincial Hospital Administration proposed to call for bids for an internally segregated, multiracial hospital on the site of the old hospital, right in town.[103] No, said chief native commissioner Van Heerden: the hospital was in "the wrong place even though plans for the location and group areas were not complete."[104] The delays dragged on until Verwoerd, the Bantu Administration minister, ruled that a "double purpose" hospital in a white area must avoid the problems of "natives visiting patients. . . . [Such a] double purpose hospital must be built outside the town's expected expansion in the direction of the location but not so that it will be in the location, because the white patients and personnel will not have it."[105] Although the hospital now proposed in Cradock was, in fact, to be in town and to serve whites, coloreds, and Africans, Van Heerden and Brownlee accepted the proposal, with the provision that a purely "Non-European" hospital would be built in the future (map 6). They failed to tell the secretary for Bantu Administration of this decision, and with bids for the hospital due to close in two months, the secretary sought to be reassured. "The nearest white houses," explained Van Heerden, "will be 200 yards away and out of sight of the hospital and the proposed non-white section of the hospital . . . will therefore cause no racial friction." The department would oppose any expansion of the "Bantu portion" of the new hospital. He understood that a site for a "separate Bantu hospital" would be provided as soon as "the Bantu township's revised boundaries were announced"; a proposed site was "tentatively" indicated on the map.[106] The Department of Bantu Administration conceded defeat: Van Heerden had taken the side of the provincial administration, and the siting was now a fait accompli.[107] His department had to accept a decision it did not want—a multiracial hospital, including beds for Africans, inside the soon-to-be-all-white town.

Cradock moved rapidly to build its new African location, noting that the present location was "shocking," particularly because no improvements to existing houses had been allowed.[108] The National Housing Board approved a loan of £175,000 to house 1,320 African families, and by June 1964, 952 new houses were up, making a total of 1,242 (including 290 in Wilken Township). This was roughly enough for 6,210 persons.[109] However, a location population of 10,314 had been estimated, assuming an increment of at least 600 per year.[110] By the end of the 1960s, local officials claimed that Africans were adequately housed. However, with Cradock's new location now housing virtually all Cradock's Africans, squatter settlements were arising on its fringes.[111]

Africans who were forced to leave houses they owned in the old location to move to the new areas beyond Wilken Township were compensated on a formula based on the market value of their confiscated property. The 1957 report of P. S. Coetzee, the health inspector, declared 35 percent of these houses uninhabitable. Considering the limited market in location property—only improvements, not land, had been sellable or heritable—the equity of the compensation payments is difficult to determine. Leaving aside the question of the justice of forced removals themselves, many location residents probably received better value for rent payments in their new houses than they had for the old site rents for which the municipality had provided few services; owners of houses built under site-and-services schemes probably did even better.

Then there was the question of the churches. Municipalities like Cradock had long resisted giving churches full legal title of the land on which their churches and schools stood. Cradock's municipal records contain a series of letters dating back long before 1948 in which church bodies sought freehold title. For example, in 1939, a town clerk's report on the "Church, School, and Similar Sites" in the Cradock location showed eight church buildings: three Anglican, three Wesleyan Methodist, and two American Methodist Episcopal. The magistrate said that the Anglican and Methodist churches claimed that they held "transfer" of their ground and consequently refused to enter into a lease with the council.[112] The issue persisted: in 1956, Ernest Butler, the chair of the committee that had produced the first proposal for a location in Sondagshoek, had been outraged when told that compensation might be refused. The African Vigilance Association protested that freehold would be denied for churches in any new location to which they were moved. The council promised from time to time to address the issue but never did. When the new location was built and the old one demolished after 1959, none of the churches were compensated.[113]

In the first ten years of the apartheid regime, to 1958, despite many delays and some retreats, the national government had achieved a rigorous plan for racial segregation in Cradock. Between them, the Department of Native Affairs (later Bantu Administration and Development) and the Cradock municipality had defined a separate area for Africans and two for coloreds. (Indians and Chinese were finally allotted to the colored area or controlled by permit.) It seemed that all that was now required was a rapid construction of a new African location and the planning of a new colored township on the site of the old "mixed" location. The boundaries of the new African location met the requirements of the apartheid doctrine for an adequate hinterland, but the area for coloreds was so limited that it ran head-on into another fiat—the necessity of an *aaneenlopende* (unfragmented) area for each separate racial group.

Apartheid doctrine was confusing to Cradock members of the National Party as well as to others, and at no point did the government itself suggest its own comprehensive plan for the town. The Department of Native Affairs had discovered that though Cradock's council was dominated by the National Party, it was unlikely to respond favorably to the peremptory demands of national bureaucrats, especially when a strict application of buffer strip doctrine would require demolition of location houses built during the Second World War, as well as destruction of most of the old location. Nor were the demands of apartheid planning always respected by other national departments: the Department of Transport flatly refused to move a road built in 1940, and the Cape Provincial Hospital Services administration had no objection to a multiracial, internally segregated, hospital in town—one that even included a hostel for colored nursing trainees. Yet another inconvenient fact on the ground had appeared when Kleefstra, the town engineer, realized that Sondaghoek was completely unsuitable for a large township and would be ruinously expensive. From the beginning, the Department of Native Affairs had made it clear that most of the cost of enforcing group areas in Cradock should be borne by Cradock and its ratepayers, certainly not by the central government, and not by the local native revenue account.

The west bank of the river had been abandoned as an area first for colored and then for African residence. The municipality had saved Wilken Township by promising not to repair houses in the buffer strip—a remarkable policy for a municipal housing provider—and by promising to demolish houses when decrepit or when paid for. Africans had lost to coloreds the central part of the "old location" with its churches and schools, where the African elite had lived, and another part to the new buffer strip a further five hundred yards south of the new colored area.

Apartheid planners had gotten their way in several respects. They had created a township with a hinterland for all Cradock's Africans and had ended the "mixed" character of the old location; they had demarcated the buffer strips that would eventually be cleared of buildings; they had resisted the National Party councilors' vehement appeals for preservation of the old "mixed" location; and they had insisted on the apartheid principle that Africans living outside the rural reserves allotted to them must limit their economic activities to working as employees, never as entrepreneurs, except in providing limited services to location residents. Cradock councilors had sometimes resisted racially defined policies that did not meet local realities, but there was a limit to their opposition. By now, they, and the town clerk also, were loyal members of the National Party, and, as such, did not challenge the overall policy of apartheid.

THE TRIUMPH OF REGENT STREET: UNSCRAMBLING THE "MIXED" TOWN

Coloreds Search for Security: Separation from Africans, Closeness to Whites

Yet the proclamation of 1961 was not the end of the story. The problem of the town itself, where whites and coloreds lived together, had yet to be resolved. A few months before the proclamation of the new group areas, buffer strips, and hinterland, the national government announced that Regent Street would no longer be the boundary between Cradock's two historically "mixed" communities, the town and the location. It was, indeed, no longer a boundary at all: it had been absorbed as a street within Cradock's first proclaimed colored group area.

After the National Party victory of 1948, coloreds in Cradock faced a new regime dedicated to segregating them from whites and Africans and also to disenfranchising them, thus reducing them to a lower political status, one close to that of Africans. Like small towns in most countries, Cradock had long been losing some of its most enterprising residents of all races to cities—in Cradock's case to Port Elizabeth and Cape Town. Colored shop-keeping families—Alexanders, Raffertys, and Butlers—who had had shops in Cradock town, were leaving for a wider world. There were no colored lawyers, doctors, or accountants in Cradock; coloreds, like Africans, found only laboring occupations, teaching, and the ministry open to them.[114] The growth of a colored skilled working population had been largely stopped by legislation that gave white trade unions control of access to most apprenticeships.[115]

The colored ministers and teachers might have become an effective local political class, but their professional work made them vulnerable and put severe limits on their political activity. The colored churches ran schools, which were subsidized and supervised by the Cape Education Department, and teachers, therefore, were dependent on official good will. Colored teachers' organizations were divided over issues of collaboration with the state; Gavin Lewis has argued that, in this period, politically active colored teachers rarely advocated the interests of working people.[116] Nor is there any record, before 1948, of vigorous organization and persistent lobbying of local authorities by Cradock's coloreds. Though represented equally with Africans on the Location Advisory Board, colored members seldom played forceful roles. The Cradock branch of the African People's Organisation (APO), which represented coloreds only, had acted only spasmodically; in 1938 it protested a proposed compulsory segregation ordinance directed at coloreds living in "mixed" areas, but it left no organization behind in Cradock and no record of joint action with Africans.[117] Yet colored politics in Cradock changed after 1943 when the United Party government established the Coloured Advisory Council (CAdC), offering colored leaders a means to demand material improvements in such areas as housing and social welfare, but with a prolongation of the political status quo; there would be no extension of the Cape franchise to the northern provinces.[118]

Cradock's colored community in 1948 had no leaders of the stature of Calata, who was important not only locally but also in the national African National Congress. A colored tailor, W. E. Lawn, had taken the initiative on colored housing in Cradock, but he had shown little capacity for leadership. Two colored organizations did emerge, one, the Coloured Peoples National Union (CPNU), led locally by Lawn, a branch of a Cape body prepared to work with authorities on welfare issues but opposed to National Party policies of compulsory segregation; the other, the Non-European Ratepayers Association (NERA), an association of colored owners of property in town who objected, in 1946, to the "layout" of a separate colored township. Both organizations seem to have had few members, and their agendas were limited to certain local issues. Neither objected publicly even to the threat to the Cape colored franchise, soon to be abolished by the apartheid government. Both groups were segregationist in relation to Africans, the CPNU explicitly demanding a new section of the location for colored residents only. Having negotiated with the municipality for segregated housing before the coming of apartheid, the CPNU would now be compromised if it sought to lead opposition to a regime that made enforced segregation of all groups its central policy issue. As for the NERA, it was concerned with its own part of Cradock *town* and, after 1948, advocated building a community hall for coloreds in the new colored area and demarcating a separate colored cemetery. It was segregationist only in seeking separation from Africans, but not from whites. It argued for equality of treatment with whites, resisting the imposition of a "whites only" rule in public facilities such as Cradock's park.[119]

After the passage of the 1950 Group Areas Act, the National Party regarded the provision of new houses as inseparable from siting them in racially defined areas. Some National Party town councilors had made colored housing an issue since 1948, with J. J. Gerber stressing that it must be segregated from Africans. Cradock and its colored community therefore faced a new situation: the National Party government, and its members on the council, wanted a colored township, one that could have required the movement and resettling of all the town's and the location's colored residents, ratepayers and tenants alike. As the group most directly affected, coloreds might have been expected to offer a spirited response, but the record of opposition is sparse.

Some of Cradock's councilors and officials seem to have regarded the group areas legislation of 1950 as simply part of a campaign against slum conditions rather than as enforced segregation. In 1952, the medical officer of health identified housing in Cradock's town for "Eurafricans," by whom he meant coloreds, as especially urgent. In July 1954, the town treasurer cautioned that a new colored township was not in the "immediate future"; surveying and approval would take "some time."[120]

Who Should Move? Whites or Coloreds?

Cradock's group areas proposal of 1955 provided "zones for five 'nationalities'": European, Indian, Chinese, Coloured, and Native (map 7). Regent Street would form the boundary between Europeans and all Non-Europeans. Apart from Indian and Chinese zones located next to Regent Street, the rest of the "Existing Native Location" was to become the new colored zone. The "European zone" would be "the remainder of the proclaimed municipal area bounded by the [other] zones."

Coloreds now living in town would be moved into the present "old location," after Africans there were evicted. Indians and Chinese would be inserted between the coloreds and the whites, a "logical" and "self-explanatory" proposal, in the words of the town clerk Van Rooyen. With most of Cradock's coloreds already in the location—only 624 lived in town—Van Rooyen explained that the plan would relocate only a minority, and that no racial group could ever be *omvleuel* (enveloped, surrounded) by another.[121] Instead, the hinterlands would absorb each group's expansion.[122] Furthermore, the plan would require no whites to move. All Indians, Chinese, and coloreds living south of Voortrekker Street in the Mixed Area would have to go further south. The whole project depended on the feasibility of a new African location in Sondagshoek.

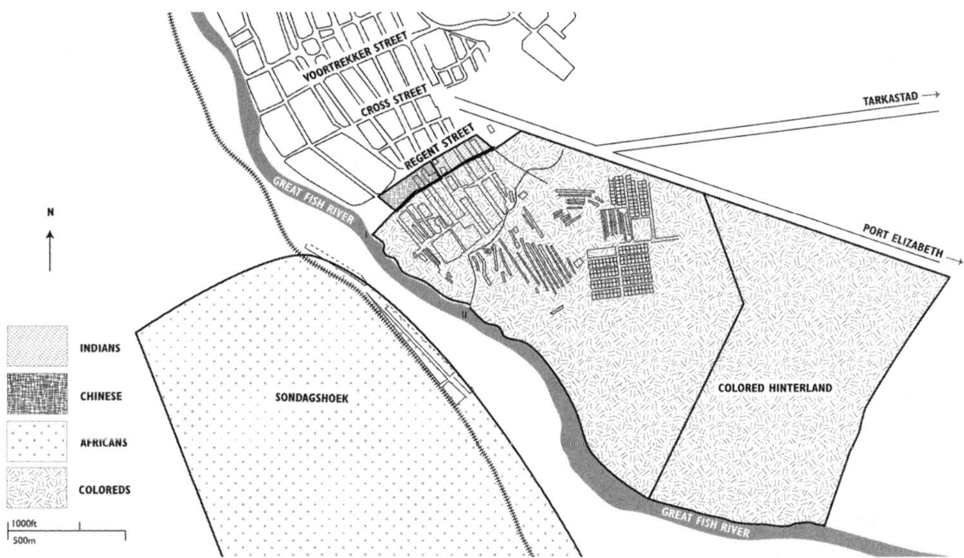

Map 7. Cradock's Proposals for Coloreds and Asians, 1955. (Map by Mariah Reisner, from point-to-point description of proposed group areas in Town Clerk to Secretary Land Tenure Advisory Board, Port Elizabeth, 30 May 1955, CAR, 3/CDK [1953–1962], 19A Group Areas)

In 1955, a subdepartment of the Department of the Interior became the Department of Coloured Affairs, an institution politically active coloreds feared would parallel the Department of Native Affairs for Africans and result in the further subordination of coloreds.[123] But officials from the new department responded critically to Cradock's proposals. One official, Jan Louw, maintained that to place Indians and Chinese between whites and coloreds would "give the coloured [businessman] little hope for business on his own."

I. D. du Plessis, an active member of Cape Town literary society, a noted Afrikaans poet, and student of Cape Malay literature and history, had been appointed the first commissioner for Coloured Affairs.[124] He now gave Cradock a straightforward option to move Africans but not coloreds; he accepted "in principle" the "native location" but rejected the *algehele verskuiwing* (comprehensive moving) of coloreds; the part of town where most coloreds now lived, in the area south of Cross Street, would become the "Coloured Zone."[125] The town clerk protested to the council that other zones would have to be found for Indian and Chinese; sixty-eight lots owned by Europeans and forty-six houses rented by poor Europeans would have to be taken in order to fashion an *aaneenlopende* (unfragmented) colored area. "I cannot see how this could be achieved unless further inroads into the proposed European Area are made," the town clerk said. Since the "area of the proposed Coloured Zone lying along the river bank is good fertile soil and adjoins the town proper or European zone," he urged the council to stick to its guns. The council decided unanimously to do just that.[126]

Coloreds, Du Plessis maintained, were not against the Group Areas Act "as such" but were apprehensive that local authorities "were too likely to shift them to somewhere outside the town." A resolution from a "Coloured Conference" that he had organized asked Coloured Affairs "to keep a watchful eye on application of the Group Areas Act to see that coloureds would not be shifted entirely out of cities and towns."[127] Some officials in the Department of Coloured Affairs and on the Eastern Cape Committee were willing to make concessions to coloreds that local politicians resisted, allowing coloreds to preserve some of the urban areas where they lived so they could profit by living and trading close to whites. Official sympathy for Cradock's town coloreds was combined with a strong antipathy to—actually a fear of—Asians, who, in Cradock's 1955 proposal, would form a "wedge" between white and colored, or even between colored and colored. One group area, cheek by jowl with another, could be damaging to a group with limited resources: Cradock's Asians were all merchants, while earlier colored merchants had virtually disappeared from the town. The Cradock town clerk and the council never explained why they considered their initial proposal of the long Asian wedge "logical and self-evident." Nor had subdepartment officials or the town clerk ever explained why they believed coloreds would gain by being close to whites.

Cradock's council could not itself define group areas; only the Eastern Cape Committee of the Group Areas Board, and the full board in Pretoria, could do that. In 1958, the year after the town engineer T. Kleefstra had recommended abandoning Sondagshoek as a site for African housing (map 5, p. 161), the town clerk sent a new proposal to the Department of Native Affairs and to the Eastern Cape Committee in Port Elizabeth. He called it a "repartition" that accumulated enough land for a colored group area, or areas, and for a further area for hinterland, between the Tarkastad and national roads. The commissioner of Coloured Affairs wrote to the Eastern Cape Committee in 1958 to object that if Cradock's coloreds could not have the area between Regent and Cross streets, they ought to be sent out to Sondagshoek, since otherwise "the necessary separation between Coloureds and Natives . . . will inevitably be delayed." The new proposal provided land too widely separated from the proposed principal layout of the colored area; and besides, the two territories would be divided by a main road, hardly providing the *aaneenlopende* (unfragmented) space on which the state insisted.

The Eastern Cape Committee was responsible for framing a proposal for Cradock that would take into account local opinion before presenting it to the Group Areas Board in Pretoria. The committee now put forward its recommendations (map 8), designating B for "Blankes" or whites, K for "Kleurlinge" or coloreds, and G for "Grenstrook" or border area.[128] Two sections of the

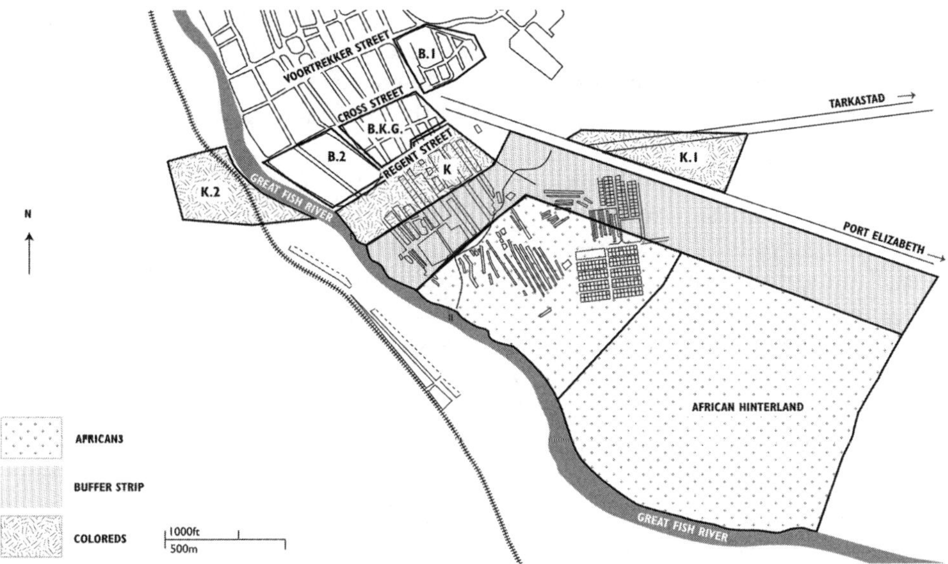

Map 8. Proposals of the Eastern Cape Committee of the Group Areas Board, 1959. (Map by Mariah Reisner, from sketch maps accompanying inquiry into a group area in Cradock District, NAR, GGR G7/283, vol. 1, 17 Sept. 1958 to 10 Nov. 1961)

"white-European" group area (B1 and B2) were to remain "controlled" since they might be declared colored in the future. The old location (K), Sondagshoek (K2), the new area (K1, along the Tarkastad road) were designated as "future colored"; and the "disputed area" between Cross and Regent (BKG), had a future yet to be decided.[129] In early 1959, the Eastern Cape Committee advertised the options in the *Midland News* and invited written representations, which were to be considered at a public meeting in Cradock's town hall.[130]

The municipality wanted the whole municipal area north of Regent Street to be declared a white area. If it were declared a colored area, whites would have to move out, and coloreds between Voortrekker and Cross Streets would also have to go. If it were a white group area, on the other hand, only the coloreds would have to move. The attorney Pieter Coetzee, spokesman for whites in the disputed area, argued that whites in that area were poor and would find it difficult to sell and then to buy in the better parts of town; if colored owners had to move, they would be selling to whites with higher incomes. Advocate Seligson, representing "the Coloured community . . . [of] businessmen, artisans and teachers . . . members of the upper middle class," rejected the "fallacious interpretation" that coloreds could move easily because they were poorer. "By allowing the area to remain as it is, by a voluntary process we shall be able to separate the groups in time to come. . . . The Europeans can easily be removed to other parts. The Coloureds have every right to remain where they are where they have schools and churches as well as their spiritual interest." Clergymen asked about the future of their church and school buildings. "What guarantee can you give us that churches and schools will not be closed?" "You must either accept or doubt the Minister's word," said the chairman, "They are going to remain there."

Identification of an area as belonging particularly to a racial or ethnic group, but with other racial groups legally entitled to buy or occupy land there, had led, ever since the 1880s, to bitter controversy over "penetration" by Indians in Natal and the Transvaal.[131] Van Rooyen now argued that, since the 1920s, coloreds had "infiltrated" the "disputed area" in Cradock. *Wrywing* (friction) between racial groups, the central problem in urban areas that apartheid was supposed to solve, was especially likely to occur, many felt, in such mixed residential areas. Van Rooyen insisted that "many complaints are received as a result of Europeans and Coloureds living next to each other." But Seligson countered that "Europeans in that area are satisfied to live . . . next to the Coloureds." On this issue, the town clerk deferred to the attorney, Coetzee, who agreed with Seligson: "The Europeans I represent do not insist on a change, they merely ask that if there is a change that it be declared a European area. They do not insist that the Coloureds be removed. They are quite happy to stay as they are."

Seligson had developed, without identifying it as such, the standard position of the United Party, now the parliamentary opposition. Unwilling to treat coloreds as social and political equals, the United Party, like Seligson, considered coloreds an "appendage" of whites: civilized people who should be treated as more closely associated with Europeans than with Africans. The coloreds in Cradock's disputed area were of the "better class . . . [and] they have a right to be regarded as a European group. . . . The municipality has just assumed that they must be moved. There may be racial dissension in Cradock because the Coloureds are known as 'God's stepchildren.' I ask you to show that the coloured people are not God's stepchildren but entitled to the same rights as others. . . . There should not be a Group area in that area." Seligson had visited a house in the disputed area: "I can ask you to come along [to a colored house] and see for yourself to what extent this person has adopted the European outlook on life."

Seligson's reference to "stepchildren" came from *God's Stepchildren,* a highly controversial 1924 novel deploring miscegenation that was written by Sarah Gertrude Millin, an author frequently at odds with South African liberals. According to one biographer, Millin's "abhorrence of miscegenation overshadowed her sympathies for the coloured outcast."[132] Seligson was rejecting Millin's view that miscegenation produced inferior beings; differences among coloreds were, in his opinion, differences of class; coloreds were "entitled" to equality and capable of adopting the "European outlook on life," closer to whites than to Africans, but not fully equal to them. He envisaged separating the racial "groups" by a "voluntary process."

In concluding the hearing, W. S. Gouws, chair of the Eastern Cape Committee, approved Cradock's preference for a "very long period of evacuation" for those who had to move. But these were questions of detail: "We recommend that the Group Areas Act be applied or not, and that is all."[133] The proceedings had been polite, no doubt because only one mobilized local group, the colored NERA, had sent a representative to protest. Apparently, no officials were present from the white political parties; no one to defend the interests of ratepayers, who were nearly all white; and no representative of the Independent (Congregational) church or of the Dutch Reformed church, whose two white congregations in town were the patrons of the colored Immanuel church and school. Nor was anyone there from the Rapportryers, a National Party organization of young men from the Chamber of Commerce or from the Afrikaanse Sakekamer (Afrikaner Chamber of Commerce). None of Cradock's colored leaders appeared, relying instead on Seligson to make their case. The disputed area apparently did not pose a serious problem for white middle-class people, who had little invested in the housing of poor whites and poor coloreds at the edge of town. Nor was the disputed area a scene of chronic violence. But the lack of protest by poor Afrikaners whose residences were at stake (many, perhaps most, of whom voted for the National Party) is surprising. So is the absence of colored teachers and ministers whose churches and schools were in the disputed area.

In an editorial after the hearing, the *Midland News* took Seligson's line: "The [Group Areas] law does not read that the Act MUST be applied in Cradock or elsewhere but only if it should be proved desirable," and, in any case, Cradock's disputed area had been a place of "complete harmony." (In fact, the act had been "deemed applicable to the whole of the Cape Province on 30 March 1951.) However, if the act were to be implemented, the editorial continued, surely it would be better to move the whites, because all the "amenities" for coloreds—schools and churches—were in the disputed area. Two months later the paper printed an "Open Letter to the Mayor" from colored "Ratepayers," whose tone was anything but benign. The writers noted the cost of declaring the disputed area white—£142,000—the taxable value of all the properties involved. Why not offer "less fortunate Whites" a housing scheme in an area "beyond doubt a white one or do you wish them to act as your buffer strip between the non-White and the prosperous whites?" F. W. Michau, Cradock's National Party mayor, replied at length in the next issue of the *Midland News*. The cited cost of expropriating colored "affected" properties was misleading, Michau said, because the Group Areas Development Board could "control, acquire and dispose of affected properties," hence the net cost of colored housing would not be total rateable (taxable) value. Enforcement of group areas was a "social necessity." A year later, with the council and Cradock residents still awaiting a decision from the Eastern Cape Committee, a new mayor, L. L. Scheepers, in his 1960 annual report, wrote that whatever the decision was, "we shall have to accept it."[134]

A Temporary Victory for Cross Street

In July 1959, Gouws, chair of the Eastern Cape Committee, completed his report on Cradock, designating the old location and the area along the national road as future colored group areas (map 8, p. 173). He reassured the commissioner of Coloured Affairs that the council had the material resources to develop "a decent coloured township" with ample room for future expansion. There was, he acknowledged, a disadvantage in creating two separate colored areas, since development would be expensive, but the required buffer strip between coloreds and Africans would make a consolidated colored area impossible. This was an additional argument for making the disputed area (BKG) colored by combining it with the old location.

The disputed area was, of course, the crucial issue. It was a choice between drawing the southern boundary of the white area at Cross Street or at Regent Street, the traditional boundary between town and location. Gouws strongly opposed Cradock's proposal to declare the area white; colored churches and schools had been there for a long time—only one colored church was outside it. Apart from the two housing schemes for poor whites, only ten properties were owned; six of these were occupied by whites, the other four vacant or undeveloped. Otherwise, the area was predominantly colored. The presence of two small white housing schemes there, while unfortunate, should not present an insuperable problem; these *huisies* (little houses, cheaply built during the war) were now "more suitable for occupation by coloreds than by whites," and it was desirable to put the whites elsewhere and give the *huisies* to coloreds. The area in dispute, bounded on the north by Cross Street, should be declared colored in line with the policy "that wherever possible a part of the town ought to be conceded to coloreds."

Between Voortrekker Street and Cross Street (the proposed new southern edge of the white area) were lower-income white houses and some Indian and colored businesses, in undesirable "mixed living." This area, Gouws said, should be declared white. Coloreds who occupied and owned thirty-two properties there should be moved south of Cross Street or into the old location. The hostel of the convent, a Catholic church, and the Immanuel church—the Dutch Reformed Mission church for coloreds—in this now-to-be-defined white area could be allowed to stay temporarily, under permit; so, too, could the small number of Asians. The area between Cross and Regent streets would have to be vacated by whites within ten years, as would the newly designated white area have to be vacated by coloreds also in ten years. But Africans in the old location (K) would be required to move in one year to allow construction of the new colored township so that coloreds could move in. Gouws's committee concluded its report with an ideological justification: group areas in Cradock, as elsewhere, were not only desirable but also essential. They would foster "parallel and independent development"; mixed living was incompatible with healthy race relations; group areas could improve planning of neighborhoods, industrial areas, and traffic routes; and Christian welfare and *opheffingswerk* (uplift), which was impossible to carry on in mixed areas, could go forward.[135]

The secretary of the Group Areas Board in Pretoria questioned the lack of a group area for Asians and raised the possibility of pushing the new location for Africans even farther out of town. But the new African location boundaries were about to be proclaimed, and the Department of Bantu Administration (formerly Native Affairs) would hardly have welcomed reopening that core issue.[136] On 25 April 1960, the board decided to proceed with an amended proposal: the old location (K) would become a colored group area, with Africans there "disqualified" and required to move out within a year. The area between Regent and Cross streets would become colored, and whites would have to vacate it in five, not ten, years; the area between Voortrekker and Cross Streets would also have to be vacated by any coloreds in five, not ten, years. The white area was now diminished in size by two "controlled" areas (B1 and B2), presently occupied largely by poor whites, which might be needed later "as a possible extension of the colored area." The board proposed that a "border strip" on Cross Street be inquired into as a place for light industry.[137] Proclamation 436, dated 30 December 1960, promulgated all these decisions, including a "border strip" on Cross Street.

No areas were defined for Indians and Chinese because of their "small number." Asians who wished to stay where they were would have to apply for permits after the "evacuation period has expired."[138] The Union cabinet had decided to allow *permit gebiede* (permit areas) as substitutes for group areas in towns with a small number of Indians.[139] Gouws reported that Cradock, with seven Indian and three Chinese households, ought to provide a permit area between the white and colored areas, which would result in "outstanding trade prospects." But the town council, representing the public and ratepayers, were strongly opposed to any kind of area for Indians and Chinese and would rather be rid of them altogether. "The council can see no reason why Indians and Chinese, after proclamation of group areas, should not be controlled by permits and be required to move [*om pad te gee,* literally, 'get out of the way']."[140]

Few in Cradock objected publicly to the group areas proclamation. The *Midland News* had taken the side of the coloreds on the Cross Street issue. Local National Party members, for their part, though somewhat chagrined that their municipality had been overridden by the Group Areas Board, were unwilling to attack their government. But some whites in the contested area did object; six ratepayers sent a petition to the town clerk protesting the boundary of the colored area as "totally unacceptable," because it would bring "the colored right into our front door." White and nonwhite children "would be mixed up in the same street," and their own lots would "have no market value and be difficult to sell." The petitioners asked that the line be shifted so that the coloreds would face onto Market Street, instead of onto High, so that all houses on High Street, where the petitioners owned nine lots, would be occupied by whites. The secretary responded that the Group Areas Board would be reluctant to change its mind and resisted a solution that would bring coloreds and whites "very close together."[141] Ultimately the white tenants were allowed to stay in the municipal houses involved, back-to-back with houses occupied by coloreds, until such time as the lots came under the provisions of the Group Areas Development Act, and the whites would have to move.[142]

"Must Move Again, After Four Years"

Under the 1960 proclamation of group areas, all "affected" properties in Cradock, that is, properties owned and occupied, or simply occupied, by racially "disqualified" people, had to be registered with the Group Areas Board within one month. The Group Areas Development Act of 1961 and the Group Areas Amendment Act of 1962 reinforced acceleration of the pace of declaring properties "affected." When a property was "affected" by the race of its occupant, the owner had a choice whether the property would be regarded as affected or not, presumably to allow white owners to continue to own land occupied by disqualified people, without forcing such property on to the market.[143] The problem remained of finding sufficient land on which to build substitute dwellings for "affected" people, those who found themselves in the wrong group area and had to move out within a stated period. As this development process began in Cradock, it soon became clear that the settlement embodied in the 1960 Proclamation had been no settlement at all.

P. W. Botha, by now the minister of Coloured Affairs (and later prime minister and president), intervened forcefully to rehouse all "Europeans who have to move from the proclaimed Coloured area." He sent a "Technical Officer (Housing)" to persuade Cradock to build, "without delay," fifty new houses for poor whites in the white area, at especially low rates of interest. The town clerk recommended to the council that the land be sold "at a reasonable figure" to the Central Housing Board; the board would erect the buildings because the municipal staff were "more than fully occupied" with building the new African location. A year later, the town clerk concluded that some whites could not afford the rents of the new houses.[144]

Meanwhile, the minister of Coloured Affairs and the Cradock municipality were simultaneously under pressure to place all coloreds in their own recently demarcated group area. Great progress had been made on the new African location—350 houses already built. But the new colored area in the old location had not yet been surveyed, let alone planned.[145] Cradock was facing a statutory gun: it was required by an order, under the Natives (Urban Areas) Consolidation Act of 1945, to remove all coloreds from the "Bantu area" by the end of 1962. This was impossible, the town clerk wrote, requesting an extension to the end of 1963.[146] He still had to find space for the coloreds who were to be moved out of the white area, but he could not use land in the old location until all Africans there were out. Cradock could still have built some housing for coloreds in the disputed area on vacant lots, but when the town engineer, Kleefstra, turned to planning the new group area, the story of Sondagshoek in 1957 was repeated: Kleefstra became the first official to face the real issue publicly: if housing in the new group area were properly planned, there simply was not enough land.[147]

In 1964, R. F. G. Allan, Van Rooyen's successor as town clerk, proposed to develop immediately the second area allocated to coloreds, the 64-morgen area along the national road, known as Taaiboschleegte.[148] Botha said that his Department of Coloured Affairs, while opposed to two colored areas in any town, was willing to consider a future single colored group area, since the existing colored group area (the former disputed area and the old location) was too small. All colored residents would ultimately go to the new colored area, and the existing colored area would be de-proclaimed.[149] In a meeting with Botha, Cradock's new mayor, Dr. G. de V. Morrison explained that the plans had seemed fine two years earlier when they needed only 350 houses. Now, considering population growth, they needed 350 more—good planning, he said, required doubling present need. The regional representative of the Department of Community Development, A. C. du Preez, then applied some apartheid planning theory: the council's proposal to expand the existing group area across the national road would make impossible an access road to the African location without traversing a colored built-up area, something the Department of Bantu Administration would not permit; this was an added argument for moving the whole colored area out of town.[150] Allan, noting that the refusal to permit two colored areas would attract a lot of opposition, even agitation, pleaded that coloreds who had already moved to the recently proclaimed colored group area be generously compensated when forced to move again, and the owners of properties in the buffer strips given the same consideration. A high school, a primary school for about 1,350 pupils, and a community center should be built promptly in the new colored area to make the movement of the colored community there easier, more acceptable, and faster.[151]

At a public meeting in September 1964, the mayor, seven councilors, and four officials faced ninety-five angry colored residents. The mayor said that two alternative schemes were under consideration—the council's scheme, a "bottleneck scheme" to join the two proposed colored areas across the national road, or a new single group area in Taaiboschleegte. (He was disingenuous in suggesting that the bottleneck scheme was still a live option.) A. B. Werner, of the Non-European Ratepayers Association, replied that schools did not require so much land and that Taaiboschleegte was hardly suitable; the colored community should be consulted when a colored residential area was to be discussed with government. Eerwaarde Kruger, the white minister in the colored Dutch Reformed Mission Church, whose church building was at stake, argued for the status quo, and R. Butler, secretary of the NERA, stated defiantly that coloreds would not leave.[152]

In October, the regional representative of the Department of Planning sent to his minister a copy of an article in the Port Elizabeth *Evening Post* headed: "Must move again, after four years." It was based on interviews with two unnamed colored Cradock residents who claimed that they had already moved—one had built a house. The town clerk, the article said, had acknowledged that the bottleneck scheme proposed by the council was "against Group Areas Act policy" because "Africans coming into town would have to go through the Coloured area."[153] A petition signed by 128 colored owners and renters appealed to the council to preserve Cross Street to Regent Street as a colored area, to develop the old location for coloreds, *and* to add enough land east of the national road. But all the principal decisions had already been taken, including the de-proclamation of the colored group area. Cradock was already energetically developing Taaiboschleegte as a separate and solely colored township, with provision for churches, schools, and a community center—and as the *only* colored group area in Cradock.

By a second proclamation of group areas in Cradock, on 20 August 1971, the recently established colored group area between Cross Street to Regent Street was changed again, from colored to white (map 9). The areas formerly set aside for future change to colored use, (B1 and B2), now became white; and Taaiboschleegte (K1 on map 8), demarcated back in 1958 for expansion of the colored area and now named Michausdal, was declared wholly colored. The former border along Cross Street was now within the white area.[154]

As far as the definition of racially defined areas in Cradock was concerned, the story was virtually complete. Regent Street, formerly the southern boundary of the municipal area, and the northern boundary of the location, had become the boundary between the white group area and the remains of the old location, now empty, no longer a new colored group area. But the drawing and the enforcing of group areas in Cradock hardly came to an end, for in 1980, yet another proclamation expanded the colored area to provide for more colored housing into Michausdal's own hinterland.[155]

The council developed Michausdal rapidly, but colored owners of twenty houses and two shops now found themselves in the "wrong" area. The municipality's efforts with sorting and resettling were energetic: according to the Mayor's Minute in 1970, 300 sub-economic houses had been completed with another 178 planned, and 28 economic houses were under construction. Still, a further 250 to 300 sub-economic houses, plus 100 privately built or economic

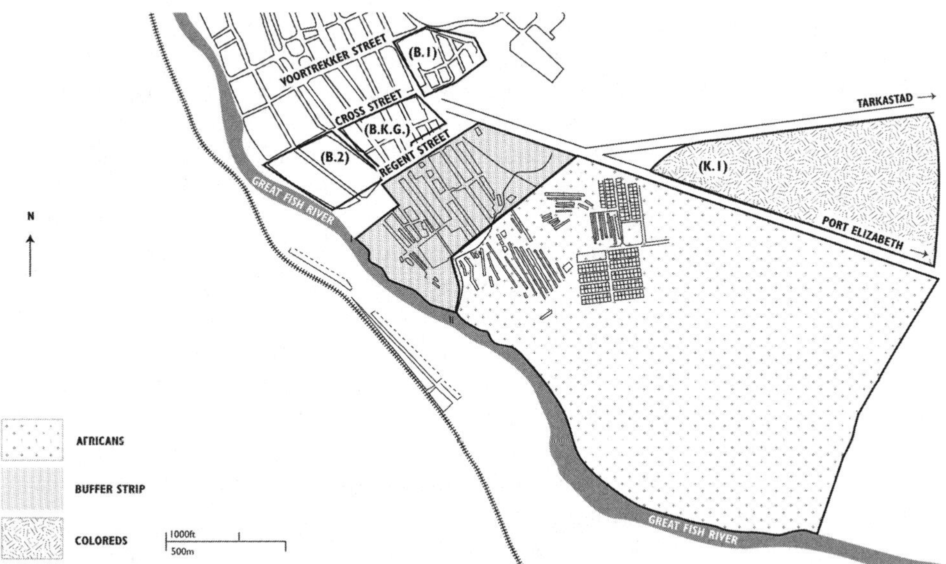

Map 9. Second Proclamation of Group Areas, 1971. (Map by Mariah Reisner, from Press Statement Map, Proclamation 178, 20.8.71, District Record Book, Magistrate's Office, Cradock, with additions by the author)

houses, were needed "to house the whole of Cradock's coloured population."[156] It was to be a long business because the 1971 proclamation provided for delays by owners who did not wish to move. In 1977, Kathleen Rayepen, a colored veteran of the Joint Council in the 1930s, was still living in town. Without leaving her house, she had lived in the Mixed Area of town until 1960, then in the new colored group area from 1960 to 1970, and finally again in town; she was now an "affected" person, a colored in a white group area, the last colored resident there, she said.[157]

The application of the Group Areas Act to Cradock from 1955 to 1971 had polarized officials and members of the public into partisans of two streets, Regent and Cross. In 1955, the municipality, reflecting the views of its white ratepayers, had proposed keeping Regent Street as the southern boundary of the town, and, in 1971, it instead became the boundary of the white group area, where only whites could own and occupy property and to which members of other races could be admitted only on temporary permits. Between the two dates, national officials in the Department of Coloured Affairs and in the group areas bureaucracy had argued for a partition of the town considerably more generous to coloreds, using Cross Street as its boundary and placing the historic Regent Street inside the new colored group area. But the enlarged space for coloreds in the municipal area turned out to be hopelessly inadequate, boxed in by the recently proclaimed new African location. Thereupon, unwilling to abandon the doctrine of a single continuous group area, the national government in 1971 restored Regent Street as the boundary, established a new colored township outside of town and over time removed all colored residences, schools, and churches from town and from the old location, many of which had been there since the early nineteenth century.

The officials took the doctrines of apartheid seriously. They were prepared to improve the welfare of colored people, but wholly in the context of white supremacy and in line with apartheid theory of frictionless living in segregated housing. The notion of a buffer strip that had caused such dispute over the boundaries of the new African location was not part of the Department of Coloured Affairs proposals. In fact, the department wanted coloreds to live near whites, expressing anxiety that coloreds who lived too close to Africans would be corrupted, and those who lived too close to Asians would suffer economically. (They may also have had a political motive—generosity to coloreds in an urban settlement would perhaps convince them of the government's good faith even though they had been removed from the common voters' roll in 1956.)

The officials gained little support in Cradock from local whites, most of whom had probably accepted the town clerk's dubious argument that coloreds had illegitimately "infiltrated" or "penetrated" a white area of town, even though there had been no legally defined white areas to infiltrate in that era. But in the public hearing on the municipality's proposal, the whites living in the disputed area had explicitly said that they had no difficulty living with coloreds, while admitting candidly that if someone had to move they would prefer it to be someone else. In 1964, the municipality, having been told by its own staff that the proclaimed colored group area in town was not big enough for present—let alone future—needs, tried to advance a "bottleneck" scheme to link the two pieces of its group area, which would have left the Cross Street boundary intact and the coloreds in the disputed area undisturbed. But there was, it seems, no popular support of coloreds from local whites, and hence the municipality buckled before the vigorous insistence of P. W. Botha, then minister of Coloured Affairs, who insisted on a single colored group area some distance from either Cross or Regent Street. The only vehement local opposition had come from the white ministers of mission churches, Roman Catholic and Anglican, and from a dying United Party, whose veteran member and former mayor, J. A. Cull, urged coloreds to press for the "bottleneck" scheme.

The return of the boundary to Regent Street symbolized the lack of any fundamental redistribution of power and resources in Cradock. In arguing for the Cross Street boundary, Coloured Affairs officials had been promoting a significant material redistribution. The disputed area was part of the old town of Cradock, receiving all the services of the rest of the town—piped water, electricity, and elimination of wastes. If the coloreds had lived there, they would have been free of the curfew and of many of the restrictions of the Liquor Act of 1928; they would have enjoyed access to Cradock's downtown and to the white residential areas where most coloreds worked. It was not to be. The new township in Michausdal achieved a rapid and complete rehousing of Cradock's colored community, some privately, some publicly built. The press release that asserted that the "new Coloured group area offers almost unlimited expansion possibilities" was strictly true of the hinterland, but it could not claim the generous augmentation of resources for the colored community promised by the Cross Street boundary.

Conclusion

The Age of Segregation and the Age of Apartheid

In partial dissent from Deborah Posel's contention that the National Party came to power in 1948 without a definite and comprehensive apartheid plan that it proceeded to implement,[1] this book has been structured around Rodney Davenport's distinction between the age of segregation, 1910 to 1948, and the age of apartheid, 1948 to 1994. From the perspective of the leading citizens of Cradock, the policies of the apartheid regime were really new, not simply an evolution and reinforcement of white supremacy and traditional racial separation.

Prior to 1948, segregation was not a bone of contention between English- and Afrikaans-speaking whites in Cradock, but it was frequently alluded to in local politics. In 1926, a colored leader complained that the new Location Advisory Board would include both Africans and coloreds; he would have preferred a board for coloreds only. In the same year, the mayor, John Deary, spoke of segregation as a settled national policy that justified separate locations for Africans and coloreds. A wide range of officials and individuals called for residential segregation of coloreds to prevent them from illicitly purveying liquor to Africans. And in discussions of public health, officials and white residents pressed for segregated clinical facilities because they believed people of color to be a threat to the health of whites—the so-called sanitation syndrome. In 1936 and 1937, in response to prodding from its Cape headquarters, the Cradock branch of the Afrikaanse Christelike Vroue Vereeniging (ACVV) noted that there was "undesirable" residential mixing in town but did not raise the issue with the town council. Organized farmers, representing the dominant interest in town and district, also had protested, from 1929 onward, that the location was a haven for work-shy layabouts and was reducing the supply of labor for farms; in 1941, they demanded a fenced location, but the council turned them down. In 1943, a group of colored residents in town pressed for housing for themselves and for location coloreds, segregated from Africans. The council was sympathetic but by 1948 had failed to settle on a scheme. None of these demands represented a coherent program of segregation. Rather, segregation was intermittently advocated in Cradock in an ad hoc and unsystematic way, often with reference to assumed national policies.

National and Local Impulses in the Age of Segregation

At least since 1855, the Cradock location had been under the autocratic control of a superintendent appointed by the municipality; the location had no representative political institutions. The Natives (Urban Areas) Act of 1923 aimed to define more clearly a municipality's responsibilities to its location: it was to control access of newcomers, provide housing, audit accounts through a native revenue account, and create a Location Advisory Board to represent residents. The implied ideal plan was to create segregated, well-managed, healthy, crime-free locations as neighborhoods for Africans—an ideology of uplift for a disenfranchised racial group. As it turned out, Cradock's Location Advisory Board, established in 1927, was a toothless body and strictly advisory.

A principal concern of the Department of Native Affairs and of the municipality, and one of the objects of the act, was to limit the number of Africans admitted to the location and allowed to reside there permanently—policies that long preceded the enunciation of the Stallard doctrine of 1922. The 1923 Urban Areas Act denied Africans the right to buy land in a *location;* the Native Laws Amendment Act of 1937—which aimed to remedy defects in the 1923 act—removed the right of Africans to buy land in a *town* and instituted a biennial census of locations, in the hope of identifying a labor "surplus." In 1938, Cradock and a large number of small towns were declared "closed" to Africans who lacked certain qualifications. The municipality then imposed increasing restrictions right up to 1948, but it failed to find the surplus African laborers who farmers insisted were living in the location.

Not all national interventions were so purely restrictive. Under the Public Health Act (1920), the Health Department appointed assistant medical officers of health with extensive powers to make two- to three-day inspections of towns and their locations; the Department of Native Affairs in 1935 appointed inspectors of urban areas. Both sets of officers visited Cradock and produced elaborate and detailed reports, studies of far higher quality than Cradock officials could have produced themselves. Responding to damning evidence in those reports, local officials took steps they would not have taken otherwise. Thus, with limited local financial support, the town acquired a location dispensary (1927), which was expanded into a clinic (1937), a full-time medical officer of health (1938), and a health center (1946).

The health center was a product of a 1944 landmark commission, headed by Dr. Henry Gluckman, that proposed a radically new, nonracial, approach to South African public health. Gluckman proposed health centers to implement a range of health and education programs, but the results of the Health Department's interventions were in fact modest. Union officials could not give orders to the municipality, and they had limited powers, if any, to incur additional expenditure. Hence, by 1946, the location had only 22 water taps, compared to

4 in 1924; and 248 lavatories in 1946, compared to 94 in 1931. The difficulties, financial and social, of applying an ambitious program such as Gluckman's in a parsimonious multiracial society had not been faced. The annual rate of infant mortality among Africans and coloreds in the location remained far higher than that among whites in town right next door.

Thus, national intervention in South African towns was both Stallardist (controlling access) and Gluckmanist (expanding health services). The latter strain aligns Cradock's history with towns throughout the Western world on the eve of the welfare state; the former lies at the root of South Africa's distinctive regimes of first segregation and then apartheid—policies designed to thwart the permanent urbanization of Africans in order to secure a supply of low-wage labor.

The dual motives of controlling residence and improving services were combined most clearly in policies of public housing, for all loans for public housing had racial labels attached. Municipalities were responsible for finding sites and for subsequently administering the loans. Some new African housing was built in the location in 1927, 145 single-roomed houses on unfenced lots. A further 288 houses—Wilken Township—were built during the Second World War, under pressure from the Department of Native Affairs, one more case of a national department pressing a reluctant municipality. But in all its public housing projects, for whites as well as Africans, the frugal municipality never made full use of the loan funds made available to it, despite urging from the Central Housing Board.

Strictly speaking, this new housing was earmarked for "Natives," but in fact it came to be occupied by both coloreds and Africans. From about 1943, loans were separately allocated to African and to colored housing, with the intent that each new development in the location would be racially exclusive. But some colored residents organized themselves to try to persuade the council to separate them from Africans on land outside, not inside, the location. Just before the election of May 1948, the municipality decided to hire a town planner to find a site for a separate colored township. The national Department of Native Affairs had long wanted towns like Cradock with mixed locations of Africans and coloreds to provide separate townships for each group. And other agencies, including the police, were pressing for action on colored housing for practical administrative reasons—above all, to stop coloreds from providing their African neighbors with liquor.

In 1948, at the end of the age of segregation, the Cradock location had changed in limited respects since the Urban Areas Act of 1923. The institutions of control remained in place and, in some cases, had been tightened: the location was still governed autocratically by a superintendent with a powerless advisory board of Africans and coloreds; African residents remained subject to a curfew; liquor consumption and production were controlled, if differently, for

Africans and coloreds; control of access to the location for both Africans and coloreds had been tightened up, and members of both groups could be denied access for long-term residence.

There had, however, been some improvements in services to the location, though most modern services still stopped at the town's edge. Although the town's new sewerage system was not extended to the location, the water supply in the location had been improved; the streets were kept cleaner; the elimination of human wastes was more efficient. In the new Wilken Township, 288 houses were on fenced lots, each with a pail lavatory and woodshed, but together they comprised only about 25 percent of all location houses—once more a municipal housing project had stopped with the job a quarter done. Colored housing, too, had stalled; the old location, housing coloreds and Africans, which Dr. Murray had described in 1924 as no credit to the town, remained.

The Union government was not the sole source of increased funding. The agitation for better water supply for the location began at least in 1913 and involved a local photographer, W. W. Lidbetter; a newspaper editor, James Butler; a magistrate, W. Vlok; and a group of English-speaking women. The leading lawyer in Cradock, Alfred Metcalf, frequently contributed to public health projects for the location in such a way that the council could not refuse. Out of this local initiative came a better water supply, the first public housing for Africans since 1903, a dispensary, and generally a local discussion of location issues unknown before. But this interest never developed into a set of more generous policies supported by Cradock's white ratepayers. The voluntary interracial Joint Council remained a small, isolated body until its demise in 1940.

In the age of segregation, white women played an important part in programs directed at poor whites and people of color. Ethnic divisions between English- and Afrikaans-speaking whites and the long commitment of the ACVV to help the white poor, who were mostly Afrikaners, meant that interest in the location was limited to a small group of English speakers. Afrikaner women in Cradock were led by an ardent member of the National Party. No such political connection was found among English-speaking women; but those who joined the Joint Council had long been involved in "native" issues, such as securing a better water supply in the location. In the mid-1920s they lost the support they initially received, and in the 1930s their Women's Civic Association died. Perhaps they were increasingly attracted to temperance activism, and after women gained the franchise in 1930, the National Council of Women made married women's property rights their central concern. In Cradock, the original WCA was crucially dependent on a few women, without whom no location dispensary would have been built in 1927. The Joint Council lost its most important single white member in 1937 when nurse Mary Butler resigned after a dispute with African nurses and location residents. With the coming of the war, interest in the location waned, and English-speaking women turned to a range of war-related activities.

In general, Union government departments cooperated with municipal officials throughout the age of segregation. Visiting officials had little to offer but the occasional public scolding and well-informed advice. They had limited powers and rarely commanded significant resources, though the salary of the nurse in the location clinic was subsidized by the government from 1929, and much more generous funding was available in the brief period of "social medicine," between 1944 and 1948. Loans for housing, though also subsidized, had to be paid back with interest. Town ratepayers stoutly resisted suggestions that the town bear financial responsibility for both the town and the location, or that the town accept deficits to narrow the gap in welfare between the two. In fact, the council, misreading the 1923 Urban Areas Act, constantly strove to make the location pay for itself. While the act aimed to ensure that all moneys raised in the location were spent there, it did not intend to set a ceiling on expenditure for the location. Always looking for increased location revenue, the council eagerly grasped at the opportunity to open a beer hall in 1938, using some of its revenue to lower the rents in a new location under construction from 1941. Although Africans made frequent requests to close the beer hall, the municipality was never willing to do so, and it was burned down by Africans in 1980. No powerfully organized local groups in Cradock advocated ambitious housing programs: the new location started in 1941 was due to a Department of Native Affairs initiative.

From Segregation to Apartheid

The 1937 Native Laws Amendment Act (restricting Africans' rights to move to town) was indeed a "triumph of Colonel Stallard," but it did not signal a decisive trend toward more restrictions in all areas of policy. In fact, in the 1930s, segregation became a matter for national debate. Under pressure from the National Party opposition, the United Party government put forward "voluntary" segregation as a solution when local conflicts arose over residential segregation of coloreds from whites. In 1938 it drafted a bill to provide for plebiscites in mixed areas where white residents were demanding segregation: if 75 percent of owners in an area wanted it, an area could be declared "white," and the municipality could expropriate property, compensate owners, and rehouse residents. Compulsory segregation had also been proposed in the Cape Provincial Council in 1938, and Cradock's African People's Organization (APO), representing coloreds, had protested against it. However problematical and evasive, this proposal favored an ad hoc approach, an attempt to meet the problem only where there was public demand, rather than an imposition of segregation on all towns, as was subsequently required by the Group Areas Act of 1950. The 1938 proposal was eventually withdrawn.

The 1948 election brought to power an Afrikaner National Party claiming to possess an appropriate set of policies—apartheid—for the governance of

South Africa. That event, and the survival of the new regime until 1994, added the word "apartheid" to the world's languages. In the Sauer Report of 1947 the National Party had synthesized an ideological justification of white supremacy, a rationale for systematic segregation to end interracial friction, and an appeal to Afrikaner social exclusiveness, which was expressed especially in conflicts between the Afrikaner poor and people of color in mixed neighborhoods in the Cape and the Transvaal.

It is true, as Posel has noted, that there were no comprehensive and coordinated planning documents in 1948. And according to Ivan Evans, policies in Native Affairs were effectively implemented in detail only after the appointment of Dr. Hendrik Verwoerd as minister in 1950.[2] Yet in its first five years, the new government passed a body of legislation that was remarkably coherent and clearly based on the principles proclaimed in 1948: enforcement of legal racial identification, prevention of mixed marriages, disenfranchisement of coloreds, and inauguration of local "Bantu authorities," to name a few statutes. Though it was not set out in explicit detail, a coherent scheme was manifested in the government's actions.

Some of this highly controversial legislation had an impact on municipal affairs, particularly when National Party councilors in Cradock began to agitate for colored housing: it had been rare in the age of segregation for any councilors to urge public housing for coloreds or indeed for the location as a whole. The question acquired urgency with the passage of the Group Areas Act of 1950, which enacted compulsory residential and commercial segregation, aiming to abolish all mixed areas throughout South Africa, rather than dealing with local problems ad hoc.

Applying such new policies required visits to Cradock by officials with different agendas from the assistant medical officers of health and the inspectors of locations in the 1920s and 1930s. These new officials were largely concerned, not with minor administrative questions, such as the curfew or admitting particular people to the location, but with the application of broad apartheid policies, especially the demarcation of racially defined residential areas. But the Cradock town clerk and the town council still had to attend to ongoing administration, and national officials frequently found them unwilling to address the government's agenda with what they regarded as proper urgency. At least one service of the national government in Cradock—the systematic inspections by medical officers—showed signs of decline. In the age of segregation, from W. A. Murray on, each report had followed a set pattern; each was carefully linked to the immediately preceding report, and each abounded in information. In 1969, an official of the health department, J. H. Steyn, made an inspection of the Cradock urban area. His report was unsatisfactory, not because he was concerned with high apartheid policy, but because he failed to follow the measured path of his colleagues in the pre-apartheid era.

In 1953, when the Cape chief native commissioner, J. van Heerden, undertook to make the boundaries of the Cradock location conform to current apartheid policy, he adopted a peremptory style unheard of in the preceding era. He virtually ordered the Cradock town clerk to provide buffer strips around the proposed African location. At a public meeting to explain these policies to the resentful African community and Cradock councilors and officials, Van Heerden arrogantly defended the boundary strips, refusing to explain why coloreds did not need strips as well. At the same meeting, one of his officials threatened the municipality with a cutoff of funds for all "purposes whatsoever." But the Native Affairs Department faced serious local opposition. The municipality dug in its heels after the town engineer declared the plan for strips impracticable. Even local National Party members opposed the strips, if they meant that an expensive new location had to be built. So Cradock was spared moving its location across the river; Wilken Township remained in the buffer strips, and the town promised to demolish houses over time.

A new Sub-Department of Coloured Affairs, founded in 1943, was responsible for administering the Group Areas Act. From the beginning of discussions concerning Cradock, its officials were prejudiced in favor of coloreds, preferring to keep the colored group area close to town. They showed none of the highhandedness of their colleagues in Native Affairs, but they were still enforcers of group area segregation. In Cradock they opposed the municipality's proposal to sustain the status quo for whites by moving the coloreds out. But the group area they chose was far too small. Their proposal was sustainable only by earmarking a second group area for coloreds, which was later vetoed by the minister, because he would not countenance two, noncontiguous colored group areas.

National Party members on the Cradock town council seemed to have little knowledge or understanding of what apartheid policy involved. When faced with the consequences of the buffer strips and the necessity of separating coloreds from Africans, members of the National Party briefly attacked the policy root and branch—Cradock's Africans and coloreds had lived together for years, they said, and buffer strips were unnecessary. But the council's oppositional stance could not be sustained. When the colored group area was defined by the Group Areas Board, the council loyally accepted the decision. The local National Party had committed itself in advance to accept the board's decision. Group areas, wrote the mayor, F. W. Michau, were a "social necessity," and Cradock would have to accept them.

Colored and African Resistance

Organizations of coloreds had always been weak in Cradock—the African People's Organization had been active from time to time, but rarely in a sustained way and never in combination with Africans. In Cradock, coloreds were undergoing a demographic decline—colored shopkeepers and tradesmen left town for such cities as Port Elizabeth and Cape Town, thereby removing individuals likely to have the requisite self-confidence for political leadership. In 1925, P. C. Goodman, an articulate and energetic colored teacher living in town, became a leader of the campaign to open a location dispensary and was active in the early days of the voluntary interracial Joint Council. But as a town resident he could not serve on the Location Advisory Board. He left Cradock in 1931, and no one of similar ability and promise succeeded him.

Coloreds were granted equal representation with Africans on the Location Advisory Board; this was actually an overrepresentation, since their population was smaller. Colored representatives did not play assertive roles on the board. They either deferred to African members or raised issues of special relevance only to themselves—hardly the basis of common action with Africans. In 1933, colored members of the board started the disputes that led eventually to nurse Mary Butler's resignation from the dispensary, but here, too, they were taking up an issue of concern chiefly to themselves only. When Africans joined the fray, the coloreds deferred to them, and the dispute went off in a direction involving Africans alone. Coloreds had been agitating for a colored nurse; Africans were protesting Butler's treatment of recently appointed African nurses.

In 1959, with the demarcation of a colored group area in Cradock virtually complete, the Department of Coloured Affairs began to encourage municipalities to set up special representative institutions for coloreds only. Asked to comment on a proposal to set up such a body in Cradock, the town clerk replied that local human and fiscal resources could not support it. Though the town clerk's judgment must be evaluated with caution, the lack of local political resources was demonstrated once more at a public hearing about a proposed colored group area for Cradock. The Non-European Ratepayers Association, an organization of colored ratepayers who, as ratepayers, lived in town, engaged a white barrister to present their case. He and the NERA were apparently unable to persuade any locals of weight to appear with him at the hearing, and much of the case against the municipality's proposal was made by local white clergy—Roman Catholic, Anglican, and Methodist—whose churches and schools, all in the Mixed Area, were likely to be expropriated without compensation.

In contrast to mild protests by coloreds, African resistance to apartheid was vehement and sustained beginning soon after the election of 1948. Cradock Africans were militantly involved in a number of local issues—rents, housing, and the proposed "removal" of the location to Sondagshoek in 1956. In local politics they acted separately from coloreds even on the Location Advisory Board, where they had equal representation. Africans frequently complained that coloreds were in a relatively favored position: for example, in the rowdy meeting of June 1956 about moving the location, Africans argued that coloreds, not Africans, should be moved. Africans showed little deference toward white authorities at this meeting; white councilors later complained of the threatening tone of a letter from the ANC Youth League and acknowledged that they feared African responses to the proposed removal. When the municipality decided, in July 1957, to drop the removal of the location to Sondagshoek, they were aware that they were giving Africans a partial victory: Wilken Township was going to continue as an African township, even though most of the old location would be bulldozed.

Apartheid, then, differed from segregation in telling ways. Its theoretical foundation was far more clearly articulated, its provisions were more precise and consistent, and it was imposed much more rapidly—too rapidly for local opinion to grasp it fully. Government officials implemented the national policy of apartheid on Cradock with a new purpose and resolve; though they occasionally bent to local reality, they never backed off entirely.

By 1970, the Cradock authorities had rehoused almost the whole of the African and colored communities in the newly designated racial areas. The ultimate justification of apartheid urban policy had been that it would eliminate social friction. Since such friction was believed to derive partly from the daily movement of people from home to work, the apartheid planners not only housed people separately by race but also tried to lay down roads for the exclusive use of one race and to site industries so that commuters would not have to cross group area boundaries. But leaving aside the slim possibility of Cradock's attracting industries, the national urban policy was sociologically inappropriate for Cradock: its workers and professionals were all in domestic, municipal, railway, and educational enterprises, with virtually all employers resident in town, now the white area. Apartheid theory forbade an African who had made bricks in Cradock for thirty years from carrying on his trade because Cradock town was in the "white area" of South Africa, not in a homeland.

Apartheid officials brought to their policy discussions a new and special vocabulary. *Wrywing* (social friction) was, they believed, the inevitable consequence of closeness of different racial groups to each other. Sound policy would avoid creating a *wig* (a wedge) between group areas; the locomotive shed, in which whites worked, should not serve as a *wig* between two settlements of Africans. Further, it was desirable to place groups on *aaneenlopende* (unfragmented) pieces of ground, a desire that made it difficult in Cradock to find enough land for the colored group area. Presumably, it was this doctrine that justified P. W. Botha's 1964 decision as minister of Coloured Affairs to insist on a single colored group area even though some coloreds had already moved to the first proclaimed group area. And J. W. van Heerden's frequent use of *drentel* (to saunter or loiter) to describe the walking of an African on a Cradock street, clearly assumed that such walking might have criminal intent.

The benign intent of many apartheid officials cannot be doubted. Nor can the material achievements of many apartheid-era municipalities in providing housing for urban Africans and coloreds. But the benefits of improved housing, clinical services, water supply, and sanitation were, for people of color, fatally tainted by the fact of being for the most part imposed. Apartheid planners seem to have assumed that their goodwill would assuage resentments against their arbitrary decisions. But Africans were insulted by the very concept of buffer strips. Coloreds were affronted that a colored group area was demarcated and then eliminated four years later, virtually without information and explanation. While the reaction of coloreds is only scantily recorded, the removal of Africans was deeply resented and publicly expressed. Improved housing, water supply, and clinical services did not mollify Africans; or if they did, the sense of reconciliation did not last.

This study of local and national policy in a small town has ended with the proclamation of the last group area in Cradock in 1971, more than two decades after the passage of the Group Areas Act. In subsequent years, the pace of change on many issues would accelerate as the central government toyed with political reform and sought to give local institutions greater powers and resources, without, however, redistributing power at the national level. The government took the radical step in 1971 of taking "native" or "Bantu" administration away from local authorities. However, such an administrative change did little to calm a society increasingly prone to outbreaks of violence, particularly by young Africans, as shown by the Soweto uprising in 1976, provoked by education policy, and the protests and riots in Cape Town following the enforcement of group areas and the bulldozing of the multiracial District Six.

Cradock produced its version of spectacular mobilizing events. As Michael Tetelman has shown, the Rev. J. A. Calata's funeral in 1983 mobilized and revived the militancy of young people.[3] And the political murder of four Cradock men in 1985—soon to become the "Cradock Four"—was to raise the political temperature even further, as authorities wrestled with urban violence in one town after another, particularly in the reef towns of the Transvaal. For a brief period, Cradock became a symbol of the national struggle. The murder of Matthew Goniwe and his colleagues was to have a long political aftermath, well into the post-apartheid era. Nothing could make clearer that the enforcement of the Group Areas Act in Cradock, and in other towns and cities, far from calming a society in *wrywing,* was one more provocation to people of color that would eventually bring down, not only the apartheid regime, but also the long-standing structures of white political supremacy in South Africa.

NOTES

Jeffrey Butler's work was based almost entirely on extensive research in unpublished archives. His notes were dense, precise, and compact, and he employed numerous acronyms, many of them mysterious to the editor for a long time. Under supervision of the editor, two researchers—Adam Tinkle working on microfilms in Middletown, and Susan Sturman working in libraries and archives in Cape Town and Pretoria—checked and corrected approximately three quarters of the references and associated passages in the text. It was not possible to check all the archives, most notably the Port Elizabeth Repository of the National Archive (PER, in Butler's terminology). And a few small collections cited by Butler have not been identified. The researchers encountered numerous errors in both the notes and the text, but virtually all of them were minor, even trivial, and had no bearing on the accuracy of Butler's assertions. This finding gave the editor confidence in the overall integrity of the notes, even those that could not be checked. It is certain that some errors remain, some derived from Butler's original manuscript, and others, perhaps, caused by the editor's attempts to clarify ambiguous references. When concerted efforts to check a source failed, this is indicated in an editor's note. In other cases, it has been deemed best to retain some notes that have not been confirmed in detail. We presume that future researchers would prefer to be given clues to the location of the sources, rather than to contend with mystifying silence.

Abbreviations

ACVV	Afrikaanse Christelike Vroue Vereeniging (Afrikaans Christian Women's Association)
AMOH	Assistant medical officer of health
ANC	African National Congress
Ann. Rept.	Annual Report
APO	African People's Organisation
CAC	Cape African Congress
CAdC	Coloured Advisory Council
CAR	Cape Archives Repository, Cape Town
CDK	Cradock
Cdk HC	Cradock Health Committee
Cen. Hsng. Bd	Central Housing Board
Cl	Council
CNC	Chief native commissioner
CPNU	Coloured Peoples' National Union
CPP	Cape Provincial Papers
DBMP	Donald B. Molteno Papers, University of Cape Town

DNA	Department of Native Affairs
DS	District surgeon
DSAB	*Dictionary of South African Biography*
EBP	Ernest Butler Papers, Rhodes University, Grahamstown
GAB	Group Areas Board
GGR	Groeps Gebiede Raad
GN	Government Notice
HAD	Hansard
HNP	Herenigde Nasionale Party
IRRP	Institute of Race Relations Papers, University of the Witwatersrand, Johannesburg
JBP	James Butler Papers, Rhodes University, Grahamstown
J. Cl. M	Joint Council Minutes (in the editor's temporary possession)
Loc. Adv. Bd.	Location Advisory Board
Loc. Sup.	Location Superintendent
LTAB	Land Tenure Advisory Board
LVM	Lady Volunteers for the Location Movement
Mag.	Magistrate
MBP	Mary Butler Papers, Rhodes University, Grahamstown
MN	*Midland News*
MOH	Medical officer of health
NAC	Native Affairs Commission
NAR	National Archives Repository, Pretoria
Nat. Comm.	Native Commissioner
Nat. Rev. Ac.	Native Revenue Account
NERA	Non-European Ratepayers Association
NGK	Nederduits Gereformeerde Kerk
NLAB	Native Labour Advisory Board
OHSA	*Oxford History of South Africa*
Ord. Cl. Mtg.	Ordinary council meeting
OUP	Oxford University Press
OYB	*Official Year Book*
PER	Port Elizabeth Repository
Prov. Sec.	Provincial Secretary
SAIRR	South African Institute of Race Relations
SAP	South African Police
SBA	Secretary for Bantu Administration
SNA	Secretary for Native Affairs
SPA	Secretary of Provincial Administration (Cape Province)
Spec. Cl. Mtg.	Special council meeting
SPH	Secretary of Public Health
SPW	Secretary for Public Works
SSW	Secretary for Social Welfare
TC	Town clerk
T. Cl. M.	Town Council Minutes
UG	Union Government
WCA	Women's Civic Association
WCTU	Women's Christian Temperance Union

Introduction

1. John Dollard, *Caste and Class in a Southern Town* (New Haven: Yale University Press, 1937; rpt., Madison: University of Wisconsin Press, 1988), xviii.

2. Ibid., 3.

3. T. R. H. Davenport, "African Townsmen? South African Natives (Urban Areas) Legislation through the Years," *African Affairs* 68 (Apr. 1969), 99.

4. David Yudelman, *The Emergence of Modern South Africa: State Capital and the Incorporation of Organized Labour on the South African Goldfields, 1902–1939* (Westport: Greenwood Press, 1983), 8–11, 19–22, 37–42.

5. T. R. H. Davenport, *South Africa: A Modern History,* 4th ed. (Toronto: University of Toronto Press), 231–33.

6. T. R. H. Davenport, "The Triumph of Colonel Stallard: The Transformation of the Natives (Urban Areas) Act between 1923 and 1937," *South African Historical Journal* 2 (Nov. 1970), 89–91.

7. Davenport, *South Africa,* 370–74, 532–33.

8. Elizabeth van Heyningen, "Public Health and Society in Cape Town, 1880–1910" (Ph.D. thesis, University of Cape Town, 1989), 14, 21–25.

9. Randall M. Packard, *White Plague, Black Labor: Tuberculosis and the Political Economy of Health and Disease in South Africa* (Berkeley: University of California Press, 1989), 72, 83, 100.

10. Union of South Africa, *Report of the Tuberculosis Commission* (Cape Town: Cape Times, Government Printer, 1914), 17, 28, 131.

11. Ibid.

12. Housing Act No. 35 of 1920, *Revised Statutes of the Union of South Africa,* vol. 3, 1917–1920 (Pretoria: Government Printer, 1935), section 7 (3), 1198.

13. Natives (Urban Areas) Act No. 21 of 1923, *Statutes of the Union of South Africa 1923* (Cape Town: Government Printer, 1923), section 7 1 (b), 150–51.

14. Department of Native Affairs, "Report of the Native Laws Commission 1946–1948" (Pretoria: Government Printer, 1948) U.G. No. 28–1948, 3.

15. For example, Department of Native Affairs, "Report of Departmental Committee Appointed to Enquire into and Report upon the Question of Residence of Natives in Urban Areas and Certain Proposed Amendments of the Native Urban Areas Act No. 21 of 1923" (mimeo, 1936), 3.

16. Cradock Municipal Voters Roll, 1921, Cape Archives Repository (CAR) 3/CDK (?).

17. Deborah Posel, *The Making of Apartheid, 1948–1961* (Oxford: Clarendon Press, 1991) 246–53.

18. Ivan Evans, *Bureaucracy and Race: Native Administration in South Africa* (Berkeley: University of California Press, 1997), 1–3.

1. Landscape, People, and Politics

1. For geographical background see J. J. Badenhorst, "A Geographical Study, Survey of the Cape Midlands and Karoo Regions," vol. 1 (Grahamstown: Institute of Social and Economic Research, Rhodes University, 1970), mimeo, 1–17, 47, 48.

2. Robert Ross, *Beyond the Pale: Essays in the History of Colonial South Africa* (Hanover, N.H.: Wesleyan University Press, 1993), 48; for farm size in 1929 see "Final Summary, 2nd General Valuation 1929: Whole Division of Cradock," (hereafter 2nd General Val.

1929), CAR, 3/CDK 6/1/2/1; for farm size generally see William Beinart, "Soil Erosion Animals and Pasture over the Longer Term: Environmental Destruction in Southern Africa," in Melissa Leach and Robin Mearns, eds., *The Lie of the Land: Challenging Received Wisdom on the African Environment* (Oxford: Curry and Heinemann, 1996), 67.

3. Richard Elphick and Hermann Giliomee, eds., *The Shaping of South African Society, 1652–1840* (Cape Town: Maskew Miller Longman, 1989), 447–49; Denis Smith, *Cradock, 1814–1965, 150th Anniversary Brochure* (Cradock: White & Boughton, 1964), 57.

4. *Cape Town Gazette and African Advertiser,* vol. 12, no. 594, 31 May 1817.

5. Smith, *Cradock, 1814–1964,* 59–61, 63–65.

6. Clifton C. Crais, *White Supremacy and Black Resistance in Pre-industrial South Africa: The Making of the Colonial Order in the Eastern Cape, 1770–1865* (Cambridge: Cambridge University Press, 1992), 68.

7. "Regulations of the Municipality of Cradock," *Cape of Good Hope Government Gazette,* no. 1656, 15 Sept. 1837, and no. 2174, 29 July 1847, CPP8/1/43.

8. Smith, *Cradock, 1814–1964,* 71, 73.

9. For Gordon, see T. R. H. Davenport, "The Consolidation of a New Society: The Cape Colony," in Monica Wilson and Leonard Thompson, eds., *Oxford History of South Africa* (hereafter *OHSA*), vol. 1 (Oxford: Clarendon Press, 1969), 290–91; *Cape of Good Hope Cape Almanac for 1855,* 252.

10. D. Hobart Houghton and Jenifer Dagut, eds., *Source Material on the South African Economy: 1860–1970,* vol. 1, *1860–1899* (Cape Town: Oxford University Press, 1972), 77, 125.

11. Smith, *Cradock, 1814–1964,* 79, 81; H. C. Hopkins, *Die N.G. Kerk Cradock, 1818–1968* (Cradock: Nederduits Gereformeerde Kerk, 1968), 55–65.

12. Alan Spencer Mabin, "The Making of Colonial Capitalism: Intensification and Expansion in the Economic Geography of the Cape Colony, South Africa, 1854–1899" (Ph.D. thesis, Simon Fraser University, 1984), 155–65.

13. David Welsh, "The Growth of Towns," *OHSA,* vol. 2, 172.

14. Office of Census and Statistics, *Third Census of the Union of South Africa, Enumerated 3rd May 1921,* Part I, Population Table V (hereafter *Census 1921*).

15. Elphick and Giliomee, *Shaping of South African Society,* 231–32, 522–24.

16. Leonard M. Thompson, *A History of South Africa* (New Haven: Yale University Press, 1990), 54–55.

17. *Cape Census 1891,* CSS 2/3/3, Census District no. 20, Urban Areas, Table XXII; *Cape Census 1904,* CSS 3/1/6, Return of Population Areas, 38–39; *Census 1911,* UG 32/1912, XI, 4–5.

18. *Census 1921,* Report, 29 UG 37–24.

19. Elphick and Giliomee, *Shaping of South African Society,* 121–22, 524.

20. *Census 1921,* Part I, Table V, 6–7; "Cradock Municipality Location Regulations," Government Notice 309, 21 Oct. 1926; *Cape Government Gazette,* 22 Oct. 1926, 650–57; Liquor Act No. 30 of 1928, sect. 175, *Statutes of the Union of South Africa 1927–1928* (Cape Town: Government Printer, 1928), 614; Union of South Africa, Bureau of Census and Statistics, *Official Year Book of the Union and of Basutoland, Bechuanaland Protectorate and Swaziland,* no. 26–1950 (Pretoria: Government Printer, 1953), 1157; *Census 1921,* Part VIII, iv.

21. Gary Baines, "The Origins of Urban Segregation: Local Government and the Residence of Africans in Port Elizabeth, 1835–1865," *South African Historical Journal* 22 (1990), 65–66; Davenport, *South Africa,* 117.

22. Thompson, *South Africa,* 77–79; interview with Godfrey Collett, 6 Nov. 1977.

23. *Census 1921,* Part VIII, iii, and Part I, Table V; Surendra Bhana and Bridglal Pachai, eds., *A Documentary History of Indian South Africans* (Cape Town: David Philip, 1984), 97; *Cradock Voters' List 1909;* Dept. of Interior, *Voters' List 1925, Electoral Division of Cradock*, State Library, Pretoria (hereafter *Cradock Voters' List 1925*). [The location of the 1909 list is not known. Butler's note places the 1925 list in the State Library, Pretoria, but we were unable to confirm this location.–Ed.]

24. Listed in the 2nd General Val. 1929, CAR 3/CDK 6/1/2/1.

25. Colin Bundy, "Vagabond Hollanders and Runaway Englishmen: White Poverty in the Cape before Poor Whiteism," in William Beinart, Peter Delius, and Stanley Trapido, eds., *Putting a Plough to the Ground: Accumulation and Dispossession in Rural South Africa, 1850–1930* (Johannesburg: Ravan Press, 1986), 103–4; Wilson School Minute Book, ACVV, Cradock.

26. Wilson School Minute Book, ACVV, Cradock.

27. Ernest Butler, "The Midland News, 1891–1926," typescript, EBP, Cory Library, Rhodes University, PR 3490; Ian Goldin, *Making Race: The Politics and Economics of Coloured Identity in South Africa* (London: Longman, 1987), 16–19.

28. Identifying voters by white last names and town addresses, the 1925 parliamentary voters' list records 60 percent of voters as Afrikaans speaking; *Cradock Voters' List 1925.*

29. Interview with L. P. Deary, John Deary's younger brother, 4 Oct. 1977.

30. For Hattingh, see *MN,* 5 Aug. 1926; for Du Plessis, see *MN,* 14 Oct. 1929.

31. See the text of the General Municipal Legislation, Ordinance 9 of 1836, in Keith S. Hunt, "The Development of Municipal Government in the Eastern Province of the Cape of Good Hope with Special Reference to Grahamstown, 1827–1862," *Archives Year Book for South African History,* 1961 (Cape Town: Government Printer, 1963), 223–35.

32. Elphick and Giliomee, *Shaping of South African Society,* 163–68, 554–59.

33. Cape Provincial Ordinance 22 of 1925, sections 4 and 7, CAR, CPP 3/1; for the parliamentary franchise, see *Official Year Book,* vol. 13, 1930–31, 65–67.

34. *Cradock Voters' List 1909; Cradock Voters' List 1925.*

35. "Report on Systematic Inspection of the Health and Sanitary Conditions in the Municipal Area of Cradock conducted by Dr. F. W. P. Cluver on 27th November, 1931," National Archives Repository (NAR), GES 627, 123/13 Sanitation Cradock; hereafter Cluver Rept. 1931.

36. 2nd General Val. 1929, CAR 3/CDK 6/1/2/1.

37. Ibid.

38. Ibid., listed under "Churches."

39. For a white protest, see P. W. Coetzer to Town Clerk (TC), 18 July 1925, 3/CDK 4/1/6, Misc. Corres. C.

40. On David Curry, see *Survey of Race Relations, 1971,* 20.

41. Interview with Dimbiti Alexander, 21 Apr. 1978.

42. P. C. Goodman (Sec. of African People's Organisation [APO]) to TC, 18 Feb. 1924, and reply, Oct. 1924, on park benches; Goodman to TC, 27 Oct. 1924 on taxis, CAR, 3/CDK 4/1/106, 1924–1938, APO.

43. Loc. Comm., 20 Jan. 1936, Town Council Minutes (T. Cl. M.) 22:23.

44. "Report on Systematic Sanitary Inspection of Cradock Municipal Area on the 8th and 9th July 1924, by Dr. W. A. Murray," NAR, Pretoria, GES 627 123/13; hereafter Murray Rept. 1924.

45. *Cradock Voters' List 1925;* for TC see *MN,* 18 Oct. 1923.

46. Valuation of town properties calculated from 2nd General Val. 1929, CAR 3/CDK 6/1/2/1.

47. "Amended Regulations for the Municipality of Cradock," *Cape Government Gazette,* no. 2597, 27 Mar. 1855, CPP 8/1/51, 368; ibid., no. 4558, 30 May 1873, CPP 8/1/69; for the curfew see Mag. to TC, 10 Sept. 1902, CAR 3/CDK, 4/1/6, Misc. Corres. C.

48. Cradock Municipality, "Regulations for the Management of the Native Location," Proc. 1334, 3 Nov. 1908; *Cape Government Gazette,* no. 9117, 10 Nov. 1908, 1847–48.

49. Gavin Lewis, *Between the Wire and the Wall: A History of South African "Coloured" Politics* (Cape Town: David Philip, 1987), chap. 1.

50. 2nd General Val., 1929, CAR 3/CDK 6/1/2/1; G. P. Wilken to TC, 4 Sept. 1935, CAR, 3/CDK 4/1/117, Municipality versus Application of J. B. Mwambo.

51. Michael S. Tetelman, "'We Can': Black Politics in Cradock, South Africa, 1948 to 1985" (Ph.D. thesis, Northwestern University, 1997), 31–33.

52. For example, Solilo represented the Vigilance Association at a hearing on Cradock's location regulations in 1925: Solilo to TC, 4 Aug. 1925, CAR, 3/CDK 4/1/28, Native Location and Finance Committee and Regulations, 1924–1928.

53. Biography of James A. Calata in Alan Cobley, "On the Shoulders of Giants: The Black Petty Bourgeoisie in the Politics and Society of South Africa, 1924–1950" (Ph.D. thesis, University of London, 1986). Made available by Gary Baines.

54. Tetelman, "Black Politics in Cradock," 58, 64.

55. Peter Walshe, *The Rise of African Nationalism in South Africa: The African National Congress, 1912–1952* (London: C. Hurst, 1970), chaps. 1 and 2.

56. Natives (Urban Areas) Act, No. 21 of 1923, Statutes of the Union of South Africa 1923, 140–96.

2. Lodgers, Layabouts, and Laborers

1. Cradock Combined Criminal Record Book, Case no. 188, 30 Mar. 1925, CAR, 1/CDK 3/1/1/33. The seventeen "Hottentots" were not mentioned again in the sources; the term had disappeared from Cradock records by the mid-1940s. "Hottentots" were increasingly treated as coloreds and counted as such by the census.

2. *Cradock Voters' List 1925.*

3. *MN,* 3 Apr. 1925, 3; 6 Apr. 1925, 3–4.

4. *MN,* 8 Apr. 1925, 2; for the "Lodger Law" see Cradock Municipality, Regulations for the Management of the Native Location, Proc. 1334, 10 Nov. 1908, 1847–48, *Cape Government Gazette,* 3 Nov. 1908.

5. Wilken to TC, 14 Apr. 1925, CAR 3/CDK 4/1/28, Native Location Finance Committee and Regulations, 1924–1928. Wilken's capitalization and punctuation have been slightly edited.

6. Special Council Meeting (Spec. Cl. Mtg.), 14 Apr. 1925, T. Cl. M. 12:584–78.

7. *MN,* 2 May 1925, 4; for the Bloemfontein events see T. Cl. M. Edward Roux, *Time Longer than Rope: A History of the Black Man's Struggle for Freedom in South Africa* (Madison: University of Wisconsin Press, 1964), 15–58.

8. Deary to Secretary for Native Affairs (SNA), 4 May 1925, NAR, 4265 114/313, Main File, vol. 1.

9. *MN,* 18 May 1925, 3–4. Deary was almost certainly wrong in claiming that Cradock was unique in granting location residents fixity of tenure.

10. SNA to TC, 10 June 1925, NAR, NTS 4265 114/313, Main File, vol. 1.

11. Mag. to SNA, 11 June 1925, NAR, NTS 4265 114/313, Main File, vol. 1; for the 1926 regulations see note 15 below; for the 1940 regulations see note 52 below.

12. [Butler's citation for the model regulations could not be confirmed.–Ed.]

13. SNA, Circular-Letter no. 201/312, Natives (Urban Areas) Act, 1923, 21 July, 1924; Circular-Letter, Location Regulations, no. 62, 10 Oct 1924, CAR 3/CDK 4/1/28, Native Location Finance Committee and Regulations.

14. SNA to Mag., 2 June 1925, NAR, NTS 4265 114/313, vol. 1.

15. Cradock Municipality, Location Regulations, Proc. 309, 21 Oct. 1926, *Cape Government Gazette,* 22 Oct. 1926, 650.

16. J. Deary to SNA, 4 May 1925, and reply, 10 June 1925, NAR, NTS 4265 114/313, Main File, vol. 1; Spec. Cl. Mtg., 16 June 1925, T. Cl. M. 12: 607–06.

17. Nicolina Best (Sec. WCA) to TC, 26 Jan. 1926, and reply 27 Jan. 1926, CAR, 3/CDK 4/1/105, Women's Civic Association, 1925–1934.

18. *MN,* 18 May 1925, 3–4.

19. Rev. John Solilo to TC, 30 Sept. 1925; Sec. Committee of the Location Coloured Residents to TC, 3 Nov. 1925; both in CAR 3/CDK 4/1/28, Native Location Finance Committee and Regulations.

20. TC to SNA, 27 Jan. 1927 and 20 Dec. 1927 saying he had received no nominations for 1928; TC to SNA, 21 Dec. 1929 saying he had a board of six members for 1930; both in CAR, 3/CDK 4/1/82, Native Affairs, vol. 1.

21. "Objections to Model Location Regulations" enclosed in Solilo to TC, 4 Aug. 1925; Manuel et al. to TC, 4 Aug. 1925; both in CAR, 3/CDK 4/1/28, Native Location Finance Committee and Regulations 1924–1928.

22. Mag. to TC, 10 Sept. 1902, CAR 3/CDK 4/1/6, Misc. Corres. C. [The regulation is referred to in this letter but not quoted. It is not clear where Butler found the quotation. –Ed.]

23. SNA to Povincial Secretary (Prov. Sec.), 5 Feb. 1926; Prov. Sec. to SNA, 3 Mar. 1926 and reply 15 Mar. 1926. [The location of this file, and those indicated in the next two notes, is not known.–Ed.]

24. TC to SNA, 29 June 1926.

25. SNA to Prov. Sec., 19 July 1926.

26. SNA to Prov. Sec., 10 Nov. 1925, NAR, NTS 4265 114/313, Main File, vol. 1; for the regulations see note 15 above.

27. *MN,* 18 Dec. 1926.

28. Cradock Joint Council, Evidence for the Native Economic Commission, 1930, CAR 3/CDK 4/1/27, Cradock Joint Council.

29. Dept. of Native Affairs, *Report of the Native Farm Labour Committee, 1937–1939,* Mimeo (Pretoria: Government printer, 1939), 39, 76–88; Sheila T. van der Horst, *Native Labour in South Africa* (London: Oxford University Press, 1942), 285.

30. Cape of Good Hope, Dept. of Public Education, *Educational Statistics, 1926* (Cape Town, 1927), 79, 93.

31. See note 28 above.

32. TC to Sec. Native Economic Committee [*sic,* Commission], 16 June 1931, CAR, 3/CDK 4/1/16, Misc. Corres. Na-Nh.

33. See note 28 above.

34. Guy Butler, *Karoo Morning* (Cape Town: David Philip, 1977), 22–24; Arthur M. Davey, ed., *Lawrence Richardson Selected Correspondence (1902–1903)* (Cape Town: Van Riebeeck Society, 1977), 4, 6, 101.

35. James Butler, "How Farmers Will Be Affected by Closer Union," Closer Union Society, Cradock, (?) Oct. 1908, James Butler Papers (JBP), Cory Library, Rhodes University, PR 3485.

36. *MN,* 26 Apr. 1926; obituary for William Ernest Cursons, *Johannesburg Star,* 9 Oct. 1940, 5.

37. Sec. Mortimer Farmers' Association to TC, 17 May 1930, and reply, 28 May 1930; Sec. Samenkomst Farmers' Association to TC, 16 May 1930; all in CAR, 3/CDK 4/1/98, Farmers' Association, 1930–1952.

38. Circular letter, TC to Secretaries of Farmers' Associations, Cradock District, 15 July 1930; "Farmers Applying for Farm Labour and Domestic Servants," n.d., but from context August or September 1930; the responses were not dated; CAR, 3/CDK 4/1/98, Farmers' Association, 1930–1952.

39. Davenport, *South Africa,* 267, 269–70.

40. TC to Wilken, 12 Feb. 1929; "Census Cradock Municipal Location," 25 July 1933; "Location Census 1935," Wilken to TC, 3 Aug. 1935; all in CAR, 3/CDK 4/1/83, Locations, vol. 1, 1928–1939.

41. T. R. H. Davenport, "The Triumph of Colonel Stallard: The Transformation of the Natives (Urban Areas) Act between 1923 and 1937," *South African Historical Journal* 2 (Nov. 1970), 84–89.

42. Ordinary Council Meeting (Ord. Cl. Mtg.), 18 July 1935, T. Cl. M. 21:359.

43. TC to M. J. Hattingh (Mayor) and others, 31 Aug. 1935, CAR, 3/CDK 4/1/83, Locations, vol. 1, 1928–1939; Ord. Cl. Mtg., 26 May 1936, T. Cl. M. 22:174. It is assumed that Glovo was an African.

44. Draft submission to Young-Barrett committee, n.d., but prepared for the visit of the committee to Cradock, 4 Oct. 1935, CAR, 3/CDK 4/1/83, Locations, vol. 1, 1928–1939.

45. Department of Native Affairs, 1936, "Report . . . upon the Question of Residence of Natives in Urban Areas" (Young-Barrett Report).

46. Davenport, "Triumph of Colonel Stallard," 85–89.

47. Evans, *Bureaucracy and Race,* 47–49.

48. "Restriction of the Right of Natives to Enter Areas under the Control of Certain Urban Local Authorities," Proclamation 115, *Government Gazette,* 12 May 1938.

49. NTS, General Circular no. 18/1938, Rights of Coloured Persons Residing in Urban Native Locations, 21 June 1938, CAR, KUS 85/5/75.

50. For Hewett see CAR, 3/CDK 4/1/11, Misc. Corres. Hen-Hez; for John Martins, TC to F. W. Grobbelaar, 4 May 1939, 4/1/73, Misc. Corres. Gr-Gz; for S. Jacobs, TC to Jacobs, 29 May 1940, 4/1/74, Misc. Corres. Ja-Jk.; for Mrs. Rainers, TC to Mrs. Rainers, 24 June 1943, 4/1/83, Locations, 1940–1946; for the town clerk in 1941, see Native Labour Advisory Board, 17 Nov. 1941, NAR, NTS 2219 415/280/34.

51. P. G. Caudwell, "Report on Inspection of the Urban Native Location at Cradock, 16 Aug. 1938," NAR, NTS 4266 114/313 Main File, vol. 3.

52. TC to SNA, 25 Nov. 1938 and 27 June 1939, NAR NTS 4265 114/313, Main File, vol. 2; GN 292, 13 June 1940, 995–96, *Cape Government Gazette,* 14 June, 1940.

53. Calculated from Native Revenue Account, 1939–1947, NAR, NTS 4960 114/313 C, Part 3.

54. “Census 1938: Cradock Municipal Location,” 6 Aug. 1938, Cradock Magistrate’s office, N 3/4/2; “Cradock Location, Census from 8/11/39 to 14/11/39—Employed and Unemployed Males Etc.,” CAR, 3/CDK 4/1/83, Locations, vol. 2, 1938–1940.

55. For the setting up of the board, Mag. to Sec. Central Farmers’ Association, Cradock, 21 May 1941, Cradock Magistrates’ Court, N 3/4/2.

56. Cull to Dr. Loock, Org. Sec. United Party (UP), Cape Town, 26 July 1941, SNA to Mag., 31 July 1942, NAR, NTS 2219 415/280/34.

57. SNA to Mag., 6 Aug. 1941, NAR, NTS 2219 415/280/34, Native Labour Advisory Board, Cradock.

58. Spec. Cl. Mtg., 13 Mar. 1942, T. Cl. M. 29:560.

59. H. R. Opperman (Sec. Cradock Farmers’ Association) to TC, 4 Sept. 1945, CAR, 3/CDK 4/1/84, Locations, vol. 4, 1945–48.

60. Note of an interview at the Department of Native Affairs, Pretoria, of Councillor Venter of Cradock, 14 June 1940, NAR, NTS 4266 114/313 Main File, vol. 3.

61. Extract of Minutes of Location Advisory Board, 21 June 1940, in TC to SNA, 9 Aug. 1940, NAR, NTS 5263 114/313 D, 30.

62. SNA to TC, 27 Aug. 1940, and reply 30 Aug. 1940, NAR, NTS 5263 114/313 D, 58, 59.

63. TC to SNA, 27 Jan. 1945; SNA repeated the refusal to approve the 1940 draft on 13 Mar. 1947, NAR, NTS 5263 114/313 D, 61, 159.

64. Memo by (?) Heald, 24 Aug. 1946; SNA to Native Commissioner (Nat. Comm.) (Cradock), 3 Dec. 1946, NAR, NTS 5263 114/313 D, 133, 136; TC to SNA, 11 June 1947, ibid., 161; TC to SNA, 17 May 1949 and reply 6 Sept. 1949, ibid., 166 and 167.

65. This material is scattered throughout the municipality’s “Miscellaneous Correspondence,” CAR, 3/CDK 4/1/1 to 4/1/81, and Location Correspondence, especially CAR, 3/CDK 4/1/82 to 4/1/85.

66. For the four examples, see note 50.

67. For example, Attorney G. C. Christie to TC, 7 Mar. 1942 on behalf of J. W. Botha, who wished to employ Willie Malata from Somerset East, a skilled smith; on 26 Mar., the town clerk refused; Botha tried again on 9 April, but on 23 April the town clerk again refused. CAR, 3/CDK 4/1/70, Misc. Corres. Ce-Ch.

68. For example, Mrs. F. van Zyl to TC, 21 July 1939, and reply 24 Aug. 1939, refusing, CAR, 3/CDK 4/1/80, vol. 2, Misc. Corres. U-V.

69. Native Labour Advisory Board, 17 Nov. 1941; NAR, NTS 2219 415/280/34.

70. TC to Mag., 28 Nov. 1940, enclosing a list of unemployed, including Moontlik Hani, NAR, NTS 4266 114/313 Main File, vol. 3.

71. Cawood Hani to Location Superintendent, “9th 9–1943,” 3/CDK 4/1/84, Locations, vol. 4, 1940–46. On the only map I have with house numbers (1949) I cannot identify Marthan Street; on this map 345 is on Mytana Street.

72. Location Advisory Board (Loc. Ad. Bd.), 6 Apr. 1949, T. Cl. M. 35:5, and Loc. Ad. Bd., 17 July 1958, T. Cl. M. 48:74. This rejection in 1958 was almost certainly because this area was due to have its houses demolished to clear a “buffer strip.”

73. See note 68 above.

74. K. T. Cremer to Mag., 9 Oct. 1946, NAR, NTS 4266 114/313, Main File, vol. 3.

75. Native Commissioner (Nat. Comm.) to TC, 9 Oct., and reply, 24 Oct. 1946; Nat. Comm. to Metcalf and Co., 25 Oct. 1946; Cremer to SNA, 18 Nov. 1946; all in NAR, NTS 4266 114/313, Main File, vol. 3. The magistrate was also the “Native Commissioner” for the Cradock district.

76. SNA to Nat. Comm., Cradock, 21 Jan. 1947, ibid.

77. TC. to Mag., 29 Jan. 1947 enclosed in Mag. to SNA., 31 Jan. 1947, ibid.

78. SNA to Mag., 27 Feb. 1947, NAR, NTS 4266 114/313, Main File, vol. 3; Loc. Cttee., 16 Sept. 1947, T. Cl. M. 33:246; TC to Mag., 25 Sept. 1947, NAR, NTS 4266 114/313, Main File, vol. 3.

79. "Approximate Location Inhabitants, June, 1946," CAR, 3/CDK 4/1/84, Locations, vol. 5, 1945–1948. The town clerk added "Gov. Census" figures.

80. See note 75 above.

81. Davenport, *South Africa,* 311–13.

82. Sec. CAdC to Sec. Social Welfare (SSW), 15 Nov. 1945; SNA to SSW, 27 Feb. 1946, CAR KUS 85/5/75, Woonbuurtes and Behuising (Residential Areas and Housing). [CAR Archivist says these KUS papers are not sorted.–Ed.]

83. David Welsh, "The Growth of Towns," *OHSA,* vol. 2 (Oxford: Clarendon Press, 1971), 187.

84. Native Labour Advisory Board (NLAB), 17 Nov. 1941, NAR, NTS 2219 415/280/34.

85. Davenport, *South Africa,* 525, 532.

3. Race and the Politics of Liquor and Beer

1. J. V. Kilian to District Commandant, SAP, 16 Sept. 1928, "Re Complaints by the Public in Cradock," CAR, 3/CDK 4/1/13, Misc. Corres. Ki to Kk.

2. Location Superintendent's Report (Loc. Sup. Report), Feb. 1942, T. Cl. M. 29:1.

3. Cradock: Beer Drinks, 1918–1928, NAR, NTS, 7045 52/322. The file ends in 1928.

4. Cradock Municipality, Regulations for the Management of the Native Location, 3 Nov. 1908, 1334, *Cape Government Gazette,* 10 Nov. 1908, 1847–48.

5. Jonathan Crush and Charles Ambler, eds., *Liquor and Labor in Southern Africa* (Athens: Ohio University Press, 1992), 24–30, 85–95.

6. *MN,* 12 Aug. 1923, 15 Aug. 1923; for a brief biography of Julia, one of the leaders of the WCTU, see *DSAB* 4:589.

7. *Official Year Book* (*OYB*), no. 7, 1910–1924, 307.

8. Crush and Ambler, *Liquor and Labor,* 19.

9. T. R. H. Davenport, "The Triumph of Colonel Stallard: The Transformation of the Natives (Urban Areas) Act between 1923 and 1937," *South African Historical Journal* 2 (Nov. 1970), 78–79. For the mayor's statement on refusal to open a beer hall, see *MN,* 18 and 25 Aug. 1924.

10. Liquor Licensing Board, Cradock, 6 Sept. 1939, CAR 1/CDK 11/8/1.

11. For the *tot* system see Hellman, *Handbook on Race Relations,* 127; *OYB,* no. 13 (1930–1931), 254.

12. See, for example, *Cape Coloured Liquor Commission of Inquiry,* UG 33/1945 (Pretoria: Government Printer, 1945), 18.

13. A colored person carrying a bottle of liquor could be challenged to prove that he was not a "native." In about 1935, I was told by a colored man that he had been stopped by a policeman who wanted to examine a bottle he was carrying, whereupon he threw his hat on the ground, pointed to his head, and said, "Baas, ek het nie peperkorrels nie!" (Sir, I don't have peppercorn hair!), that is, "I am not an African."

14. Ian Goldin, *Making Race: The Politics and Economics of Coloured Identity in South Africa* (London: Longman, 1987), 19–24.

15. Crush and Ambler, *Liquor and Labor,* 85–95.

16. Prov. Sec. to SNA, 25 Jan. 1924, and reply, 7 Feb. 1924, NAR, NTS 5406 114/313 G.

17. Mag. to SNA, 7 Feb. 1925; NAR, NTS 5406 114/313 G. The new regulation was published as Provincial Notice 234, 30 July 1925, 155, *Cape Government Gazette,* 9 July 1925, CPP 2/32.

18. TC to SNA, 30 May 1927, and reply 7 June 1927, NAR, NTS 114/313 Main File, vol. 1.

19. Michael Tetelman, "The Burial of Canon J. A. Calata and the Revival of Mass-Based Opposition in Cradock, South Africa, 1983," *African Studies* 58, 1 (1999), 6–7. "Rev. James Arthur Calata" in Alan Cobley, "On the Shoulders of Giants: The Black Petty Bourgeoisie in the Politics and Society of South Africa, 1925–1950" (Ph.D. diss., University of London, 1986); made available by Gary Baines.

20. Joint Council Minutes Book (J. Cl. M.), 1927–1934, 6 Dec. 1928 to 14 Mar. 1929, Mary Butler Papers (MBP), temporarily in the editor's possession.

21. Ibid.

22. Ord. Cl. Mtg., 26 Feb. 1929, T. Cl. M. 14:(?); *MN,* 1 Mar. 1929.

23. Ibid.

24. J. Cl. M., 2 May 1930.

25. Ibid., 6 May 1930.

26. Ibid., 19 June 1930. The minutes contain copies of memoranda: (1) "Memorandum" addressed to Mayor and Councillors, supporting beer brewing, signed by Gould, Calata, and Mary Butler, 16 Aug. 1930; (2) "Minority Report" signed by Evans and Bam, both Methodists, and Jordan, Baptist, n.d.

27. For farmers' resistance and town clerk's response see, e.g., Sec. Mortimer Farmer's Assn. to TC 17 May 1930, and reply TC to Sec. Mortimer Farmers' Assn., 28 May 1930, CAR, 3/CDK 4/1/98, Farmers' Assn., 1930–1952.

28. Ord. Cl. Mtg., 27 May 1930, T. Cl. M. 15: (?); TC (Queenstown) to TC (Cradock), 20 May and reply 22 May 1930, CAR, 3/CDK 4/1/19 Misc. Corres. Q.

29. Dept. of Native Affairs, "Report of Departmental Committee Appointed to Inquire into and Report upon the Question of Residence of Natives in Urban Areas and Certain Proposed Amendments of the Natives Urban Areas Act No. 21 of 1923" (Mimeo, 1935)," Young-Barrett Report, Draft Bill, Clause 17, p. 22.

30. Native Laws Amendment Act, no. 46 of 1937, *Statutes of the Union of South Africa,* 1937, 662–728.

31. *MN,* 25 Sept. 1937.

32. Report Back by Cradock delegates to National Conference of Municipal Councillors and Officials in Pretoria, 26–29 Sept. 1937, CAR 3/CDK4/1/82, vol. 1, Native Affairs, 1926–1938; Ord. Cl. Mtg., 23 Nov. 1937, T. Cl. M. 25:323; TC to SNA, 6 Dec. 1937, and telegram 6 Jan. 1938, NAR, NTS 5406 114/313 G.

33. *MN,* 23 Oct. 1937; Butler, *Karoo Morning,* 2; personal reminiscence; obituary for Charles Butler, *MN,* 8 Jan. 1949; *DSAB* 4:70–71.

34. Ord. Cl. Mtg., 25 Jan. 1938, T. Cl. M. 25:414–402 (?).

35. G. P. Wilken, "Location Advisory Boards Congress of South Africa at Port Elizabeth, 19th to 22nd Dec. 1937," 13 Jan. 1938, CAR, 3/CDK 4/1/83, Locations, vol. 1, 1928–1930.

36. For the meeting, see *MN,* 19 Feb. 1938; Ord. Cl. Mtg., 22 Feb. 1938, T. Cl. M. 25:492; TC to SNA, 26 Feb. 1938, NAR, NTS 5406 114/313 G.

37. Cape African Congress, "Petition to the Town Council," 14 Mar. 1938, CAR, 3/CDK 4/1/82, Native Affairs, vol. 1, 1926–1938.

38. Loc. Cttee., 15 Mar. 1938, T. Cl. M. 25:515.

39. Ibid.

40. J. A. Calata to TC, 17 Mar. 1938, NAR, NTS 5406 114/313 G; Loc. Cttee., 19 Jan. 1943, T. Cl. M. 30:271–72.

41. TC to SNA, 9 Feb., 24 Feb., and 31 Mar. 1939; SNA to TC, 20 Apr. 1939, NAR, NTS 5406 114/313 G.

42. TC to SNA, 6 Apr. 1940, NAR, NTS 4266 114/313 Main File, vol. 3.

43. See map of location in Annual Report, Cradock Health Centre, NAR, TBPA, GES 1643 54/32.

44. Hellman, *Handbook on Race Relations,* 258–59; Crush and Ambler in *Liquor and Labor,* 19, overstate when they write, "The 'Durban System' became a model for urban control . . . by the 1930s throughout the Union of South Africa." Department of Native Affairs (DNA), *Report of the Committee Appointed to Enquire into the Use of Profits Derived from the Manufacture, Sale and Supply of Kaffir Beer 1945–1946* (Pretoria: Government Printer, 1948), hereafter *Kaffir Beer Profits 1945–1946.*

45. Circular Letter, 19 Oct. 1944, and SNA to Mag., 31 July 1945, NAR, NTS 114/313 C.

46. Davenport, *South Africa,* 524–29.

47. "Town Council of Cradock . . . Exclusive Municipal Supply of Kaffir Beer," GN 2009, *Gov. Gazette,* 2710, 15 Dec. 1939.

48. Prov. Sec. to SNA, 5 Mar. 1940; NAR, NTS 114/313 G.

49. SNA to Mag., 24 July 1940 reiterating refusal to promulgate; TC to Mag., 12 Sept. 1940 and SNA to Mag., 26 Sept. 1940 agreeing to promulgate; all in NAR, NTS 5406 114/313 G; "Regulations relating to . . . sprouted grain into Cradock," GN 555, 14 Nov. 1940, 768, *Cape Government Gazette,* 1910, 15 Nov. 1940.

50. Calculated from Native Revenue Account (Nat. Rev. Ac.) 1940, NAR, NTS 114/313 C; for estimate 1941, see Spec. Cl. Mtg., 21 Nov. 1940, T. Cl. M. 29:73.

51. NAC, Report of the Native Affairs Commission Appointed to Enquire into the Working of the Provisions of the Natives (Urban Areas) Act Relating to the Use and Supply of Kaffir Beer, 1942, para. 109.

52. A. M. Bester (Sec., Cape Coloured Defence Link Committee) to TC, 12 Aug. 1943; TC to Chairman, Advisory Board, 28 June 1945; both documents in CAR, 3/CDK 4/1/84, Locations, vol. 4, 1940–1946; Minutes of Cradock Liquor Control Board, 4 Dec. 1935, and, for examples, on 6 Dec. 1944, and 3 Dec. 1947, CAR 1/CDK 11/8/1.

53. SNA to TC, 16 Aug. 1940, NAR, NTS 4266 114/313 Main File, vol. 3.

54. Wilken to TC, 6 Mar. 1941, CAR, 3/CDK 4/1/84, Locations, vol. 4, 1939–1951.

55. Particulars of Natives and Hottentots Residing in the Railway Camp . . . ," 17 Oct. 1932, CAR 3 CDK 4/1/82, Native Affairs, vol. 1, 1926–1938. [This document could not be located in this file.–Ed.]

56. Loc. Sup. Rept., Ord. Cl. Mtg., 25 Mar. 1941, T. Cl. M. 29:200.

57. Wilken to TC, 19 June 1941, CAR, 3/CDK 4/1/84, Locations, vol. 4, 1939–1951.

58. Ord. Cl. Mtg., 23 Sept. 1941, T. Cl. M. 29:440.

59. Mag. to TC, 12 June 1943 reporting refusal by Adjutant General, Pretoria, CAR, 3/CDK 4/1/84, Locations, vol. 4. 1940–1946.

60. "Social Welfare Location," Wilken to TC 21 July 1944, CAR, 3/CDK, 4/1/84, Locations, vol. 5, Apr. 1945–48.

61. E. S. Mvambo to D. B. Molteno, 5 and 31 Mar. 1945; Annexure "A": statement by plaintiff in Njawi vs. Wilken and others; Annexure "B": statement by plaintiff in Njawi vs. Gugu Poni (Assistant policeman); Mvambo to Molteno, 4 June 1945; Donald B. Mol-

teno Papers (DBMP), Bc579 A10 142 ff. For Molteno, see *DSAB,* 5, 516–17; E. S. Mvambo may be related to the Rev. J. B. Mvambo, who in 1935 tried to gain recognition for the Bantu Methodist church in Cradock: Mvambo to TC, 30 Aug. 1935, CAR, 3/CDK 4/1/117, Municipality vs. Application of J. B. Mvambo.

62. Mvambo to Molteno, 5 Mar. and 31 Mar. 1945, and reply, 5 Apr. 1945, DBMP, Bc579 A10 146 and 148; Molteno to TC, 3 Sept. 1945, DBMP Bc579 A10 153, and reply, 27 Sept. 1945; TC to Wilken, 27 Sept. 1945, CAR, 3/CDK, 4/1/84, Locations, vol. 4, 1940–1946; Loc. Cttee., 18 Sept. 1945, T. Cl. M. 32:11.

63. DNA, *Kaffir Beer Profits 1945–1946* (Pretoria: Government Printer, 1948); questionnaire signed by Town Clerk, 26 Oct. 1945; evidence submitted by Cradock Town Council to the Beer Hall Profits Inquiry at Cradock, 2 Nov. 1945, 1–3; for Ngumbela, 7; South African Institute of Race Relations (SAIRR) reel 28 (hereafter, Cradock Evidence [1945]).

64. For the sprouted grain regulation, see TC to Nat. Comm. (Cradock), 8 Nov. 1945, NAR, NTS 114/313 6330 P, 76; *Cape Gazette,* 1 Feb. 1946.

65. Annual Statements, Native Revenue Account, Cradock 1940–1948, NAR, NTS 114/313 C.

66. For the National War Memorial Health Foundation (NWMHF) see Hellman, *Handbook on Race Relations,* 393, 662; O. H. Walters to D. B. Molteno, 21 Oct. 1947, DBMP Bc579 A10, 199–201.

67. D. B. Molteno to O. H. Walters, 6 Nov. 1947, and Walters to Molteno, 21 Dec. 1947, DBMP Bc579 A10, 199–201.

68. L. T. Philips to D. L. Smit (SNA), 2 June 1944, NAR, NTS 5406 114/313 G.

69. For price of beer in the Cape in 1945 see ibid.; for price of beer in Cradock in 1945, see "Cradock Evidence (1945)," 2.

70. "Cradock Evidence (1945)," 3; *MN,* 20 May 1980.

71. *MN,* 20 May 1980.

72. NAC, *Use and Supply of Kaffir Beer (1942),* para. 42.

4. Water, Slops, and Night Soil

1. "Perseverantia Vincit (the Cradock Motto)" published by Lidbetter as an illustrated pamphlet. [The pamphlet was in Jeffrey Butler's possession. Butler thanked Professor Arthur Upgren of Wesleyan University's Astronomy Department for calculating the time of the Lidbetter picture. The original Lidbetter photo is reproduced here.–Ed.]

2. Guy Butler, *Karoo Morning: An Autobiography (1918–1935)* (Cape Town: David Philip, 1977), 113; J. Cl. M., 16 July 1929; Obituary for W. W. Lidbetter, *MN,* 3 Feb. 1959.

3. J. G. Gamble, "Water Supply in Cape Colony," *Proceedings of the Institute of Civil Engineers,* 1886–1887, vol. 90, Part IV, 255–94, CAR, 3/CDK 2/1/1/5, General Correspondence.

4. Ord. Cl. Mtg., 22 Sept. 1914, T. Cl. M. 11.

5. Great Fish River Irrigation Board, "Facts about the Valley of the Great Fish River," Nov. 1922; this copy marked "Written by C. E. Lawford," Keith Collett Papers, Grassridge; obituary for Lawford, *MN,* 9 Aug. 1951.

6. Keith Collett Papers, Grassridge.

7. *Eastern Province Herald,* "The Miracle of the Great Karoo: Whole Future of the Great Fish River Valley Changes," 29 and 30 Sept. 1925; 1, 3, 5, 6, 10, 13, and 17 Oct. 1925.

8. Elizabeth van Heyningen, "Public Health and Society in Cape Town, 1880–1910" (Ph.D. diss., University of Cape Town), 1989, introduction and chapter 5.

9. Queen's Central Hospital, Cradock, Report and Financial Statements of the Board of Management for the Year ended December 31st, 1923, p. 5, NAR, GES 564 123.

10. Cape of Good Hope, Department of Public Education, *Educational Statistics 1926* (Cape Town, 1927), 17–18, 79, 93.

11. Ord. Cl. Mtg., 28 April, 1936, T. Cl. M. 22:149.

12. Municipality of Cradock, Summary of Receipts and Payments for the Year 1926, CAR, 3/CDK 4/1/429, Audit, 1925–1931.

13. "Report on Systematic Sanitary Inspection of Cradock Municipal Area on the 8th and 9th July, 1924, by Dr. W. A. Murray," NAR, GES 627, 10/123/13A, para. 15 (hereafter Murray Rept. 1924).

14. Water Cttee., 14 Sept. 1925, T. Cl. M. 1/1/1 13:645–42.

15. Location Regulations, 3 Nov. 1908, *Cape Government Gazette,* no. 9, 1334, 10 Nov. 1908; Location Regulations 1926, no. 25, *Cape Gazette*, 309, 21 Oct. 1926.

16. J. E. Manuel and P. C. Goodman (Joint Secs., APO) to J. Deary (Mayor) 18 Feb. 1924; P. C. Goodman (Joint Sec., APO) to Town Council, 27 Oct. 1924; both in CAR, 3/CDK 4/1/106.

17. Public Health Act No. 36 of 1919, *Statutes of the Union of South Africa 1919* (Cape Town: Government Printer, 1919), 184–329.

18. *MN,* 13 Oct. 1923; Butler, *Karoo Morning,* 23, 68, 149, 161, 162; interview with Mary Butler, 7 July 1977; obituary for Mary Butler, *MN*, 9 Aug. 1977.

19. Mag. (W. J. Vlok) to SNA, 22 Oct. 1923; Act. SNA (J. S. Allison) to Administrator (Cape), 7 Nov. 1923; Act. SNA (J. S. Allison) to Sec. Pub. Health (SPH), 7 Nov. 1923; SPH to TC, 17 Nov., 1923; all in NAR, NTS 4265, 114/313 vol. 1.

20. TC to SPH, 22 Nov. 1923, NAR, NTS 4265, 114/313 vol. 1; SPH to TC, 30 Nov. 1923, NAR, GES 627, 123; TC to Prov. Sec., 1 Dec. 1923, NAR, NTS 4265, 114/313 vol. 1; TC to SPH, 4 Jan. 1924, NTS 4265, 114/313, vol. 1.

21. Minute by official, 4 Jan. 1924, NTS 4265, 114/313, vol 1. [Citation uncertain.–Ed.]

22. For William's father, Charles, see *DSAB* III, 644; *University of Cape Town Calendar 1930*, 122; J. Currie, Assistant Librarian, Edinburgh University Library to Jeffrey Butler, 28 Oct. 1992.

23. Union of South Africa, *Public Service List* 1921, 1924, 1934; Saul Dubow, *Scientific Racism in Modern South Africa* (Cambridge: Cambridge University Press, 1995), 177–79.

24. "Report of a meeting of Councillors to meet Dr. Murray of the Health Department, held on Wednesday, 9 July, 1924," NAR, GES 627,123/13.

25. Murray Rept. 1924, 11.

26. Ibid., 15.

27. "Assistant MOH's Report, October 12th/24," signed by Dr. P. de Wet, NAR, GES 627, 123/13.

28. "Report of Sanitary Committee Meeting held 4/11/24," NAR, GES 627, 123/13.

29. Ibid.

30. Cursons to Murray, 14 Aug. 1924, ibid.

31. Ibid.; and *MN,* 1 Sept. 1924.

32. Spec. Mtg., 11 Jan. 1924, T. Cl. M. 12.

33. Spec. Mtg., 15 Sept., and 28 Sept. 1925 to authorize visit of Deary, Hattingh, and Town Clerk to Pretoria, T. Cl. M. 13.

34. *MN,* 21 Aug. 1925; Ratepayers meeting, 16 Oct. 1925; *MN,* 17 Oct. 1925. [Citations uncertain.–Ed.]

35. *Official Yearbook,* no. 13, *1930–1931,* 88.

36. *MN,* 28 May 1926; for the legend on the roof, personal reminiscence.

37. Mayoral Minutes, 1928–1929, 20 Aug. 1929, T. Cl. M. 14.

38. Minute by Murray, 15 Oct. 1931, NAR, GES, 627, 123/13.

39. "Report on Systematic Inspection of the Health and Sanitary Conditions in the Municipal Area of Cradock conducted by Dr. F. W. P. Cluver on the 27th of November, 1931," dated 30 Dec. 1931, NAR, GES 627, 123/13 (hereafter Cluver Rept. 1931).

40. SPH to TC, 7 Mar., 10 and 28 Nov., 30 Dec. 1932; the suggested threat is a minute on SPH to TC, 30 Dec. 1932. Both in NAR GES 627, 123/13.

41. TC to SNA, 29 Nov. 1932, enclosing S. J. Kelly (Town Engineer) to TC, 28 Nov. 1932; SNA to TC, 7 Dec. 1932, approving expenditure; all in NAR, NTS 114/313 C.

42. Meetings of Joint Council, 2 Feb. 1930 and 21 Nov. 1932, J. Cl. M.; for 1935, see Petition to Chairman, Advisory Board, 2 Feb. 1935, CAR, 3/CDK 4/1/83, Locations, vol. 1, 1928–1938.

43. Ratepayers meeting, 20 Jan. 1936 authorizing loan, T. Cl. M. 22:34.

44. P. G. Caudwell, "Report on Inspection of the Urban Native Location at Cradock on 16 Aug. 1938," 30 Aug. 1938, NAR, NTS 4265, 114/313, Health Conditions, vol. 2 (hereafter Caudwell Rept. 1938).

45. *Proposed Sewerage Scheme for Cradock: Full Text of Engineer's Report* (Cradock: Midland News, 1944), "Cradock's Water Supply," 14–15, 22–23; hereafter Clinton Rept. 1942. [Citations not clear.–Ed.] It is difficult to accept even this figure as a measure of the amount of water that had to be carried to a location home—a five-member family would have needed 50 gallons, twelve 4-gallon "paraffin tins," every day.

46. Medical Officer for Health (MOH) Annual Report (Ann. Rept.), 30 June, 1953, NAR, NTS 6627, 114/313 U.

47. MOH Ann. Rept., 30 June, 1944; MOH Ann. Rept., 30 June, 1950; both in NAR, GES 565 123/13/B.

48. "Report on Re-Inspection of the Municipal Location Cradock and Matters connected therewith, on 7th and 9th September, 1946" by G. I. Nel, NAR, NTS 4266, 114/313 Main File, vol. 3 (hereafter Nel Rept. 1946).

49. A. Hyam and Co. (acting for municipality) to TC, 6 Feb. 1929 and 4 July 1929, listing purchase of stoves, toasters, hot plates, and heaters, CAR, 3/CDK 4/1/12, vol. 8, Misc. Corres. Hu-Hz.

50. Murray Rept. 1924, 5, 11.

51. *Amended and Additional Regulations Framed by the Municipal Council of Cradock* (Cape Town: W. A. Richards and Sons, 1899), 12–14; see Murray Rept. 1924, 5.

52. Charles Tapp to MOH, Cape Colony, 29 Jan. 1910; TC to Sec. for Interior, 1 Aug. 1910; both in NAR, GES 547 123/13.

53. Murray Rept. 1924, 3; personal information.

54. Murray Rept. 1924, 6.

55. Cluver Rept. 1931, 3.

56. Cradock Location Regulations, 1926, no. 25.

57. Cluver Rept. 1931, 9.

58. See note 49 above.

59. TC to Chief Health Officer, 5 Nov. 1935, and H. S. Gear, "Health Inspection: Cra-

dock Municipal Area, 16 Dec. 1935," NAR, GES 627, 123/13 A, 3–5 (hereafter Gear Rept. 1935).

60. Gear to SPH, 16 Dec. 1935; SPW to SPH, 15 Jan. 1936, NAR, GES 627, 123/13 A, 3–5.

61. Ord. Cl. Mtg., 28 Apr. 1936, T. Cl. M. 22:148–49.

62. J. J. Claassen: "Report on Sewerage Scheme Cradock," 31 July, 1936, NAR, GES 627, 123/13 A.

63. Clinton Rept. 1942, 4.

64. Nel Rept. 1946, 29.

65. Murray Rept. 1924, para. 25; TC to SNA, 10 Jan. 1928, NAR NTS 4960, 114/313C vol. 1, Nat. Rev. Ac.

66. Calculated from Nat. Rev. Ac., Annual Statements, 1934 to 1939, ibid.

67. Caudwell Rept. 1938, and response by municipality, TC to SNA, 25 Nov. 1938, NAR, NTS 4265, 114/313 vol. 2, Health Conditions.

68. "Cradock Native Location," blueprint by municipality signed "C. H. Marais, 20/2/49", Ernest Butler Papers (EBP).

69. Nel Rept. 1946, paras. 29, 60.

70. Ibid.

71. "Annual Report of the Medical Officer of Health [Dr. A. Budler] Ending 30/6/27," 20 Sept. 1927, NAR, GES 627 123/13.

72. Cluver Rept. 1931, para. 26.

73. MOH Ann. Repts. 1939 and 1940, NAR, GES 627 123/13A.

74. MOH Ann. Rept. 1943, ibid.

75. MOH Ann. Rept. 1945, ibid.

76. MOH Ann. Rept. 1943, ibid., 3.

77. MOH Ann. Rept. 1945, ibid., 3.

5. Charity and Welfare in the Age of Segregation

1. See H. C. Hopkins, *Die N.G. Kerk Cradock 1818–1968* (Cradock: Nederduits Gereformeerde Kerk, 1968), 90; Census 1926, Part VII, Religions (Europeans), 13; General Valuation, 1929.

2. Rev. Lionel B. Fletcher (Evangelist) to TC, 9 Nov. 1938, CAR, 3/CDK 4/1/16, Misc. Corres., Na to Nh; for a service for rain, see *MN,* 25 Feb. 1927.

3. For a comprehensive study of the ACVV, see Marijke du Toit, "Women, Welfare, and the Nurturing of Afrikaner Nationalisms: A Social History of the Afrikaanse Christelike Vroue Vereeniging, c. 1870–1939" (D. Phil. diss., University of Cape Town, 1996).

4. Johann Kinghorn, "Modernization and Apartheid: The Afrikaner Churches," in Richard Elphick and Rodney Davenport, eds., *Christianity in South Africa: A Political, Social, and Cultural History* (Berkeley: University of California Press, 1997), 138–39.

5. Rev. J. A. van Niekerk to TC, 20 Aug. 1925, CAR, 3/CDK 4/1/105, Immanuel Church.

6. Rev. J. A. van Niekerk to Superintendent, Union Education Dept., 5 Feb. 1935; report on Immanuel Te Huis (Immanuel Home), by C. Kempff, Inspector of Institutions, 5 Dec. 1934 and 18 May 1935; cutting from the *Star,* 1 June 1935; all in CAR, SWC A30 50/2/8; Hopkins, *N.G. Kerk Cradock*, 104.

7. Ord. Cl. Mtg., 7 Sept. 1935; Notules van die Kerkraad (Minutes of the Kerkraad), Dutch Reformed Church, Cradock; Social Welfare Office (Graaff-Reinet) to Dept. of Social Welfare (Pretoria), 29 June 1949, CAR SWC A30 50/2/8.

8. Rev. J. P. Jacobs to TC, 27 July 1937, CAR, 3/CDK 4/1/12, Misc. Corres., Ja-Jk; Hopkins, *N.G. Kerk Cradock,* 99–107.

9. Du Toit, "Women and Welfare," chap. 1. [The author's copy of this thesis is not paginated. Hence in the notes that follow he cites it by chapter, followed by the footnote closest to the text he wanted to indicate.–Ed.]

10. John Dollard, *Caste and Class in a Southern Town,* 3rd ed. (1949; reprint, Madison: University of Wisconsin Press, 1988), 74.

11. Du Toit, "Women and Welfare," chap. 2, n. 14, 23; chap. 3, n. 49. Jeffrey Butler, "Afrikaner Women and the Creation of Ethnicity in a Small South African Town," in Le Roy Vail, ed., *The Creation of Tribalism in Southern Africa* (Berkeley: University of California Press, 1989), 58–64.

12. Du Toit, "Women and Welfare," chap. 2, n. 124.

13. Ibid., chap 3, n. 49.

14. Hopkins, *N. G. Kerk Cradock,* 114–15; Butler, "Afrikaner Women," 68–69.

15. Butler, "Afrikaner Women," 69; *MN,* 3 Apr. 1926.

16. Hopkins, *N. G. Kerk Cradock,* 117; Butler, "Afrikaner Women," 69–70.

17. Notule van die ACVV Bestuur (Minutes of the ACVV Executive), Sterling Library, Yale University, film no. 824 (hereafter ACVV Bestuur).

18. Ibid., 4 Sept. 1926.

19. Ibid., 6 Aug. 1927; 2 Feb. 1929; 4 June 1932; 3 Aug. 1935.

20. *MN,* 20 Jan. 1927.

21. *MN,* 27 July 1931; St. Peter's Lay Council Minutes, 14 June 1929, 5 June 1930; St. Peters, Cradock; Census 1926, Part VII, Religions (Europeans), 13; General Valuation, 1929; Circular letter, Rev. Clarence W. Wallace, 23 Oct. 1926, St. Peters, Cradock; St. Peters' Lay Council, Car Committee, 12 May 1948. [These citations were not checked.–Ed.]

22. *MN,* 19 Feb. 1927.

23. H. Philips, "South Africa's Worst Demographic Disaster: The Spanish Influenza Epidemic of 1918," *South African Historical Journal* 20 (Nov. 1988), 57–73; *MN,* 29 Nov. 1920.

24. *MN,* 7 Mar. 1924, 5 Dec. 1924, 9 Apr. 1926.

25. *MN,* 16 Aug. 1924.

26. For Deary, see *MN,* 18 and 25 Aug. 1924; for Waters see *MN,* 22 Aug. 1924.

27. *MN,* 9 Sept. 1924; "Petition To: The Mayor and Councillors of the Cradock Municipal Council," 16 Sept. 1924, CAR, 3/CDK 4/1/163, Location Women Voters (*sic:* Volunteers) (hereafter Lady Volunteers for the Location Movement [LVM]).

28. TC to LVM, 23 Oct. 1924, ibid.; *MN,* 18 Sept. 1924.

29. LVM to TC, 2 Nov. 1924, ibid.

30. LVM to TC, 5 Dec. 1924, ibid; *MN,* 24 Dec. 1924.

31. *MN,* 4 Oct. 1924.

32. *MN,* 28 Nov. 1924; L. F. Brown (Pres. WCA) to TC 20, Feb. 1929, suggesting a deputation of herself, Mrs. Hattingh, and Mrs. P. J. J. Coetzee to discuss an infectious diseases hospital, CAR 3/CDK 4/1/105, Women's Civic Association (WCA).

33. Hendrickse et al. to the Mayor and Councillors, 21 Oct. 1925, CAR, 3/CDK 4/1/105, WCA. [Item not located.–Ed.]

34. N. Best to TC, 26 Jan. 1926, ibid.

35. Ord. Cl. Mtg., 23 Feb. 1926, T. Cl. M. 13.

36. *MN,* 31 May 1926; Ord. Mtg., 25 (?) May 1926, T. Cl. M. 13.

37. R. M. Benjamin to TC, 20 Apr. 1926; Ethel Heffard to MOH (Cradock), 15 Apr.

and 27 May 1926; TC to Benjamin, 22 May 1926; all in CAR, 3/CDK 4/1/28, Native Location: Finance Cttee. and Regulations. Benjamin to TC, 26 May 1926, CAR, 3/CDK 4/1/105, WCA.

38. M. Furmidge (Sec. WCA) to TC, 3 July 1926, CAR, 3/CDK 4/1/9, Misc. Corres. Fr-Fz; L. Brown (Pres. WCA) to TC, 21 July 1926, CAR, 3/CDK 4/1/105, WCA. The latter letter is incomplete but in Brown's hand.

39. TC to Sec. WCA, 26 Aug. 1926. [Item not located.–Ed.]

40. Brown (Pres. WCA) to TC, 18 Oct. 1926 in reply to a letter from TC of 1 Oct., missing from this file, CAR, 3/CDK 4/1/105, WCA.

41. Ord. Cl. Mtg., 26 Oct. 1926, T. Cl. M. 13.

42. Loc. Cttee, 8 Mar. 1927, T. Cl. M. 13; TC to Brown (Sec. WCA), 31 Mar. 1927, CAR, 3/CDK 4/1/105, WCA.

43. L. L. Russell (Sec. WCA) to TC, 20 Oct. 1927; K. O. Hughes (Acting Sec., WCA) to TC, 17 July 1929, enclosing tender and diagrams; TC to Hughes, 25 Sept. 1929; all in CAR, 3/CDK 4/1/105, WCA; *MN,* 5 Mar. 1930.

44. Second General Valuation, 1929.

45. The first document in a "Soup Kitchen" file is TC to Rev. A. Hendrickse (Congregational), Rev. J. W. Owen (Methodist), and Rev. C. W. Wallace (Anglican), 18 May 1927, asking for numbers of children in their location schools, CAR 3/CDK 4/1/28, Soup Kitchen, Location, 1929–1938.

6. "Is It Nothing to You?"

1. Jeffrey Butler, "Interwar Liberalism and Local Activism," in Jeffrey Butler, Richard Elphick, and David Welsh, eds., *Democratic Liberalism in South Africa: Its History and Prospect* (Middletown: Wesleyan University Press, 1987), 93–94; Mary Butler to J. D. Rheinallt-Jones, 15 Feb. 1931, University of the Witwatersrand, South African Institute of Race Relations Papers (IRRP), AD 1433 Cc 5, Cradock Joint Council.

2. "Report on Systematic Inspection of the Queens Central Hospital Cradock on 9th July, 1924 by Dr. W. A. Murray," NAR, GES 1142 11/19; for 1946 see "Report of Visit to Cradock on 5th and 6th February, 1946 by G. W. Gale etc.," NAR, GES 2210 60/70.

3. Statement by TC, 4 Jan. 1927, CAR, 3/CDK 4/1/64, Location Dispensary, 1927–1944.

4. "Report on Work in the Location Dispensary, February-March 1927," J. Cl. M.

5. Minutes Combined Location Committee, 30 July 1927, J. Cl. M.; L. L. Russell (Sec. WCA) to TC, 9 Oct. 1927, CAR, 3/CDK 4/1/105, WCA.

6. Report to WCA, 18 Apr. 1927, CAR, 3/CDK 4/1/105, WCA.

7. Quarterly Meeting (Qtly. Mtg.), 30 July, 15 Aug., 21 Nov. 1927, J. Cl. M.

8. Qtly. Mtg., 30 July 1927, ibid.

9. Qtly. Mtg., 28 Jan. 1928, ibid.

10. Qtly. Mtg., 4 May 1928, ibid.

11. Ibid.

12. Qtly. Mtg., 20 Nov. 1928, ibid., J. Cl. M.; *MN,* 23 Nov. 1928.

13. M. Butler to J. D. Rheinallt Jones, 25 Nov. 1928, and reply, 5 Dec. 1928, IRRP, Cc 5, Cradock Joint Council.

14. Minutes of the Last Qtly. Mtg., 6 Dec. 1928, J. Cl. M.; Richard Haines, "The Politics of Philanthropy and Race Relations: The South African Joint Councils, c. 1920–1965" (Ph.D. thesis, London University, 1991), 15–16.

15. TC to SNA, 10 Mar. 1931, NAR NTS 114/313 C.

16. Joint Council Meeting, 6 Dec. 1928, J. Cl. M.

17. Location Advisory Board (Loc. Adv. Bd.), July 1933, T. Cl. M. 18:7, 41.

18. Spec. Cttee., 15 Aug. 1933, T. Cl. M. 18:7, 71.

19. Loc. Adv. Bd., Sept. 1933, T. Cl. M. 18:7, 90.

20. Dr. W. Scholtz to TC, 28 May 1934, CAR, 3/CDK 4/1/21, Misc. Corres. Sc; Dr. Budler, Special Report, 4 Apr. 1935, T. Cl. M. 20:288; Finance Cttee., 19 Aug. 1935, T. Cl. M. 21:387.

21. Ord. Cl. Mtg., 4 June 1935, T. Cl. M. 21:321, 319; Finance Cttee., 5 Dec. 1935, T. Cl. M. 21:569–70.

22. Report by Mary Butler on confinements, 17 July 1936, T. Cl. M. 22:221.

23. Rev. N. Mhlomi to Loc. Sup., 25 Feb. 1937; Mary Butler to TC, 9 Mar. 1937; J. Sitela (Sec. CAC) to TC, 8 Mar. 1937; all in 3/CDK 4/1/64, Location Dispensary.

24. Finance and Health Cttee., 19 Aug. 1935, T. Cl. M. 21:387; Loc. Cttee., 16 Mar. 1936, T. Cl. M. 22:92.

25. Loc. Cttee., 20 Apr. 1936; TC, "Re Anonymous Gift to Build New Dispensary or Clinic in the Location," 15 April 1936, T. Cl. M. 22:126, 112–15.

26. Spec. Mtg., Loc. Adv. Bd., 27 Apr. 1936, T. Cl. M. 22:138.

27. Loc. Cttee., 31 July 1936, T. Cl. M. 22:291; Loc. Cttee., 26 Nov. 1936, T. Cl. M. 23:410; Helen Mtombeni to TC, 9 Nov. 1936, CAR 3/CDK 4/1/64; for the CAC see Spec. Cttee. Mtg., 27 May 1937, T. Cl. M. 24:108–9.

28. TC to Osary Hokwana, 28 Jan. 1937; Hokwana to TC, 1 May 1937; M. Butler to TC, 3 May 1937; Town Clerk's rough notes (n.d.); all in CAR, 3/CDK 4/1/64, Location Dispensary. [A number of items that Butler places in CAR 3/CDK 4/1/64 were not found by the endnote checkers.–Ed.]

29. J. Sitela (Sec. CAC) to TC, 2 Mar. 1937, and reply, 4 Mar. 1937; Sitela to TC, 8 Mar. 1937, CAR, 3/CDK 4/1/64, Location Dispensary.

30. TC to Sec. CAC, 30 Apr. 1937, CAR, 3/CDK 4/1/64, Location Dispensary; Ord. Cl. Mtg., 22 April 1937, T. Cl. M. 24:16; Loc. Cttee., 15 Mar. 1937, T. Cl. M. 24:560; and 3 May 1937, T. Cl. M. 24:77.

31. M. Butler to TC, 4 May 1937; Hokwana to TC, 4 May 1937; M. Butler to TC, 14 May 1937; all in CAR, 3/CDK 4/1/64, Location Dispensary.

32. J. Sitela (Sec. CAC) to TC, 8 May 1937, ibid.

33. S. P. Akena, E. Macembe, A. Pokomela, Native Members of the Adv. Bd. to TC, 8 May 1937. [Possibly in ibid.–Ed.]

34. Spec. Cttee., 27 May 1937, T. Cl. M. 24:86.

35. Report Postponed Special Committee Meeting Held on 21 June 1937; TC to Hokwana, 24 June and 3 Aug. 1937; both in CAR, 3/CDK 4/1/64; Loc. Cttee., 19 July 1937, T. Cl. M 24:134.

36. Loc. Adv. Bd., 8 Sept. 1937, T. Cl. M. 24:227.

37. O. Walters to J. D. Rheinallt Jones, 24 June 1937, IRRP, Cradock Joint Council, Cc 5.1.

38. Dorothy Butler to Lynn Saffery, 24 Nov. 1938, ibid.; J. D. Rheinallt Jones to Charles Butler, 10 Dec. 1940, ibid.

39. MOH Ann. Rept., 30 June 1939, NAR, GES 627 123/13A; ACVV Bestuur Min., 4 Feb. and 15 Aug. 1939.

40. Ord. Cl. Mtg., 24 Sept. 1937, T. Cl. M. 24:235.

41. Thornton's first report for a full year ending 30 June 1939, NAR, GES 627 123/13 A.

42. *Census 1936,* vol. I, Table 7; *Census 1946*, vol. I, Table 7.

43. Shula Marks, "South Africa's Early Experiment in Social Medicine: Its Pioneers and Politics," *American Journal of Public Health* 87 (1997), 452–54; *Official Yearbook* no. 26–1950, 151.

44. Marks, "Social Medicine," 453.

45. Copy Cull's resolution TC to Hon. Sec. Cape Midlands Development Assn., 13 Mar. 1945, NAR, GES 2210, 60/70, Health Centres, Cradock, 1945–1948.

46. Molteno to H. G. Lawrence (Min. of Public Health), 16 Oct., 1945, and reply, 20 Oct. 1945, NAR TBPA, GES, vol. 30, 43/1 B, District Surgeon, Cradock.

47. TC to Magistrate, 15 Nov. 1945, ibid.

48. DS to Mag., 6 Dec. 1945, ibid. (Van Rensburg signed this letter as District Surgeon).

49. TC to SPH, 25 Jan. 1946, and Secretary Divisional Council (Sec. Div. Cl.) to SPH, 11 Feb. 1946; both in ibid.

50. G. W. Gale, "Report of Visit to Cradock on 5th and 6th February 1946," n.d., ibid.

51. "Petition for a Health Centre at Cradock to His Hon. the Minister of Health," 18 Feb. 1946, ibid.

52. B. J. van Rensburg to Mag., 29 Mar. 1946, NAR TBPA, GES, vol. 30 43/1 B.

53. Margery Cooper to Mag., 18 Sept. 1946; unsigned memo to Minister, 18 Sept. 1946; SPH to Mag., 25 Sept., 1946; Sec. Div. Cl. to Mag., 9 Oct. 1946; Mag. to SPH, 17 Oct. 1946; all in NAR TBPA, GES 943, 43/17, Tuberculosis Cradock.

54. Randall M. Packard, *White Plague, Black Labor: Tuberculosis and the Political Economy of Health and Disease in South Africa* (Berkeley: University of California Press, 1989), 35, 39.

55. *Report of the Tuberculosis Commission 1914* (Cape Town: Cape Times Ltd., Government Printers, 1914 U.G. 34–14), para. 64, 28–29.

56. For WCA see L. F. Brown (Sec.) to TC, 20 Feb. 1930, CAR, 3/CDK 4/1/105. For the Joint Council see Mary Butler (Sec. to TC), 4 May 1930; Rev. Charles Gould (Pres.) to TC and to Sec. Div. Cl., 1 June 1934; both in CAR, 4/CDK 4/1/27, Location Joint Council, 18 Mar. 1929–22 June 1937.

57. L. Oosthuizen, "The Tuberculous Menace in Cradock," 30 Apr. 1947, NAR GES 1035, 43/17, Tuberculosis. This date is inaccurate: B. A. Dormer used material in it on 28 Mar. 1947.

58. B. A. Dormer (Chief: Division of Tuberculosis) to SPH, 28 Mar. 1947, ibid.

59. Cdk HC Ann. Rept., 1946–47, 2, NAR, GES 1918 5/54/32.2.

60. Ibid.; "Approximate Location Inhabitants," June 1946; both in CAR, 3/CDK 4/1/84, Locations, vol. 5, 1945–1948.

61. Cdk HC Ann. Rept. 1946–47, 5–6.

62. Ibid., 7.

63. Ibid., 5.

64. Ibid., 2.

65. Cdk HC Ann. Rept. 1950–51, 1, NAR, GES 1918 4/54/32.1.

66. Sec. Mortimer District Nursing Society to SPH, 12 Jan. 1954, NAR, GES 2210 60/70 A, Baroda and Mortimer Nursing Society, 1949–1957.

67. MOH Ann. Rept., 30 June 1953, NAR, GES 565 123/13 C, Sanitation; MOH Ann. Rept., 1953, NAR NTS 6627 114/313 U.

68. See note 58 above.

69. Marks, "Social Medicine," 458n28.

70. Ibid., 455.

71. Shula Marks and Neil Anderson, "Industrialization, Rural Health and the 1944 National Health Services Commission in South Africa," in Steven Feierman and John M. Jansen, eds., *The Social Basis of Health and Healing in Africa* (Berkeley: University of California Press, 1992), 157–58.

72. Cdk HC Ann. Rept. 1950–51, NAR GES 1918 54/32.2.

7. Improvement or Removal?

1. *MN,* 19 Oct. 1926.

2. David Welsh, "The Growth of Towns," *OHSA,* vol. 2, 187–89.

3. For Mrs. Solly, see *MN,* 3 Oct. 1922, 27 Feb. 1923, 12 Aug. 1924.

4. T. R. H. Davenport, "The Beginnings of Urban Segregation in South Africa," Institute of Social and Economic Research, Occasional Paper no. 15 (Grahamstown: Rhodes University, 1971), 21–23; on the act, see *MN,* 3 Nov. 1924.

5. Hellman, *Handbook on Race Relations,* 242, 387.

6. E.g., *OYB,* no. 13 (1930–1931), 209.

7. "Report on Systematic Sanitation Inspection made of Cradock Municipal Area on the 8th and 9th July 1924, by Dr. W. A. Murray," NAR, GES 627/123/13.11 (hereafter Murray Rept. [1924]); "Meeting of councillors to meet Dr. Murray . . . 9/7/24," NAR, GES 627/123/13.

8. TC to SNA, 7 Aug. 1926, and reply, 15 Sept. 1926, NAR, NTS, vol. 1, 114/313 H; obituary for Van Heerden, *MN,* 7 Jan. 1948.

9. Ord. Cl. Mtg., 25 May 1926, T. Cl. M. 13:(?).

10. Jeffrey Butler, "Housing in a Karoo Dorp: A Survey of Sources and an Examination of Developing Segregation before the Group Areas Act, 1950," *South African Historical Journal* 17 (1985), 105–7.

11. Kelly to TC, 18 Oct. 1926, CAR, 3/CDK 4/1/28, Native Location Finance Committee and Regulations, 1924–1938.

12. *MN,* 26 Nov. 1926; Kelly to TC, 22 Nov. 1926, NAR, NTS 55/2, 114/313H, vol. 1; Sec. Central Housing Board (Cen. Hsng. Bd. to TC 4 June 1927, and reply, 30 June 1927, and Sec. Cen. Hsng. Bd. to Prov. Sec., 20 July 1927, NAR, NTS 55/2 114/313 H, 31–42; Cen. Hsng. Bd., 19 Nov. 1927, NAR, GEM 10 4/182.

13. Reg. no. 7, Mun. of Cradock, *Location Regulations,* AN 309, 1926; Sec. Cen. Hsng. Bd. to TC, 4 June 1927, NAR, NTS 55/2 114/313H, 40. [The first citation is not clear; see also chapter 2, notes 13 and 15.–Ed.]

14. Butler, "Housing in a Karoo Dorp," 106; untitled memorandum by TC, evidence for Young Barrett Committee, n.d., in response to Sec. Young-Barrett Committee to TC, 18 July 1935, CAR, 3/CDK 4/1/83, Locations, vol. 1, 1929–1939.

15. TC to Prov. Sec. 27 July 1928, NAR, NTS 55/2 114/313 H, 43.

16. SNA to Mag., 13 Aug. 1928, 46, and reply, 20 Aug. 1928, 47, ibid.

17. Petition to Chmn., Loc. Adv. Bd., 2 Feb. 1935, CAR, 3/CDK 4/1/83, Locations, vol. 1, 1929–1939; Applications Sub-Economic Houses—Coloured, 1944, CAR 3/CDK 4/1/30, Housing Coloureds, 1944–52.

18. Murray Rept. (1924), 2–3.

19. TC to Prov. Sec., 5 July 1939, CAR, 3/CDK 4/1/163 European Housing. [This may indicate the wrong file.–Ed.]

20. Cluver Rept. (1931), 2; Blair Rept. (1949), 12. [Location of Blair Report not determined.–Ed.]

21. ACVV Bestuur Minutes, 12 Oct. 1929.

22. For the petitions, see CAR, 3/CDK 4/1/85 European Housing, vol. 1, 1927–1930.

23. Metcalf to TC, 7 Feb. 1930, CAR, 3/CDK 4/1/85, European Housing, vol. 1, 1927–1930.

24. Spec. Cl. Mtg., 26 Feb. 1930, T. Cl. M. 15:48; Butler, "Housing in a Karoo Dorp," 115–16; *De Middelandsche Afrikaander,* 28 Feb. 1930.

25. Questionnaire dated 27 Oct. 1929, CAR, 3/CDK 4/1/163, European Housing Applications, vol. 1, 1929–1938. In these calculations I used a 26-day month.

26. Fin. Cttee., 21 Aug. 1936, T. Cl. M. 23:279; Hlth. Cttee., 15 Mar. 1938, T. Cl. M. 25:518.

27. TC, Schedule Applications Economic Housing Scheme: dated 17 Oct. 1938, 3 CAR 3/CDK 4/1/86; *MN,* 29 Oct. 1938.

28. For application of the act to locations, see Caudwell Rept. (1938), NAR NTS 4265 114/313 Main File, vol. 2.

29. TC to Sec. Cen. Hsng. Bd., 23 Oct. 1940, NAR NTS 4266, vol. 3.

30. *Report of the Carnegie Commission of Investigation on the Poor White Question in South Africa,* vol. 1, *Economic Report*: J. F. W. Grosskopf, *Rural Impoverishment and Rural Exodus* (Stellenbosch: Pro-Ecclesia, 1932), 8, 13, 71–76.

31. TC to Sec. Cen. Hsng. Bd., 23 Oct. 1940, applying for funds for 33 houses, CAR, 3/CDK 4/1/87, vol. 3, Sub-Economic Housing, 1938–1942. According to layout plans, 32 were built.

32. TC to SNA, 21 Nov. 1940, NAR, NTS 114/313 C.

33. TC to Prov. Sec., 3 Mar. 1941, CAR, 3/CDK 4/1/87, vol. 3, Sub-Economic Housing, 1938–1942; Spec. Cl. Mtg., 6 Mar. 1941, T. Cl. M. 29:187; Hsng. Cttee., 19 Jan. 1942, T. Cl. M. 29:54; Report by TC, 22 Aug. 1942, CAR, 3/CDK 4/1/88, vol. 4, Housing Loan, 1942–1944.

34. "Petition to the Cradock Municipal Council," 16 July 1943, signed by 15 residents, CAR, 3/CDK 4/1/88, vol. 5, Sub-Economic Housing Scheme, 1942–1944.

35. ACVV Minutes, 16 Sept. 1933, 2 Dec. 1933, and 1 May 1937.

36. Mayoral Minute, August 1945, T. Cl. M. 32:522.

37. Henriette J. Lubbe, "Vergeet die arbeiders en wen die 'Kleurlinge': Die 'swart gevaar' propaganda in Kaapland gedurende die parlementêre verkiesingstryd van 1928 tot 1929." ("Forget the Workers and Win the 'Coloureds': 'Black Peril' Propaganda during the Parliamentary Election Campaign from 1928 to 1929"), *Kronos* 18 (Oct. 1991), 15, 27–28.

38. Gavin Lewis, *Between the Wire and the Wall: A History of South African "Coloured" Politics* (Cape Town: David Philip, 1987), 160–61, 209–11.

39. M[artjie] Van Rensburg (Sec. ACVV, Cradock) to Miss Ida Theron (Sec. ACVV Executive, Tulbagh), 14 June 1938; ACVV *Jaarverslag* (Ann. Rept.), 1937, 1937–1938, ACVV collection, CAR, A 1952.

40. Ord. Cl. Mtg., 9 Feb. 1939, T. Cl. M. 27:505.

41. Lewis, *Between Wire and Wall,* 171–73.

42. Loc. Cttee., 20 Sept. 1937, T. Cl. M. 25:211; Report by Loc. Sup. to Loc. Cttee., 3 Dec. 1937, T. Cl. M. 25:372; Loc. Cttee., 18 Jan. 1938, T. Cl. M. 25:413.

43. P. G. Caudwell, "Report on Inspection of the Urban Native Location at Cradock, 16 Aug. 1938," NAR, NTS, Main File, 4266 114/313, vol. 3.

44. TC to Mag., 28 July 1939, NAR, NTS 114/313 H, 57; Application Sub-Economic Scheme £15,000, 13 June 1940, ibid., 80–82.

45. TC Report, 22 Aug. 1942, 3/CDK 4/1/88, Housing Loan, vol. 4, 1942–1944; TC to SPH, 6 July, 1944, CAR, 3/CDK 4/1/86, vol. 2, Economic Housing Scheme, 1937–1947; CAR, 3/CDK 4/1/29, Non European Housing Loan, 1943–1945.

46. F. W. J[ameson], "Cradock Muncy. Coloured and Native Housing Scheme," 17 Sept. 1940, ibid., 100. [No indication given of location of this file.–Ed.]

47. Loc. Cttee., 25 Sept. and 25 Oct. 1941, T. Cl. M. 29:455 and 462; F. Walton Jameson to Sec. Cen. Hsng. Bd., 12 Oct. 1941, NAR, NTS 114/313 H, 136. Ord. Cl. Mtg., 28 Oct., 1941, T. Cl. M. 29:469.

48. Lewis, *Between Wire and Wall,* 173.

49. Hsng. Cttee., 19 Feb. 1945, T. Cl. M. 31:371; Ord. Cl. Mtg., 27 Feb. 1945, T. Cl. M. 31:385–90.

50. W. E. Lawn, T. Bester, J. Jarson, and A. Adams to Mayor and Councillors, 26 Mar. 1945 enclosing petition, CAR, 3/CDK 4/1/30, Housing Coloureds, 1944–1952.

51. Constitution of Coloured Peoples National Union, CAR 3/CDK 4/1/30, Housing Coloureds, 1942–1952; Lewis, *Between Wire and Wall,* 208, 223, 237.

52. Athol J. K. Sauls (Hon. Sec. CPNU Cradock Branch) to TC, 19 Mar. 1946, CAR, 3/CDK 4/1/30, Coloured Housing Scheme, 1944–1952.

53. H. C. A. Cloete, "The Case for the Coloured People of Cradock on the question of separate Housing in a Coloured township," 15 June 1946, ibid.

54. Coloured Advisory Council (CAdC), "Report of an Interview with Major Collings . . . on . . . 5th September, 1946, at Cradock, signed by H. C. A. Cloete," 10 Sept. 1946, ibid.

55. W. A. J. van Heerden (Sec. NERA) to TC, 2 Nov. 1946; TC to Cloete, 29 Nov. 1946, ibid.

56. Cloete to TC, 4 Dec. 1946, ibid.

57. G. R. Butler (Assn. Sec. NERA) to TC, 5 Jan. 1951, ibid.

58. TC to Prov. Sec., 30 Mar. 1950, ibid.

59. TC to Secretary for the Interior, 5 Sept. 1951, ibid.

60. Lewis, *Between Wire and Wall,* 177, 206, 211.

61. J. S. Furnivall, *Colonial Policy and Practice: A Comparative Study of Burma and Netherlands India* (New York: New York University Press, 1956).

8. Apartheid Comes to Cradock

1. T. R. H. Davenport, *South Africa: A Modern History,* 4th ed. (Toronto: University of Toronto Press, 1991), 320; *MN,* 21, 24, 28 Feb. 1947.

2. Newell M. Stultz, *Afrikaner Politics in South Africa, 1934–1948* (Berkeley: University of California Press, 1974), 60–66.

3. Kenneth A. Heard, *General Elections in South Africa, 1943–1970* (London: Oxford University Press, 1974), 32–35.

4. T. R. H. Davenport, "The Triumph of Colonel Stallard: The Transformation of the Natives (Urban Areas) Act between 1923 and 1937," *South African Historical Journal* 2 (Nov. 1970), 92–96.

5. T. R. H. Davenport, "Racial Policies of the Smuts Governments, 1939–1948," (mimeo, n.d.), 14a, 15, 30.

6. Dept. of Native Affairs, "Report of the Interdepartmental Committee on the Social,

Health and Economic Conditions of Urban Natives" (Smit Committee), G.P.S. 7272 (Pretoria: Government Printer, 1942), paras. 146–207.

7. Dept. of Native Affairs, "Report of the Native Laws Commission 1946–1948" (Fagan Commission), U.G. No. 28–1948 (Pretoria: Government Printer, 1948), 49–51; for Smuts's speech see J. C. Smuts, "The Basis of Trusteeship," Hoernlé Memorial Lecture, January 1942, New Africa Pamphlet no. 2 (Johannesburg: Institute of Race Relations, 1942).

8. Davenport, *South Africa,* 306–7.

9. Margaret Ballinger, *From Union to Apartheid: A Trek to Isolation* (New York: Praeger, 1969), 82.

10. Gavin Lewis, *Between the Wire and the Wall: A History of South African "Coloured" Politics* (Cape Town: David Philip, 1987), 165–73; G. I. Nel, "Report on Re-Inspection of the Municipal Location Cradock, . . . on 7th and 9th September, 1946," NAR, NTS 4266 114/313, Main file, vol. 3, para. 20, p. 152.

11. Lewis, *Wire and the Wall,* 208–11.

12. Stultz, *Afrikaner Politics,* 137.

13. Ibid., 137.

14. For the United Party manifesto, see Stultz, *Afrikaner Politics,* 137, quoting *Rand Daily Mail,* 26 Apr. 1948.

15. Deborah Posel, *The Making of Apartheid, 1948–1961* (Oxford: Clarendon Press, 1991), 1–6, 261.

16. "Verslag van die Kommissie aangestel deur die H.N.P. van Kaapland insake beleid van die Nasionale Party teenoor die Kleurlinge" (Report of the Commission Appointed by the H.N.P. of Cape Province on Policy of the National Party towards the Coloureds), (Cape Town: mimeo; 1945), South African Library, Cape Town.

17. "Verslag van die Kleurvraagstuk—Kommissie van die Herenigde Nasionale Party" (Report of the Colour Problem Commission of the Re-united National Party), (Cape Town: mimeo, 1948), South African Library, Cape Town, hereafter "Sauer Report."

18. D. W. Kruger, ed., *South African Parties and Policies, 1910–1960* (London: Bowes and Bowes, 1960), 402–7.

19. Voters' List, Electoral Division of Cradock, 1953. [Archive unknown.–Ed.] Colored voters were listed separately after 1936. I was unable to find a Cradock voters' list closer to 1948 than 1953.

20. *MN,* 2 Apr. 1948, 4.

21. *MN* editorial, 21 May 1948, 4 and reports 19 Mar. 1943, 2, 4–5, 3 May 1943.

22. *MN,* 28 Apr. 1948, 2.

23. *MN,* 28 Apr. 1948, 2; 7 May 1948, 7, 4; and 28 May 1948, 1.

24. *MN,* 15 Nov. 1951, 3.

25. Stultz, *Afrikaner Politics,* 131–32; *MN,* 31 May 1948, 2.

26. John Lazar, "Conformity and Conflict: Afrikaner Nationalist Politics in South Africa, 1948–1961" (D. Phil. thesis, Oxford University, 1987), 346.

27. Stultz, *Afrikaner Politics,* 161–62.

28. Davenport, *South Africa,* 327–40.

29. Ibid., 328.

30. Ivan Evans, *Bureaucracy and Race: Native Administration in South Africa* (Berkeley: University of California Press, 1997), 6, and chapter 2, "Reviving the Department."

31. Davenport, *South Africa,* 518–24.

32. Ballinger, *From Union to Apartheid,* 132; Davenport, *South Africa,* 327–38.

33. For the town clerk, *MN,* 24 Mar. 1955, 1; Blair Rept. (1949), 1, 12.

34. Blair Rept. (1949).

35. Census 1946, vol. 1, 84–85, Table 10.

36. Act 41 of 1950, *Statutes of the Union of South Africa 1950,* 407–69.

37. Hansard (HAD), 29 May 1950, 7433–34.

38. Ibid., 7451.

39. Ibid., 7453–74.

40. Uma Mesthrie, "Tinkering and Tampering: A Decade of the Group Areas Act (1950–1960)," *South African Historical Journal* 28 (1993), 179–84.

41. Mabel Palmer, *The History of the Indians in Natal* (Westport: Greenwood Press, 1977), 64, 85–87, 122–24, 55.

42. TC (Port Elizabeth) to TC (Cradock), 26 Oct. 1951; TC (Cradock) to Sec. Eastern Cape Cttee., 30 Nov. 1951, supporting demand for an Eastern Cape office; both in CAR, 3/CDK 19/A, Group Areas.

43. Mesthrie, "Tinkering and Tampering," 183.

44. Ibid., 184–85.

45. SNA to TC, 2 Aug. 1947; boundaries approved, 10 Dec. 1948 and proclaimed in GN 2771, 24 Dec. 1948, NAR, NTS 114/313 N, vol. 1, 48, 70, 74.

46. Board of Works, 20 Oct. 1947, T. Cl. M. 32:282; J. H. C. Hofmeyr to TC, 8 June 1949, CAR, 3/CDK 4/1/32, Town Planning.

47. Evans, *Bureaucracy and Race,* 56–66, 74.

48. Chief Native Commissioner (CNC) to TC, 6 June 1952, NAR, NTS 114/313 N, vol.1, 83; TC to CNC, 27 June, 1952, CAR, 3/CDK 4/1/30, Coloured Housing; Report of Visit to Cradock by G. A. Brand (DNA), (?) Page (Housing) and J. Louw (Coloured Affairs) on 4 Sept. 1952, CAR, KUS 85/5/75, Residential Areas and Housing, vol. 2.

49. TC to CNC, 3 Dec. 1952, enclosing a "Layout Plan," PER, CNC (24) N 1/2/2; CNC to SNA, 9 Apr. 1953, NAR, NTS 114/313 N, vol. 1, 88. [PER references have not been checked.–Ed.]

50. CNC to TC, 26 Mar. 1953, NAR, NTS 114/313 N, vol. 1, 86–87.

51. SNA to CNC, 24 Mar. 1953, and reply, 9 Apr. 1953, ibid., 88; Ord. Cl. Mtg., 28 Apr. 1953, T. Cl. M. 40:185; TC to CNC, 30 Apr. 1953, and reply, 25 May 1953, NAR, NTS 114/313 N, vol. 1, 91, 92.

52. Ord. Cl. Mtg., 23 June 1953, T. Cl. M. 40:265; TC to CNC, 26 June 1953, NAR, NTS 114/313 N, vol. 1, 96.

53. CNC to SNA, 1 July 1953, NAR, NTS 114/313 N, vol. 1, 97.

54. Die Afrikaner, 4 Mar. 1954, 1–2.

55. "Establishment and Extension of Urban Locations: Buffer Requirements," 14 July 1954, general circular no. 27 of 1954 sent by Magistrate to TC, 13 Apr. 1955, NAR, NTS 114/313 N, vol. 1, 117.

56. Spec. Cl. Mtg., 14 Sept. 1954, T. Cl. M.

57. CNC to SNA, 22 Jan. 1954, NAR, NTS 114/313 N, vol.1, 108; Ord. Cl. Mtg., 22 Mar. 1955, T. Cl. M.; TC to Mag., 29 Mar. 1955, NAR, NTS 114/313 N, vol. 1, 145.

58. TC to SNA, 31 Mar. 1955, CAR, 3/CDK (1953–1962), 25/NA/2, Misc.

59. CNC to Mag., 4 Apr. 1955, NAR, NTS 114/313 N, vol. 1, 142–43; Mag. to CNC, 9 Apr. 1955, and Sec. for Transport to SNA, 17 June 1955, ibid., 146–47, 153–54.

60. TC to Sec. E. Cape Cttee., Land Tenure Advisory Board (LTAB), 30 May 1955, CAR, 3/CDK (1953–1962), 19A, Group Areas.

61. Presidential Address to African National Congress (ANC) (Cape), n.d., July 1948, Carter-Karis Collection, 2:DA17:30/6; *MN,* 10 Jan. 1948, 3.

62. Peter Walshe, *The Rise of the African Nationalism in South Africa: The African National Congress* (Berkeley: University of California Press, 1971), 399–400.

63. Calata to Sec. Gen. (ANC), 16 June, 1950, Carter-Karis Collection, 2:XC3:41/72; MN, 13 June 1950, 1.

64. For banning from teaching see *The Friend,* 2 Jan. 1953, quoting *Rand Daily Mail* (Johannesburg), 25 Nov. 1952, MBP; for the trial see Thomas Karis, *The Treason Trial in South Africa: A Guide to the Microfilm Record of the Trial* (Palo Alto: Hoover Institution, 1965), 32, 49; interview with W. Lombard, 10 Mar. 1978.

65. *MN,* 27 Nov. 1952; SNA to TC, 1 May 1953, CAR, NTS 114/313 C, vol. 4, Nat. Rev. Ac., 390.

66. Ord. Cl. Mtg. 24 Feb. 1953, T. Cl. M. 40:87.

67. *MN,* 6 Nov. and 18 Dec. 1952, 8; David Carter, "The Defiance Campaign—A Comparative Analysis of the Organization, Leadership and Participation in the Eastern Cape and the Transvaal," *Collected Seminar Papers on the Societies of Southern Africa in the 19th and 20th Centuries,* vol. 2 (London: University of London, Institute of Commonwealth Studies, 1971), 97, appendix III; Lodge, *Black Politics,* 46.

68. Meeting of Ratepayers, 4 Mar. 1953, T. Cl. M. 40:91; *MN,* 12 Mar. 1953, 1.

69. TC to CNC, 28 Oct. 1954, and reply, 3 Nov. 1955, CAR, 3/CDK (1953–1962) 25/NA/2, Misc.

70. Spec. Cl. Mtg., 15 Nov. 1955; T. Cl. M. 44:224–26; TC to CNC, 25 Nov. 1955, and reply, 29 Nov. 1955, CAR, 3/CDK (1953–1962) 25/NA/2, Misc.

71. TC to SNA, 27 Aug. 1956, CAR, 3/CDK (1953–1962) 25/NA/2, Misc., vol. 1, 174.

72. Loc. Cttee., 20 Feb. 1956, ibid., 355; Protest dated 22 Feb. 1956, T. CI. M. 44:3384. [Minutes for these meetings not found.–Ed.]

73. Spec. Cl. Mtg., 14 Mar. 1956, on occasion of fire that day; ibid., 386; Spec. Cl. Mtg. 28 Apr. 1956, ibid., 500. [Minutes not found.–Ed.]

74. Statement of Cradock Vigilance Association (mimeo), 29 June, 1956, EBP; also in PER, CNC N 9/15/3/23, vol. 3.

75. *MN,* 3 July 1956, 1–3 for an extended account of the meeting of 29 June.

76. SNA to CNC, 23 July 1956, and TC to SNA, 27 Aug. 1956; both in NAR, NTS 114/313 N, vol. 1, 172, 174; MN, 28 Aug. 1956, 3–4.

77. TC to SNA, 29 Oct. 1956; NAR NTS 114/113 N, vol. 1, 176.

78. Ord. Cl. Mtg., 29 Oct. 1956, T. Cl. M. 45:379; MN, 20 Nov. 1956, 3–4.

79. W. M. Lombard, "Confidential Report of ANC Youth League Concert: 24 Aug. 1956," NAR, NTS 4266 114/313 Main File, vol. 3, 249.

80. Spec. Cl. Mtg., 18 Jan. 1957, T. Cl. M. 46:57. [Minutes not found.–Ed.]

81. Ord. Cl. Mtg., 26 Feb. 1957, ibid.,105; MN, 22 Jan., 1 and 5 Feb. 1957; *Eastern Province Herald,* 21 Jan. 1957, 1.

82. *New Age,* 7 Mar. 1957, 3; Municipality of Cradock, Audit for years ended 31 Dec. 1956 and 31 Dec. 1957, NAR, NTS 114/313 C, Nat. Rev. Ac., vol. 5, 166.

83. Michael Tetelman, "'We Can': Black Politics in Cradock, South Africa, 1948–85" (Ph.D. thesis, Northwestern University, 1977), 154.

84. Spec. Cl. Mtg., 2 Apr. 1957, T. Cl. M. 46:171–227; *MN,* 2 April. 1957.

85. Evans, *Bureaucracy and Race,* 126.

86. P. S. Coetzee (Chief Health Inspector) to Mayor, 25 April 1957, CAR, 3/CDK (1953–1962), 25/NA/2, Shifting of Location.

87. Ord. Cl. Mtg., 30 Apr. 1957, T. Cl. M. 46:219–20.

88. Report, Town Engineer's Department, signed by T. Kleefstra, 1 July 1957, CAR, 3/CDK (1953–1962), 25/NA/2, Shifting of Location.

89. Loc. Cttee., 23 July 1957, T. Cl. M. 46:356; Ord. Cl. Mtg., 30 July 1957, T. Cl. M. 46:328.[These page numbers are probably wrong.–Ed.]

90. TC to CNC, 30 Aug. 1957, NAR, NTS 232 114/313 N, vol. 1, 233.

91. Tetelman, "'We Can,'" 134, 140–45.

92. Ord. Cl. Mtg., 25 Feb. 1958, T. Cl. M. 47:373.

93. TC to CNC, 29 July 1958; PER, CNC N 9/15/3/23.

94. Brownlee to CNC, 22 Aug. 1958, NAR, NTS 272 114/313 N, vol. 1, 252–55.

95. Memo by Minister of Bantu Administration, 26 Jan. 1959, ibid., 272–75.

96. Govt. Notice 794 in Government Gazette, vol. 204 6094, 26 May, 1961, 27.

97. Report of visit to Cradock by G. A. Brand (DNA), (?) Page (Housing) and Jan Louw (Coloured Affairs) on 4 Sept. 1952, CAR, KUS 85/5/75, Residential Areas and Housing, vol. 2, 9.

98. CNC to TC, 20 May 1958; NAR, NTS 231 114/313 N, vol. 1, 234–37.

99. SNA to CNC, 30 Nov. 1953, CAR 3/CDK (1953–1962), 25/NA/2, Shifting of Location.

100. P. R. Hattingh, Secretary for Bantu Administration (SBA), to TC, 30 May, 1959, NAR, NTS 114/313 N, vol. 2, 2–3.

101. TC to SBA, 7 July 1959, and reply, 15 Oct. 1959, ibid., 10, 12.

102. Prov. Sec. to SBA, 27 Apr. 1957, NAR, NTS 114/313 U, Medical and Clinical Services, 35.

103. Ibid.

104. SNA to CNC, 10 May 1957, and reply, 8 June 1957, ibid., 36, 38.

105. P. K. Olivier (Admin. of Cape) to Dr. H. Verwoerd (Min. of Native Affairs), 18 Oct. 1957, ibid., 46; Verwoerd to Admin., 13 Feb. 1958, ibid., 57.

106. CNC to SBA, 24 Oct. 1959, ibid., 67–69.

107. Prov. Sec. to SBA, 2 Feb., 1960, ibid., 81.

108. TC to SNA, 26 Feb.1959, NAR, NTS 114/313 N, vol. 1, 292–93.

109. Lombard (Loc. Sup.) to TC, 28 Nov. 1964, PER 3/CDK (1963–1976), 25/NA/2A, Native Affairs.

110. TC to Postmaster (Cradock), 10 Jan. 1964, ibid.

111. MOH Ann. Rept., 1969; Spec. Cl. Mtg., 14 Jan. 1970, T. Cl. M. 67:557; Mayor's Minute, 31 Aug. 1970, ibid., 343.

112. TC to Mag., 5 May 1939; Mag. to CNC, 2 Apr. 1940; both in PER, CNC N 9/10/3/24, Church and School sites.

113. K. T. Cremer to Jeffrey Butler, 17 Nov. 1997, quoting Dennis Burkinshaw, former Diocesan Secretary of the Diocese of Grahamstown.

114. Interview with David Curry, Cape Town, 23 Jan. 1978.

115. Lewis, *Wire and the Wall,* 161–62.

116. Ibid., 216, 219.

117. Interview with Reuben Butler, Cape Town, 10 Aug. 1982.

118. Lewis, *Wire and the Wall,* 173.

119. Community hall: Sec. Soc. Welfare to TC, 5 Aug. 1948, CAR, 3/CDK 4/1/30, Housing Coloureds, 1944–1952. Public facilities: Commissioner for Coloured Affairs to Mayor, 21 Apr. 1954, CAR, KUS 85/5/75, Residential Areas and Housing, vol. 2, 20. Colored cemetery: M. W. Curry (Act. Sec. NERA) to TC, 23 June 1952, CAR, 3/CDK

4/1/30, Housing Coloureds, 1944–1952. Improvements: G. R. Butler (Ass. Sec. NERA) to TC, 5 Jan. 1951, ibid.

120. MOH Ann. Rept., 1952, CAR 3/CDK 5/2/5/1; T. Cl. M. 39:318; *MN,* 4 Dec. 1952, 20 July 1954.

121. TC to Sec. E. Cape Cttee., LTAB, 30 May 1955.

122. Davenport, *South Africa,* 309, 344; David Welsh, "The Growth of Towns," *OHSA,* vol. 2, 240–41.

123. Lewis, *Wire and the Wall,* 257–59; Davenport, *South Africa,* 316.

124. *Dictionary of South African Biography* (*DSAB*), vol 5, 217–19 (Johannesburg: Van Rensburg, 1987); *Who's Who of Southern Africa 1970,* 317.

125. Comm. for Col. Aff. to TC, 4 July 1955, CAR, KUS, 85/5/75K 110/17, Comm. for Col. Aff., 50.

126. TC to Mayor and Councillors, 13 July 1955, T. Cl. M. 43:444; Ord. Cl. Mtg., 26 July 1955, T. Cl. M. 43:466.

127. Ibid.

128. W. J Gouws to Sec. Group Areas Board (GAB), 17 Sept. 1958, and reply, 17 Jan. 1959, NAR GAB G 7/283, vol. 1.

129. Sec. GAB (Pretoria) to Sec. E. Cape Cttee., 17 Nov. 1958, NAR, GAB G 7/283, vol. 1.

130. Sec. E. Cape Cttee. (GAB) to TC, 21 May 1959, CAR, 3/CDK (1953–62) 19/A, Group Areas.

131. Davenport, *South Africa,* 317–20.

132. Martin Rubin, Sarah Gertrude Millin (Johannesburg: Ad Donker, 1977), 82; *DSAB,* vol. 4, 363.

133. Inquiry into Demarcation of Group Areas in Cradock, Monday and Tuesday, 8 and 9 June 1959, CAR, 3/CDK (1953–1962) HA 31/A, GAB.

134. For the "Open Letter" see *MN,* 18 Aug. 1959; for Michau's response, see *MN,* 25 Aug. 1959; Mayoral Minute, 1960, T. Cl. M. 51:9, Afrik., 12 Aug. 1960.

135. "Report and Recommendations of Eastern Cape Committee Concerning the Establishment of Group Areas in the Municipal Area ('Regsgebied') of Cradock," 10 July 1959, CAR, PAA (AK) H/10 26/1.

136. Sec. GAB to Sec. E. Cape Cttee., 3 Nov. 1959 and 12 Mar. 1960, NAR, GGR G 7/283, Application for Group Area, Cradock, vol. 1.

137. Minutes, 45th General Meeting, Groeps Gebiede Raad, 25–28 Apr. 1960, ibid.

138. Proclamation No. 436, 1960, Government Gazette, vol. 202, no. 6602, 1–3, 30 Dec. 1960; Press Statement, Group Areas: Cradock, CAR, 3/CDK (1952–1963) 19/A/1, Group Areas.

139. Gouws to Sec. GAB, 3 Nov. 1959, NAR, GGR G 7 283, vol. 1.

140. Ibid.

141. H. C. Coetzer et al. to TC, 24 June 1961; TC to Sec. E. Cape Cttee. (GAB), 3 July 1961, and reply, 13 July 1961; both in CAR, 3/CDK (1953–1962) 19/A, Group Areas; Ord. Cl. Mtg., 27 June 1961, T. Cl. M. 52:282.

142. Reg. Under-Sec., Department of Community Development to TC, 19 Aug. 1961, CAR, 3/CDK (1953–1962) 19/A, Group Areas.

143. *MN,* 12 Sept. 1961, 3; 12 June 1962, 1.

144. TC to Mayor and Councillors, 25 Sept. 1961, CAR, 3/CDK (1953–1962) 19/A/1, Group Areas; MN, 3 Oct. 1961, 1; 14 Aug. 1962, 1.

145. Ord. Cl. Mtg., 29 Aug. 1961, T. Cl. M. 52:367; TC to Secretary School Board,

Cradock, 28 May 1963, CAR, 3/CDK (1953–1962) 10/C/1, New Coloured Township; *MN,* 21 Aug. 1962.

146. TC to Mag., 2 Apr. 1962, NAR, GGR G 7/283, vol. 2.

147. Secretary, Department of Community Development to TC, 28 July 1962; NAR, GGR G 7/283, vol. 2, Afrik., 13 Mar. 1964, 1.

148. R. F. G. Allan (Town Clerk), "Memorandum in connection with the problems of payment of compensation to Coloureds whose houses must be demolished, proclamation of a new Coloured group area, and the type of houses which must be erected for Coloureds," 26 Mar. 1964, PER, 3/CDK (1963–1976), 10/B/1, Coloured Affairs, Miscellaneous.

149. Report of Deputation to Cape Town, 16 and 17 Apr. 1964, PER, 3/CDK (1963–1976), 42/1, Township Board.

150. Report of meeting, 5 May 1964, "Identifiseering van Kleurlingwoonbuurt," PER, 3/CDK (1963–1976) 19/A, Group Areas.

151. Memorandum by TC, 11 May 1964: Interview with senior officials of state departments on 5 May 1964, concerning proposed Coloured group area in Taaiboschleegte, PER, 3/CDK (1963–1976) 21/1, Dept. of Community Development.

152. Mayor's Minute, Year ended 31 Aug. 1964, T. Cl. M. 57:513; Meeting of Members of the Town Council and Coloured Owners and Occupiers held in the Coloured Methodist Church, 24 Sept. 1964, PER, 3/CDK 10/B/1, Authorities Miscellaneous.

153. A. L. du Preez to Sec. for Planning, 14 Oct. 1964, enclosing news cutting, NAR, GGR G 7/283, vol. 1.

154. Ibid. For the first border area on the edge of the colored area see Proc. 21, 1962, NAR, GGR G 7 283, vol. 2.

155. Proc. 45, 7 Mar. 1980, added a block of new streets and lots in Michausdal's hinterland.

156. Mayor's Minute, 31 Aug. 1970, T. Cl. M. 67:343; for population see TC to Sec. Road Safety Board, 9 Aug. 1968, PER, 3/CDK (1963–1976), 10/B/2 Coloured Affairs Misc.

157. Interview with Kathleen Rayepen, Cradock, 28 Oct. 1977.

Conclusion

1. Deborah Posel, *The Making of Apartheid, 1948–1961: Conflict and Compromise* (Oxford: Clarendon Press, 1991), 1–6 and passim.

2. Ivan Evans, *Bureaucracy and Race: Native Administration in South Africa* (Berkeley: University of California Press, 1997), 6 and passim.

3. Michael Stanley Tetelman, *The Burial of Canon J. A. Calata and the Revival of Mass-Based Opposition in South Africa, 1983* (Johannesburg: University of the Witwatersrand, Institute for Advanced Social Research, 1998).

INDEX

Figures, maps, and tables are indicated by f, m, and t (respectively) following the page number.

Abrahamson, Clara, 100
ACVV. *See* Afrikaanse Christelike Vroue Vereeniging (Afrikaans Christian Women's Association; ACVV)
African Methodist Episcopal church, 23, 166
African National Congress (ANC): African identity and, 25; Cradock ban on all public meetings of, 157; Defiance Campaign, 157; representation of Cradock Africans by, 157; Youth League, 157, 159, 193
African People's Organisation (APO), 29–31; alcohol control and, 57–58; coloreds represented by, 30, 191; Coloured Peoples National Union (CPNU) formed from dissident members of, 137; ineffectual role in Cradock, 169; objection to compulsory residential segregation (1939), 139, 189; objection to lodger's permits and other regulations on the location (1925), 34–35; protesting on behalf of colored ratepayers (1924), 22, 69; seeking colored nurse to attend to coloreds in the location, 111
African Political Organisation (later African People's Organization), 25
Africans: access and residence in age of segregation, 28–46; demographics of, xi, 15; failure to ally with coloreds, 6, 24, 25–26, 36, 62, 101, 192; franchise not extended to, 4, 19, 124; identity development among, 25; male workers, legislation and procedures focused on, 28, 38; national representation for, 144; in 1921 census, 14; occupations of, x; as racial category, 6, 14; resistance to apartheid, 157–58, 162, 192, 194. *See also* alcohol control; apartheid era (1948–94); housing (1910–48, segregation era); housing (1948–94, apartheid era); "location, the" (1910–48, segregation era); "location, the" (1948–94, apartheid era); public health (1910–48, segregation era); sanitation and sewage (1910–48, segregation era); segregation era (1910–48); water supply (1910–48, segregation era); women, African; youth, African
African Vigilance Association, 167. *See also* Location Vigilance Association
Afrikaanse Christelike Vroue Vereeniging (Afrikaans Christian Women's Association; ACVV), 87, 88–95, 89*f*, 103–4, 114; aid for poor whites, 130, 131, 133–34, 188; on Mixed Area's demographics, 134, 140, 185; old people's home, 132
Afrikaanse Sakekamer (Afrikaner Chamber of Commerce), 175
Afrikaners (whites speaking Afrikaans): apartheid designed by, 7; class divisions among, 92; housing for poor whites and, 128–34; local Cradock government's change to Afrikaans as working language (1948), 147; majority and political roles in Cradock, 16; nationalism, 90, 104; water supply and, 68–69. *See also* poor whites; United Party; whites; women, Afrikaner
agriculture and farming: alcohol control advocated by farmers, 48–49, 62;

agriculture and farming (*continued*)
annual agricultural show as joint Anglo-Afrikaner event, 87; farmers advocating influx control to make farm labor available, 37–40, 185, 186; grazing land of commonage, 69; health care for farm workers, 108, 115; historical development of, 11–12; impoverishment, 16; ostrich farming, 67; pastoralism, 67; vegetables, 69
Akena, A., 42, 45, 54, 59
alcohol control, 7, 48–63, 187–88; African tradition of home brewing beer, 48, 50–61; ban on sale of liquor to Africans, 49–50, 62; beer hall, 53–62, 189; beer hall boycotts by Africans, 57, 159; beer hall revenues, 56, 60–61, 62, 63, 156; beer raids in the location (from 1920s through 1940s), 47, 58–59; burning down of beer hall (1980), 62, 189; coloreds as liquor couriers for location Africans, 50, 62, 155, 185, 187; curfew requirements and, 35, 50; drunkenness and disorderly conduct, 47, 57–62; Durban system, 49; end of prohibition, 53–57; hotel system, 54–55, 56; Kaffir Beer Profits Inquiry (1945), 60; Liquor Licensing Board, 57–58; local option, parliamentary vote on, 49; prohibition in Cradock, 49, 50, 53; temperance movement, 48–50, 98, 188. *See also* Liquor Act (1928)
Alexander, Piet, 20
Alexander family (colored), 168
Allan, R. F. G., 179
Allison, J. S., 71
ANC. *See* African National Congress (ANC)
Anglican denomination, 88, 95, 96, 104, 166, 182, 192. *See also* St. James church (Anglican); St. Peter's Mission (Anglican church)
Anglo-Boer War (1899–1902), 3, 18; ACVV roots in, 90; coloreds in Cradock siding with British in, 19; contentions continuing after, 87; memorial, x
apartheid era (1948–94), 142–83, 189–90; African resistance, 157–59, 162, 192, 194; Asians' treatment in, 162, 167, 170, 176; buffer strips, imposition of, 8, 154–56, 158–60, 161–62, 182, 191, 194; businesses, conduct of, 164–65; churches, policy toward colored or African churches when population relocated, 158, 160, 162, 166–67, 174, 175, 176, 192; compensation to African residents forced to move, 166; confusion over apartheid doctrine, 143, 150–51, 167, 191; Cradock's slow-moving agenda, 7, 168–78, 182, 185; disqualified persons, time allowed for relocation of, 151, 178–83; in first ten years (1948–58), 167–68; group areas, decision to create, 161–64; hospital siting and, 165–66; housing construction and, 166; industrial area, establishment of, 164, 177; map of apartheid plan for Cradock (proposed 1953), 154*m;* map of apartheid plan for Cradock (proposed 1957), 161*m,* 162; map of colored and Asian group areas in Cradock (proposed 1955), 171*m;* moves of colored and African communities to newly designated areas, 193; 1960 proclamation by Group Areas Board on division of Cradock by race, 163*m,* 177, 178–83; political foundations of, 144–48; post-1971 policies, 194; replacing segregation as racial model after 1948, 6–7, 185; sociological inappropriateness for Cradock, 193; town, relocations within, 149, 168–81; town access required by African and colored workers, 164; whites not required to move in town, 170. *See also* coloreds (1948–94, apartheid era); Group Areas Act (1950); housing (1948–94, apartheid era); "location, the" (1948–94, apartheid era)
APO. *See* African People's Organisation (APO)
Armesorg Kommissie (Poverty Relief Commission), 103
Asians: alcohol access of, 50; in apartheid era, location of, xii, 162, 167, 170, 176; demographics of, xi, 15–16; fear of and antipathy toward, 172; franchise,

electoral, 4, 19–20, 146, 148; Group Areas Act (1950) and, 16, 146, 151; immigration from India banned, 146; living in town in 1920s, 26; as merchants, 172; in Mixed Area, 20, 21; Natal's and Transvaal's limits on ownership and occupation of, 150, 151; Natives (Urban Areas) Act and, 26; in 1921 census, 14, 15; Orange Free State's exclusion of, 151; property and political rights, limits on (1946), 144, 148; as racial category, 6, 14; return to India, policy for, 146
Asiatic Land Tenure and Representation Act (1946), 144, 148
Asiatic Laws Amendment Act (1948), 148

Bam, J., 53
Bantu Administration, Department of (formerly Department of Native Affairs), 164–67, 177, 179
Bantu Authorities, establishment of, 148, 190
Bantu Authorities Act (1951), 148
Bantu Education Act (1953), 148, 159
Baptist denomination, 88
Baroda Rural Society, 117
Bartman, Alex, 41
Basuto Methodist church, x, 21
beer. *See* alcohol control
Bekker, Gerard, 146, 156
Benjamin, R. M., 101
Best, Nicolina, 101
Beveridge Report (Britain 1942), 115
bilingualism, 86, 87
Bloemfontein, 31, 53, 56, 61
blueprint of Township of Cradock (1924), 20
Botha, Louis, 142
Botha, P. W., 178, 182, 193
Brand, G. A., 152–53
brickmaking, 164–65
British Commonwealth, 142
Brown, Mrs. L., 98, 101, 102, 108
Brownlee, F. H., 157–60, 162–64
Budler, A. H., 82, 111
Buffelskop, ix
Butler, Charles (author's great-uncle), x, xi, 18, 37; on alcohol control, 54, 56, 57, 61, 156; involvement in nursing dispute involving his niece Mary, 113; location amenities promised by, 156
Butler, Dorothy (author's sister), 114
Butler, Ernest (author's father), x, xi, 16, 105, 156–60, 166–67
Butler, Guy (author's brother), *Karoo Morning: An Autobiography (1918–35)*, xii
Butler, James (author's grandfather), xi, 18, 37, 70, 117, 188
Butler, Mary (author's aunt), ix, xi, 105–14; Africans and coloreds raising complaints about, 110–11, 192; alcohol control and, 52–54; background of, 70–71, 105; Calata's relationship with, 110, 113; in conflict with Hokwana (trained African nurse), 105, 112–13; departure from Cradock, 113; drug stocking for dispensary and, 107–8, 110; on infant mortality rates in the location, 105; as nurse for dispensary in the location, 101–2, 105, 107; photograph of, 102*f*; resignation from nursing position, 113, 188; water supply and, 70–71; WCTU and, 98
Butler, R., 180
Butler, R. E., 28
Butler Brothers (shop of author's family), x
Butler family (colored), 168
Butlers (author's family) as Quakers, 65

CAC (Cape African Congress), 54, 55, 112–13, 116
Calata, James A.: as Africanist and activist, 51; on alcohol access for Africans, 54–55, 59; as Anglican minister in Cradock, 50; funeral of, effect on young people, 194; indictment for high treason, 156; involved in dispute between Mary Butler and African trained nurse, 105–6; Joint Council role of, 52; as leader of African National Congress, 25, 55; local and national prominence of, 169; Natives and Coloured Peoples Conference organized by, 36, 51; on new housing construction for the

Calata, James A. (*continued*)
location, 135; on 1948 election, 156; opposing government intervention in missionary schools, 159; opposing move of Africans to Sondagshoek, 156, 158; portrait/photograph of, 51*f*, 96*f*; relationship to Mary Butler, 110, 113–14; water supply and, 77
Cape African Congress (CAC), 54, 55, 112–13, 116
Cape Colony, 3–4; demographics, topography, and history of, 12–15; liberal tradition of, 19–20
Cape Coloured Commission report (1937), 137
Cape Coloured Defence Link Committee, 57
Cape Dutch, settlement of Cradock, 11–12
Cape Education Department, 169
Cape franchise, 3–4, 169
Cape Government Railway, 13
Cape Municipal Ordinance (1836), extending self-government to towns, 19
Cape of Good Hope Annual Register, The (1855), 12
Cape Province: apartheid enforcement in, 151–52, 175; colored people's rights in, 2, 124, 134, 137; franchise, 3–4, 169; friction in big cities between whites and Asians or coloreds, 149
Cape Provincial Administration, 88
Cape Provincial Council, 189
Cape Provincial Hospital Administration, 165, 167
Cape Times on water situation in Cradock, 74
Cape Town, 53, 56, 61, 149, 168, 191, 194
Carnegie Commission, 72
Carolus, E. C., 136–37
Catholics. *See* Roman Catholic Convent of the Sacred Heart
Caudwell, P. G., 40, 77–78, 135
census: 1921 census, 14; 1933 Wilken's census of the location's population, 38; 1936 compared to 1946 numbers, 115; 1938 location census, 40; 1946 Union census of the location's population, 44; 1946 Wilken's census of the location's population, 43; biennial instituted to identify African male surplus under Native Laws Amendment Act (1937), 39, 186
Central Farmers' Association, 37, 41
Central Housing Board, 126, 133, 135, 139, 154, 178, 187
Chambers of Commerce, 175
charity and welfare (1910–48, segregation era), 87–104; individuals making donations to the location, 95–96, 102–3. *See also* Afrikaanse Christelike Vroue Vereeniging (Afrikaans Christian Women's Association; ACVV); churches; Women's Civic Association (WCA)
Child Welfare Society (CWS), 108–9
Chinese. *See* Asians
cholera, 4, 68
churches: apartheid policy toward colored or African churches when population relocated, 158, 160, 162, 166–67, 174, 175, 176, 192; comparative poverty of English-speaking churches, 96; English-speaking ministers of town churches, 95; failure to unite Africans and coloreds, 24–25; lack of cooperation between Methodists and Anglicans, 96; in the location (African churches), 23, 25; missionaries, apartheid's policy toward, 145; in Mixed Area in 1920s, 21, 24–25; as most important nongovernmental organizations, 87–88; temperance movement and, 48–49, 53, 57; thanksgiving bazaars for fund-raising by, 95; voluntary organizations allied with, 87, 104. *See also specific names and religious groups*
Citizenship Act (1949), 147–48
civil rights and status: erosion of coloreds' rights, 3, 8, 33, 39, 134–36, 145, 146, 168–69; Ordinance 50 (1828), extending to freed blacks, Khoikhoi, and Africans, 19
Clinton, J., 78
Cloete, H. A. C., 138–39

clothes washing, 64–65, 66*f*, 73–74, 77*f*, 78, 165
Cluver, F. W. P., 76–77, 80, 82–83
Coetzee, P. S., 160, 166
Coetzee, Mrs. P. J. J., 108
Coetzee, Pieter, 173, 174
coloreds (1910–48, segregation era): access and residence for, 2, 28–46; alcohol and beer hall access of, 50, 53, 54, 57–59, 61–62; civil rights and status, erosion of, 3, 8, 33, 39, 134–36, 145, 146; "closing" the location, effect on (1938), 39–40, 48; curfew and pass laws, application to, 2, 24, 35, 45, 50, 136, 182; demographics of, xi, 14–15; desire to be separate from Africans, 36, 44, 134–36, 140, 145; employment color bar and, 4, 134; failure to ally with Africans, 6, 24, 25–26, 36, 62, 101, 192; franchise based on income or property ownership, 19, 145; living in town (not required to live in the location), 2, 44, 125, 138–39, 149, 170; in the location in 1920s, 26; lodgers' raids and, 29, 136; in Mixed Area, 8, 20, 26; municipal influence of, 6; Natives (Urban Areas) Consolidation Act (1945) and, 164; in New Brighton, 127; in 1921 census, 14; orphanage for colored girls, 89–90; as racial category, 6, 14, 26; United Party and, 141, 143, 144. *See also* franchise, electoral
coloreds (1948–94, apartheid era): arguing against town relocation of, 173–74, 191; arguing for equality with whites in town, 170, 174–75; church access, 158, 160, 162; civil rights and status, erosion of, 168–69; colored businesses, conduct of, 171–72; desire to be separate from Africans, 169–70, 185, 187; employment color bar and, 168–69; failure to ally with Africans, 169; failure to lobby local authorities for better conditions, 169; inadequacy of municipal area designated for, 181–82, 191; Michausdal (new township housing all coloreds), xii, 180–81, 183; moving to other cities, 168, 191; relocation to newly designated colored area, 8, 137, 145, 153–55, 162, 167–70, 171*m*, 176, 179, 192; second move required to achieve consolidated single group area for, 179–80, 182, 191, 193
Coloured Advisory Council (CAdC), 136–39, 143, 169
Coloured Affairs, Department of, 143, 171–72, 178–79, 181–82, 191–92
Coloured Methodist church, 21, 25, 59
Coloured Peoples National Union (CPNU), 137, 169
Coloured Representative Council, 145
Combined Location Committee, 108–10
Community Development, Department of, 179
Congregational "Independent" church, 25, 29, 30, 175
constitutional changes after 1948 election, 147
Convent of the Holy Rosary, 133
Cooper, Margery, 117
CPNU (Coloured Peoples National Union), 137, 169
Cradock, John, 11
Cradock, municipality of: access to, ix, 11; age of apartheid distinguished from age of segregation in, 7, 8, 146, 189–91, 193–94; blueprint of Township of Cradock (1924), 20; climate, 11; coloreds' rights in segregation era, 146; demographics in 1800s, 12; demographics in 1921, 14; description in 1920s, 16–18; farms in district of, 11; history of establishment of, 11–12; map of (segregation era), 153*m*; map of apartheid plan (proposed 1953), 154*m*; map of apartheid plan (proposed 1957), 161*m*, 162; map of colored and Asian group areas (proposed 1955), 171*m*; map of group areas (1960 proclamation), 163*m*; map of group areas (1971 proclamation), 171, 181*m*; 1948 election, issues for, 146–47; optimism of future growth, 18; racial attitudes from founding through 1800s, 14; reluctance to impose segregation regulations on the location, 33, 125,

Cradock, municipality of (*continued*) 140, 190; topography in region of Great Karoo, 11; town council's role, 5. *See also* apartheid era (1948–94); Cradock, town proper of; "location, the" (1910–48, segregation era); "location, the" (1948–94,, apartheid era); Mixed Area of Cradock town; segregation era (1910–48); town council; *and specific street names*

Cradock, town proper of: Africans living in town in age of segregation, 2; apartheid and relocations within town, 149, 168–81; coloreds living in town in age of apartheid, 169–70, 181; coloreds living in town in age of segregation, 2, 44, 125, 138–39, 149, 170; demographics of, xii, 2, 16, 20; entirely white after apartheid implemented, 8; historic core from 1930s, x; photograph of (1933), 131*f;* property ownership trends in 1920s, 20; racial composition in 1920s, 16, 26; regional hospital, location proposed in town for, 165–66; responding to apartheid system's introduction (late 1940s and 1950s), 2; responding to segregation system (1920s to 1940s), 2, 45; zoning of (1920s and 1930s), 128–30, 129*m*

Cradock African Political Organization, 134

Cradock Board of Executors, 74

"Cradock Four" (1985), xi, 194

Cradock Handelskool (Commercial School), 94

Cremer, Keith, 43

Cross Street: as boundary of white area in age of apartheid, 176–77, 182; colored petition trying to preserve as colored area from Cross Street to Regent Street (1964), 180; in Eastern Cape Committee's proposal to create group areas for different races (1959), 173; Group Areas Act, effect on, 181; within white area (1971 proclamation), 171

Cull, James A., 41, 116, 133, 137, 138, 141, 146–47, 182

Culldene (Mixed Area), 133, 134

"Cupido" name, 15

curfew in the location and application to coloreds, 2, 24, 33, 35, 45, 50, 136, 182, 187

Curry, David, 21

Curry, M. W., 136–37

Cursons, William, 31, 37, 71, 77

Cypressenhof hostel for indigent girls, 92–93

Davenport, Rodney, 4, 44, 143, 148, 185

De Aar railway junction, 98, 100

Deary, John: as Cradock's mayor, 18; criticizing Waters's call for improvements in the location's conditions, 99; disagreeing with Murray on sanitary standards of Cradock, 74; fixity of tenure for Africans extolled by, 38, 42; Natives (Urban Areas) Act enforcement by, 30–34; on separate housing locations for coloreds and Africans, 123, 125, 127–28, 141, 185

death rates. *See* mortality rates

Defence, Department of, 59

Defiance Campaign (ANC and South African Indian Congress), 157

De Kock, Hester, 99, 100

De Kock, Max, 81, 86, 99, 113, 131

demographics. *See* census; races, division of population into; *and specific racial designations*

De Wet, P., 74, 84

diarrhea, 84, 84*t*

Die Afrikaner (newspaper, formerly *De Middlelandsche Afrikaander*), 17–18

diphtheria, 68, 84, 84*t*

Dollard, John, *Caste and Class in a Southern Town,* 1–2, 92

Dönges, T. E., 150, 151

Dorman, Miss, 100

Dormer, B. A., 118, 120, 121

Drury, Allen, 8

Du Plessis, H. P., 18

Du Plessis, I. D., 171–72

Du Preez, A. C., 179

Durban, 49, 99

Dutch Reformed church, 12, 13*f,* 88–92, 175; in 1920s, 16; evangelical preach-

ers from overseas at, 88; largest of all English-speaking churches, 88, 96; no English-speaking members, 88; relationship with Immanuel Church, 95; school for poor white children (Poor School), 16; serving colored and African Dutch Reformed congregations, 89–90; welfare system of, 103
Dutch Reformed Mission church (for coloreds). *See* Immanuel Church
Du Toit, Marijke, 94

Eastern Cape Committee, 151; approval of long period for relocations, 175; proposals to create group areas for different races (1959), 172–73, 173*m;* report (1959) designating colored area, 176
Eastern Province Herald, on Great Fish River Valley irrigation development, 68
economic development, 37, 45
education. *See* schools and education
Elandsdrift rural hostel for boys, 93
electricity: as municipal service, 8–9, 75–76; pumping water, requirements of, 75–76; town's need to provide, 68; in town's new dwellings (1929), 128
Els, Johannes, 60
employment. *See* labor; wages
energy sources, 69–70
English-speaking population. *See* whites; women, white
enteritis, 84, 84*t,* 98
Evans, Ivan, *Bureaucracy and Race,* 7, 190
Evening Post (Port Elizabeth), on second move required for Cradock colored residents, 180

Fagan Commission, 44, 143, 144
farming/farmers. *See* agriculture and farming
Fish River. *See* Great Fish River
franchise, electoral: Africans, 4, 19, 124; in apartheid era, end of colored franchise, 169; Asians, 4, 19–20, 146, 148; in Cape Colony, 3–4, 169; coloreds, 2, 4, 19, 143, 145, 148; in Cradock (1925), 19; as major issue for whites, 20; municipal vs. parliamentary, 5, 19; property or income qualifications, 2, 3, 19; white immigrants, 141, 148; women, 5, 100
Frank, G., 43
Froom, Ethel, 119, 120, 122
Furnivall, J. S., 141

Gale, George, 115, 117, 121
gas-and-water socialism, 3
George VI (king), 142
Gerber, J. J., 156, 159–60, 170
Gie, S. F. N., 94
Gluckman, Henry, 115, 116, 121, 122, 186–87
Gluckman Health Commission's report, 116, 186–87
Goniwe, Matthew, 194. *See also* "Cradock Four" (1985)
Goodman, P. C., 29–31, 34, 101, 104, 108, 109, 192
Gordon, R. J., 12
Gouws, W. S., 175, 176–77
governance: municipalities, 3; self-governance to towns under Cape Municipal Ordinance (1836), 19. *See also* apartheid era (1948–94); segregation era (1910–48)
Government Relief Works, 38
Great Depression, 37–38, 92, 127, 132
Great Fish River, 11–12, 58, 79, 129, 146, 154; brickmaking location on east bank, 165; water supply and, 65–68, 74–75
Great Fish River Irrigation Board, 67
Great Karoo, 2, 11
Great Trek, 90, 91*f*
Groeps Gebiede Raad (GGR). *See* Group Areas Board
group areas, decision to create, 161–64
Group Areas Act (1950), x, xi; African protests against, 157–59; Asians and, 16; colored churches in town or in location off limits to coloreds, 160; coloreds forced into single area due to requirements of, 180; enforcement of, 191, 194; Mixed Area, effect on, 20, 21; multistep procedure allowed for

Group Areas Act (1950) (*continued*) implementation, 155; National Party's plan to separate all races, 7–8, 149–52; polarizing effect of, 181; rationale for, 149, 177, 190, 193; residential separation of colored and African populations, 137, 139, 148–52, 170, 190
Group Areas Amendment Act (1962), 178
Group Areas Board, 151, 164, 172, 175, 177–78, 191. *See also* Eastern Cape Committee
Group Areas Development Act (1961), 178

Haines, Richard, 109
Hani, Cawood, 42–43, 45
Hani, Moontlik, 42
Hattingh, M. J., 18, 52, 53, 74–76, 86, 131
Hattingh, Mrs., 100, 103
Health, Department of. *See* Public Health, Department of
health services. *See* public health (1910–48, segregation era)
Helpmekaar (Help One Another), 103
Hendrickse, Adrian, 101
Hertzog, J. B. M., 30
Hewett, Edward, 40
Hobhouse, Emily, 90–92
Hobson, J. A., 92
Hofmeyr, J. H. C., 152
Hokwana, Osary, 112–13
Holtzhuisbaaken farm with spring, 65, 68
Holy Rosary Mission, 21, 25. *See also* Convent of the Holy Rosary
hospital, regional, location of, 165–66. *See also* Metcalf Clinic; public health (1910–48, segregation era); Queen's Central Hospital
Hottentots, use of term, 12, 14–15, 24, 28, 35
housing (1910–48, segregation era), ix, 123–41; for Africans, 4, 123, 187; Africans prohibited from town residence, 4; for aged white poor, 133; beer hall revenues used to subsidize housing for whites, 56; colored demands for separate township, 136–39; for coloreds, 5, 82, 134–36, 187, 188, 190; Joint Council, role in, 6; local authorities to provide housing for the poor, 5; as municipal service representing South African racial order, 8–9; Murray's recommendations on minimally adequate housing, 125; for poor whites (1929), 123, 128–34, 139; race as factor, 7, 187; separation of coloreds and Africans, 123, 136–39; site-and-service schemes, 125, 166; Special Economic Housing Scheme, 132; subsidized housing, Cradock's failure to fully access state funding for, 124, 132, 187, 189; substandard dwellings in MOH report (1938), 132–33; Waters identifying as problem needing reform in the location, 99; zoning of (1920s and 1930s), 128–30, 129*m*. *See also* "location, the" (1910–48, segregation era); rental fees
housing (1948–94, apartheid era), 123; African squatter settlements, 166; compensation to African residents forced to move, 166. *See also* apartheid era (1948–94); coloreds (1948–94, apartheid era); Wilken Township (in the location)
Housing Act (1921), 124

Immanuel Church, 21, 25, 59, 89–90, 91*f*, 95, 133, 175, 176, 180; Church Council, 90*f*
Immanuel Te-Huis (Immanuel Home), 89–90
Immigration Restriction Act (1903), 15
Immorality Act (1927), 4
Indianola (Mississippi), 1–2
Indians. *See* Asians
Industrial and Commercial Workers' Union of Africa, 18
infant mortality, 73, 74, 82–86, 99, 105, 107, 108, 114, 121, 121*t*, 187
influenza epidemic (1918), 70, 98, 124
influx control, 4, 5, 7, 186, 188; farmers advocating to stop Africans moving to towns, 37–40; Native Affairs Department's disagreement with municipality over, 43–44; Native Labour Advisory Board and, 41; post–World War I,

124; for sewering and waste disposal purposes, 81, 85. *See also* Stallardism
Institute of Race Relations, 109, 143
Interior, Department of, 139, 171
intermarriage between whites and all people of color prohibited, 145, 148, 190
Irrigation Act (1912), 67, 74

Jabavu, D. D. T., 108
Jabavu, Florence Makiwane, 108
Jacobs, J. P., 90
Jameson, F. W., 135
Johnson, William E. ("Pussyfoot"), 48
Joint Council: on African children attending school, 37; Africans as focus of, to exclusion of coloreds and Asians, 109; alcohol control and, 52–55, 59–61; collapse of, 106, 114; effectiveness of, 188; formation of, 6, 52; isolation hospital, proposal for, 117; Lidbetter on, 65; public health dispute and, 109–14; water supply and, 77, 85
Jordaan, Elizabeth, 92–95, 93*f*, 100, 133

"Kaffer," use of term, 18
Kaffir Beer Profits Inquiry (1945), 60
Karg, A., 59
Kark, Emily and Sidney, 121
Karoo, ix, 66–67
Karoo Garden, x
Kelly, S. J., 126, 128
Kilian, J. V., 47, 48
King George V Hospital (Durban), 118
Kirby, J., 69
Kleefstra, T., 161–62, 167, 172, 179
Kleurvraagstuk Kommissie (1945), 145
Kruger, Eerwaarde, 180

labor: African and colored domestic servants, 98; Africans as supply of low-wage labor, 187; Africans not needed for in-town jobs, mandatory return to original habitat in country, 145; Afrikaner women as domestic servants, 93–94; apprenticeships, 4, 16, 169; color bar, 4, 134, 168–69; English-speakers' loss of dominance in, xi; in-town work opportunities, 36–37; poor whites, 4, 6; skilled trades, 4; surplus alleged to reside in towns, 4, 36–39, 186. *See also* Stallardism; wages; *and specific occupations and professions*
Lady Volunteers for the Location Movement, 89, 99–100
Land Tenure Advisory Board, 151, 156. *See also* Group Areas Board
Lawford, C. E., 67–68
Lawn, W. E., 136–37, 169
Lawrence, H. G., 116
Lazar, John, 147
Lewis, Gavin, 169
Lidbetter, W. W., 64–66, 70, 73, 188; photographs by, 13*f*, 17*f*, 22*f*, 65*f*, 66*f*, 70*f*, 75*f*, 77*f*, 91*f*, 97*f*, 101, 102*f*, 107*f*; self-portrait photograph, 67*f*
Lingelilhe (new township housing all Africans), xii
liquor. *See* alcohol control
Liquor Act (1928), 15, 49–50, 61, 182–83
Liquor Licensing Board, 57–58
"location, the" (1910–48, segregation era), 152–56; applications of Africans to stay in, 42–46; beer hall revenues and, 56, 60–61, 62, 63, 156; birth and death reporting, 33; birthright to residence in, 42–43, 45; in blueprint of Township of Cradock (1924), 20; boundaries approved (December 1948), 152; capital expenditures for the location to be separate from town's financing, 126; "closing" of (1930s), 39–42; coloreds' treatment in, 33, 42, 44; Combined Location Committee, 108; during Depression, 38; dispensary (clinic) in, 98, 99–100, 101–6, 103*f*, 106*f*, 108, 186, 192; governance of, 2, 187; health conditions in, 5, 98; health reporting in, 33; Health Society proposed for, 109; history of establishment of, 12; house construction, 158; housing conditions in, 22, 33, 126, 135; improvement applications (1954), 157; lack of amenities in, 6, 22–23, 76; land ownership not allowed in, 1–2, 124, 149; lodger's permit requirements

"location, the" (1910–48, segregation era) (*continued*)
(1925–40), 24, 28–32, 34–36, 40, 42, 44, 60; losing residential rights in, 42–46; Magquba quarter, 23–25; map (1926–29), 21*m*, 23; ministers in, 25; mix of Africans and coloreds in, xii, 8, 26, 32, 149–50, 168; Model Regulations applicable to, 32–36, 125; Murray's recommendations for, 125; racial structure from time of town's founding, 1; raids and arrests for living in the location without lodger's permit, 28–32, 35–36; regulation of, from founding through early 1900s, 24–25, 27; rental rates in, 126; residence permits, 33; soup kitchen in, 104; street names not used in, 23; superintendent of, 2, 24; visitors to report in, 33; zoning area, 130. *See also* New Brighton (Cradock location); public health (1910–48, segregation era); sanitation and sewage (1910–48, segregation era); water supply (1910–48, segregation era); Wilken Township (in the location)
"location, the" (1948–94, apartheid era): buffer strips, 8, 154–56, 158–60, 161–62, 182, 191, 194; end of mix of Africans and coloreds in, 168; funding of new location, 157–58; hinterland for future growth, 154, 161, 163, 167–68; old location (disposition after apartheid), x, 81, 149–50, 170, 176, 193; population to be accommodated in new location (1956), 157; rate of construction of, 178; timeline for Africans to move out so coloreds can move in, 176–77. *See also* Wilken Township (in the location)
Location Advisory Board: alcohol control and, 52–55, 57; colored representation on, 169, 192; coloreds' and Africans' reaction to, 34, 35, 109, 185; creation and composition of, 2, 30, 32, 34, 169, 186; dispute over location rents to pay for nursing services, 112–13; on loans to improve location housing, 135; naming numbered streets in the location, 23; proposing African trained nurse to replace Mary Butler, 110; refusing to allow repairs to location home, 42; registration of service contracts and location as residence for all Africans, 41; role of, 33–34, 69, 186
Location Vigilance Association, 25, 34, 52, 157, 167
"Loco" (railway land on which Africans lived), 150, 153, 155
lodger's law and permit, 24, 28–32, 34–36, 40, 42, 44, 60
Lombard, A. C. A., 41
Lombard, W., 159
Loram, Charles, 99
Lottering, J., 137
Louw, Jan, 171
Lwana Memorial Methodist church, 23, 25
Lwana Street, 64, 101

Mackenzie, L. M., 109
Macombring, Joseph [Joel], 31
Malan, D. F., 144
Malan, N., 146–47
Manuel, J. E., 28, 31–32
Marenge, Chrissie, x
Market Square, 13*f*, 16–17, 17*f*
Market Street, 178
Mass Radiographic Survey (1947), 119–20
Mdlimela, Eric, 60
measles, 105
medical officers of health (MOH): appointment of, under 1920 Health Act, 5, 186; decline of inspections by, 190; failure of, 114, 116–17; identification of "Eurafrican" (colored) housing as urgent need, 170; reports required, 33, 124; role of, 5, 186. *See also* Murray, William A.
Mentor, Walter, 34
Metcalf, Alfred: dispensary in the location, providing funding for, 101, 103, 111–12, 188; in housing dispute over location of new housing for poor whites, 130, 133; St. James church (in

the location), donating to, 96; water supply, giving grant for, 77, 188
Metcalf Clinic, 114–17, 122, 186
Methodist denomination, 88, 95, 96, 104, 166, 192. *See also* African Methodist Episcopal church; Basuto Methodist church; Coloured Methodist church; Lwana Memorial Methodist church
Mfengu ("Fingo"), 15, 22*f*
Mhlomi, N., 111
Michau, F. W., 175–76, 191
Michausdal (new township housing all coloreds), xii, 180–81, 183
Midland News: on Africans' access to towns, 37; author's father as publisher, xi; Mary Butler (author's aunt) as columnist on health and family issues in, 71; Cluver's inspection report published in, 76; on coloreds' side in Cross Street issue, 177; on Eastern Cape Committee hearing on moving coloreds vs. moving poor whites, 175; Eastern Cape Committee's proposal to create group areas for different races (1959) published in, 173; founding of (under name *Midland News and Karoo Farmer*), xi, 17; health bulletins from Public Health Department in, 98; on infant mortality rates in the location, 105; on influenza epidemic (1918) and other epidemics, 98; on irrigation development of Fish River Valley, 68; Lidbetter's complaints in, 64; Michau writing on costs of colored housing, 175; on Native Affairs officials' threats for not complying with apartheid, 160; on 1948 election, 146, 147; objections to moving the location to Sondagshoek published in, 158–60; protesting over raid on the location for males without lodger's permit, 28–30; on relocation of the location vs. building new houses on present site (1926), 123; role of, 17–18; on royal visit of George VI to South Africa, 142; on systematically segregated municipality, 128; temperance movement and, 49, 53; thirty-fifth anniversary celebration, 16; on Waters asking for women volunteers to improve conditions in the location, 99; on water situation, 71, 74; on WCA initiative to help sick and poor both coloreds and whites, 101
migration of Africans to town, 36–37
Millin, Sarah Gertrude, *God's Stepchildren,* 174
miscegenation, 174
missionaries, apartheid's policy toward, 145
missionary schools for Africans, 36–37, 104, 145, 146, 148, 159
Mixed Area of Cradock town, 20–27; age of segregation characterized as "golden age" in, 21; alcohol control and, 63; apartheid and abolishment of, 149, 152–56, 190; colored people forced to relocate from after apartheid policy, 8, 170; coloreds living in during age of segregation, 44, 136, 138, 139; demographics (1938), 131; institutions located in, 21; location of, 20; map (1926–29), 21*m;* Natives (Urban Areas) Act (1923) recognizing, 26; poor whites' housing constructed in, 131, 133; property ownership trends in 1920s, 20; public housing in, 124; white acceptance of, 26, 140; white Afrikaner women objecting to, 6; zoning of, 129
Mlanjeni's War (1850), 15
Model Regulations for the location, 32–36, 125
Molteno, Donald B., 60–61, 116
Moolman, J. H., 41
morality, 98–99, 107
Morrison, G. de V., 121, 179
mortality rates: causes in the location, 101; causes of death by race (1944), 84, 84*t;* infant mortality, 73, 74, 82–86, 99, 105, 107, 108, 114, 121, 121*t,* 187; by race (1931 and 1946), 82–83, 83*t;* by race (1946 and 1953), 121, 121*t*
Mortimer Rural Society, 117, 120
Msikinya, Charles, 101
Mtombeni, Helen, 112

municipalities: as agents to implement segregationist housing policies, 124; challenges of showing municipal policy as embodiment of South Africa's uniqueness, 8; governance of, 3; pressure to provide better services to racially delineated locations, 4, 83–86. *See also* Cradock, municipality of
Murray, William A.: on adequacy of new water scheme, 73, 76; background of, 72; the location described by, 23; photograph of, 72*f;* sanitary inspection and recommendations by, 71–74, 79, 81, 98, 106, 121, 125, 128, 188, 190
Mvambo, E. S., 60

"Nachtmaal" vote, 68–69, 73, 75, 85
Natal, 3, 49, 121, 141; Indians in, 174; racial conflict in, 149–51
National Council of Child Welfare (NCCW), 88
National Day of Protest (1950), 156
National Health Services Commission (1944), 115–16
National Housing Board, 166
National Party, 142–52; Bantu policy, 145–46; colored vote and, 143, 148, 169, 190; in Cradock 1948 election, 146–48; Cradock town council and town clerk as members of, 168; Dutch Reformed male members likely to vote for, 103; forming United Party by joining with South African Party, 132, 134; local members' reaction to group areas designations (1960), 177; Race Relations Policy of the National Party, 145; registration of service contracts and, 42; Sauer Report and, 145; segregation demands 1938–48, 62–63; social medicine and, 122; Stallardism and, 143; in Swart Gevaar (Black Peril) election (1929), 134; victory of 1948 and apartheid policy, 7–8, 139, 141, 144, 147, 149–52, 170, 185, 189–90; women members not joining WCA, 100
National Road Board, 154
National Tuberculosis Commission (1914), 117
National War Memorial Health Foundation (NWMHF), 60, 119
Native Affairs, Department of: alcohol control and, 50, 52, 58, 60; apartheid policy and, 152–57, 167, 190; change of policies 1925–40s, 46; on colored area proposal sent by town clerk, 172; coloreds prohibited from moving to the location, 40; colored township separate from African location, support for, 138, 187; health center, creation of, 116; housing plans to meet requirements of, 133; influx to location limited by, 186; inspection of the location by, 135, 186; lodger's permit, enforcement of, 31–32; medicines, stocking of, for location residents, 110; Model Regulations for municipalities, 33–34, 125; name change to Department of Bantu Administration, 165; Native Farm Labour Committee, 36, 40–41; nursing services, subsidies for, 113; opposition to Location Advisory Board restrictions during World War II, 41–42; public housing for the location and, 56, 125–27, 139; sanitary conditions and charges and, 82; schools for Africans and, 159; urban area inspectors to be appointed, 5; Verwoerd's reorganization of, 148; water supply and, 71, 76–78. *See also* Bantu Administration, Department of (formerly Department of Native Affairs)
Native Affairs Commission, 57, 61, 62
Native Affairs Committee (Durban system), 49
Native Farm Labour Committee, 36, 40–41
Native Labour Advisory Board, 40–42
Native Laws Amendment Act (1937), 4, 39–40, 45–46, 134; biennial census of locations, 39, 186; prohibition ended by, 54; restricting Africans' right to move to town, 186, 189
Native Laws Amendment Act (1944), 56
Native Laws Commission. *See* Fagan Commission
Native Representation Act (1936), 113

Native Representative Council, 55, 144, 145, 148
Native Revenue Account, 32
Natives Abolition of Passes and Coordination of Documents Act (1952), 159
Natives (Urban Areas) Act (1923): Africans banned from freehold ownership in locations, 124, 149, 186; alcohol control and, 49, 50, 52; "closing" locations under section 5 of, 39; coloreds' position in locations, 26, 46, 125; curfew and pass laws, application to coloreds, 35; Deary's enforcement of, 30; dispensary costs charged to native revenue account, 106; enforcement of, 33–35, 187; franchise not allowed to Africans, 124; housing loans for locations provided by, 124; housing to be provided to employed Africans, 43; Location Advisory Board established, 2; on locations to be solely African occupied, 139; "native locations," terminology of, 26; native revenue account, income and expenses of, 5, 99, 106, 189; proposed amendments to, 39; purpose of, 186; racial classifications and, 15; Stallard doctrine and, 4, 38; urban Africans defined, 26. *See also* influx control
Natives and Coloured Peoples Conference (1926), 36, 51
Natives (Urban Areas) Consolidation Act (1945), x, 41, 149, 164, 165, 179
Native Services Levy Act (1952), 157–58
Native Welfare Society (Port Elizabeth), 110
NCCW (National Council of Child Welfare), 188
Nel, G. I., 78, 143
NERA. *See* Non-European Ratepayers Association (NERA)
New Brighton (Cradock location), 58, 76–77; annex to old location, 130; housing construction and financing, 126–27; mix of coloreds and Africans living in, 127, 140
New Brighton (Port Elizabeth), 110
newspapers, 17–18
New Township area, proposal to locate housing for poor whites in, 129–30
Ngumbela, Medicine, 60
Njawi, Elizabeth, 59–60
Non-European Ratepayers Association (NERA), 138–39; opposed to second move of coloreds, 180; opposed to separate colored township, 169–70, 175, 192
nongovernmental organizations, 87–88. *See also* charity and welfare (1910–48, segregation era); public health (1910–48, segregation era); *and specific organizations*
Nongqawuse (Xhosa girl prophet), 15
Ntsikana (Xhosa Christian prophet), 51
nursing services for the location, 99–100, 101–3, 103*f*, 105, 189

Oakes, A. G., 105
Official Yearbook of the Union (1950), 15
Oosthuizen, L. V., 117–18
Orange Free State, 3, 31, 44–45, 150, 151
Ordinance 50 (1828), 19
Osche, Charles, 157–58, 165
Ossewabrandwag, 41, 61

Pact government (1924), focus on Afrikaner poor, 128
Parade Street (Mixed Area), 131
Pass Laws: coloreds exempt from 1923 law, 35, 41; not promulgated (1940), 41. *See also* curfew in the location and application to coloreds
Paterson, G. B., 71
Pegging Act (Natal 1943), 151
Philips, L. T., 61
plague, 4, 98, 100
Planning Department, 180
pneumonia, 84, 84*t*
Pokomela, Alfred, 29, 135
Polela (Natal) as example of TB control, 121
Poni, Guqu, 60
poor whites, 88–96; ACVV caring for poor youth, 95; Afrikaans-speaking, 88, 92, 128, 188; in apartheid era, new

poor whites (*continued*)
housing to be provided for, 178; in apartheid era, relocation to create colored area, 171, 173, 175; demographics of, 16, 18; Dutch Reformed Church and, 92; housing for, 56, 128–34, 139; in Mixed Area, 20; schools for, 68; social services for welfare of, 88
Poplars, The (Butler family home), x
Population Registration Act (1949), 148
Port Elizabeth, 13, 53, 56, 61, 133, 168, 191
Posel, Deborah, *The Making of Apartheid,* 7, 144, 185, 190
prohibition (liquor). *See* alcohol control
Prohibition of Mixed Marriages Act (1949), 148
public health (1910–48, segregation era), 105–22, 150; ACVV interest in, 95; Cape African Congress's intervention, 110–14; children's health, 94, 95; coloreds and Africans preferring to replace Mary Butler with their own nurses, 111; crises in large cities, 4–5; expanded staffing of health center, 119; health center for African and colored population, 115, 119–21, 120*t,* 122, 186; isolation facilities for patients with TB or venereal diseases, 23, 116–18, 120–21; Joint Council, role in, 6; local implementation of, 5, 107–8; location blamed for poor health of its inhabitants, 107; Metcalf Clinic, 114–17, 122, 186; midwives, shortage of, 119, 120; MOH/DS (medical officer of health/ district surgeon), appointment of and failure of, 114, 116–17; movement in South Africa, 5; post-1930s expansion of interest in, 104; race as factor, 7, 8–9, 86, 122; reports between 1927 and 1939, inaccuracy of, 82; reports from health center on prenatal care, mother-child care, and syphilis treatment, 120, 120*t;* sanitation syndrome and, 185; social medicine and, 60, 114–18, 122, 189; voluntary organizations involved in, 122; water as bearer of fatal infections, 68. *See also* mortality rates; nursing services for the location; Queen's Central Hospital; sanitation and sewage (1910–48, segregation era); *and individual diseases*
Public Health, Department of: dispensary and nursing services for the location and, 104; establishment of, 5; health bulletins in *Midland News* by, 98; housing loans for whites, coloreds, and Asians from, 124–26; improved housing conditions, advocating for, 56; supervisory role of, 106, 186–87; waste disposal and sanitation and, 80–86; water supply and, 71–74, 76. *See also* Central Housing Board
Public Health Act (1919), 5, 70, 71
Public Health Act (1920), 124, 186
Public Health (Amendment) Act (1935), 114
public housing. *See* housing (1910–48, segregation era); housing (1948–94, apartheid era)
Public Works Department, 81
Purified National Party, 134–35; anti-British stance of, 141; residential segregation policy of, 134–35

Quakers, 6, 18, 37, 49, 53, 65
quarry, in the location, 164
Queen's Central Hospital, 68, 106–7, 107*f,* 117, 165
Quengwa, Edward, 47

races, division of population into, 6–7, 14–16, 26, 46, 170; Group Areas Act (1950), effect of, 8, 151, 170–76; housing policy to sustain, 124–25; identity cards and national register to indicate race of each person, 148, 190; United Party's view on, 140–41. *See also* Africans; Asians; coloreds (1910–48, segregation era); coloreds (1948–94, apartheid era); whites
Rafferty, Thomas, 29, 31
Rafferty family (colored), 168
railroads, 13, 16, 76
Railway Reserve area, 129
Rainers, Elizabeth, 40

Rapportryers (National Party organization), 175
ratepayers: apartheid policy, costs to relocate to satisfy requirements of, 167; colored population as, 22, 69, 140, 175; dispensary in the location, not charged to, 106; Eastern Cape Committee and, 175; group areas designations (1960), objections to, 177–78; location subsidy from, 156–57; water supply improvements and, 68–69, 73, 75, 85. *See also* Non-European Ratepayers Association (NERA)
Rayepen, Kathleen, 181
Red Cross, 87, 119, 122
Regent Street, 131*f;* in apartheid era, in area designated for colored population, 161–62, 168, 181; in apartheid era, boundary between town and buffer strip, 154, 180; in apartheid era, boundary to separate Europeans from Non-Europeans, 152, 154, 170, 176–77, 181, 182; colored petition trying to preserve as colored area from Cross Street to Regent Street, 180–83; in Eastern Cape Committee's proposal to create group areas for different races (1959), 173; Group Areas Act, effect on, 181; municipal proposal to make area north of a white area, 173; in segregation era, boundary of town and the location, 8, 20, 22, 69, 98, 124, 152
regional hospital, location of, 165–66
registration of service contracts, 41–42
rental fees: average rents of whites, 132, 139; colored rental housing, 137, 138; location rent (1927), 127; location rent increases (1947, 1948, and 1953), 156; lodger's permits, 24, 28; in New Brighton housing, 127; poor whites, new housing built for after 1960 proclamation, 178
residence, right of. *See* apartheid era (1948–94); housing (1910–48, segregation era); housing (1948–94, apartheid era); segregation era (1910–48)
Rheinallt Jones, J. D., 109, 114
River Street slums, 16, 131
road construction for access to town from location, 155
Roman Catholic Convent of the Sacred Heart, 88, 94, 176, 182, 192
rugby teams, 25, 87
Rusoord (1943 housing for old poor whites), 133–34

St. James church (Anglican), 25, 96, 96*f,* 157
St. John's Ambulance Brigade, 87
St. Peter's church (in town), 96, 97*f*
St. Peter's Mission (Anglican church), 23, 25
sanitation and sewage (1910–48, segregation era), 71–76, 79–82; double-pail system, 79–82; infant mortality linked to, 84–85; in the location, changes 1924–48, 80–82, 86, 186–87, 188; mandatory services in the location, 33; as municipal service representing South African racial order, 8–9; in New Brighton housing construction, 127; new sanitary system for town, 80–82; pit closets, 80; public lavatories, availability of, 79–80; street storm-water gutters or gardens for disposal of waste water, 80–81; systematic sanitary inspection, 71–76; tank collection of slops, 79, 80; in town (1920s), 79, 80, 128; water-borne sewerage system, 68, 81, 82, 86
SAP. *See* South African Police (SAP)
Sauer, P. O., and Sauer Report (1947), 144–45, 190
Sauls, A. K., 137
Sauls, C. M., 28, 31, 110
Scheepers, L. L., 159, 176
Scholtz, W., 111
schools and education: Adult Education Movement, 119; for Afrikaner girls, 92–94; church-run schools, 23, 25, 88, 169; colored schools, 134, 169, 174, 175, 176; colored teachers' organizations, 169; Cradock Handelskool (Commercial School), 94; enrollment levels in town vs. in the location, 37, 68; missionary schools for Africans,

schools and education (*continued*) 36–37, 104, 145, 146, 148, 159; poll tax supposed to support, 54; state control under apartheid regime, 146, 148, 159; teachers' training college, 68; vocational education, 94; Wilson school for the poor, 92
Schreiner, Olive, ix, 90
segregation era (1910–48), 7, 11–27; Africans prohibited from town residence, 4; alcohol control in, 48–63; charity and welfare in, 87–104; coloreds' housing during, 44; friction not an issue between English- and Afrikaans-speaking whites in Cradock, 6–7, 185; governance during, 189; housing in, 123–41; job color bars, 4; lack of coherent plan for, left to ad hoc enforcement, 185, 189; national and local impulses in, 186–89; public health in, 105–22; sanitation and sewage in, 71–76, 79–82; Schreiner's criticism of, ix; transition to age of apartheid, 189–91; water supply in, 64–78. *See also* alcohol control; housing (1910–48, segregation era); public health (1910–48, segregation era); sanitation and sewage (1910–48, segregation era); water supply (1910–48, segregation era)
self-governance to towns under Cape Municipal Ordinance (1836), 19
Seligson, Advocate, 173–75
Separate Representation of Voters Act (1951), 148
sexual relations, interracial restrictions, 4, 14, 145, 174
Sitela, John, 112–13
slaves, 14
Slums Act (1934), 119, 132–33
smallpox, 4, 98
Smit, D. L., 57, 61, 143
Smuts, Jan, 34, 54, 142, 146, 147
social medicine, 60, 114–18, 122, 189
social services. *See* charity and welfare (1910–48, segregation era)
Social Welfare, Department of, 44, 119, 136, 137
Solilo, John, 25, 34, 35, 101
Solly, Julia, 124
Somerset, Charles, 12
Sondagshoek: African opposition to move of the location to, 157–58, 162, 192; Africans, apartheid proposal to locate in, 156–60, 157, 170; coloreds, apartheid proposal to locate in, 154, 155, 172; unsuitability for site of location, 161–62, 167, 172, 193; waste disposal in trenches in, 79
South Africa Act (constitution 1909), 19
South African Indian Congress, Defiance Campaign, 157
South African Party, 89, 132, 134
South African Police (SAP), 5, 28, 47, 58, 59
South African Railways, 149, 150, 153, 155, 160
South African Temperance Alliance, 49
South African War. *See* Anglo-Boer War (1899–1902)
"Southerntown," USA (Indianola, Mississippi), compared to Cradock, 1–4, 7
South West Africa (later Namibia), 147
Soweto uprising (1976), x, 194
Special Economic Housing Scheme, 132
spinal meningitis, 98
sports and race, 25, 87
Stallard, Charles, 4
Stallardism, 4, 32, 38–39, 44, 85, 127, 142–44, 186, 187, 189
Stewart, Shand and Oliver (engineering firm), 81
Steyn, J. H., 190
Strauss, J. G. N., 150
Stringer, Alice (author's mother), xi
Stultz, Newell, 144
Swart Gevaar (Black Peril) election (1929), 134
syphilis. *See* venereal diseases

Taaiboschleegte (new colored area), 179–80. *See also* Michausdal (new township housing all coloreds)
Tapp, Charles, 79
Tarkastad Road, 137, 162, 163, 172, 173; in Eastern Cape Committee's proposal

to create group areas for different races (1959), 173
taxation: Location Advisory Board and, 2; water rates, 68–69. *See also* lodger's law and permit; ratepayers
Tembu Tribe, 37
temperance, 48–50, 98, 188. *See also* alcohol control
Tetelman, Michael, 194
Tgintgi, Jan, 43–44, 46
Thallie, Sam, 165
theft of stock, 38–39, 40
Thembu, 15
Thornton, G. O., 83, 114
Toekoms hostel for indigent boys, 93
town council: alcohol control and, 52, 55; cautious approach of, 6, 190; colored site in town considered by, in age of apartheid, 172; colored township separate from African location, consideration of, 137; group area designations outside powers of, 172; Location Advisory Board, relationship with, 2; Location Committee, 112, 126, 135, 156–59, 162; provision of health services to the location, 100; provision of municipal services to the location, 6, 69; refusing to yield immediately to national proposals for group areas and buffer strips, 191; on relocation of the location (1937), 135; on relocation of the location vs. building new houses on present site (1926), 123; role of, 5; water supply and, 76; WCA relationship with, 101
Transport, Department of, 155–56, 167
Transvaal, 3, 58, 90, 141; Indians in, 174; racial conflict in, 149, 190, 194
tuberculosis, 4, 5, 23, 82, 84*t*, 108, 110, 115, 117–19, 118*t*, 121
Tuberculosis Commission (1914), 5
typhoid fever, 68, 82, 84–85, 98
typhus, 68, 82, 84*t*, 98

Union of South Africa, creation of, 3, 19, 142
United Party: colored population, relationship with, 140, 143, 144, 148; on coloreds as "appendage" of whites, 174; in Cradock 1948 election, 146–48; creation of, 132, 134; housing subsidies and, 132; local actions in Cradock not priority of, 141; Native Labour Advisory Board representation, 41; 1948 platform of, 143–44; opposed to second move of colored population, 182; proposed legislation to segregate coloreds if local whites voted to enforce, 143; residential segregation policy of, 134, 141, 150, 151, 189; social medicine and, 122; Stallardism, rejection of, 142–44. *See also* Coloured Advisory Council (CAdC)
Urban Areas Act. *See* Natives (Urban Areas) Act (1923)
urban areas inspectors, 5
Urie, A. J., 28–29

Van der Horst, Sheila, 36
Van Heerden, J., 152–57, 159–60, 164–66, 190–91, 193
Van Heerden, P. de K., 38–39, 125–26, 128, 156
Van Heerden, P. L., 128
Van Heerden, W. A. J., 138
Van Niekerk, J. A., 31, 89–90, 90*f*, 91*f*
Van Rensburg, B. J., 84–85, 114–20, 122
Van Rensburg, Martjie, 99
Van Rooyen, G. W., 139, 147, 155, 162, 170, 174
Van Zyl, Mrs., 43
venereal diseases, 23, 115, 117, 119, 120, 120*t*
Venter, G. L. E., 41
Verwoerd, Hendrik, 7, 148, 152, 154, 160, 165, 190
Victoria Hotel, 16, 17*f*
Vigilance Association. *See* Location Vigilance Association
Viljoen, Dr., 74
Vlok, W. J., 31, 71, 188
Volkskas (bank), 147
Voortrekker centennial celebrations (1936–38), 90, 91*f*
Voortrekker Street: as boundary of Mixed Area, 8, 170; construction of housing

Voortrekker Street (*continued*)
for poor whites, location of, 130–31; mixed area adjacent to, to be changed to white in age of apartheid, 176, 177
voting rights. *See* franchise, electoral

wages: farm workers vs. in-town jobs, 36, 41; in-kind supplements discontinued, 36; Native Farm Labour Committee investigating, 36; Native Labour Advisory Board and, 41; whites, average income (1930s), 132
Walters, Owen H., 54–55, 60–61, 114
Warm Baths sulfur springs, 64–66, 66*f*, 73, 78
washerwomen. *See* clothes washing
waste disposal. *See* sanitation and sewage (1910–48, segregation era)
Waters, Mary, 98–99
water supply (1910–48, segregation era), 6, 64–78, 65*f*; dams and, 66–69, 74; distribution between town and location, 69–70, 76–78; droughts, 68; financing needed for, 56; first reservoir (1928), 75*f*; as government function, 65; historical shortages of, 11; infant mortality linked to, 84–85; Irrigation Act (1912), 67, 74; irrigation systems, 67, 114; in the location, 64, 69, 86, 186–87, 188; mandatory services in the location, 33; as municipal service representing South African racial order, 8–9; Murray's reaction to and recommendations on the location's water situation, 72–74; New Brighton construction and, 126; in 1948 election campaign, 146; race as factor, 7; ratepayers and "Nachtmaal" vote on improvements, 68–69, 73, 75, 85; standpipes for location residents, 69, 70*f*, 73; in town, 64, 86; in town's new dwellings (1929), 128; townspeople vs. farmers over, 68; urgent need for water, 66–71, 99
WCA. *See* Women's Civic Association (WCA)
WCTU. *See* Women's Christian Temperance Union (WCTU)
Werner, A. B., 179–80
whites: alcohol access of, 49–50; ascendancy of English-speaking minority, 16–17; demographics of, xi, 14, 16–17; moves required to accommodate group areas in age of apartheid, 176; political roles in Cradock, 16; as racial category, 6, 14; segregation not generating friction between English- and Afrikaans-speaking whites in Cradock, 185; settlers, ix; superintendent of the location, 2; white supremacy, commitment to, 142, 147, 156. *See also* Afrikaners (whites speaking Afrikaans); apartheid era (1948–94); poor whites; ratepayers; segregation era (1910–48); women, white
whooping cough, 84*t*, 98, 119
Wilken, G. P.: as acting location superintendent conducting raid and arresting those without lodger's permit, 28–31, 35–36, 45; alcohol control and, 47, 54, 58–60; census of the location's population, 38, 43; church list compiled by, 25; nursing services, raising location rents to cover and, 112; ordering Tgintgi to leave the location, 43
Wilken Township (in the location): apartheid era and, 150, 155, 161–64, 191, 193; construction of, 136, 187; data collected, 122; located in buffer strip, 155; mix of coloreds and Africans living in, 140; saved from demolition, 166, 167, 191; tuberculosis pilot project in, 118–19; waste disposal in, 81–82, 188
Willard, Frances, 98
women, African: alcohol purchase by, 54, 56–57, 59, 124; as beer brewers, 48, 50, 99; morality of, 98–99; protesting pass law's applicability to women, 159; in water line and transporting water, 64, 78, 86
women, Afrikaner, 6, 88–96, 188
women, colored, 5
women, white, 5; alcohol access of, 50; divided into Afrikaans-speaking and English-speaking, 87; English-speaking, 88–89, 188; English-speaking women

concerned with welfare and health of the poor, 97–103, 188; franchise, electoral, 5, 100; location as focus of social initiatives of, 89; nongovernmental institutions providing social welfare and, 87, 188; promoting social initiatives for the poor, 97–104; property rights of married women, 188; on racial separation, 89; temperance movement and, 48, 124, 188; town shop employees, lavatory facilities for, 79; World War II–related activities of, 188
Women's Christian Temperance Union (WCTU): background of, 97–98; beer hall opposition of, 57; both English- and Afrikaans-speaking women participating in, 87, 88; continual opposition to alcohol production and sales, 62, 97; establishment of, 97; founding in South Africa, 48; on housing site for poor whites, 131; on locations' conditions, 124; resolution to ban "Kaffir" beer, 52
Women's Civic Association (WCA): alcohol control and, 52; demise of, 188; dispensary (clinic) established by, 89; establishment of, 100; first leaders of, 101; on housing location for poor whites, 130; isolation hospital, proposal for, 117; limited effectiveness of, 104; Medicine and Nourishment Fund, 108; supporting colored representation on Location Advisory Board, 34
Women's Enfranchisement Association of the Union, 100
wool industry, 12, 67
Worcester sewerage system, 81
World War II, 41–42, 57
wrywing (friction) between racial groups, 149–50, 174, 193, 194

Xhosa, 15, 51. *See also* Africans

Young-Barrett Committee (1935), 38–39
youth, African: ANC Youth League, 157, 159; beer halls and beer production, 58; Calata's funeral, effect on, 194

Zambodla, A. B., 59

RECONSIDERATIONS IN SOUTHERN AFRICAN HISTORY

Milton Shain, *The Roots of Antisemitism in South Africa*

Timothy Keegan, *Colonial South Africa and the Origins of the Racial Order*

Ineke van Kessel, *"Beyond Our Wildest Dreams": The United Democratic Front and the Transformation of South Africa*

Benedict Carton, *Blood from Your Children: The Colonial Origins of Generational Conflict in South Africa*

Diana Wylie, *Starving on a Full Stomach: Hunger and the Triumph of Cultural Racism in Modern South Africa*

Jeff Guy, *The View across the River: Harriette Colenso and the Zulu Struggle against Imperialism*

John Edwin Mason, *Social Death and Resurrection: Slavery and Emancipation in South Africa*

Hermann Giliomee, *The Afrikaners: Biography of a People*

Tim Couzens, *Murder at Morija: Faith, Mystery, and Tragedy on an African Mission*

Diana Wylie, *Art and Revolution: The Life and Death of Thami Mnyele, South African Artist*

David Welsh, *The Rise and Fall of Apartheid*

John Edwin Mason, *One Love, Ghoema Beat: Inside the Cape Town Carnival*

Eric Allina, *Slavery by Any Other Name: African Life under Company Rule in Colonial Mozambique*

Richard Elphick, *The Equality of Believers: Protestant Missionaries and the Racial Politics of South Africa*

Hermann Giliomee, *The Last Afrikaner Leaders: A Supreme Test of Power*

Meghan Healy-Clancy, *A World of Their Own: A History of South African Women's Education*

Ruramisai Charumbira, *Imagining a Nation: History and Memory in Making Zimbabwe*

Jeffrey Butler, edited by Richard Elphick and Jeannette Hopkins, *Cradock: How Segregation and Apartheid Came to a South African Town*